Syntax and Semantics of Spanish Presentational Sentence-Types

D1715874

Margarita Suñer

Georgetown University Press, Washington, D.C. 20057

Library of Congress Cataloging in Publication Data

Suñer, Margarita.
    Syntax and semantics of Spanish presentational
sentence-types.

    Bibliography: p.
    1. Spanish language--Syntax. 2. Spanish language--
Semantics. 3. Spanish language--Discourse analysis.
4. Spanish language--Existential constructions.
5. Spanish language--Topic and comment. I. Title.
II. Title: Presentational sentence-types.
PC4369.S9 1982   465   82-12122
ISBN 0-87840-084-2

International Standard Book Number: 0-87840-084-2

To Erik

CONTENTS

ACKNOWLEDGMENTS

During the five years of work on this manuscript, I had numerous opportunities to discuss many of the ideas embodied in it with friends, colleagues, and students. Among them I would like to mention Christian Adjémian, Len Babby, Erik J. Beukenkamp, Dwight Bolinger, Ivonne Bordelois, Wayles Browne, Amanda Chacona, Heles Contreras, John Goldsmith, Wayne Harbert, Julie Herschensohn, Larry King, Carlos Piera, Carol Rosen, and Marisa Rivero. To all of you my most sincere thanks.

I am also grateful to the Cornell University Department of Modern Languages and Linguistics, the Latin American Studies Program, and the College of Arts and Sciences for Faculty Research grants which were essential to the preparation of the final version of this book.

A special thanks goes to Beth Giddings, for editing the manuscript, and to Jacqui Hall and Stephanie Doucett, for their efficient clerical work.

Margarita Suñer

ACKNOWLEDGMENTS

[faded, largely illegible text]

0

INTRODUCTION

0.1 Purpose and theoretical framework. The purpose of
this study is to present a thorough study of two types of presentational sentences in Spanish: those which are constructed
with impersonal haber, and those which contain a semantically
intransitive verb which precedes its subject. Presentational
sentences are functionally defined as those which introduce the
referent of the noun phrase into the universe of discourse.
Their verb serves to assert this appearance. These sentences
obey the somewhat vague principle that no more than one NP
can be introduced at a time, regardless of whether it displays
a subject or an object function; therefore, due to their mono-
valency, both impersonal haber and intransitive verbs are
suited for participation in the presentative function.

The theoretical framework presupposed in this research is
that of transformational generative grammar--in particular, the
Revised Extended Standard Theory (REST) as developed in
Chomsky (1975, 1976, 1977b, 1979b, 1980a), Chomsky and Lasnik (1977), and related work. Although the analysis proposed
here will be justified at each step, some familiarity with the revised EST is assumed. Within this model, the grammar is
assumed to adhere to the organization shown in (1).

(1) 1.   Base
     2.   Transformations
     3a. Deletion   3b. Construal
     4a. Filters   4b. Quantifier
     5a. Phonology   Interpretation
     6a. Stylistic rules   5b. Conditions on
                                  binding
     (Chomsky and Lasnik 1977:431; Chomsky 1980a:3)

The rules of the base generate base structures to which
transformations apply; the outcome consists of S-structures,

1

that is, surface structures which contain traces. This model
assumes trace theory, which postulates that a phrase moved by
a transformation leaves behind a trace which is controlled by
the moved phrase. Furthermore, the base rules conform to
some version of the $\overline{X}$ theory (Chomsky 1970, Jackendoff 1977).
Together, the rules of the base and the transformations form
the syntactic component of the grammar. After the level of
S-structures, the grammar subdivides into two further independent components: the phonological component, which associ-
ates S-structures with phonetic representations (rules (3a)-
(6a)), and the interpretive component which links S-structures
to representations in logical form (LF). Logical form is understood 'to be a universal system of representation that incorporates whatever aspects of meaning [are] strictly determined
by sentence grammar, not involving situational context, background beliefs, speaker's intentions, etc.' (Chomsky and Lasnik 1977:428). Because of the way in which the different components of the grammar are displayed in (1), the phonological
component is also known as the left side or left branch of the
grammar, and the interpretive component is the right branch
of the grammar.

Diagram (1) provides us with a model for sentence grammar
only. Presentationalism, however, is a functional notion that
concerns the function of a certain type of sentence in the discourse. It is evident, therefore, that in this study it is necessary to go beyond sentence grammar and into the discourse.

Chomsky (1976:336) suggested that after rules of semantic
interpretation, SI-1, have applied to S-structures and given
the representations in LF, these representations interact with
other cognitive representations to render complete semantic
representations by rules of SI-2. I consider these rules of
SI-2 to be part of the discourse, where discourse is understood
in its wide denotation and encompasses not only previous linguistic discourse but also extralinguistic context.

One of the claims to be substantiated in this study is that
the interpretation of presentational sentences takes place in
stages, that is to say, in LF, or sentence grammar, as well
as at SI-2, or discourse grammar. This, in turn, means that
some sentences are filtered out in LF while others are not discarded until SI-2.

In general, not much formal work has been done to pursue
the study of a particular problem beyond sentence grammar
into the discourse.[1] To achieve this aim I make use of some
of the insights provided by the European linguists of the
Prague School. Their theory of functional sentence perspective (FSP), especially, can be fruitfully incorporated into the
transformational framework, once one begins to strive for total
semantic interpretation. In order to fully accomplish this objective without undue disruption, I first provide a discussion
of some of the linguistic terminology which is relevant to this
analysis.

0.1.1 The dichotomies subject vs. predicate, theme vs.
rheme, old vs. new. It seems to be a tradition that some linguistic terminology gives rise to confusion and misinterpreta-
tions.[2] The dichotomies theme vs. rheme and old vs. new are
no exception. I am of the opinion that this confusion is due
mainly to two factors: first, to a lack of clear definitions, and
second, to the failure of some linguists to distinguish different
levels of analysis. In what follows, I outline a proposal which
incorporates at different points of the analysis the notions
theme vs. rheme, old vs. new, and also subject vs. predicate.

The pair 'subject' and 'predicate' is the least controversial
of the three. If 'subject of' is defined as the [NP, S] and
'predicate of' as the [VP, S] (Chomsky 1965), it can safely be
assumed that this pair belongs to the grammatical or syntactic
level. It is there that it plays a major role. These grammatical functions are necessary for such operations as NP-Prepos-
ing, Subject-Verb Agreement, Case Marking, Subject Raising,
and many others.

The terms 'theme' and 'rheme' come to us from Mathesius and
his disciples of the Prague School.[3] These scholars developed
a theory of Functional Sentence Perspective (FSP) which 'makes
it possible to understand how the semantic and grammatical
structures function in the very act of communication' (Daneš
1964:225). But even within the Prague School, not all linguists
define theme vs. rheme in exactly the same way. For example,
'Mathesius defines the theme as "that which is known or at
least obvious in a given situation, and from which the speaker
proceeds" in the discourse' (Firbas 1964:268). Thus, Mathesius
equates theme with old information[4] (and rheme with unknown)
within a given context. Firbas (1964:272) alters Mathesius' definitions to free the notion of theme from contextual dependency:

> the theme is constituted by the sentence element or elements
> carrying the lowest degree(s) of C[ommunicative] D[ynamism]
> within the sentence. It follows from this definition that the
> theme need not necessarily convey known information or such
> as can be gathered from the verbal or situational context.
> It can convey even new, unknown information. The essen-
> tial feature of the theme is the lowest degree of CD, not the
> conveyance of known information.[5]

Unfortunately, while Firbas succeeds in separating theme from
old and rheme from new information, he postulates a gradience
of themeness and rhemeness which, because of its arbitrariness,
renders these notions operationally useless (cf. Contreras 1976:
16, Adjémian 1978:266).

Another linguist who has found the theme vs. rheme opposition useful for linguistic analysis is Halliday (1967). He too
segregates rhematic structure from informational structure. For
him, the pair theme vs. rheme belongs to the realm of the
clause, whereas old vs. new information pertains to the

discourse.[6] Although at times I find Halliday's writings rather unclear and lacking in precision, he is the linguist who comes closest to my own beliefs of how theme and rheme should be defined in linguistic theory. Therefore, I quote him at length (1967:205):

> The functions 'given' and 'new' are however not the same as those of 'theme' and 'rheme'. The two are independently variable. But there is a relationship between them such that in the unmarked case the focus of information will fall on something other than the theme; it will fall at least within the rheme, though not necessarily extending over the whole of it...while given means what you were talking about or what I was talking about before, theme means what I am talking about now.

And, in talking specifically about English, he states (1967:223):

> English is structured simultaneously on the dimensions of given-new and theme-rheme, the former determining its organization into discourse units and the status of each such unit as a component in the discourse, the latter starting from its organization in sentence structure and framing each clause into the form of a message about one of its constituents, with the further possibility of an optional 'key signature' in the form of a theme relating to discourse or speech function.[7]

Since the goal of this manuscript is the study of presentational sentences, I define the rheme of an affirmative presentational sentence as that portion of the sentence which coincides with the scope of assertion (Givón 1975b,[8] Babby 1978 and 1980). Conversely, the theme of a presentational sentence is the unasserted part, that segment which falls outside the scope of assertion. These definitions do not necessarily relate to truth conditions but to conditions for successful communication.[9] Thus, in organizing a sentence in terms of theme vs. rheme, the speaker makes certain assumptions with respect to what is important, to what will carry the communication forward.

Having provided the definition for the terms of the dichotomy under study, it is now necessary to establish the level of analysis at which theme vs. rheme play a role. According to the definitions given, it should be possible to determine the theme vs. rheme structure of a sentence at the sentence level of analysis independently of the total discourse. More specifically, assuming the Extended Standard Theory (EST) model of grammar, I believe that theme vs. rheme enter into the analysis immediately after the level of logical form (LF). Recall that LF is arrived at from S-structures by rules of semantic interpretation; it incorporates those semantic properties that are strictly determined by linguistic rules, by grammatical structure (Chomsky 1976, 1980, and references therein). Grammatical structure plays a crucial role in the determination of theme vs. rheme. But since this dichotomy more appropriately relates to the act of communication in which the speaker's assumptions must be considered, I locate theme vs. rheme after the level of LF but still within sentence grammar, i.e. before the level of total discourse.

There remains one dichotomy: old vs. new. As opposed to theme vs. rheme, the pair old vs. new must take into account discourse context. When a sentence is considered in isolation, it is impossible to decide whether the whole sentence conveys exclusively new information or whether just a portion of it provides us with something new. Faced with a sentence like (2), it is difficult to ascertain what is old and what is new.

(2) Mis hijas están en la Florida con los abuelos.
'My daughters are in Florida with their grandparents.'

It is only after taking the discourse into account that it becomes possible to separate old from new. If (2) is a reply to (3), then the whole sentence constitutes new information. If (2) is given as an answer to (4), then only the prepositional phrases are new.

(3a) Se te ve muy descansada.
'You look very rested.'

(3b) La casa parece muy silenciosa.
'The house seems very quiet.'

(3c) ¿Qué hay de nuevo?
'What's up/new?'

(4) ¿Dónde están las niñas que no las oigo?
'Where are the girls that I don't hear them?'

Thus, old and new become relevant beyond sentence grammar, at a level where complete semantic representations are rendered through the interaction of semantic rules and other cognitive systems that draw from real world knowledge, beliefs, and context. For the sake of exposition I would call this level of complete semantic representations 'pragmatics', to keep it distinct from 'semantics'. The latter term I use in connection with sentence semantics up to the level of theme vs. rheme assignment (i.e. LF plus the determination of the scope of assertion).

Schematically, the three sets of dichotomies are 'located' as shown in (5).

Certainly, all three dichotomies might coincide and 'partition' a given sentence in exactly the same way.

(5)

Dichotomy	Level of relevance	
subject vs. predicate	syntactic level:	grammatical structure
theme vs. rheme	post-LF, sentence semantics:	rhematic structure[10]
old vs. new	discourse-level pragmatics:	information structure

(6a) -¿Qué sabes de Paco?
   what you-know of Paco
   'What's up with Paco?'

(6b) -Paco encontró un trabajo interesante.
   Paco found (3 sg.) a job interesting
   'Paco found an interesting job.'

In (6b), Paco is the grammatical subject, the theme, and moreover, given the question in (6a), he constitutes old information.
Encontró un trabajo interesante is the predicate, the rheme
(i.e. the portion of the sentence within the scope of assertion),
and it also provides new information. It is to be expected that
instances such as the foregoing, where all three dichotomies
coincide, constitute the most common state of affairs and, as
such, the unmarked case. But this is a statistical fact, not a
syntactic dictum. It is easy to show that the three dichotomies
are independent of each other. Note that the 'freer' the word
order exhibited by a given language, the easier it should become to demonstrate this. Consider the examples in (7).

(7a) En el jardín hay un elefante.
   'In the garden there-is an elephant.'

(7b) En el jardín apareció un elefante.
   in the garden appeared (3 sg.) an elephant
   'In the garden an elephant appeared.'

The underlining in (7) is meant to show the rheme. But
notice that while the rheme in (7a) encompasses the verb and
the direct object, in (7b) it includes the verb and its subject.
Both sentences have en el jardín as the theme.[11] But without
a larger context, it is impossible to determine what is given
and what is new information in (7). For example, if the examples in (7) were uttered out of the blue or in response to (8),
then the entire sentence would convey new information and,
consequently, both the theme and the rheme would carry new
information.

(8) ¿Por qué estás tan sorprendida?[12]
   'Why are-you so surprised?'

On the other hand, if (7) answers (9), the theme would
represent old information and the rheme new information.

(9) ¿Qué ves en el jardín?
    'What do-you-see (2 sg.) in the garden?'

Or, if (7) responds to (10), only the rhematic NP would
constitute new information.

(10) ¿Qué $\begin{Bmatrix} \text{hay} \\ \text{apareció} \end{Bmatrix}$ en el jardín?

     'What $\begin{Bmatrix} \text{is-there} \\ \text{appeared} \end{Bmatrix}$ in the garden?'

To further confirm the hypothesis that new and rheme are
independent of each other, a slightly different type of example
with impersonal <u>haber</u> is given in (11).

(11a) Era una muchacha como ya no <u>las</u> hay. (CT 155)[13]
      She-was a young-woman like already no them there-are
      'She was a young woman the likes of whom no longer
      exist.'

(11b) Ha habido muchas dificultades y aún <u>las</u> hay.
      there-have been many difficulties and still them
         there-exist
      'There have been and still are many difficulties.'

(11c) ...En Mallorca...los turistas han ido allí desde hace
      mucho tiempo...o sea...el turista rico...típico inglés
      etc. Esto es del siglo pasado,...iban a Mallorca...
      --...con su...
      --<u>Los</u>...<u>los</u> había mucho tiempo antes. (VEA 59)
      '...In Mallorca...the tourists have gone there for a
      long time...that is...the rich tourist...typically
      English etc. This is from the last century...they
      went to Mallorca...
      --...with their...
      --They were there from a long time before.'
      (Lit: them...them there-were...)

The examples of (11) constitute instances in which existential
<u>haber</u> cooccurs with an anaphoric clitic. Anaphoric clitics[14]
convey old information; their referents can only be identified
by taking into account the preceding context or situation.
Notice that while the referents for the clitics in (11a) and
(11b) are to be found in the immediately preceding clause, the
one for (11c), <u>los turistas</u>, is to be found at a considerable
distance. In spite of this fact, all of these clitics are still
part of the rheme, that is, they are within the scope of assertion of their respective sentences. The speaker uses these
anaphoric clitics to signal to the addressee something like 'I
haven't shifted my attention to another matter; I'm still talking
about the same situation.' The clitics reintroduce (part of) the

rheme into the discourse; and this reintroduction is done anaphorically because this is one of the ways in which recoverable
information tends to be presented in the discourse.[15]

As a matter of fact, it is possible to envision sequences in
which the entire sentence is old information. They might be
highly redundant, but they do occur in actual speech. For
example, picture a child who has been waiting for a present
sent by grandma and who has been asking the same question
(12a) every five seconds. The child may receive (12b) as an
answer.

    (12a) ¿Ya vino el cartero?
           already came (3 sg.) the mailman?
           'Has the mailman already come?'

    (12b) Sí, vino el cartero (pero no te trajo nada.)
           yes, came the mailman (but not to-you brought nothing)
           'Yes, the mailman came (but he didn't bring you any-
              thing).'

In (12b), vino el cartero is still the rheme although the information is old in view of the question it answers.[16] There might
be all kinds of reasons for reiterating old information in the
asserted part of the sentences. Some might be purely syntactic, others of a pragmatic nature; but the fact is that it happens in natural languages, since these are not known for their
conciseness, precision, and economy.[17]

Finally, observe that just as there are sentences in Spanish
that are syntactically subjectless and all rheme (see Chapter 1
for discussion and justification), for example (13), there are
other sentences that, even though they manifest the dichotomy
subject vs. predicate, are all rheme (14).

(13) Hay $\begin{Bmatrix} \text{un libro} \\ \text{varios libros} \end{Bmatrix}$ sobre la mesa.

    'There $\begin{Bmatrix} \text{is a book} \\ \text{are several books} \end{Bmatrix}$ on the table.'

    (14a) Salió el sol.
           came-out (3 sg.) the sun
           'The sun appeared.'

    (14b) Manaba sangre.
           oozed (3 sg.) blood
           'Blood was seeping out.'

These facts show that it is not necessarily the case that all
sentences need to be completely balanced and have both parts
of the dichotomies under discussion.[18] Therefore, there are
sentences which do not have a subject (cf. (7a) and (13)),

some which are all rhematic (cf. (13) and (14)), and some
which convey exclusively old information (cf. (12b)).
To sum up, it has been shown that the three dichotomies
under discussion (subject vs. predicate, theme vs. rheme, old
vs. new) may work independently of each other, and that each
of them belongs to a different level or dimension of analysis.
Most of the facts pointed out in this section have, at one time
or another, been discussed by various scholars.[19] This contribution consists of providing an unambiguous definition for
theme vs. rheme, having separated different levels of analysis,
and restating these concepts within EST. The analysis confirms the need for distinguishing sentence from discourse phenomena as hypothesized by Williams (1977), since it has been
demonstrated that while theme vs. rheme assignment belongs to
sentence grammar, old vs. new information pertains to the
larger realm of the discourse.

**0.1.1.1 The relationship between the determiner and the
dichotomy old vs. new.** The confusion arising from the practice of using the dichotomy old vs. new for sentence-level
semantics has had its repercussions in the analysis of the
determiners. Thus, the definitive article has been equated
with known information more often than not (Chafe 1976,
Kempson 1975, Bello 1970). The problem is that 'definiteness'
is an exclusively syntactic feature which does not always correspond to semantic definiteness (cf. Chapter 1, especially Section 1.3.1.3.1.5; Bolinger 1977; Herschensohn 1979). Definiteness may correspond to known information because of a purely
linguistic factor such as context (cf. (15)) or because the noun
referent represents some shared knowledge between speaker
and hearer (cf. (16)), a purely pragmatic factor.

(15)   Vienen un hombre y una mujer. El hombre lleva
       sombrero, la mujer una cartera enorme.
       come (3 pl.) a man and a woman the man carries hat,
       the woman a purse huge
       'A man and a woman are coming. The man has a hat,
       the woman a huge purse.'

(16)   A medianoche llegaron los abuelos.
       at midnight arrived (3 pl.) the grandparents
       'The grandparents arrived at midnight.'

Notice that in both examples we have gone beyond a single
sentence: into the discourse in (15), and into pragmatics in
(16). Once again it becomes evident that old vs. new does
not play a part in sentence grammar.
As a matter of fact, the determiner in presentationals is not
syntactically constrained at all. Although it might be argued
that the 'ideal' presentational should introduce its NP with an
indefinite determiner, such indefiniteness is by no means

required. Examples are found with indefinite as well as definite determiners (cf. Section 1.3.1).

Even proper names--both animate (17b) and (17c), and inanimate (17a) and (17d)--appear in the type of presentational sentence discussed in Chapter 2.

(17a) Y a la derecha de los hipopótamos empieza Asia. (H 8)
     and to the right of the hippopotamus begins (3 sg.)
     Asia
     'And Asia begins to the right of the hippopotamus.'

(17b) Ya salió Roberto. (H 13)
     already went-out (3 sg.) Roberto
     'Roberto already went out.'

(17c) Y cuando en nuestro siglo surgen Freud y... (H 13)
     and when in our century appear (3 pl.) Freud and
     'And when Freud and...appear in our century...'

(17d) Iba anocheciendo; surgía Madrid,... (H 13)
     was becoming-dark; emerged (3 sg.) Madrid,...
     'It was becoming dark; Madrid was emerging...'

In sum, it will be shown that there are no syntactic constraints on the determiner of presentationals. Any determiner, and even proper names, may appear in them. The concepts of new vs. old cannot be used to control the choice of the determiner, first, because this information is not available at the level of sentence grammar;[20] and second, because for the most part pragmatic factors enter into the decision as to what is new or old.

0.1.2 Focus. Intertwined with the concepts theme vs. rheme and old vs. new is that of 'focus'. Focus is often understood to be the specific word in the sentence that receives the main sentential stress, lluvia in (18a) and desgracias in (18b).[21]

(18a) Llegó la lluvia.
     came (3 sg.) the rain
     'The rain came.'

(18b) Supongo que no habrán ocurrido desgracias. (H 9)
     I-assume that no will-have (3 pl.) occurred mishaps
     'I assume that no mishaps have occurred.'

It has already been noticed by Firbas (1964) that even within the theme and the rheme the degrees of communicative dynamism are not homogeneous. Halliday (1967) calls the element which receives prominence within the message the 'information focus'. This focus 'reflects the speaker's decision as to where the main burden of the message lies' (1967:204). Within the Spanish tradition, Bolinger (1954 and 1954-1955) studied the effects of both sentential stress and word order. He writes (1954:125) that sentential stress signals the 'information point':

mark the 'point' of the sentence where there is the greatest concentration of information, that which the hearer would be least likely to infer without being told.

It is this 'information focus' or 'information point' which is labeled as 'focus' in this book. It represents the most important or 'loaded' element in the sentence, and it tends to fall within the rheme under conditions of neutral stress and intonation.[22] Thus, focus is a semantic notion.

A certain confusion traditionally surrounds the use of this term. For example, Jackendoff (1972:230) defines the 'focus' of a sentence as that part which denotes 'the information in a sentence that is assumed by the speaker not to be shared by him and the hearer'. His counterpart to 'focus' is 'presupposition'--that part which denotes 'the information in a sentence that is assumed by the speaker to be shared by him and the hearer'. Thus, 'focus' and 'presupposition' are reminiscent of Chafe's definition of 'new' and 'given' (cf. note 4).

Halliday himself (1967:204) states: 'What is focal is "new" information; not in the sense that it cannot have been previously mentioned, although it is often the case that it has not been, but in the sense that the speaker presents it as not being recoverable from the preceding discourse'. And then he adds, 'But the non-predictability of the new does not necessarily imply factually new information; the newness may lie in the speech function, or it may be a matter of contrast with what has been said before or what might be expected' (1967: 205-206).

I think that to equate focus with 'new' is a mistake that can only lead to more confusion. Even Halliday admits that in this use 'new' does not mean 'factually new information'. Moreover, focus (at least noncontrastive focus, which is the type that interests us here) can be determined within sentence grammar independently of the discourse; as already shown, old and new pertain to the larger context of the discourse. If I am correct in making this distinction, and if we accept with Williams (1977) the principle of 'strict utterance' which maintains that rules of discourse grammar must apply only after all the rules of sentence grammar, then focus could not be identified with or assigned on the basis of new information, since this information would not be available at the point at which focus assignment takes place.

Observe that, although nothing prevents semantic focus and phonological focus from coinciding (cf. Bolinger's quote already cited), there is in principle nothing which requires that this should be the only possibility, especially since each type of

focus belongs to a different side of the grammar (cf. (1)).
More is said about this notion of focus in the following chapters.

   0.2 Scope and organization. The two types of Spanish presentational sentences are studied against a background both of
descriptive insights and of ample data, so that most of the
analysis should survive any refinements of the theory. This
treatise also shows what should be considered if an account of
Spanish presentational sentences is undertaken within a theoretical framework other than the one employed here.
   This investigation does not claim to represent the linguistic
competence of any one native speaker or even of a group of
speakers (i.e. of any one dialect); on the contrary, its purpose is to explore and determine the parameters of the Spanish
language as a system, at least in that portion of the language
which pertains to the two types of presentational sentences
under examination. This is the reason for collecting the data
from different sources (cf. list of sources of data). Therefore,
it is to be expected that not all native speakers will judge uni-
formly or unequivocally the grammaticality or appropriateness
of some of the examples.
   This work is organized in the following way. Chapter 1 investigates the presentational construction par excellence: impersonal haber sentences. After a consideration of the syntactic and semantic characteristics inherent in these sentences,
their constituent analysis is determined. The syntax and the
semantic interpretation of haber sentences is given, and the
determiners which occur with the NP argument are examined in
detail. As a result of this analysis, the Definiteness Restriction is shown to be ill founded. The chapter closes with a
look at impersonal haber sentences in nonstandard Spanish,
   Chapter 2 explores the second type of presentational sentences: those manifested by the sequence of intransitive verb
plus subject. The peculiarities of this construction are stated,
and these sentences are shown to be distinct from declarative
sentences. It is determined that their surface structure is
arrived at by a syntactic movement rule of Subject Postposing.
The grammar of intransitive presentational sentences follows,
and the chapter concludes with an examination of the theoretical implications of leftward traces.
   Chapter 3 grapples with the fact that some presentational
sentences of the intransitive kind cannot be paired with a
corresponding well-formed declarative sentence. As a result,
the Naked Noun Constraint (NNC) is born. [23] Its pertinent
parameters and its reason for being are the main concern of
this chapter. Since contrastive sentences do not adhere to
this constraint, their grammar is outlined and compared to
that of presentational sentences. Finally, it is concluded that
the NNC should be stated as a filter.
   Spanish is known as one of the languages with so-called 'free'
word order. Therefore, it is relevant to determine whether it

has a basic word order and, if so, what this basic word order is. This is the purpose of Chapter 4. Different basic word order possibilities are investigated, both within the ordered base hypothesis and within the unordered base hypothesis. In the end it is determined that Spanish is SVO and that the ordered base hypothesis provides for a more consistent and principled analysis.

Chapter 5 summarizes the principal results and defines areas for future research related to the two types of presentational sentences examined.

Two appendices are included in this book. The first is related to Section 1.3.1.1. Similarities and differences in the usage of the three verbs, hay-estar-ser, all of which are translated as English 'be', are pointed out, and Bull's proposal is refined in order that all the relevant data can be accounted for. The second appendix investigates three types of Spanish sentences which have no subject in outer structure. One of them is impersonal haber. The analysis adheres to Chomsky's (1980b) assertion that:

> The investigation of properties of 'missing elements' is of particular interest for the study of mental representations. Their properties presumably are not derived by the language learner from actual expressions, since the elements in question are not physically present. Rather, they derive from properties of the system of grammar, and thus give unique insight into the nature of the principles of grammar.

In this appendix it is hypothesized that Spanish has three kinds of null subjects--PRO, trace, and ∅; and, moreover, that [± obligatory subject] is one of the significant parameters along which languages may vary.

NOTES

1. There are some exceptions, of course; see Guéron (1978, 1980). Williams' (1977) valuable work concentrates on the interaction between sentence grammar and discourse grammar. Kuno (1978, 1979 and references therein) has been one of the first linguists to show how pragmatics interacts with syntax.
2. As an example within generative grammar, consider the case of the terms deep and surface structure.
3. For a critical survey of the development of the notions theme vs. rheme in linguistic theory (with an emphasis on French), see C. Adjémian's (1978) article.
4. Chafe (1974:119), while discussing the Prague School terms theme and rheme, equates 'theme' of a sentence with that information assumed to be in the addressee's consciousness, and 'rheme' with material being newly introduced into the

addressee's consciousness. Therefore, for Chafe, it is also the case that theme = given and rheme = new.

5. By degree of communicative dynamism, Firbas (1964:270) means 'the extent to which the sentence element contributes to the development of the communication, to which it "pushes the communication forward"'.

6. Quite a few other linguists have used theme vs. rheme in their analysis. Just to name a few: Gundel (1977), Chafe (1974), Babby (1980), Contreras (1976), Adjémian (1978-1979), and, of course, Kuno (see References). This does not mean that all of them define the terms in the same way. For example, both Contreras and Adjémian blend 'theme' with 'old' and 'rheme' with 'new' in agreement with Chafe's definitions (cf. note 4).

7. Halliday's 'key signature' appears to be related to Williams' notion of 'discourse-conditioned' rules (cf. Williams 1977:102-103).

8. Givón (1975a:185) also manifests a certain amount of confusion and identifies assertion with new information. He writes, 'It is normally assumed, for the "neutral" sentence pattern of a language, that the predicate phrase ("verb phrase") contains the new information or asserted portion [emphasis mine, M.S.], while the subject is the topic or presupposed portion with respect to which the assertion is being made.'

9. For example, Kempson (1975) separates logical presupposition from speaker presupposition. This latter type is in contrast to assertion. Notice that I prefer to define 'theme/rheme' as 'nonassertion/assertion' rather than 'presupposition/assertion'. The difference might be subtle, but nonassertion is a more neutral term and avoids confusion with logical and philosophical terminology.

10. In previous versions of this work I used 'thematic structure' in accordance with Prague School linguists. I have replaced this terminology with 'rhematic structure' to avoid any confusions with thematic structure as it relates to thematic relations in the sense of Jackendoff (1972) and more recent work within the EST.

11. Halliday (1967:212) identifies the 'theme' with what comes first in the clause, with what is being talked about (vs. 'given', which represents what was talked about), with the point of departure of the clause as message. But theme does not necessarily need to precede everything else in a clause. Right-dislocated structures are thematic, since they are inherently resumptive in nature, sort of clarifications or afterthoughts. See the discussion in Chapter 3 and also Gundel (1977), for example.

12. Conceivably, (8) could also be answered with (i).

(i)   Un elefante apareció en el jardín.
      'An elephant appeared in the garden.'

The difference between the presentational sentence (7b) and the declarative sentence (i) consists of a difference in what is included in the scope of assertion (i.e. rheme). In (7b) the speaker considers un elefante to be more important or relevant than its location, while in (i) the reverse is true.

13. Throughout this book I include in parentheses the source and page number of pertinent examples. The sources of data are listed after the references.

14. Spanish clitics are always unstressed (a fact which is implied in the label 'clitic'), so that they could not even be considered to be contrastive.

15. Other ways are by substitution or deletion. The reader should keep in mind that the NP argument which appears with hay is the object argument (see Section 1.1.1.3). Clitics can only 'replace' object arguments in Spanish.

16. Silva-Corvalán's (1978) study of spoken Mexican-American Spanish includes the following table which cross-tabulates subject position by old and new information. Her corpus included a total of 338 expressed subjects out of a total of 795 tokens.

	Old information			New information		
	50+	35-45	Total	50+	34-45	Total
Postverbal	$\frac{52}{127}$ 40.9%	$\frac{58}{158}$ 36.7%	$\frac{110}{285}$ 38.6%	$\frac{15}{29}$ 51.7%	$\frac{19}{24}$ 79.2%	$\frac{34}{53}$ 64.2%
Preverbal	$\frac{75}{127}$ 59.1%	$\frac{100}{158}$ 63.3%	$\frac{175}{285}$ 61.4%	$\frac{14}{29}$ 48.3%	$\frac{5}{24}$ 20.8%	$\frac{19}{53}$ 35.8%
Significance ($p < 0.001$)						

Of specific interest here is the fact that 38.6 percent (representing 110 instances out of 285) of postverbal subjects constitute old information, while 35.8 percent (19 out of 53) of preverbal subjects stand for new information. Thus, this work supports my claim that theme vs. rheme should be kept separate from new vs. old.

17. One of the factors that might have led the utterer of (12b) to reiterate vino el cartero could have been the fact that s/he was talking to a young child. Many times we tend to repeat things to young children in the hope that the message gets across.

18. Some Prague School linguists were already aware of this possibility (although Firbas (1964) maintained that all sentences have theme and theme). Contreras (1976) also points out the potential for having sentences which consist exclusively of rheme (but keep in mind that he equates rheme with new information).

19. For example, Firbas (1966:241) says, 'The function of the sentence in the act of communication can be successfully interpreted if three levels are kept separate: those of the semantic and the grammatical structure of the sentence and that of FSP.' If the level of Functional Sentence Perspective (FSP) is interpreted in the sense of organization of the utterance as the rhematic structure level, Firbas' three levels translate into

four in my framework, since after the levels of grammatical
structure and FSP (my rhematic structure), his semantic structure is equivalent to the two levels of LF and SI-2 within the
EST.

To demonstrate that there is very little new under the sun, I
cannot resist the following by Daneš (1964), in which he expands
on the autonomy of the syntax.

> As for the grammatical level, it can be characterized by the
> fact that it is autonomous, and not onesidedly dependent on
> the semantic content; consequently, it is a rather self-
> contained and determining component. Thus, the grammati-
> cal categories such as subject, etc. are not based on the se-
> mantic content, but on the syntactic form only; they are
> bearers of a linguistic function in a given system. The
> autonomy of the grammatical form reveals itself in the fact
> of diversity of languages (while the semantic categories,
> being extra-linguistic, seem to be universal, or nearly so).
> The autonomy and dominance of grammar does not mean that
> there is no correspondence between both levels; but it must
> be underlined that, e.g. the relation between the grammati-
> cal sentence elements and the respective semantic categories
> is not that of identity, but of close or distinct affinity.

As a matter of fact, Daneš criticizes Chomsky (1962) for not
respecting 'the difference between the grammatical and the semantic level in syntax' (1964:226).

20. Of course, it goes without saying that this implies the
acceptance of Williams' (1977) model.

21. Thus, this characterization of focus coincides with Chomsky's (1971), which maintains that the focus of an utterance is
the phrase that contains the intonational center.

22. Observe that 'focus' and 'rheme', as defined in this
paper, cannot be equated as one and the same thing. At
most, it is possible to say that under neutral, noncontrastive
stress and intonation the focus falls on one of the elements of
the rheme.

23. The predecessor of this chapter was presented at the
Colloquium on Hispanic and Luso-Brazilian Linguistics in
Oswego, New York in July, 1976 in the form of a paper en-
titled 'The Spanish Naked Noun Constraint'.

1

IMPERSONAL *HABER*

1.0 Introduction. The purpose of this chapter is to provide an in-depth study of the syntax and semantics of impersonal haber sentences in Spanish. To achieve this aim, the discussion has been divided into four major sections. Section 1.1 examines the properties which characterize this existential verb. Section 1.2 explores the constituent structure of haber sentences: the obligatoriness of its object argument and the kinds of modifications which it allows. This part closes with a brief look at clitics and at the word orders adopted by this type of sentence. Section 1.3 presents the grammar of impersonal haber sentences. It is shown that while their syntax is extremely uncomplicated, their semantic interpretation is achieved in stages. A thorough study of the determiners which cooccur with the NP object is included, after which the Definiteness Restriction is examined and evaluated. Section 1.4 contains an investigation of impersonal haber in nonstandard Spanish. Finally, the chapter concludes with a summary of its principal findings (Section 1.5).

1.1 Characterization of impersonal *haber*

1.1.1 Syntactic traits. Syntactically speaking, haber in its impersonal use[1] is a one-argument verb which invariably adopts the third person singular form. Since its only NP functions as a direct object, this is a syntactically subjectless verb. In the following subsections, I examine each of the characteristics of this verb in turn.

1.1.1.1 Third person singular. In that variety of Spanish sanctioned by the official grammars of the language, impersonal haber appears only in the third person singular, regardless of its syntactic environment.

(1a) Hay mucho sol hoy.[2,3]
there-is much sun today
'It's very sunny today.'

(1b) Junto al cordón de la vereda había un gran automóvil
negro. (R 51)
by to-the curb of the sidewalk there-was a big car
black
'By the sidewalk curb there was a big black car.'

(1c) Hubo un arreglo entre ellas. (TE 166)
'There-was an agreement between them (f. pl.).'

The form of the verb is 'frozen' in the third person singular
in standard Spanish, even when its NP argument is plural.[4]

(2a) Aquí no habrá lujos, pero hay corazones sinceros que
la quieren.
here not there-will-be luxuries, but there-is hearts
sincere that her (acc.) love (3 pl.)
'Here there may not exist luxuries, but there are
honest hearts that love her.'

(2b) ...y de pronto hubo dos personas... (IM 30)
'...and suddenly there-were two persons...'

(2c) A mi llegada había centenares de peces muertos...
(IM 21)
on my arrival there-was hundreds of fishes dead...
'On my arrival there were hundreds of dead fish.'[5]

1.1.1.2 Syntactically subjectless. The examples in (2) can
also serve to show that impersonal haber is syntactically subjectless. Since all subjects in Spanish trigger subject-verb
agreement, the NP argument which accompanies impersonal
haber must not be a subject. Compare (3) with examples
containing hay in (4) and (5).

(3a) El niño llegó (3 sg.) a las cinco.
'The boy arrived at 5 o'clock.'

(3b) Los niños llegaron (3 pl.) a las cinco.'
'The boys arrived at 5 o'clock.'

(3c) Nosotros llegamos (1 pl.) a las cinco.'
'We arrived at 5 o'clock.'

(4a) Hay un testigo.
'There-is one witness.'

(4b) Hay tres testigos.
'There-are three witnesses.'

(5a) Había una casa magnífica...
'There-was a magnificent house...'

(5b) Había dos casas magníficas...
'There-were two magnificent houses...'

Since the plural NP argument does not cause the verb to
pluralize in (4b), (5b), and in the examples in (2), the foregone conclusion is that this NP must not be the subject of the
sentence. [6]
Moreover, the NP argument strictly subcategorized by haber
does not govern subject-verb agreement in Subject-Raising environments, precisely because this NP is an object and as such
it cannot be raised to the subject position of the matrix sentence. To illustrate the process of Subject-Raising in Spanish,
observe what happens with parecer 'to seem' in example (6).

(6a) Parece que los niños están dormidos.
'It-seems that the children are asleep (3 pl.).'

(6b) Los niños parecen estar dormidos.
'The children seem to be asleep.'

(6c) Parecen estar dormidos, los niños.
seem (3 pl.) to be asleep, the children

Sentence (6a) is an instance of parecer followed by an embedded que clause. Example (6b) shows that the subject of
the embedded clause (los niños) has been raised to subject
position of the matrix sentence; this, in turn, has caused the
main verb to take the third person plural ending to agree with
its subject. Sentence (6c) illustrates a slightly more complicated structure; here los niños is right-dislocated, but the
subject of the infinitive clause (a third person plural pronominal) has been raised to matrix subject position, triggering
subject-verb agreement. After an anaphoric relationship is
established between the matrix subject and the right-dislocated
NP (cf. Rivero 1980), this pronominal subject is deleted by the
Subject PRO-Drop rule. In essence, the structure of (6c) is
that given in (7) (details aside).

(7) $[_S \begin{bmatrix} PRO_i \\ 3\ pl \end{bmatrix}$ parecen $[_S [_{NP_i} t]$ estar dormidos]]

$[_{NP_i}$ los niños]...

What happens with an hay sentence embedded under parecer is shown in (8).

(8a) Parece que hay muchas quejas.
'It-seems that there-are many complaints.'

(8b) *Muchas quejas parecen haber.

(8c) *Parecen haber muchas quejas.

Regardless of the preverbal (8b) or postverbal (8c) position of muchas quejas, these two sentences are ungrammatical because an 'illegal' agreement has taken place between the NP muchas quejas and parecer. Such ungrammaticality results from the function of this NP. Being an object, it cannot undergo Subject-Raising and thereby trigger Subject-Verb agreement. Crucially, the grammatical sentence (9a) differs from (6c) in that the NP in final position is not right-dislocated; the structure of (9a) is shown in (9b) (again, details omitted).

(9a) Parece haber muchas quejas.
it-seems there-to-be many complaints

(9b) [$_S$ parece [$_S$[$_{VP}$ haber muchas quejas]]]

An argument similar to the one developed with Subject-Raising can be presented by using Equi. If the NP argument of hay had a subject function, it should be possible to interpret it as coreferential with the matrix subject. That is, given examples such as those found in (10a) and (10b), it should be the case that (11) would be a grammatical sentence.

(10a) Mucha gente quiere X.
'Many people (sg.) want (3 sg.) X.'

(10b) Haber mucha gente en la fiesta.
there-to-be many people in the party

(11) *Mucha gente quiere haber en la fiesta.

It is obvious that (11) is ungrammatical. Its starred status is a natural consequence of the nonsubject function of the haber argument.

At least three other facts follow from the subjectless nature of this verb. In the first place, hay cannot cooccur with impersonal se. Impersonal se is used only with those verbs which may occur with a [+human] subject.

(12a) Se vivía mejor en otros tiempos.
'One / PRO} lived better in times past.'

(12b) <u>Se</u> tiene más conciencia de la contaminación hoy en día.

$\left.\begin{array}{l}\text{'One}\\\text{'PRO}\end{array}\right\}$ is more aware of pollution nowadays.'

(12c) *<u>Se</u> nieva en enero.

$\left.\begin{array}{l}\text{'One}\\\text{'PRO}\end{array}\right\}$ snows in January.'

Since <u>hay</u> does not take a subject (human or otherwise), it can be predicted that it will never appear with impersonal <u>se</u>. This prediction is borne out in (13).

(13)   *<u>Se</u> hay un lobo afuera.
       there-is a wolf outside

The second piece of evidence comes from the reflexive use of <u>se</u>. On the premise that reflexive interpretation takes place between the clitic and the subject argument (14), one can predict, as well as explain, the nonexistence of sentences with <u>hay</u> and a reflexive clitic.

(14)   Las niñas_i se_i peinaban en la sala.
       the girls (f. pl.) themselves combed in the living room
       'The girls were combing their hair in the living room.'

The third fact is a consequence of the subjectlessness of <u>hay</u> in conjunction with its invariably third person singular trait. <u>Hay</u> never appears in the imperative form. A command requires a being (subject) who is able to carry out the command; moreover, direct orders are given to an implicit <u>you</u> (second person).[7] Since <u>hay</u> does not take a subject and invariably appears in the third person, it does not fulfill either of these prerequisites. Thus, it comes as no surprise that there do not exist commands with <u>hay</u>.

(15)   *¡Hay (tú) más helado!
       there-is (you) more ice-cream

Impersonal <u>haber</u> is not the only subjectless verb in Spanish. Minimally, there is at least one other verb of this type: impersonal <u>hacer</u> 'to do, make'. This verb also appears only in the third person singular in standard Spanish.[8]

(16a) Hace (3 sg., present) frío hoy.
       it-makes cold today
       'It is cold today.'

(16b) ¿Qué tiempo hizo (3 sg., preterit) ayer?
       what weather made yesterday
       'What was the weather yesterday?'

Subjectless verbs show that the subject argument is not obligatory in Spanish; in its absence the verb adopts the unmarked features of person and number (third person singular). As in the case of hay, hacer does not appear with impersonal se, nor with reflexive clitics, nor in the imperative form.[9]

1.1.1.3 Object function of the NP argument. To further disprove any hypothetical claims of subjecthood for the NP argument of hay, it can be shown that this NP functions as direct object. Spanish direct objects may be cliticized to the verb by means of the appropriate accusative clitics: lo (m. sg.), la (f. sg.), los (m. pl.), and las (f. pl.).

(17a) ¿Compraste un regalo (m. sg.) para María?
      --Sí, lo (m. sg.) compré ayer.
      'Did you buy a present for Mary?
      --Yes, I bought it yesterday.'

(17b) ¿Conseguiste flores (f. pl.) para la fiesta?
      --Sí, ya las (f. pl.) conseguí.
      'Did you get flowers for the party?
      --Yes, I got them already.'

In (17a) un regalo is referred to by the clitic lo, and in (17b) flores is alluded to by the clitic las. Precisely the same type of cliticization occurs in reference to the NP argument of impersonal haber.

(18a) Hay magníficas perspectivas en la cordillera, y no las
      hay menos hermosas y variadas en los valles.
      (Ramsey, PP 22.5)
      'There are magnificent views (f. pl.) in the mountains,
      and there are no less beautiful and varied ones (f.
      pl.) in the valleys.'

(18b) ¿Hay un médico en este pueblo?
      Sí que lo hay.
      'Is there a doctor (m. sg.) in this town?
      Of course there is one (m. sg.).'

In (18a) magníficas perspectivas is referred to by the anaphoric clitic las, and in (18b), un médico is cliticized by the corresponding masculine singular clitic lo. If the haber NP argument were a subject, the cliticization illustrated in (18) could not have taken place; direct object clitics can never refer to subject arguments. Consequently, there are two pieces of evidence that conclusively prove that the NP argument of impersonal haber is an object: (1) the NP does not trigger verb agreement in standard Spanish, and (2) the NP may be cliticized by means of an accusative clitic.[10]

1.1.1.4 Further properties. There is still another peculiarity about <u>hay</u> that can be taken to follow from its subjectless nature. It has to do with the so-called 'personal a'. It is a well-known fact about Spanish that personal <u>a</u> is used before specific human objects.[11]

(19a) Vio $\begin{cases} \text{al niño} \\ \text{a un estudiante} \\ \text{a dos personas} \end{cases}$ en la tienda.

'S/he saw $\begin{cases} \text{the child} \\ \text{a student} \\ \text{two persons} \end{cases}$ at the store.'

(19b) Vio $\begin{cases} (\text{*a) la camisa azul} \\ (\text{*a) un libro nuevo} \end{cases}$ en la tienda.

'S/he saw $\begin{cases} \text{the blue shirt} \\ \text{a new book} \end{cases}$ at the store.'

Thus, the direct objects in (19a) require the personal <u>a</u> but those in (19b) do not. However, this <u>a</u> may also emerge when both subject and object are nonhuman.

(20a) El rojo pasó <u>al</u> azul.
'The red passed the blue (one).'

(20b) El perro mordió <u>al</u> gato.
'The dog bit the cat.'

(20c) El pronombre suplanta <u>al</u> nombre.
the pronoun replaces the noun
'Pronouns replace nouns.'

Obviously, it is not possible to maintain that personal <u>a</u> appears in (20) because the direct object is human. Examples such as those found in (20), together with those in (19) and others, have given rise to different hypotheses. The most widespread hypothesis maintains that the function of personal <u>a</u> is to set direct objects apart from subjects (Ramsey 1956, Roldán 1971a). A different claim is made by Luján (1978), who states that a descriptively adequate analysis must be based on the selectional restrictions of the verb with respect to both subjects and objects.

Regardless of where the ultimate answer for personal <u>a</u> lies, I now return to impersonal <u>haber</u>. It is important to the discussion that this verb <u>never</u> takes personal <u>a</u>, not even when it has a specific human object.

(21a) Hay (*a) un médico en el pueblo.
'There-is a doctor in (the) town.'

(21b) ...y de pronto hubo (*a) dos personas...
'...and suddenly there-were two persons...' (IM 30)

(21c) No hay ya (*a) los grandes poetas de otros tiempos
(Bello, 295)
no there-is already the great poets of other times
'The great poets of yesteryear do not exist anymore.'

(21d) También había (*a) los hombres de extrema derecha y
los de extrema izquierda.
'There were also the men of the extreme right and
those of the extreme left.'

Why should this be so? It is possible to speculate that hay
never cooccurs with personal a because this verb never appears
with an NP subject. In other words, due to its subjectlessness,
there is no need to set an object NP unequivocally apart from
a subject NP, nor is it necessary to take selectional restrictions
into consideration. The sole criterion that must be kept in
mind to explain this idiosyncrasy about hay is that it is a
subjectless verb.[12]
The inability of impersonal haber to cooccur with personal a
might be construed by some as an argument against the direct
object function of its single NP. This would be a mistake.
Since it has already been shown that this NP cannot perform
the subject function, the only viable possibility left to be considered (other than direct object) is for the NP to be a predicate nominal. This hypothesis can be proven wrong by showing that the NP does not behave like a predicate nominal. Observe the behavior of a predicate nominal argument under
cliticization.

(22a) ¿Paco es un médico?
'Paco is a doctor?'

Sí, lo es.
Yes, it (neuter) he-is
'Yes, he is.'

(22b) ¿Susana es una arquitecta?
Susana is an architect (f. sg.)?

Sí, lo/*la es.
Yes, it (neuter) she-is
'Yes, she is.'

(22c) ¿Paco y Susana son dos profesionales?
'Paco and Susana are two professionals?'

Sí, lo/*los son.
Yes, it (neuter) they-are
'Yes, they are.'

In sum, a predicate nominal argument can be referred to only
by the invariable neuter clitic lo. This is in marked opposition
to the behavior of clitics vis-à-vis the argument of hay (cf.
Section 1.1.1.3). Recall that in this latter case the clitics
must coincide in number and gender with the noun they allude
to. Consequently, despite the fact that hay never selects a
personal a to introduce its NP argument, this argument is a
direct object.

Aside from the traits just discussed, which for the most part
stem from its subjectless nature, impersonal haber behaves just
as any other verb in the language. For example, it may appear
in any tense and aspect.

(23a) ...a veces hay pequeñas sorpresas. (CH 126)
'...sometimes there-are (present) small surprises.'

(23b) ...a la puerta había una muchacha. (R 81)
'...at the door there-was (imperfect) a young woman.'

(23c) En 15 días hubo tres grandes inundaciones. (IM 27)
'In 15 days there-were (preterit) three huge floods.'

(23d) ...habrá completa separación entre la Iglesia y el
Estado... (LP 12)
'...there-will-be (future) complete separation between
Church and State...'

(23e) ...iba a haber una oportunidad. (VEA 39)
'...there-was-going-to-be a chance.'

(23f) -Claro que sigue habiendo arrozales... (VEA 58)
'Of course (that) there-continue-to-be rice fields...'

(23g) ...ahora último ha habido mucho entusiasmo... (VEA 48)
'...lately there-has-been (present perfect) a lot of
enthusiasm...'

(23h) ...que...aunque sea indirectamente...está habiendo
un eh...proselitismo, ¿no? (VEA 47)
'...that...although indirectly...there-is-(being)
(present progressive) (a) uh...proselytizing, isn't
there?'

The sentences in (23) are just a few examples which serve to
illustrate the freedom that this verb exhibits with respect to
tense and aspect. Moreover, it is also used in 'periphrasis':
in (23e) it turns up in the shape of an infinitive and in (23f)

as a present participle. And, contrary to what prescriptive
grammars maintain, it can even be found in the progressive
(23h).[13]
It can also be shown that impersonal haber is not restricted
with respect to mood. The examples in (23) are instances of
the indicative mood; but should the situation warrant it, hay
also occurs in the subjunctive.

(24a) Usted se lo dirá más adelante cuando ya no haya
peligro. (R 84).
'You will tell it to her later when there-is (present
subjunctive) no more danger.'

(24b) ...como si no hubiera escape posible. (VEA 88a)
'...as if there-weren't (imperfect subjunctive) any
possible way out.'

(24c) ...querían que allí hubiese también otras instituciones
de cultura. (LP 18)
'...they-wanted there also to be (imperfect subjunctive) other institutions of culture there.'

The examples in (24) also show that hay is free to occur in
nonmatrix clauses. In (24a) it is embedded in an adverbial
clause, in (24b) in an if clause, and in (24c) in a noun clause.
To sum up the defining syntactic characteristics of impersonal
haber in standard Spanish, it has been shown that this is a
verb which never takes a subject argument and that its finite
form is always third person singular. The single NP argument
in the sentence functions as direct object, since it may be
cliticized by an accusative clitic of the appropriate gender and
number. Furthermore, this verb never cooccurs with the so-
called personal a.

1.1.2 **Semantic conditions.** Hay is an interesting verb not
only because of its peculiar syntactic characteristics (discussed
in Section 1.1.1), but also because of its semantic ones. This
verb is the existential verb par excellence. In an affirmative
sentence it serves to assert the existence of the referent of
its NP argument.[14] In order to gain a comprehensive picture
of this verb, I examine some examples with impersonal haber.
When speakers utter sentences like those in (25), they are
more often than not introducing a new topic[15] of conversation;
they are trying to establish a common ground with the addressee
from which to start a meaningful exchange of ideas.

(25a) Hay en Belgrano una mansión toda cubierta de
hiedra... (R 129)
'There-is in Belgrano a mansion all covered with
ivy.'

(25b) Había un muchacho conocido, y... (VEA 24)
    'There-was an acquaintance [a young male], and...'

(25c) Hay una situación explosiva. (VEA 2)
    'There-is an explosive situation.'

(25d) Hay algo que Cárdenas no entiende... (VEA 28)
    'There-is something that Cárdenas does not under-
    stand...'

As utterances which introduce a new topic or referent into
the discourse, hay sentences constitute instances of the 'presentative function' (Hetzron 1975). According to this linguist
(1975:374), the presentative function

...means calling special attention to one element of the
sentence for recall in the subsequent discourse or situation. This recall may be needed because the element is
going to be used, directly or indirectly, in the ensuing
discourse, because what is going to be said later has some
connection with the element in question,--or because that
element is relevant to what is going to happen or be done
in the reality.

This quote clearly reflects the role of Spanish hay sentences.
They are used to introduce the referent of the NP into the
universe of discourse.[16] To show this, one needs to explore
the context in which the sentences in (25) were said. Those
examples were continued as in (26).

(26a) ...y yo he ido a esa mansión a restaurar el retrato
    de una muerta. (R 129)
    '...and I have gone to that mansion to-restore the
    portrait of a dead-person [female].'

(26b) ...tomó nota sobre lo que dijeron los industriales.
    (VEA 24)
    '...he-took note of what the industrialists said.'

(26c) Las barriadas hoy están cargadas de gente descontenta.
    (VEA 2)
    'The neighborhoods today are loaded with dissatisfied
    people.'

(26d) ...el público no está en contra de la selección nacional
    ni en favor del Guadalajara. (VEA 28)
    '...the public is not against the national team nor in
    favor of-the-one-from Guadalajara.'

In (25a) hay introduces the argument mansión by means of
the indefinite article una 'a', which in (26a) becomes definitized

with esa 'that'. The common ground having been established
in the introductory sentence, the speaker makes the second
mention of 'mansion' definite in order for the hearer to know
that the same mansion is still under consideration. A similar
situation occurs in (25b): after un muchacho conocido is presented into the discourse, the sentence is continued (26b) by
reintroducing the same character in subject position, as evidenced in the verb agreement.[17] The third example, (26c),
explains what constitutes the explosive situation of (25c), and
(26d) expands on the algo that Cárdenas does not understand
in (25d). These two latter examples are instances of what
Hetzron means by the indirect use of the element introduced
through the presentative function of an utterance.

Consequently, it is clear that hay sentences are presentational in nature, since they conform to all of the characteristics of this type of construction. What they present to the
addressee is an 'object' for consideration. This 'object' is
embodied in the NP argument subcategorized by hay. Hay
sentences have been variously described by the established
Spanish grammars as constructions which denote 'the existence
of what follows' (Ramsey 1956:403), or as a means of indicating 'vague existence or presence' (RAE 1974:383), or as a way
of suggesting the 'existence of the object that appears in the
accusative' (Bello 1970:264). I define (affirmative) hay sentences as those which assert that the referent of the object
NP exists.[18] This existential assertion may be absolute (cf.
(27)) or relative; in the latter case the place and/or time are
stated (cf. (28)).

> (27a) Hay una película.
>   'There-is a movie.'

> (27b) Hay un dios omnipotente.
>   'There-is an omnipotent god.'

> (28a) Hay una película $\begin{cases} \text{en la televisión.} \\ \text{a las ocho.} \end{cases}$
>   'There-is a movie $\begin{cases} \text{on (the) television.'} \\ \text{at eight o'clock.'} \end{cases}$

> (28b) Habrá una reunión el miércoles próximo a las tres.
>   'There-will-be a gathering (the) next Wednesday at
>   three o'clock.'

Thus, minimally, HAY NP ≡ NP exists; that is to say, uttering an hay sentence represents a commitment on the part of the
speaker as to his/her belief in the existence of whatever is
represented by the referent of the NP. Consider (29) and
(30).

(29a) Hay una médica muy buena...
'There-is a very good doctor [female]...'

(29b) ..., es la dra. Pérez.
'..., she is Dr. Pérez.'

(29c) ..., *pero aún no existe.
'..., but she doesn't exist yet.'

(30a) Hay un determinado autor que me gusta...
'There-is a particular author whom I like...'

(30b) ...; escribe micro-cuentos.
'...; he writes micro-stories.'

(30c) ...; *todavía no ha nacido.
'...; he hasn't been born yet.'

Sentences (29a) and (30a) assert the existence of the entity
to which the NP refers; they may thus be continued as (29b)
and (30b) without any semantic clash resulting. Precisely the
opposite outcome arises with the rejoinders found in (29c) and
(30c). In these cases direct contradictions result: the (c)
sentences deny the existence of what has been asserted by the
hay sentences. From this one can conclude that there must
exist an 'object' in the universe of discourse that fits the
reference of the NP.

In an effort to distinguish English existential there from
other kinds of existential sentences, Bolinger (1977:92)
narrows its characterization from 'bringing something into
existence' to 'bringing something into awareness'. This more
restricted definition, which aims at capturing the psychological
effect of this type of existential sentence, is perfectly consonant with Spanish hay sentences.

In sum, Spanish impersonal haber sentences are inherently
existential. Furthermore, they are presentational by virtue of
their function in the discourse.

1.2 The constituent structure of *haber* sentences. Having
already discussed the syntactic and semantic traits which
characterize this existential impersonal verb, the investigation
now considers the constituent structure of the sentences in
which hay occurs. Given the two facts, (1) that hay sentences are subjectless and their NP argument is a direct object,[19] and (2) that verbs strictly subcategorize their object
NP argument if they take one, the minimum lexical entry for
hay should be as in (31).

(31) $\begin{bmatrix} /hay/ \\ +V \\ +[\_\_NP] \\ SI \end{bmatrix}$

I take lexical entries to be a composite of at least three types of information: phonological, syntactic, and semantic (cf. Jackendoff 1972, 1975). In (31), /hay/ stands for the phonological properties of this verb. The category [+V] and the type of syntactic environment in which this verb is inserted constitute the syntactic information. And finally, SI is the abbreviation for its semantic interpretation, which should be something like the statement in (32).

(32) Assert the existence of the referent of NP.[20]

1.2.1 Obligatoriness of the NP argument. Before proceeding, observe that the examples in (33) justify the postulation of the object NP as obligatory in (31).[21]

(33a) *Hay entre ellas.
'There-is among/between them (f.).'

(33b) *Había en Buenos Aires.
'There-was in Buenos Aires.'

(33c) *Había pintado de azul.
'There-was painted (of) blue.'

Moreover, notice that although (34a) is ungrammatical because ayer 'yesterday' is analyzed as an adverb, (34b) is not, because in this instance ayer (and mañana 'tomorrow') has been inserted under the NP category.[22]

(34a) *Hubo [$_{Adv}$ ayer].
'There-was yesterday.'

(34b) Hubo [$_{NP}$ ayer] y habrá [$_{NP}$ mañana].
'There-was a yesterday and there-will-be a tomorrow.'

Other sentences which at first glance seem to constitute counterexamples to the obligatoriness of the NP argument are given in (35) and (36).

(35a) Hay donde sentarse.
there-is where to-sit-down
'There is a place to sit down.'

(35b) Habrá donde ir.
there-will-be where to-go
'There will be somewhere to go.'

(36) Habrá con que secarse.
there-will-be with what to-dry-oneself
'There will be something to dry oneself with.'

In (35) a free relative is introduced by an adverbial (donde 'where'), and in (36) the relative is introduced by a complex of preposition plus que. Both cases lack an expressed antecedent. Free relatives are discussed in Section 1.2.2.2.3, where it is shown that they are not counterexamples to the obligatoriness of the NP object.

As should be expected, the object position of hay may be occupied by more than one NP, as (37) shows.

(37a) Siempre habría casas y caminos, autos y surtidores de nafta,... (TE 150)
'There would always be houses and roads, cars and gas pumps,...'

(37b) ...hubo algunos episodios, algunos hechos... (R 94)
'...there-were some episodes, some doings...'

(37c) ...acaso en sus ojos hay esa vaga melancolía, esa dulzura... (SXX 30)
'...perhaps in her eyes there-is that subtle melancholy, that tenderness...'

Taking for granted that the grammar must provide for the phrase-structure generation of conjoined NPs,[23] it is only necessary to indicate the possibility of the recursiveness of this object argument by means of the asterisk convention: +[_NP*]. Having shown that hay must obligatorily cooccur with an NP term at the level of sentence grammar, larger contexts can now be considered. At times hay sentences emerge with more than just an NP object. Thus, assuming that their environment is +[_NP X], we next explore what shape X may adopt.

1.2.2 Elucidation of the term X

1.2.2.1 Adverbials. Perhaps the commonest (and least controversial) manifestations of X are locative and time adverbials.

(38a) Hubo un gran conflicto allí.
'There-was a big conflict there.'

(38b) Habrá un desfile mañana.
'There-will-be a parade tomorrow.'

These adverbs are quite free to move around in the sentence provided they do not break up certain constituents.[24]

(39a) Allí hubo un gran conflicto.
(39b) Hubo allí un gran conflicto.
(39c) *Hubo un allí gran conflicto.
(39d) *Hubo un gran allí conflicto.

(40a) Mañana habrá un desfile.
(40b) Habrá mañana un desfile.
(40c) *Habrá un mañana desfile.

Locative and time expressions are equally well represented by prepositional phrases, which are also quite free to crop up in different positions in the sentence.

(41a) Va a haber una película en el Cine Capital...
'There-is going to-be a movie in the Capital Theatre...'

(41b) En el Cine Capital va a haber una película...

(41c) Va a haber en el Cine Capital una película... (VEA 6)

(42a) Hubo mucho viento durante la noche.
'There-was a-lot-of wind during the night.'

(42b) Durante la noche hubo mucho viento.

(42c) Hubo durante la noche mucho viento.

And, of course, locative and time elements may cooccur in a single sentence, thus indicating the need for different slots.

(43a) Mañana habrá una fiesta allí.
'Tomorrow there-will-be a party there.'

(43b) Ayer hubo una película extraordinaria en la televisión.
'Yesterday there-was an extraordinary movie on (the) television.'

(43c) Hay muchos asaltos por la noche en Nueva York.
'There-are many assaults at night in New York.'

(43d) Allí hubo canto y baile hasta la madrugada.
'There there-was singing and dancing till dawn.'

Intuitively, the difference between adverbs (like allí 'there', ayer 'yesterday', etc.) and some prepositional phrases seems to be that the latter are part of the VP while the former behave more like sentence adverbials generated outside the VP. Spanish is a language which allows for different word order possibilities, a fact which makes a conclusive proof of this intuitive judgment extremely difficult to produce (see also the discussion under Section 2.3.3.1.3.2). However, this impression is to a certain degree corroborated by the judgments given in (44).

(44a) ?En la televisión hubo una película extraordinaria <u>ayer</u>.
'On (the) television there-was an extraordinary movie yesterday.'

(44b) ?En la televisión <u>ayer</u> hubo una película extraordinaria.

(44c) <u>Ayer</u> en la televisión hubo una película extraordinaria.

Compare (44a) to (43b); the latter appears to be more natural. And (44c) is better than (44b). What the data show is that the preposing of a VP adverbial attached to S produces less felicitous results than the preposing of a sentence adverbial attached to the same node. Moreover, if both types of adverbials are attached to S, the preferred order has the sentence adverbial in the periphery of the sentence (cf. (44c) vs. (44b)). Assuming the correctness of this analysis, and associating it with the fact that more than one prepositional phrase may arise in a single sentence (cf. (43c)), we arrive at the possible string with <u>hay</u> given in (45).

(45a) [$_{VP}$<u>hay</u> NP* (PP)*] (Loc) (Time)[25]

(45b) Hubo una gran exhibición en el museo en Ithaca ayer.
'There-was a great exhibit in the museum in Ithaca yesterday.'

Up to this point the prepositional phrases examined indicate only location or time. These are not the only options allowed in Spanish; a few other possibilities are listed in (46).

(46a) ...hay otro lugar <u>con</u> muchas flores. (IM 38)
'...there is another place with many flowers.'

(46b) ...hubo una conferencia <u>para</u> industriales... (VEA 24)
'...there was a lecture for industrialists...'

(46c) ...hubo un arreglo <u>entre</u> ellas... (TE 160)
'...there was a deal among them...'

(46d) ...hay un libro nuevo <u>por</u> ese autor...
'...there is a new book by that author...'

Nevertheless, there is a difference between the PPs in (46) and those discussed previously. While the latter PPs provide some kind of modification to the verbal element, those in (46) modify the NP. This points to a difference in structure. Diagram (47) represents the structure of PPs of the type found in (46), while diagram (48) represents the structure of a locative PP.

(47)

(48)

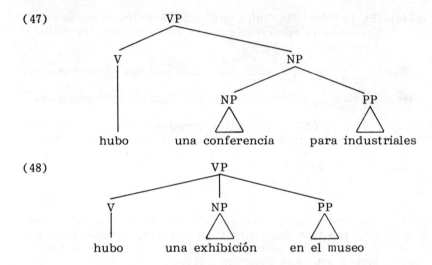

Before bringing this section to a close, and for the sake of completeness, I would like to examine briefly the merits of Kuno's proposal (1971). Kuno, while hypothesizing that locatives are in subject position in existential sentences, explicitly mentions Spanish to give credence to his thesis. He offers the example shown here as (49) (his number (135)).

(49)   Jorge dice que no hay vacas en el Japón,
         says that   cows

     pero a mí me   parece que $\left\{ \begin{array}{l} \text{las} \\ \text{them} \\ \text{*ellas} \\ \text{they} \end{array} \right\}$ hay.
     but to me to-me seems

    'George says that there are no cows in Japan, but it
      seems to me that there are (them).'

Then Kuno expands (1971:375):

Note that the accusative pronoun las, and not the nominative pronoun ellas, appears before hay. This otherwise mysterious phenomenon seems to be accountable for if we assume that the existential sentence has the basic word 'locative + NP$_{indef}$', and that the locative occupies a subject-like position, and the indefinite NP an object-like position, in the sentence.

There is not a single piece of evidence in Spanish that could support Kuno's contention that 'the locative occupies a subject-like position'. Besides the existence of hay messages without a locative (a problem in itself for Kuno), locatives never trigger subject-verb agreement in Spanish. The only 'subject-like' trait I can find is that locatives, if definite, tend to appear preverbally, in keeping with the most natural trend in discourse of starting sentences with thematic information (a fact which Kuno himself notes).[26] This cannot be taken seriously as a subject-like property in a language like Spanish, which has a relatively much 'freer' word order than English. The confusion here can only be due to a misunderstanding of 'this otherwise mysterious phenomenon'. It is not so mysterious after all. It is a direct consequence of there being syntactically subjectless sentences in Spanish, of which hay is just one example.

1.2.2.2 Finite clauses in *hay* sentences

1.2.2.2.1 Relative clauses. When looking for instances of hay sentences plus a finite sentence, one finds that hay occurs with what to all appearances look like relative clauses.

(50a) Hay gente que enfoca este problema... (VEA 5)
'There-are people who focus on this problem...'

(50b) Aquí hay eso que buscan. (spontaneous conversation)
here there-is that that they-are looking for
'Here is what they are looking for.'

(50c) Y también hay esas tres autoras a quienes ya
mencioné.
and also there-are those three authors (f.) whom I
have already mentioned.

(50d) Pero hay el par de horas que pasaron desde que el
hombre bajó de la habitación... (TE 161)
'But there-is the couple of hours that went by since
(the time) the man came down from his room...'

Assuming that the sentences in (50) are examples of (restrictive) relative clauses, their structure would be roughly that of (51).[27]

(51)

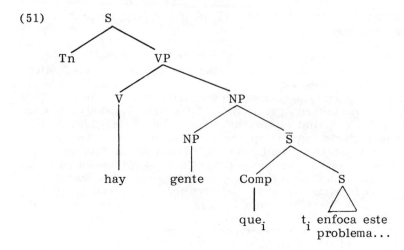

One characteristic of Spanish relative clauses is that the head noun may remain unexpanded (cf. Rivero 1979). Therefore, the existence of the sentences in (52) allows us to predict those in (53).

(52a) Aquí hay <u>unos libros</u> que acabo de recibir.
'Here there-are several books that I-have-just received.'

(52b) Hay <u>los hombres</u> que viven sólo de rentas.
'There-are the men who live only from rentals.'

(52c) Luego hay <u>la otra</u> chica que estudia abogacía.
'Then there-is the other woman who studies law.'

(53a) Aquí hay <u>unos</u> que acabo de recibir.
'...several...'

(53b) Hay <u>los</u> que viven sólo de rentas.
'...those...'

(53c) Luego hay <u>la (otra)</u> que estudia abogacía.
'...the (other)...'

The structure of the sentences in (53) is totally parallel to that found in (51), with the exception of the unexpanded noun. To illustrate, the relative clause in (53a) is diagrammed in (54).
    Free relatives also occur in <u>hay</u> sentences. However, a discussion of this type of relatives is postponed until after the examination of another construction which, although it also has the form of a relative clause, turns out to be an S̄ complement.

(54)

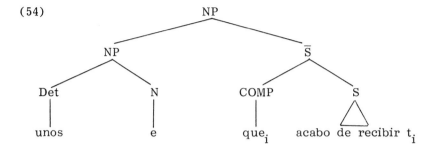

1.2.2.2.2 S̄ complements. At first glance the underlined part of the sentence in (55) appears to be another instance of a restrictive relative clause.

(55) ¿Te parece que aún hay libros que cuestan $2?
      to-you (dat.) seems that still there-is books that cost
      (3 pl.) $2
      'Do you think that there are still books that cost $2?'

Nevertheless, this apparent parallelism breaks down upon close examination. For example, it is possible to respond to (55) as shown in (56).

(56) Sí, y también los hay que cuestan $1.
      yes, and also them (acc. m.) there-is that cost $1
      'Yes, and there also exist those that cost $1.'

Crucially, observe that the alleged head of the relative clause (underlined in (56)) has been cliticized. But heads of true relative clauses are not subject to cliticization; hence the ungrammaticality of the sentences in (58) vis-à-vis the grammatical ones in (57).

(57a) ¿Conoces al hombre que toca la tuba?
       'Do-you-know the man who plays the tuba?'

(57b) ¿Consiguió el vino que viene de La Rioja?
       'Did-he-get the wine that comes from La Rioja?'

(58a) *Sí, lo conozco que toca la tuba.
        him (acc.)

(58b) *No, pero lo consiguió que viene de Alsacia.
        no, but it (acc. m.) he-got that comes from Alsace.

The possibility for cliticization is one of the properties that segregates relative clauses from the sequence NP plus S̄ complement. There are at least two other traits which differentiate these constructions. First, in relative clauses the relative pronoun can fulfill different types of functions: for example, subject relativization (cf. (59a)), object relativization (cf. (59b)), relativization of an indirect object (goal) argument (cf. (59c)), etc. However, the missing element in the struc-ture clitic + hay + que... can only be a subject (cf. (60)).

(59a) El hombre que llega es el profesor X.
'The man who is-arriving is (the) professor X.'

(59b) Ese libro que compramos es malísimo.
'That book that we-bought is extremely-bad.'

(59c) La niña para quien traje este regalo cumple 10 años.
'The girl for whom I-brought this present is 10
years old.'

(60a) Los hay que viven como reyes.
them (acc.) there-is that live (3 pl.) like kings
'There are those who live like kings.'

(60b) *Los hay que acabas de recibir.
them (acc.) there-are that you-have-just received
'There are those which you have just received.'

Second, on the assumption that topicalization is a movement rule of some sort, it is possible to extract a direct object argu-ment from the que clauses embedded under hay (cf. (61)). Observe that the same extraction out of a relative clause pro-duces an ungrammatical sentence (cf. (62)) because this move-ment is in violation of the Complex NP Constraint, i.e. Sub-jacency.[28]

(61) Dinero, hay un banquero que sí que tiene Δ.
money, there-is a banker that yes that he-has Δ
'As for money, there is a banker who does have it.'

(62) *Dinero, conozco al banquero que sí que tiene Δ.
money, I-know the banker that yes that he-has Δ
'As for money, I know the banker who does have it.'

Along the same lines of argumentation, note that in (63) there is relativization of an element in the embedded que clause.[29]

(63) Este artículo de Chomsky en el cual hay mucha gente
que está interesada [t] es demasiado complicado para
mí.
'This paper by Chomsky in (the) which there-are many
people that are interested [t] is too complicated for
me.'

It goes almost without saying that if the que clause in (63) were a relative clause, such an extraction would be impossible.

In sum, the differences in behavior exhibited by true relative clauses and what I have termed S̄ complements justify the positing of two different constructions. The hypothesis embodied in the foregoing discussion is that hay sentences with relative clauses are characterized by the bracketing hay [NP NP S̄], while hay sentences with S̄ complements are best captured by a constituent analysis of hay NP S̄. Note that what differentiates both structures is just the NP which dominates NP S̄ in the case of true relative clauses. Hence it should be expected that structural ambiguity could arise in some instances.

This is not the sole instance in Spanish of apparent identical surface structures which behave differently with respect to some syntactic process(es). There is a very similar problem involving perception verbs which led me to the postulation of the strict subcategorization ___ NP S̄ in addition to the more familiar ___ S̄ (see Suñer 1978 for details and discussion).[30] The parallelism between hay NP S̄ and perception verbs plus NP S̄ is striking. Compare (64) with (56), (65) with (60), and (66) with (63).

(64) Lo oigo que toca la guitarra.
    him (acc.) I-hear that he-plays the guitar
    'I hear the one (m.) who is playing the guitar.'

(65a) Lo ví que venía.
    him I-saw that was-coming
    'I saw the one (m.) that was coming.'

(65b) *Lo ví con que hablabas.
    him I-saw with that you-were-talking
    'I saw the one (m.) you were talking with.'

(65c) *Lo ví que acababas de retar.
    him I-saw that you-have-just scolded
    'I saw the one (m.) you have just scolded.'

(66) Esta guitarra la cual/que lo ví que tocaba [t] está
    muy desafinada.
    this guitar the which/that him I-saw that was playing
    [t] is very out-of-tune
    'This guitar which I saw the one (m.) who was playing it is very much out of tune.'

In addition to the behavior exemplified in (64) through (66), perception verbs in the ___ NP S̄ frame also adhere to certain tense limitations and to restrictions with the pseudomodals poder 'to be able', soler 'to be used to', deber 'must', etc. These latter peculiarities seem to be an automatic consequence

of the direct perception reading that obtains in such a
frame.

The questions raised by the need to posit two different
bracketings for the hay NP S̄ sequence (and that of perception
verbs plus NP S̄) are not unique to Spanish. For example,
Quirk et al. (1972:959) notice the special status of the relative
clause in the there + BE + noun phrase + relative clause structure. They mention that in There's something (that) keeps up-
setting him, the relative pronoun that may be omitted even
though it is the subject of the clause, contrary to what is the
norm for relative clauses: 'This omissibility is a sign of the
special status within the main clause here, as in cleft sentences' (Quirk et al. 1972:959). Jenkins (1975) maintains that
a man in the garden in There is a man in the garden is a remnant of a cleft sentence. As evidence for his claim he presents
two main arguments; the first is based on intonation and the
second is the observation attributed to Chomsky that reduced
relatives do not follow full relatives. Thus, one can contrast
the grammatical existential sentence There is a girl who knows
you standing on the corner and the grammatical That-Cleft
That's a girl who knows you standing on the corner, to the ungrammatical *A girl who knows you standing on the corner is
waiting for a bus.[31] And Stockwell et al. (1973:422) specifically segregate true relatives from what they call pseudorela-
tives (among which they mention there sentences), which they
do not discuss.

1.2.2.2.3 **Free relatives.** Free relatives are relative clauses
which have no surface antecedent. Traditional grammars of
Spanish state that the relative pronoun 'includes its antecedent'
(Ramsey 1956:196), or that there is an 'implicit antecedent'
(RAE 1974:220).[32] Impersonal haber sentences cooccur with
free relatives of the kind shown in (67)-(69).

(67a) Hay quienes contemplan la vida pasivamente.
     there-is who (pl.) contemplate (3 pl.) the life pas-
       sively
     'There are those who contemplate life passively.'

(67b) Hay quien la quiere.
     there-is who (sg.) her (acc.) loves (3 sg.)
     'There is one who loves her.'

(67c) Hay cuanto quieras.
     'There-is all that you-want.'

(68a) Hay con los que yo no jugaría.
     there-is with the (m. pl.) that I not would-play (1 sg.)
     'There are those with whom I would not play.'

(68b) Hay <u>por los que</u> (yo) no pondría la mano en el fuego.
there-is for the (m. pl.) that (I) not would-put (1
sg.) the hand in the fire
'There are those I would not trust.'

(69a) No hay <u>donde</u> sentarse.
not there-is where to-sit-down
'There isn't a place to sit down.'

(69b) Hay <u>con que</u> taparse.
there-is with what to-cover-oneself
'There's something to cover oneself with.'

(69c) No hay <u>por quien</u> votar.
not there-is for whom to-vote
'There's no one to vote for.'

The examples included in (67)-(69) are representative: those
in (67) include free relatives which begin with a WH-phrase;
those in (68) are prepositional compound relatives; and those
in (69) are infinitival relatives. All of them have in common
the lack of an antecedent. This trait immediately presents a
problem. Recalling that in Section 1.2.1 it was claimed that
the NP argument of <u>haber</u> sentences is obligatory, how can
one reconcile this claim with the data in (67)-(69)? Before
providing an answer to this question, it is necessary to
examine the different proposals that have been advanced for
the analysis of free relatives. There are two main competing
hypotheses: the head proposal and the COMP proposal.

Bresnan and Grimshaw (1978) are the proponents of the first
alternative. According to their analysis, the WH-phrase is
generated as head of its clause in antecedent position and a
rule different from WH-movement interprets the necessary gap.
Thus, sentence (67a) can be displayed in the tree shown in
(70). This hypothesis automatically accounts for the 'matching
effect' between the phrase and its head, since in this analysis
free relatives are headed. Moreover, it explains the absence
of a complementizer by not providing a COMP node.

By contrast, in the COMP proposal the WH-phrase is in
COMP and the head remains empty. This second alternative
makes the implicit claim that the only difference between regular relatives and free relatives is the presence or absence of a
lexical head; their constituent structure is the same. Under
this analysis, sentence (67a) would be diagrammed as in (71).

(70)

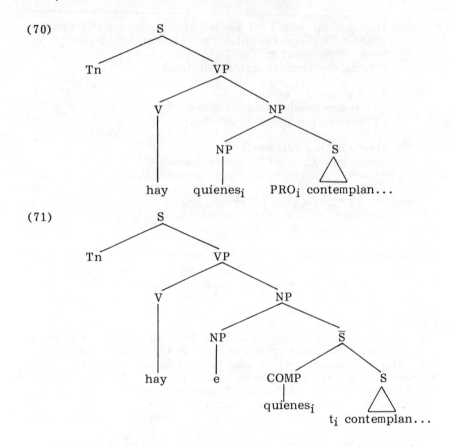

(71)

Hirschbühler and Rivero (1980) reject the head analysis for Catalan on the basis that it requires an additional phrase-structure rule (NP → NP S) which makes the wrong predictions with regard to both headed relatives and noun complements. This same argument applies to Spanish. The sentences in (72) are ungrammatical precisely when the complementizer is missing.

(72a) Hay un niño *(que) llora.
      'There-is a boy *(that) cries.'

(72b) El hecho *(que) llegó tarde me enojó.
      'The fact *(that) he-arrived late annoyed me.'

Nevertheless, acceptance of the COMP proposal implies that the matching effect must be accounted for by another mechanism. Following the lead of Groos and Van Riemsdijk, Hirschbühler and Rivero hypothesize that in free relatives the COMP position must be accessible to the subcategorization requirements of the matrix clause. But note that although this

suggestion beautifully takes care of (67a) and (67b) (because
quien/es 'who (sg./pl.)' works as a noun and hence fulfills
the subcategorization requirement of hay), it still does not explain the grammaticality of the remaining examples (that is,
(67c), (68), and (69)).
  Without pretending to give a full account of free relatives, I
suggest that the solution to the puzzle lies elsewhere. This
sketch of a solution is in accordance with the intuitions of traditional grammarians. In the first place, I agree with Hirschbühler and Rivero, and accept the COMP hypothesis as my working analysis, because I think headed and headless relative
clauses should have parallel structures. To bring this point
home, I show that for every free relative in (67)-(69) there is
a corresponding headed relative which conveys the same meaning. The sentences appear in the same order as those in (67)-
(69); the head is underlined.

(73a) Hay $\left\{ {los \atop \underline{hombres}} \right\}$ que contemplan la vida...

  there-is $\left\{ {the \; (ones) \atop men} \right\}$ that contemplate the life...

(73b) Hay alguien que la quiere.
  there-is somebody that her (acc.) loves

(73c) Hay todo $\left\{ {cuanto \atop lo \; que} \right\}$ quieras.
  there-is all that you-want

(74a) Hay hombres con los que yo no jugaría.
  there-is men with whom I not would-play

(74b) Hay hombres por los que yo no pondría...
  there-is men for whom I not would-put...

(75a) No hay lugar donde sentarse.
  not there-is place where to-sit-down

(75b) Hay algo con que taparse.
  there-is something with which to-cover-oneself

(75c) No hay $\left\{ {persona \atop \underline{nadie}} \right\}$ por quien votar.

  not there-is $\left\{ {person \atop nobody} \right\}$ for whom to vote

  My hypothesis goes as follows. On the basis of the equiva-
lency of the free relatives in (67)-(69) and the headed relatives in (73)-(75), I maintain that the head position of free
relatives in Spanish is taken up by PRO. This PRO is indeterminate in nature, almost as indeterminate and general as

the heads of the relatives in (73)-(75); the only difference between these heads and PRO is that the former have lexical
matrices while the latter does not. Consequently, free relatives can be represented as in (76).

(76)

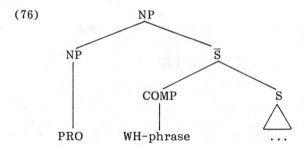

This proposal implies that I was correct in claiming that the
NP subcategorized by <u>hay</u> is obligatory (Section 1.2.1). Moreover, I would like to propose that the subcategorization condition imposed by impersonal <u>haber</u> is fulfilled by the top NP in
(76) and not by the lower one (i.e. PRO), and furthermore
that free relatives do not provide any hard evidence for maintaining that COMP position should be accessible to the subcategorization requirements of the matrix clause in Spanish.
    To claim that it is the entire relativized NP and not the head
NP which meets subcategorization requirements is not such a
radical claim. Note that subcategorization is met by categories
of certain types (i.e. NP, S̄, AP, etc.) but not generally by
any given structure found inside these categories. To put it
differently, subcategorization is blind as to whether the NP is
composed of just N, Det N, or [NP NP S̄], as long as there is
an NP. Under this analysis, the case of relatives is completely
parallel to that of embedded clauses. For example, the verb
<u>querer</u> 'to want' requires an object NP; this subcategorization
condition can be met by a plain NP (77a), or by an NP which
dominates NP S̄ (77b). Given the appropriate discourse situation, both types of NPs react in the same way to cliticization;
that is, <u>lo</u> in (78) is capable of referring to the direct object
argument in (77a) or to that in (77b).

(77a) Quiero [_{NP} un libro interesante].

    'I-want an interesting book.'

(77b) Quiero [_{NP} un libro [_{S̄} que sea interesante]]

    I-want a book that is (subjunctive) interesting
    'I-want an interesting book.'

(78) Sí, lo quiero.
    yes, it (acc.) I-want
    'Yes, I want it.'

Hay behaves similarly regardless of whether its object is a plain NP (79a), or a headed or headless relative clause, (79b) and (79c), respectively. All of these objects can be referred to by the appropriate object clitic (80).

(79a) Hay un niño...
'There-is a boy...'

(79b) Hay un niño que quiere verte.
'There-is a boy who wants to-see-you.'

(79c) ¿Hay con que taparse?
is-there with what to-cover-oneself?
'Is there something to cover oneself with?'

(80) Sí, lo hay.
'Yes, there is (it).'

The question in (79c) can also be answered as in (81).

(81) Sí, hay.
'Yes, there-is.'

Nevertheless, (81) does not represent a problem for my proposal. It is a property of hay that it can take determineless and, therefore, nonspecific NPs as its direct object. In this case the clitic might become unnecessary at the discourse level precisely because clitics tend to refer to specific referents.

(82a) ¿Hay sol?
Is-there sun
'Is it sunny?'

(82b) Sí, hay.
yes, there-is
'Yes, it is.'

Consider also example (83), taken from a play.

(83)   --De acuerdo.   Pero aquí lugar no hay.
fine but here place not there-is
'Fine.   But here there is no room.'

¿O hay? (EL 83)
'Or is-there?'

Here the question ¿O hay? is asked without a clitic referring to lugar 'place, room', because in context the determineless character of lugar makes the occurrence of a clitic unnecessary.

There is a further question that one needs to address when postulating structure (76) for free relatives.   Why should it be

the case that some verbs accept free relatives in subcategorized
positions more readily than others? Compare examples (84)-
(87).[33]

(84a) Invito a quien tú invitaste.
I-invite to whom you invited
'I invite (the one) whom you (have) invited.'

(84b) *Invito con quien tú te irás.
I-invite with whom you-will-leave
'I invite (the one) whom you will leave with.'

(85) Compré donde tú vives.
I-bought where you live
'I bought a place close to where you live.'

(86) Tienen con quien hablar.
they-have with whom to-talk
'They have someone to talk to.'

(87) Hay por los que no votaría.
'There-are (those) for whom I would not vote.'

Hirschbühler and Rivero use the Catalan examples parallel to
those in (84) to argue in favor of the hypothesis that Catalan
adheres to the matching requirement and that material in COMP
must satisfy the conditions of the matrix verb. Nevertheless,
notice that despite the fact that comprar 'to buy' and tener
'to have' as well as hay are verbs that subcategorize an object
NP,[34] the examples in (85), (86), and (87) are grammatical
even though there is no object NP. Therefore, the matching
effect is used to explain the ungrammaticality of (84b), when
the grammaticality of the sentences in (85), (86), and (87)
speaks against such a hypothesis. This inconsistency in the
treatment of the data leads me to believe that the solution must
be sought elsewhere.

First, it is necessary to point out that, although the assumption that PRO heads the free relatives in (84)-(87) can explain
the grammatical sentences in the set, this assumption does not
help with the ungrammaticality of (84b) vis-à-vis the well-
formedness of (84a). I outline a possible explanation which
solves the puzzle posed by the examples in (84). These examples are totally parallel to the following ones with querer 'to
love'.

(88a) Quiero a quien tú quieres.
I-love to whom you love
'I love (the one) whom you love.'

(88b) *Quiero con quien tú vienes.
       I-love with whom you come
       'I love (the one) whom you come with.'

I assume that the ungrammaticality of the (b) member of each
pair is due to the fact that <u>invitar</u> and <u>querer</u> require the personal <u>a</u> whenever their direct object is human. Under this
hypothesis, the structure of (84a) after personal <u>a</u> insertion
would be (89).

(89)

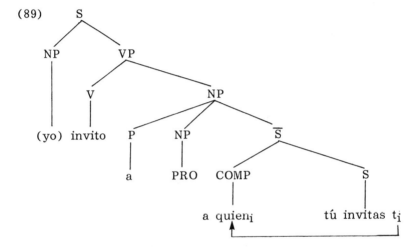

After the verb's demand for personal <u>a</u> is fulfilled, this preposition must be deleted, since Spanish does not allow dangling
prepositions.
  Justification for the deletion of the preposition is found in
the assertion of traditional grammarians that a preposition is
often deleted when the antecedent and the relative pronoun
appear with the same preposition (see RAE 1974:529). Observe
what happens with <u>soñar con</u> 'to dream of', a verb which is
subcategorized for the preposition <u>con</u> 'with'.[35]

(90a) Soñé con mi amante.
       I-dreamed with my lover
       'I dreamed of my lover.'

(90b) *Soñé mi amante.

(90c) Soñé con quien tú soñaste.
       I-dreamed with whom you dreamed
       'I dreamed of (the one) whom you dreamed of.'

(90d) *Soñé quien tú soñaste.

The structure of the free relative in (90c) must be something like (91).

(91)

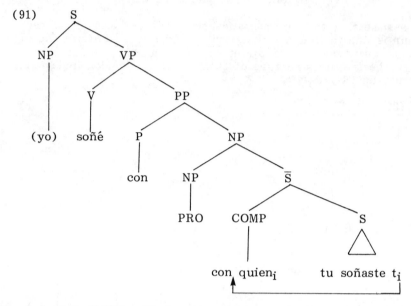

The outcome of (91) with two prepositions con (one because of the matrix verb, the other because of the embedded one) is ungrammatical (92a); but since both prepositions are identical, one of them deletes, rendering the grammatical (92b).[36]

(92a) *Soñé con con quien tú soñaste.
(92b) Soñé con quien tú soñaste.

This preposition deletion cannot take place, however, unless both prepositions have the same phonological matrix. Thus, the ungrammaticality of both (84b) and (88b) results from the impossibility of having the examples in (93) as well-formed surface Spanish sentences.

(93a) *Invito a con quien tú te irás.
(93b) *Quiero a con quien tú vienes.

Sentence (93) presents a paradox: on the one hand, a must delete because it is dangling, and on the other, it cannot delete because it is not identical with the preposition that accompanies the WH-phrase. Either way the sentences are unacceptable, with or without the preposition (compare (93) with (84) and (88b)). Therefore, this explanation, based on the insights of traditional grammarians, neatly accounts for the data without need to resort to COMP accessibility.

In short, the free relative construction is parallel to that of headed relatives. The only difference is that headed relatives have a lexical head while free relatives have PRO. This analysis renders the COMP accessibility principle unnecessary (at least, in this case). Furthermore, I have maintained that the relative clause itself fulfills the subcategorization conditions established by the matrix verb, a fact which gives credence to the claim that hay obligatorily subcategorizes an object NP (cf. Section 1.2.1).

1.2.2.3 Gerundives and participles. Continuing with the examination of the term X, I next explore the cooccurrence of hay with what has the appearance of a reduced clause.

(94a) ...hay una mujer mirando las puestas de sol...
(IM 26)
'...there-is a woman looking at the sunsets...'

(94b) ...había muchos chicos jugando en el parque.
'...there-were many kids playing in the park.'

(95a) Hay varios estudiantes sentados en el suelo.
'There-are several students sitting on the floor.'

(95b) Hay dos policías parados en la esquina.
'There-are two policemen standing on the corner.'

(95c) Hay ese pueblito tan alejado de la civilización...
'There-is that village so far-removed from civilization...'

(95d) Hay dos ratas encerradas en la trampa.
'There-are two rats enclosed in the trap.'

(96a) Había un muchacho conocido... (VEA 24)
'There-was a guy known...'

(96b) Hay esos tulipanes traídos de Holanda.
'There-are those tulips brought from Holland.'

The underlined words in the foregoing examples are gerunds (94), and past participles ((95) and (96)). Each of these sets of sentences is discussed in turn.

Gerunds (-ndo forms) raise by far the most interesting questions. Gerunds in Spanish have two main uses. They occur with the verb estar to form the progressive (97a), and they also function as adverbials to express the cause, manner, or means of an action ((97b) and (97c)).

(97a) Pepe estaba manejando sin carnet.
'Pepe was driving without a (driver's) license.'

(97b) Paco salió $\begin{cases}\text{corriendo.}\\\text{gritando.}\end{cases}$

'Paco left $\begin{cases}\text{running.}\\\text{shouting.}\end{cases}$'

(97c) Briana hace gimnasia cantando.
Briana does exercises singing
'Briana exercises while singing.'

In contrast to English, however, Spanish gerunds cannot in general be used as noun modifiers.

(98a) *Un viejo muriéndose de hambre llamó a la puerta.
'An old man dying of hunger knocked at the door.'

(98b) *Una niña gritando a todo pulmón corría por el parque.
'A girl screaming her lungs out was-running through the park.'

Nevertheless, in the environment of certain verbs, gerunds perform a function which is indeterminate between adjectival and adverbial modification. Curiously enough, the verbs with which the gerunds allow themselves this double interpretation are precisely the verbs of perception and impersonal haber.[37] Recall that in the section on S̄ complements (Section 1.2.2.2.2) the parallellism in the structures of these verbs was pointed out; therefore, the fact that they behave in a similar fashion with respect to gerunds also should come as no surprise. Compare the sentences in (94) with those in (99).

(99a) Ví a una mujer mirando las puestas de sol...
'I-saw a woman looking at the sunsets...'

(99b) Ví a muchos chicos jugando en el parque.
'I-saw many kids playing in the park.'

This indeterminacy between the adjectival and adverbial interpretation of gerunds with perception verbs and hay automatically emerges if one assumes that the adjectival reading arises from the __[NP NP S̄] subcategorization frame of these verbs while the adverbial reading falls out from the __NP S̄ frame. In other words, the adjectival interpretation would follow from tree (100), and the adverbial from (101).[38] If one assumes that only constituents can move and that this PRO has to be controlled, then it follows that the preposing of the gerundive phrase by itself should render an unambiguous reading. This is exactly correct, since the preposed gerundives give only an adverbial interpretation in (102).

(100)

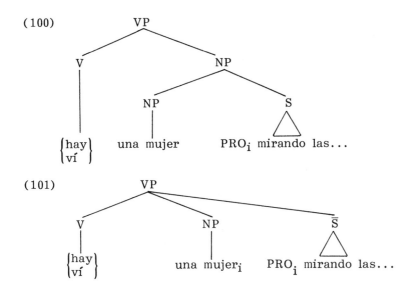

(101)

(102) Mirando$_i$ las puestas de sol $\left\{ \begin{matrix} \text{hay} \\ \text{ví} \end{matrix} \right\}$ una mujer$_i$. [39]

'Watching the sunsets $\left\{ \begin{matrix} \text{there-is} \\ \text{I-saw} \end{matrix} \right\}$ a woman.'

Moreover, well-known syntactic tests which are used to discover the constituent structure of given strings should tell us
that una mujer mirando... can behave as a single constituent
or as two constituents. Again this prediction is borne out by
the facts in (103) and (104). [40]

(103a) Pseudo-cleft:

  Lo que hay es una mujer mirando las puestas de sol.
  'What there-is is a woman watching the sunsets.'

(103b) WH-movement:

  --¿Qué había?
  'What was-there?'

  --Había una mujer mirando las...
  'There-was a woman watching...'

(104a) Pseudo-cleft:

  Lo que hay mirando las puestas de sol es una mujer.
  'What there-is watching the sunsets is a woman.'

(104b) WH-movement:

--¿Qué había mirando...?
'What was-there watching...?'

--Había una mujer (mirando...)
'There was a woman (watching...).'

Observe that Pseudo-cleft and WH-movement show the string under consideration as forming a single constituent in (103), but as two constituents in (104).[41] This potentially puzzling situation finds a natural answer in the assumption that the examples in (103) have the constituent analysis found in (100), and those in (104) have the structure diagrammed in (101).

There is one additional interpretation of gerundives which segregates hay from perception verbs and which also falls out naturally from my analysis. Note that a sentence with a perception verb is, in fact, ambiguous in three ways.

(105) Ví a muchos chicos caminando por el parque.
'I-saw many kids walking through the park.'

The gerundive in (105) may have an adjectival interpretation (thus, structure (100)), or an adverbial interpretation (thus, structure (101)); but it can also have an adverbial reading in which the gerund is controlled by the subject of ver. In the latter case, sentence (105) should have the structure in (106).

(106)

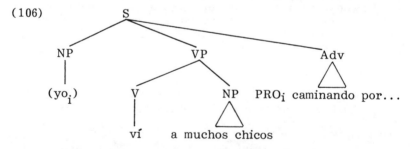

That the gerundive structure must hang from S and not from VP follows from the fact that the matrix subject must C-command the gerundive for the desired interpretation to take place. Crucially, structure (106) cannot be interpreted as having muchos chicos controlling the gerundive PRO, because the matrix direct object does not C-command the adverbial.

My assumption that hay is a subjectless verb (cf. Section 1.1.1.2) immediately explains the impossibility of this latter adverbial reading of the gerundive arising in an hay sentence; there is no matrix subject which could possibly control the gerundive PRO. Consequently, (107) could never be an instance of the structure (108), but only of the one found in (101).

(107) Hay muchos chicos jugando en el parque.
'There-are many kids playing in the park.'

(108)

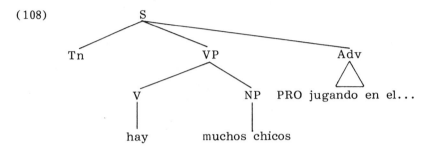

This concludes the discussion of hay sentences with gerundives. Taking as a basis the analogous behavior and interpretation of gerundive complements with respect to relative clauses and S̄ complements, I have proposed that gerundives come from two distinct sentential sources, (100) and (101). This position explains naturally their ambiguous adjectival/adverbial surface interpretation, as well as their divergent behavior as one or two constituents (cf. (103) vs. (104)).[42]

Next, let us turn to the examination of past participles in hay sentences. The examples in (95) and (96) are repeated here for convenience.

(95a) Hay varios estudiantes <u>sentados</u> en el suelo.
'There-are several students sitting on the floor.'

(95b) Hay dos policías <u>parados</u> en la esquina.
'There are two policemen standing on the corner.'

(95c) Hay ese pueblito tan <u>alejado</u> de la civilización.
'There-is that village so far-removed from civilization.'

(95d) Hay dos ratas <u>encerradas</u> en la trampa.
'There-are two rats enclosed in the trap.'

(96a) Había un muchacho <u>conocido</u>...   (VEA 24)
'There-was a guy known...'

(96b) Hay esos tulipanes <u>traídos</u> de Holanda.
'There-are those tulips brought from Holland.'

Among their diverse usages, Spanish past participles function as adjectives, in which case they agree in number and gender with the noun they modify. It is in their adjectival use that they occur in the foregoing examples. In (95a) and

(95b) the past participles describe body positions, and in (95c) and (95d) they denote location and a condition, respectively. The examples in (96) have participles which in some way modify the direct object noun.

The immediate problem posed by the type of sentences found in (95) and (96) is whether the participle (and whatever follows) is generated with the noun as part of the direct object or whether it arises from a reduced clause. Moreover, if it were to arise from a reduced clause, one would still need to determine whether it has a reduced relative or an $\bar{S}$ complement source. The ultimate answer to this inquiry may have to wait until the origin of postnominal adjectives is established beyond reasonable doubt.[43] In the meantime, I limit myself to pointing out some facts that must be taken into account in any analysis.

In the first place, notice that for every sentence in (95) and (96) there exists a parallel sentence with a que clause.

(109a) Hay varios estudiantes que están sentados en el suelo.
'There-are several students who are sitting on the floor.'

(109b) Hay dos policías que están parados en la esquina.
'There-are two policemen who are standing on the corner.'

(109c) Hay ese pueblito que está tan alejado de la civilización...
'There-is that village which is so far-removed from civilization...'

(109d) Hay dos ratas que están encerradas en la trampa.
'There-are two rats that are enclosed in the trap.'

(110a) Había un muchacho que era conocido (por todos)...
'There-was a guy who was known (by everybody)...'

(110b) Hay esos tulipanes que fueron traídos de Holanda (por los floristas más ambiciosos).
'There-are those tulips which were brought from Holland (by the most ambitious florists).'

If full clauses were the origin of the participles in (95) and (96), one would have to say that those in (95) originate in a relative clause or an $\bar{S}$ complement, while those in (96) are what is left after reduction has applied to a passive sentence, which itself might come from either a relative clause or an $\bar{S}$ complement.

One of the problems encountered by the full-clause analysis is the potential ambiguity that arises from a sentence like (111).

This sentence could have as its source any of the full clauses listed in (112).

(111) Hay varias personas sentadas en el suelo.
       'There-are several people seated on the floor.'

(112) Hay varias personas que $\left\{\begin{array}{l}\text{están}\\ \text{estaban}\\ \text{estuvieron}\\ \text{estarán}\\ \text{habían estado}\end{array}\right\}$ sentadas
       en el suelo.

       'There-are several people who $\left\{\begin{array}{l}\text{are}\\ \text{were (imperfect)}\\ \text{were (perfect)}\\ \text{will-be}\\ \text{had been}\end{array}\right\}$
       sitting on the floor.'

This ambiguity seems to be quite an undesirable possibility.[44]
Alternatively, the participles could originate from a tenseless sentential source. On analogy with the structure posited for gerundives (113a), the participles could come from something like (113b).

(113a) $[_{\bar{S}}[_S$ PRO -NDO Verb...]] gerundives

(113b) $[_{\bar{S}}[_S$ PRO -DO Verb...]] participles

And (113b) could itself be part of a relative clause or fill the $\bar{S}$ complement slot in the ___ NP $\bar{S}$ subcategorization frame. That participles fulfill this double role just as gerundives do is confirmed by testing their constituency by means of a preposing movement rule.

(114a) ?*Conocido por todos había un muchacho...
        'Known by all there-was a guy...'

(114b) Traídos de Holanda hay esos tulipanes...
        'Brought from Holland there-are those tulips...'

(114c) Parados en la esquina hay dos policías...
        'Standing on the corner there-are two policemen...'

Although the participles in (114b) and (114c) can be preposed without difficulty, the result obtained in (114a) is less felicitous. This appears to indicate that the participle in (114a) originates in a relative clause while those in (114b) and (114c) come from an $\bar{S}$ complement.

As a matter of fact, there exist some arguments which can be used to support the sentential origin for participles. First, it is a well-known fact that Spanish passives obey severe constraints. In particular, verbs of emotion, perception, change, memory, and motion are barred from occurring with the <u>ser</u> passive if the agent is human and 'when the meaning of the verb implies the subject's deliberate or non-deliberate involvement or participation in the action' (Solé and Solé 1977:258-259). Therefore, the unacceptability of the following sentences is explained by the ungrammaticality of the corresponding full passive.

(115a) *Hubo varios prisioneros (*que fueron) oídos por los guardias.
'There-were several prisoners (who were) heard by the guards.'

(115b) *Había una casa enseñada por el Sr. Pérez que nos gustó mucho.
'There-was a house shown by Mr. Pérez that we liked very much.'

Furthermore, the same constraint on the passive explains why the participles in (116) can only be interpreted as arising from <u>estar</u> + past participle, and never from a <u>ser</u> passive.

(116a) Había algunos estudiantes $\left\{ \begin{array}{l} \text{que estaban} \\ \text{*que fueron/*que eran} \end{array} \right\}$ preocupados por los parciales.
'There were several students (who were) worried by the mid-terms.'

(116b) Había dos estudiantes $\left\{ \begin{array}{l} \text{que estaban} \\ \text{*que fueron/*que eran} \end{array} \right\}$ ofendidos en clase hoy.
'There were two offended students in class today.'

Another piece of evidence emerges from the fact that, in contrast to English, Spanish indirect objects cannot be passivized. Consequently, it is possible to predict the ungrammaticality of example (117) because of the nonexistence of a corresponding full passive (118).

(117) *Había un niño dado un premio por su valor.
'There was one child given a prize for his courage.'

(118) *Un niño fue dado un premio por su valor.
'A boy was given a prize for his courage.'

Therefore, the positing of a tenseless underlying passive structure for (some instances of) past participle modification in <u>hay</u> sentences appears to be justified by the data given in (115) through (118). This assumption would obviate the need to express twice the constraints to which true passives must conform.

On the other hand, it could also be argued that Passive is not a transformation in Spanish but rather a lexical redundancy rule, since the severe constraints that it must adhere to make it a much less general rule than for English. Under this alternative point of view, past participles would be considered derived adjective phrases having the structure found in (119), which is introduced by one of the base rules which rewrites AP.

(119) $AP \rightarrow [_A -DO [_V V]]...$

The difference in behavior of the participles with respect to preposing (cf. (114)) can still be accounted for by assuming that AP can be generated both inside an NP (120a) and as an independent constituent (120b).

(120a) $[_{NP} NP \; AP]$

(120b) NP AP

In short, because of the many open questions which concern the ultimate source of postnominal adjectives, I have not taken a firm stand on the origin of the past participle. What I have done is to present two alternatives: the tenseless sentential proposal and the adjectival phrase hypothesis. The advantage of the former is that participles and gerunds would have totally parallel structures (cf. (113)). Its disadvantage is that it is more abstract than the AP proposal. Both alternatives appear to account for the limited data examined during the discussion of participles. The choice of one alternative over the other is left open to future research.

1.2.2.4 Summary and conclusion. This section has been devoted to the constituent analysis of impersonal haber sentences. Once it was posited that hay + NP is a mandatory syntactic unit (Section 1.2.1), the main task was limited to the elucidation of the term X in the sequence hay NP X. It was found that X adopts many forms. It can be represented by locative and time adverbials as well as by PPs (Section 1.2.2.1); although none of these terms is necessarily subcategorized by this impersonal verb, it appears to be the case that some PPs are optionally subcategorized by hay because they are capable of taking a position inside the VP. Finite clauses also occur in hay sentences. It was discovered that while some of them are relative clauses (Section 1.2.2.2.1), others form an independent S̄ complement constituent (Section 1.2.2.2.2). Several syntactic processes which differentiate these two types of clauses were

examined. The striking parallellism between complements of
hay and of perception verbs was also pointed out. Free relatives were the topic of the discussion in Section 1.2.2.2.3.
There the proposal that free relatives have a PRO head was
advanced. This hypothesis has the advantage that it makes it
possible to claim that headed and headless relatives have the
same constituent structure. Finally, gerundives and participles
in hay sentences were examined (Section 1.2.2.3). Arguments
were presented which suggest a sentential tenseless origin for
gerundives. This stand automatically explains their adjectival
and adverbial functions as well as their different controllers.
I was quite cautious with respect to participles. The possibilities of their being derived from a tenseless sentential source
and of their being directly generated as one of the expansions
of AP were explored. The choice between the two alternatives
was left open to future research.

In sum, the following seems to be the most accurate and
reasonable strict subcategorization for impersonal haber:

(121)   hay, + V, + [__NP ($\left\{ \begin{array}{c} \bar{S} \\ PP \\ AP \end{array} \right\}$)]

The optional AP is included just in case it is decided that
participles are APs. If, on the contrary, it is conclusively
shown that participles should originate in a tenseless clause,
this AP option becomes unnecessary.

1.2.3 Clitics and word order. These are two syntactic
facets which must be taken into account in any complete treatment of hay sentences. They are treated together here because they become intertwined in some instances.

Without attempting to provide any comprehensive analysis of
Spanish clitics, I simply note that impersonal haber does co-
occur with clitics (see also discussion under Section 1.1.1.3).
As can be predicted by the direct object function of the single
NP subcategorized by haber, these clitics are accusative ones.
I assume without further ado that Spanish clitics are base-
generated (cf. Rivas 1977, Strozer 1976).

(122a) Ayer lo había.
       yesterday it (m. sg.) there-was
       'Yesterday, there-was.'

(122b) Ayer la había.
       it (f. sg.)

(122c) Ayer los había.
       them (m. pl.)

(122d) Ayer las había.
   them (f. pl.)

In general, clitics in hay sentences emerge because of previous
context. For example, sentences such as those in (122) could
be perfect answers to questions such as those asked in (123).

(123) ¿Sabes si había
   ayer?[45]

(a) pescado (m. sg.)
(b) langosta (f. sg.)
(c) tomates (m. pl.)
(d) uvas (f. pl.)

en el mercado

'Do you know whether there
market yesterday?'

was { (a) fish
  (b) lobster

were { (c) tomatoes
   (d) grapes

in the

The clitic and the referent of the NP with which it is coreferential (at the discourse level) must agree in the features
of number and gender.

Other examples in which the clitic is coreferential with an
argument in a previous noninterrogative sentence can be seen
in (124). Again, note the matching in features.

(124a) Eran unas muchachas$_i$ como ya no las$_i$ hay.
   they-were young-females as already not them there-is
   'They-were females the likes of whom no longer
   exist.'

(124b) Es cierto que ha habido muchas dificultades$_i$ y que
   las$_i$ hay para que... (VEA 79)
   it-is true that there-has been many difficulties (f.
   pl.) and that them (f. pl.) exist in order to...

Still another instance in which a clitic surfaces with hay can
be seen in (125). In this case, the NP with which the clitic
is coreferential has been base-generated in TOP position. This
example has the constituency of a left-dislocated structure
(Rivero 1980), exemplified in (126), where the clitic is anaphorically linked to the phrase in TOP position. The base-
generation of the left-dislocated structure of (126) can be motivated by observing that if it were produced by a movement
rule, it would violate Subjacency (i.e. the Complex NP Constraint) (see (127)).

(125) ...problemas$_i$ los$_i$ hay en todas partes. (VEA 37)
   ...problems (m. pl.) them (m. pl.) there-is everywhere
   '...problems exist everywhere.'

(126) [$_{S''}$[$_{TOP}$ problemas] [$_{S'}$[$_S$ los hay en todas partes]]]

(127)   ...problemas$_i$ me cuesta aceptar [$_{NP}$ la premisa
        [$_S$ de que [$_S$ los$_i$ hay en todas partes]]]
        '...problems I have a hard time accepting the premise
        that they exist everywhere.'

As opposed to the base-generated left-dislocated structure of
(125), the examples in (128) seem to be instances of Topicalization.[46] The word order in this case is arrived at by a movement rule which leaves a gap at the removal site. Observe that
no anaphorically related clitics surface in topicalized structures.
The constituent structure of topicalized sentences is found in
(129). Topicalization as a movement rule can be justified by
observing that although (130a) is grammatical, (130b) is not.
This is because in (130a) the moved NP has gone iteratively
from COMP to COMP (Chomsky 1977); but since NPs do not
have a COMP, (130b) is ungrammatical. This falls out from the
fact that movement rules obey Subjacency.

(128a) Algo raro hay en ese idilio. (R 71)
       'Something strange there-is in that idyll.'

(128b) Gente hay en todos lados. (EL 53)
       'People exist everywhere.'

(128c) --Y peligro de peste no hay, ¿no es cierto, Willi?
          (EL 102)
       'And pest danger there isn't, isn't it true, Willi?'

(128d) --Lugar hay.
       'Place there-is.' (EL 11)

(129) [$_{S'}$ [$_{COMP}$ algo raro] [$_S$ hay en ese idilio t]]

(130a) Algo raro dicen que hay en ese idilio.
       'Something strange they-say that there-is in that
       idyll.'

(130b) *Algo raro me cuesta aceptar [$_{NP}$ la premisa [$_{S'}$ de
       que [$_S$ hay t en ese idilio]]]
       'Something strange I have trouble accepting the
       premise that there-is in that idyll.'

This closes the discussion of clitics in hay sentences. Notice
that clitics and word order interact in an example such as (125).
And the examples in (128) represent cases in which the direct
object of hay has been preposed by a movement rule.
Different word order possibilities for locative and temporal
prepositional phrases and adverbials have been discussed in
Section 1.2.2.1. All that I want to point out here is that the
word order exemplified in (131)--hay PP NP, in which the

direct object argument and the PP have switched places--might constitute an effort to establish a more perfect match between the hay sentence and the presentative function (cf. Section 1.1.2).

(131) ...había en su origen una incomprensible humillación...
       (TE 129)
       '...there-was in its origin an incomprehensible humili-
       ation...'

Sentence (131) adheres to the loose principle that whatever is going to be recalled in the subsequent discourse comes last (see also discussion under Section 2.1.4).

1.3 **The grammar of *hay* sentences.** After having examined in great detail the constituent structure of impersonal haber sentences, one is in a position to investigate the grammar of this type of sentence.

The claim is that the grammar of existential haber is a maximally simple one. Working within the theoretical framework outlined in the Introduction, this means that haber sentences are base-generated; because of their basic nature no major transformations apply to simply hay sentences of the type found in (132).

(132) Hay una mosca.
       'There-is a fly.'

When this sentence reaches the level of sentence semantic interpretation, its S-structure is mapped onto its logical form (LF) by rules of semantic interpretation. Recall that in Section 1.1.2 it was said that part of the semantics of hay sentences consists in asserting the appearance of the referent of the NP in the universe of discourse. Since this assertion carries an existential implication, it follows that one of the rules of semantic interpretation must formally state this fact. I assume along with Milsark (1977) and Chomsky (1980) that hay sentences give rise to a structure of existential quantification.[47]

(133) $\exists\, x$, x an NP

When applied to (132), this renders (134) (details aside).

(134) $(_S\ (_{VP}\ \exists\ (_{NP}\ \text{una mosca})))$

In other words, the verb hay itself acts as an existential quantifier.[48] Observe that it would be undesirable to extract the existential quantifier out of the VP, because it seems wise to claim that the assertion of existence remains intact even under the scope of other logical operators. Consider the negation of sentence (132), for instance.

(135)   No hay una mosca.
        no there-is a fly
        'There isn't a fly.'

It seems desirable for the existential quantifier to be under the scope of NO, because what obtains is equivalent to sentence negation (cf. discussion in Section 2.2.4). Therefore, the LF of (135) is (136).

(136) $(_S$ NO $(_{VP}$ $\exists$ $(_{NP}$ una mosca$)))$

The structure in (136) provides the correct interpretation for (135); the negative operator denies the assertion of the existence of a fly. If one were to extract the quantifier $\exists$, one would immediately have to face the problem of the order of the two (or more operators, i.e. NO $\exists$ vs. $\exists$ NO. This question never arises if $\exists$ is left in place. The implicit claim is that any other logical operator would merely modify the existential assertion.

Notice that since impersonal haber sentences are basic, their NP is automatically in argument position in LF, as required by the theory (cf. Freidin 1978).[49]

Before proceeding with the LF of hay sentences, let us first examine some slightly more complicated examples. In Section 1.2.2.4 the following strict subcategorization for hay was posited.[50]

(137)   __NP $(\left\{ \begin{array}{c} PP \\ AP \\ \overline{S} \end{array} \right\})$

A representative example of each kind is given in (138).

(138a) Hay una mosca [$_{PP}$ en mi cerveza.]
        'There is a fly in my beer.'

(138b) Hay una mosca [$_{AP}$ muerta de hambre].
        'There-is a fly dying of hunger.'

(138c) Hay una mosca [$_{\overline{S}}$ zumbando alrededor mío].
        'There-is a fly buzzing around me.'

What the PP, AP, and $\overline{S}$ do in the sentences in (138) is to modify the NP or the whole sentence in one way or another. The PP in (138a) helps locate the NP, the AP in (138b) tells us the condition in which the NP is, and the $\overline{S}$ in (138c) explains where the NP exists by stating what the NP is doing.

In other words, these complements relativize the existence of
the referent of the NP by giving more information about it, so
that one can appropriately 'pick out' the referent of the NP
object. Therefore, these complements modify the assertion from
'within' the VP, just as a logical operator such as NO modifies
the assertion from 'outside' the VP. In this respect, notice
that it is immaterial whether a PP or an adverb is strictly subcategorized by hay (and therefore inside the VP) or not (in
which case it would be outside the VP and would be subsumed
directly under S). Suppose ayer in (139) is a sentence adverbial.

(139)   Hubo un partido]$_{VP}$ ayer]$_S$.
        'There-was a game yesterday.'

The adverb ayer still relativizes the existence of the NP
referent by locating it in time. This modification qualifies the
existential assertion from within the sentence.
    There are thus two types of modification that can affect the
existential assertion which emerges from hay--'exterior' modification imposed by logical operators (e.g. NO, but also others
such as conditional, subjunctive, etc.), and 'interior' modification realized by the PPs, APs, and S̄ subcategorized by hay,
as well as by sentential modifiers or complements. One can
now resume the discussion of the rules of semantic interpretation.
    To account for the way in which hay sentences are inter-
preted--as asserting the appearance of the referent of the NP
in the universe of discourse--it is necessary to devise a rule
which selects the object NP as the one which is being introduced in the discourse. For this purpose, I posit the following rule of Focus Assignment.[51]

(140)   Focus Assignment (LF)

        Mark the NP argument of hay sentences Focus of S.

Furthermore, one needs another rule in LF to establish the
modification relationship that obtains between the core of the
hay sentence (hay + NP) and any other modifiers that cooccur
with this core (cf. (138) and (139)). This is achieved by the
following rule.

(141)   Complement Linking (LF)

        Mark any PP, AP, S̄, or Adv to the right of [hay +
        NP] Complement of the Focus of S.[52]

The combined effect of (140) and (141) in a sentence like
(138a) is (142).

(142) $(_S (_{VP}$ hay $(_{NP} \underline{\text{una mosca}}) (_{PP} \underline{\text{en mi cerveza}})))$
$\phantom{(142) (_S (_{VP}}$ hay $\phantom{(_{NP}}$ Focus of S $\phantom{(_{PP}}$ Compl. F. of S

A similar outcome is obtained for (139).

(143) $(_S (_{VP}$ hubo $(_{NP} \underline{\text{un partido}})) (_{Adv} \underline{\text{ayer}}))_S$ F of S
$\phantom{(143) (_S (_{VP}}$ hubo $\phantom{(_{NP}}$ Focus of S $\phantom{(_{Adv}}$ Compl.

On considering the types of sentences exemplified in (144), it could be argued that the rule of Focus Assignment (140) is inadequate.

(144a) No hay donde sentarse.   (free relative)
no there-is where to-sit-down
'There is no place to sit down.'

(144b) El postre que hay en la heladera...   (relative clause)
'The dessert that there-is in the refrigerator...'

(144c) Ayer las había.   (cliticized direct object)
yesterday them (f. sg.) there-were

(144d) Problemas los hay en todas partes.   (left-dislocation)
problems them (m. pl.) there-are everywhere

Indeed, if logical focus (which is the one determined by rule (140)) and phonological focus (which supposedly establishes sentential stress) were to coincide in every instance, rule (140) would be hopelessly inadequate. Nevertheless, I am going to maintain that (140) serves my purpose for two reasons. First, notice that the theoretical model I have chosen for this study is the one characterized in Chomsky and Lasnik (1977) (cf. Introduction to this study). This means that while logical focus belongs in the right-hand side of the grammar, phonological focus pertains to the left-hand side. In this framework, logical focus could never determine sentential stress because each side of the grammar is blind with respect to the other side; therefore there must be two distinct types of focus. Second, rule (140) attempts to capture formally the invariant meaning carried by every hay sentence--that of the existential assertion of the referent of the NP. This meaning persists in the sentences in (144) even when they do not have a surface NP in argument position. I propose that the sentences in (144) have the following S-structures (details not pertinent to the discussion have been omitted).

(145a) No hay $(_{NP}$ PRO $[_{\bar{S}} [_{COMP}$ donde] $[_S$ sentarse]])

(145b) el postre que$_i$ hay $[_{NP_i}$ t] en la heladera

(145c) ayer las había [$_{NP}$ PRO][53]

(145d) problemas los hay [$_{NP}$ PRO] en todas partes

Provided the analysis in (145) is on the right track, it can be assumed that Focus Assignment applies and marks the object in each of these sentences as Focus of S,[54] just as it does when the NP has a lexical matrix. Since this proposal makes the intuitively satisfactory claim that the presence or absence of phonological matrix in the pertinent NP makes no significant difference in the interpretation of impersonal haber sentences, I conclude that the sentences in (144) are not counterexamples to the rule of Focus Assignment (140). Moreover, note that the objects in (145) are independently needed to fulfill the subcategorization conditions of hay (cf. Section 1.2.1).

The two rules, (140) and (141), are the only ones of LF pertinent to the discussion of impersonal haber sentences. No semantic restrictions of any kind are placed on this type of sentence at the LF level of sentence semantics.

In keeping with the stated goal of this investigation as an in-depth study of the syntax and semantics of presentational sentences in Spanish, it is necessary to go beyond the level of LF. In the first place, recall that in the Introduction it was hypothesized that subject vs. predicate, theme vs. rheme, and old vs. new become relevant at different levels of analysis: syntactic, post-LF, and pragmatic levels, respectively. Consequently, one has to see whether any of the rules of the post LF-level (which is still part of sentence semantics) plays a role in the interpretation of the sentences under scrutiny. Since I have identified the scope of assertion with rheme (cf. Section 1.1.2), it is obvious that a rule which would mark the rheme of an affirmative sentence is needed.

(146)   Rhematization (post-LF)

Mark as Rheme the VP and anything that follows it inside of S. Anything outside the Rheme becomes part of the Theme.[55]

This rule has the following effect on the already partially analyzed sentence (143).

(147) $(_S [(_{VP}$ hubo $(_{NP} \underline{\text{un partido}}))$ $(_{Adv} \underline{\text{ayer}})$ F. of S$]_S)$

Focus of S   Compl. F. of S

Rh

Because of the identification of the scope of assertion of an affirmative sentence with the rheme, it can be maintained that a noncontrastive negative sentence merely negates the rheme of its affirmative counterpart. This seems to be correct (see also Section 2.2.4), and is shown schematically in (148).

(148)   NO [$_\text{Rh}$ hubo un partido ayer]

Finally, it is necessary to move to the next stage of analysis, SI-2, the level of complete semantic representation. This
stage takes into account previous discourse, knowledge of the
world, and whatever other linguistic and extralinguistic information is pertinent for the complete interpretation of what is
generated by the syntax. It is at this level that the dichotomy
old vs. new becomes relevant and analyzable. Even more important to my immediate concern, at SI-2 a sentence is judged
according to its adequacy as a presentational statement.
Remember that all hay sentences function as presentationals,
since their mission is to introduce the referent of their NP object into the universe of discourse (cf. Section 1.1.2). The
pertinent rule of interpretation is given in (149).

(149)   Presentational Sentence Interpretation (SI-2)

Interpret S as presentational if it asserts the
appearance of the referent of the NP in the universe of discourse.

Rule (149) has a filtering effect: if a sentence does not
qualify, it is marked as ill-formed. Thus, while the sentences
in (150) properly fit the presentational sentence interpretation
(149), those in (151) do not, because the NP cannot be interpreted as being heralded into the discourse. On the contrary,
the NPs in (151) refer to entities which must already have
been part of the total discourse.

(150a) Allí hay más cartas.
        'There there-are more letters.'

(150b) ...hay un analfabetismo de gente que sabe leer.
        (VEA 16)
        '...there-is an illiteracy of people who know how to
        read.'

(150c) ...en sus ojos había el fuego de la esperanza.
        '...in her eyes there-was the fire of (the) hope.'

(150d) ...en Madrid es donde hay los mejores medios de
        trabajo...   (VEA 2)
        '...in Madrid is where there-exist the best means
        of work...'

(151a) *Hay los niños.
        'There-are the kids.'

(151b) *Había Sills.
        'There-was Sills.'

By examining the determiners which occur with the object NPs in (150) and (151), one can see that 'definiteness' by itself cannot be what rules out the sentences in (151). Definite determiners accompany the objects in (150c) and (150d), and these sentences are perfectly well-formed as presentationals. I come back to this problem after examining in detail the types of determiners permitted in hay sentences.

In the meantime, let me say that I am of the opinion that, contrary to what Milsark (1977) and Stowell (1978) claim, the sentences in (151) cannot be marked as ungrammatical in LF. As a matter of fact, they should not be filtered out at that point, because in order to make a principled decision on acceptability, one needs to make use of information that is not available to sentence grammar.[56]

In short, the syntax of hay sentences is very simple. These sentences are base-generated by the phrase structure rules of the grammar, and no transformations play a major (and/or exclusive) role in their derivation. Their semantic interpretation is far more interesting because it takes place in stages. At the level of LF, two rules help determine their sentence semantics: Focus Assignment (140) singles out the NP argument as the logical Focus of S, and Complement Linking (141) marks any adjectival or adverbial phrases to the right of [hay + NP] as Complement of the Focus of S. Moreover, the verb hay itself acts as an existential quantifier. Immediately after the rules of LF have finished operating, Rhematization (146) takes place; this rule parcels out the rhematic from the thematic part of the sentence. And finally, in SI-2 Presentational Sentence Interpretation (149) applies. This rule judges sentences according to their appropriateness as presentationals. If they are not well-formed presentationals, the sentences are filtered out.

Before demonstrating that the Definiteness Restriction has no place in the grammar of Spanish, it is necessary to pursue an investigation of determiners in hay sentences. This is done in Section 1.3.1.

1.3.1 The determiners. This section on the determiners that occur with the NP object of impersonal haber is subdivided as follows. In Section 1.3.1.1 the analysis proposed by the Hispanist William Bull (1943, 1965) is presented. To my knowledge, he offers the only treatment of Spanish hay to date.[57] The indefinite determiners are examined in Section 1.3.1.2, the definite ones in Section 1.3.1.3. In the next section (1.3.2), the Definiteness Restriction is evaluated in the light of the previous discussion.

1.3.1.1 Bull's proposal. Bull's main concern is the devising of pedagogical rules that would help in the teaching of Spanish. He advocates studying impersonal haber together with two other verbs, ser and estar, both of which translate as English 'to be'.

For him, ser-estar-haber form a complex unit. In mentioning
that there are differences in language which have no contrasting function, he says, 'the difference between haber and
estar for location is not a meaningful contrast. It is the product of useless specialization' (1965:174). He asserts that the
choice between one or the other is made based on the concept
of definiteness and indefiniteness. According to him, estar is
used to locate a definite entity, haber an indefinite one, and
ser is chosen to locate a definite event. Therefore, Bull urges
that the student learning Spanish be taught to distinguish between definite and indefinite grammatical concepts, since this
distinction triggers the rule for the use of haber, ser, and
estar. In his own words (1965:205):

> He must learn that haber and ser are used with events;
> haber and estar with entities, and the choice between each
> member of the two pairs depends on the subset of limiting
> adjectives used. The cues are unmistakably clear: entity
> vs. event; definite vs. indefinite.

Anyone not fully aware of the facts of Spanish could very
easily extrapolate Bull's useful practical rules and hypothesize
that the complex ser-estar-haber is but the surface reflex of
a single underlying verb of location. This abstract verb (call
it LOC) would manifest itself as one of the 'alloverbs' according to the schema in (152).

(152)

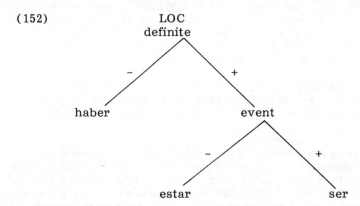

But pedagogical rules meant to guide students during the first
steps of foreign language learning sometimes do not accurately
reflect all usage possibilities of the language. Because of previous research he had conducted on haber vs. estar, Bull was
well aware that his rule would only work in approximately 95
percent of the cases.

This division of function is observed in 417, or 95.3 percent, of the 438 examples of the locative estar encountered

in the present study. Twenty-one examples of estar were
found in which the subject was indefinite. In contrast, the
haber predicate is indefinite in 677, or 95 percent, of the
713 examples encountered. (1943:122)

Consequently, a comprehensive and accurate grammar of Spanish should not ignore the 5 percent that is not covered by
Bull's pedagogical rules. Ideally, it would be necessary to
find an explanation for all of the uses of ser, estar, and
haber (see Appendix A).
　There is another problem with Bull's approach, a problem
of which he was aware also. In the 5 percent not covered by
his pedagogical rules, it is not the case that [± definite] was
used indiscriminately, or that haber and estar could be interchanged without a concomitant change in meaning. Bull writes:

...a point is reached where haber and estar may not be
interchanged by substitution of the definite for the indefinite. When haber approaches almost absolute synonymity
with existir its predicate may be definite.

Hay, pues, primero la necesidad de conocer para vivir...
(Unamuno)

...sin éste no hay aquél. (Ortega y Gasset)

Similarly when estar closely approaches the meaning of its
Latin etymon its subject may be indefinite.

A su lado estaba un caballero anciano (Palacio Valdés)
Cien veces dijo que no quería ver más indios; y menos a
uno que estaba ahí... (Abreu Gómez)
Unos están en las puertas... (Azorín)[58]

One way to narrow the gap between posited rules and actual
usage would be to maintain that there are two verbs hay, one
which means 'location' that adheres to Bull's rules, and a
second one which signifies 'existence'. But this seems to be a
less than ideal solution. How would the dividing line between
location and existence be determined? Things do not exist in
a vacuum, they tend to be somewhere. Let us examine the
two sentences in (153).

(153a) Hay hielo.
　　　'There-is ice.'

(153b) Hay hielo en el balde.
　　　'There-is ice in the bucket.'

Would one be justified in saying that (153a) implies mere existence but that (153b) implies location? The only difference is

that (153b) has a prepositional phrase which explains where
the ice is to be found. Furthermore, prepositional phrases
(and locative adverbs also) are not barred from appearing in
sentences where hay cooccurs with a definite NP.

(154a) Además de este yerro hay en esta frase el otro no
        menos chocante del plural habían. (Bello 1970:264)
        'Besides this mistake there-is in this phrase the other
        one not less shocking of the plural habían.'

(154b) ...y allí no hay el problema de... (VEA 75)
        '...and there there-isn't the problem of...'

Hence, the possibility of splitting hay into two lexical items--
one denoting location, the other denoting existence--is rejected
as an artificial construct and receives no further attention here.
Nevertheless, it can easily be seen how Bull's pedagogical
analysis could have given rise to a myth: the myth of the
Definiteness Restriction in hay sentences.

1.3.1.2 On indefiniteness. Because the primary function of
hay sentences is to introduce the referent of the NP into the
world of discourse, it comes as no surprise that this construction is highly compatible with an indefinite argument. 'Indefinite' is used here as a rough equivalent to 'nonidentifiable'.[59]
In other words, given the discourse, the speaker assumes that
the hearer cannot properly identify or select the referent under
consideration from among all other referents that might be denoted by the noun (cf. Chafe 1976:39). Since hay sentences
are presentational by nature, it turns out that at the discourse
level (i.e. SI-2) the indefinite NP argument is interpreted as
conveying new information. And it is a well-known fact that a
high correlation exists between new information and indefiniteness. Since there is no controversy about the compatibility of
hay with indefinite modifiers, the task is therefore limited to
exploring the signals used to mark a given argument as indefinite.[60]
    In the first place, there is the indefinite article un/una.
This article in Spanish has essentially the form and function
of the number one. Compare (155a) and (155b).

(155a) un hombre
        'a/one man'

(155b) una mujer
        'a/one woman'

It goes without saying that if the number one is compatible
with hay, then all other cardinal numbers should be so, too.
This is warranted by the examples in (156).

(156a) Hubo un arreglo entre ellas,... (TE 66)
'There-was a deal between them,...'

(156b) Hay uno por ciento de la población de esquizofrénicos.
(VEA 73)
'One percent of the population is schizophrenic.'

(156c) ...hay dos operados en el segundo piso. (CH 124)
'...there-are two individuals-who-have-been-operated-
on on the second floor.'

(156d) Hay nueve cámaras iguales... (IM 25)
'There-are nine identical chambers...'

Nevertheless, two types of expressions of cardinality exist.
On the one hand, the 'objective' numbers (one, four, ninety-
two, etc.) represent exactly the same concepts for everybody.
On the other hand, there are the 'subjective' numbers (expressions like unos 'some', muchos 'many', varios 'several',
pocos 'a few', algunos 'some', tantos 'so many', etc.) which
might refer to relatively different quantities for different
people.[61] What might be 'many presents' for one child might
be 'a few' for another. The point is that just as hay is compatible with objective numbers, it is also compatible with subjective numbers.

(157a) ...hay muchos lugares donde practicar ese deporte
... (VEA 29)
'...there-are many places in which to practice that
sport...'

(157b) ...sabemos que hay mucho capital oculto,... (VEA 38)
'...we know that there-is a lot of hidden capital,...'

(157c) ...hubo algunos episodios, algunos hechos... (R 94)
'...there-were some episodes, some deeds...'

(157d) ...hay unas rocas muy resbaladizas...
'...there-are some very slippery rocks...'

Among the expressions of cardinality, it is necessary also to
consider the limiting adjective otro 'another'. At first glance
this adjective seems to teeter between an objective and subjective number. It is not an objective number in the same sense
as 'seven' or 'twenty' because it is not possible to assign an
immutable numerical value to it that would be valid in every
circumstance. On the other hand, sometimes it is possible to
infer an exact numerical value for it, as in example (158).

(158) Hay cinco dormitorios arriba pero también hay otro
dormitorio más chico en la planta baja.
'There-are five bedrooms upstairs but also there-is
another smaller bedroom on the first floor.'

In the context of example (158), otro implies a sixth bedroom.
Nevertheless, the context is not always that explicit. In most
cases the number cannot be exactly pinpointed and otro conveys merely the idea of 'one more', 'an extra one', 'another',
or the like.

(159a) Pero hay otro aspecto igualmente importante...
(VEA 142)
'But there-is another equally important aspect...'

(159b) ...también hay otra organización que funciona...
(VEA 76)
'...also there-is another organization that functions
...'

(159c) Hay otra consideración más que tener en cuenta...
(VEA 160)
'There-is one more consideration that needs to
be taken into account.'

Thus, although an explicit enough context may allow us to
infer a numerical value for otro, this value is not part of the
lexical meaning of this expression.
Proceeding with the discussion of indefiniteness, it becomes
clear that plurality as manifested by the plural suffix is also a
subjective expression of cardinality. The only information it
conveys is that there are at least two, but maybe more, of
something.

(160a) ...hay opiniones divergentes... (VEA 4)
'...there-are divergent opinions...'

(160b) Hay sillas de paja,... (IM 21)
'There-are straw chairs...'

Recalling that otro means 'an additional one', what would the
plural morpheme add to this meaning?

(161a) Hay otros problemas con esa hipótesis.
'There-are other problems with that hypothesis.'

(161b) Hay otras organizaciones que se ocupan de eso.
'There-are other organizations that deal with that.'

Evidently, the outcomes of juxtaposing otro and the plural
suffix is 'at least two more'. Hence, the common denominator

of plurality as exemplified in (160) and (161) must be 'more than one'. All other inferences are part of the context and/or the elements with which the plural suffix is combined.[62]

Having discussed the effect of determineless plural nouns, I have yet to explore the opposite phenomenon: the effect an unmodified singular noun has when used with hay. The examples gathered seem to fall into two major groups. In the first group, the negative particle no appears and the result is very similar to using the number zero.

(162a) No hubo respuesta. (LP 88)
       'There-was no answer.'

(162b) Por lo menos allí no hay viento. (TE 169)
       'At least there there-is no wind.'

(162c) ...hay hielo... (TE 141)
       '...there's no ice...'

(162d) No hay dinero... (VEA 48)[63]
       'There's no money...'

In the second group, the unmodified [-count] nouns stand for some 'indefinite quantity' or 'unspecified amount'.

(163a) ...si hay viento. (IM 39)
       '...if there-is wind.'

(163b) --¿Hubo jaleo en su casa? ¿Hubo pelea? (R 84)
       '--was-there quarreling in your house? Was-there fighting?'

(163c) Había sangre en el suelo.
       'There-was blood on the ground.'

Thus, whether the implied meaning is zero (as in (162)), or some indefinite quantity (as in (163)), once more this is an instance of cardinality.

So far, it has been shown that one way to signal indefiniteness in Spanish is by using expressions of cardinality, and that in turn, cardinality may be manifested in either of two ways: by means of objective numbers, and by means of subjective numbers. Although in the examples these expressions modify the noun, it is also possible for many of them to assume a pronominal function. A few sentences suffice to exemplify this use.

(164a) Hay uno sobre la mesa y hay otro en el primer cajón.
       'There-is one on the table and there-is another in
        the first drawer.'

(164b) ¿Había mucho para discutir?
      'Was-there a lot to discuss?'

(164c) No, había poco.
      'No, there-was little.'

(164d) Hay algo que no dices.
      'There-is something that you're not telling.'

(164e) ¿Había alguien a la puerta?
      'Was-there anybody at the door?'

(164f) No, no había nadie.
      'No, there-was no-one.'

Another way of signaling indefiniteness in Spanish was
hinted at in the discussion of free relatives (Section 1.2.2.2.3).
The relative pronouns quien 'who', donde 'where', etc. may appear without an antecedent when they make reference to an
indeterminate person/group or place.

(165a) Hay quien critica a los profesores...   (VEA 50)
      there-is who criticize professors...
      'There-are those who criticize professors...'

(165b) No hubo quien le arrancara la dirección de Rosaura.
      (R 111)
      no there-was who him could-get the address of
        Rosaura.
      'Not a soul could get Rosaura's address from him.'

(165c) No hay donde ir.
      no there-is where to-go
      'There isn't a place to go'.

In conclusion, it has been shown that Spanish signals indefiniteness in several ways, all of which constitute instances
of cardinality. Impersonal haber sentences are highly congruous with all these expressions of cardinality.[64]

1.3.1.3 On definiteness. In recent literature it has become
common practice to exclude (as ungrammatical) definite modification from existential sentences of the type under discussion
(cf. Bull 1943 for Spanish; and Bresnan 1970, Wasow 1975,
Kuno 1971, Milsark 1977, Jenkins 1975, Stowell 1978 for English).[65]   Since this is such a prevalent trend, I find it necessary to examine the devices that Spanish employs to signal
definiteness before proceeding to a full discussion of hay and
definiteness.

Syntactic definiteness is morphologically marked in Spanish. Although one of the most obvious ways to convey definiteness in Spanish is by means of the definite article, this is by no means the only way. Bull (1965:205) has already noticed that the definite determiner, possessives, and demonstratives belong to the same set:

> The Spaniard feels (and the student must learn) that they share some common function in his way of organizing reality, and it may be assumed, as a result, that he is very likely to generalize this feeling and treat them in a similar fashion ...

One of the problems with definiteness is that syntactic definiteness does not show a one-to-one correlation with semantic definiteness (see Section 1.3.1.3.1.5). This has led Pope (1976), for example, to suggest that semantic definiteness be considered anaphoricity. She states that an NP should be taken as anaphoric not only when it has been mentioned in the preceding discourse but also if it is known to both speaker and hearer. Anaphoricity in this sense appears to be synonymous with 'identifiable', that is, the speaker assumes that the listener can pick out the particular referent the speaker has in mind (cf. Chafe 1976). Syntactic and semantic definiteness do coincide in this use.

The Spanish definite article serves well to establish anaphoricity.

(166a) Los niños ya están en casa.
'The children are already home.'

(166b) Llevé los (tres) gatos al veterinario.
'I took the (three) cats to the veterinarian.'

(167a) El presidente está de vacaciones.
'The president is on vacation.'

(167b) El marido de Pepa está en la cocina.
the husband of Pepa is in the kitchen
'Pepa's husband is in the kitchen.'

(168) Vi una camisa y unos pantalones en una boutique pero sólo tenía plata para comprar la camisa.
'I saw a shirt and a pair of pants in a boutique but I only had enough money to buy the shirt.'

(169) Ayer fuimos al cine. La película era malísima.
'Yesterday we went to the movies. The film was extremely bad.'

As examples (166)-(169) show, there are several ways to
establish an argument as 'identifiable'. Both speaker and
hearer might share knowledge about the referents (166); given
cultural and situational context, there might be a unique referent (167); or anaphoricity may be determined by prior mention, whether direct (168)[66] or inferred (169). Note that while
in (166) and (167) identifiability is not linguistic, in (168) and
(169) it is, although in the latter case it can only be determined at the discourse level and not at the level of sentence
semantics. Therefore, these examples already give us a clue:
anaphoricity or identifiability must be part of SI-2, since they
are pragmatic notions.

To prove that possessives and demonstratives pattern with
the definite article, examples (170)-(173) are arranged to illustrate situations similar to the ones displayed in (166)-(169).

(170a) Tus herramientas están tiradas por todas partes.
'Your tools are thrown all over the place.'

(170b) Estas sillas están muy destartaladas.
'These chairs are falling apart.'

(171a) Mi hija ya perdió tres dientes.
'My daughter has already lost three teeth.'

(171b) Este traje es muy chillón.
'This suit is very loud.'

(172a) Me robaron una pulsera y varios anillos. Lo que
más siento es la pérdida de mi pulsera porque era
un recuerdo de familia.
'They stole a bracelet and several rings from me.
What I regret the most is my bracelet because it
was a family keepsake.'

(172b) Compré varias cosas en una liquidación incluso una
pollera larga, pero esta pollera resultó ser un clavo
pues se arruga.
'I bought several things on sale, including a long
skirt, but this skirt happened to be a bad buy because it wrinkles.'

(173a) Participé en una exhibición de arte. Mis acuarelas
fueron muy bien recibidas.
'I participated in an art exhibit. My watercolors were
very well received.'

(173b) Ayer fuimos al teatro. Nos gustó más esta obra que
la del mes pasado.
'Yesterday we went to the theater. We liked this
play better than the one (presented) last month.'

The examples listed in (166)-(169) do not exhaust the possible usages of the definite determiner in Spanish. It is also used for definite descriptions with a relative clause (174) and with superlatives (175).[67]

(174) El libro que te regaló Paco...
'The book that Paco gave you...'

(175) Hoy ví la mejor película de mi vida.
'Today I saw the best movie in my life.'

There is one additional instance of the definite determiner which will become quite relevant in the discussion of hay sentences: the generic.

(176a) Las vicuñas viven en los Andes.
'(The) vicuñas live in the Andes.'

(176b) La vicuña vive en los Andes.
'The vicuña lives in the Andes.'

(176c) Los hombres son mortales.
'(The) men are mortal.'

(176d) El perro es un mamífero.
'The dog is a mammal.'

As evidenced in (176), generic statements can be expressed in Spanish by either a singular or a plural form.[68] A generic statement not only includes the whole set of X (i.e. the genus) but it also highlights characteristic or defining properties of X.

There is a marked difference between the generic use of the definite determiner and the uses previously discussed (cf. (166)-(169), (174), and (175)). In the earlier cases, the definite NPs refer to particular individuals or objects; therefore, the referents are specific. The statements in (176), however, refer to the class X without any specific reference to individual members of X. Hence, the utterance of a generic statement does not represent the speaker's commitment as to the existence of a given item of X. Observe (177).

(177a) Ya se sabe que los 'blacos' destruyen los virus...
'It is already known that the "blacos" destroy (the) viruses...'

(177b) ...pero desgraciadamente aún no se ha inventado los 'blacos'.
'...but unfortunately the "blacos" have not been invented yet.'

(177c) ...pero desgraciadamente los 'blacos' no existen aún.
'...but unfortunately the "blacos" don't exist yet.'

As (177) shows, it is possible to concoct a generic statement
and then to deny the existence of members of X. No contradiction results from the juxtaposition of (177b) or (177c) with
the generic sentence (177a). This is not what happens if one
attaches a remark of the type found in (177b) or (177c) to a
sentence like (166a) (repeated here as (178a)).

(178a) Los niños ya están en casa...
'The children are already home...'

(178b) ...pero desgraciadamente los niños no han nacido aún.
'...but unfortunately the children have not been born
yet.'

(178c) ...pero desgraciadamente los niños no existen aún.
'...but unfortunately the children don't exist yet.'

In this case, the outcome of concatenating (178b) or (178c) to
(178a) is nonsensical, because by uttering (178a) the speaker
presupposes the existence of a certain number of children.
The referent of the NP is specific. The significance of the
distinction between definite specific and definite nonspecific
(i.e. generic) plays a crucial role in the discussion of hay
with definiteness (cf. Section 1.3.1.3.1.5).

Nevertheless, all of the uses of the definite determiner have
something in common. The definite determiner always expresses
the totality of Xs, that is to say, it makes reference to all the
members of a given set. Totality might range from the generic
whole (cf. (176)), to any total determined by context (cf.
(166)), to one unique entity (cf. (167)). In a unique reference the total equals one. This single item may be something
common to mankind (el sol 'the sun'), to a given culture (only
one spouse in a monogamous society), or to the situation (for
example, something previously mentioned, cf. (168)).

Finally, for the sake of completeness, any discussion of
definiteness must mention proper names. Proper names are
semantically very much akin to common nouns with a unique
referent. They identify particular referents and are thus
definite by definition. If somebody says:

(179) Llegó Pepe.
'Pepe arrived.'

the assumption is that the listener knows who Pepe is. This is
essentially the function of proper names; they are meant to
have a unique referent.[69]

Using this discussion as a foundation, it is now possible to
examine the cooccurrence of hay with definite NPs.

1.3.1.3.1 *Hay* and definiteness. As already mentioned in
Section 1.3.1.1, hay does appear with definite determiners--
although not as frequently as it occurs with expressions of
cardinality. To ignore this possibility is to leave aside pertinent data. During the following discussion it should become
evident that a concept such as syntactic definiteness is not
crucial to judgments of either grammaticality or appropriateness for hay sentences. The answer to the problem resides
in the interpretation of these sentences, not in their form.
If the sentence complies with the semantics and pragmatics of
impersonal haber sentences--that of asserting the existence of
the NP referent while being presentational in function--it is
judged well-formed and interpretable.

For ease of exposition, the present section is subdivided
into four parts: superlatives, cataphoric reference, anaphoric
reference, and lists.

1.3.1.3.1.1 Superlatives. Superlatives provide us with one
instance of hay involving definite morphology. There are two
kinds of superlatives in Spanish: (1) the true superlative,
which conveys the highest or the lowest degree of a given
quality as compared with any other degrees of the same scale,
and (2) the absolute superlative, which also expresses a very
high degree but without reference to any other (cf. Ramsey
1956:153).

(i)   Tiene los ojos más lindos del mundo.
      'S/he has the most beautiful eyes in the world.'

(ii) Tiene un acento peculiarísimo.
      'S/he has the most peculiar accent.'[70]

For the purposes of the present discussion, only the former
type of superlative is of interest. This true superlative of adjectives is formed by adding the definite determiner (or a
possessive) to the corresponding comparative, as in example
(180).

(180a) Este libro es mejor (que ésos).
       'This book is better (than those).'

(180b) Este libro es el mejor.
       'This book is the best.'

Example (180a) is a comparative while (180b) is a superlative.
Thus, since the definite determiner is required by the language
system to segregate superlatives from comparatives, its semantic
definiteness (i.e. 'identifiability' of the NP) might be open to
question.[71]

I now turn to the Spanish data with hay. As will become evident, the examples have been arranged in a more or less decreasing scale of semantic definiteness for ease of exposition.

(181a) Según me contaron, había el diamante más grande del
      mundo en esa exposición.
      'According to what they told me, there-was the
      largest diamond in the world at that exhibit.'

(181b) En la clase hoy, había el olor más peculiar que te
      puedas imaginar. No sé a que se debería.
      'In class today, there-was the most peculiar smell
      that you can imagine. I don't know what it was
      due to.'

The two examples in (181) single out a unique item to be at the topmost of its corresponding scale. Qualifying expressions such as del mundo 'in the world' and que te puedas imaginar 'that you can imagine' leave no room for doubt about the superlative's position on the scale. Hence, in this instance, grammatical and semantic definiteness appear to coincide.

(182a) ...en Madrid es donde hay los mejores medios de
      trabajo... (VEA 2)
      '...in Madrid is where the best working conditions
      exist...'

(182b) En sus estantes había las más diversas mercaderías.
      (cf. Kany 1969:257)
      'On its shelves there-were the most diversified goods.'

(182c) También hay sus altamente ridículas proposiciones de
      casamiento.
      'There-are also his extremely ridiculous proposals of
      marriage.'

The sentences in (182) contain plural NPs; precisely because of their plurality they cannot refer to unique specific entities, but only to whole classes. Thus, they are somewhat less definite semantically than unique entities.

(183a) No hubo (ni) la más mínima indicación de que
      despedirían al presidente de la compañía.
      'There-wasn't (even) the slightest sign that they
      would fire the president of the company.'

(183b) Nunca hubo la más remota posibilidad de que Paco
      ganara la carrera.
      'There-was never the remotest possibility that Paco
      would win the race.'

(183c) Todavía no hay <u>los</u> mejores tomates de esta temporada
en el mercado.
'The best tomatoes of this season aren't in the market
yet.'

All the examples in (183) are negated. Negating an <u>hay</u> sentence (as already explained in Section 1.3.1.2) has the effect of saying 'zero' or 'no' quantity/amount. This zero-producing effect of negation is completely transparent in (183a) and (183b). It is even possible to replace the superlative expressions there with those in (184) without radically changing the idea of the message conveyed.[72]

(184a) ...ninguna indicación...
'...any indication...'

(184b) ...ninguna posibilidad...
'...any possibility...'[73]

The inference in (183c) is also zero, but the statement is ambiguous in the sense that it could be zero quantity of the best tomatoes or, alternatively, zero quantity of any tomatoes at all. This latter interpretation is the only one possible if (183c) is continued with (185).

(185) ...en realidad, ni siquiera hay tomates aún.
'...actually, there-aren't even any tomatoes yet.'

Therefore, since the statements in (183) deny the existence of the referent of their NP, it is impossible to identify the referents successfully. Hence, these examples could be considered semantically indeterminate despite the presence of the definite determiner.

The conclusion that can be extracted from (181) through (183) is that definiteness in superlatives is a matter of degree.[74] Superlatives cover the entire span, from identifying a single specific item to conveying a general idea of nonexistence when used in conjunction with a negative expression. One must note, however, that regardless of their degree of semantic definiteness, superlatives cooccur with <u>hay</u>. By keeping in mind that the function of superlatives is to place something at the unsurpassable extreme (whether top or bottom) of some evaluative scale, it becomes possible to explain their compatibility with <u>hay</u>. The sentences in (181) through (183) introduce the referent of the NP into the discourse; it just happens that the speaker has chosen to put this NP at the extreme of a given scale. Maybe because the language demands the presence of the definite determiner for the superlative reading to obtain, no clash with the function of <u>hay</u> sentences arises; the sentence can be interpreted as presentational.

Finally, let me point out a peculiarity of superlatives. Native speakers do not feel completely at ease when the superlative refers to a uniquely identified human being.

(186a) ??Hay el profesor más insoportable del mundo al
       frente de mi clase de psicología.
       'There-is the most intolerable professor in the world
       in front of my psychology class.'

(186b) ??En la película de anoche había el actor más guapo
       del mundo.
       'In last night's film there was the most handsome
       actor in the world.'

This might be due to a conglomerate of factors, among which the absence of personal a might play an important role. Recalling that personal a is required before a direct object NP which refers to a specific human being, it is easy to understand why the sentences in (186) produce doubts. The NP referent is being uniquely identified, yet personal a is barred from hay sentences (cf. Section 1.1.1.3).

Nonetheless, superlatives with human referents may cooccur with hay without any problems. I found two of these examples cited in Ramsey (1956:140, 163).

(187a) O eres el hombre más malo que hay en el mundo, o
       no sé lo que eres.
       'Either you are the worst man that there-is in the
       world, or I don't know what you are.'

(187b) Soy el hombre más infeliz más infeliz que hay bajo la
       capa del cielo.
       'I am the most unhappy, the most unhappy man that
       there-is/exists under the sky.'

No doubt the grammaticality of (187)--as opposed to the sentences in (186)--is due to the fact that in (187) the superlative is part of the matrix sentence and hay belongs in the relative.

In conclusion, hay and superlatives may cooccur because their functions--to introduce the NP referent and to place something at one extreme of a scale, respectively--are compatible in spite of the form of the superlative in Spanish (i.e. definite morphology).

1.3.1.3.1.2 Cataphoric reference. Quirk et al. (1972:155) mention the cataphoric use of the determiner as that one which 'has forward reference to a post-modifying prepositional phrase or relative clause'. Their examples are the following.

The wines { of France
             { that France produces

The Philadelphia which Mr. Johnson knows so well is a
heritage of colonial times.

Cataphoric reference is pertinent to this discussion because of
the role it plays in existential sentences with definite modification.

(188a) Había el caso del emigrante que tenía contrato ya...
     (spontaneous conversation)
     'There-was the case of the emigrant who already had
     (a) contract...'

(188b) Pero hay el par de horas que pasaron desde que el
     hombre bajó de la habitación... (TE 161)
     'But there-is the couple of hours that went by since
     the man came down from his room...'

(188c) Luego hay la otra chica que no ha hecho su tesis;...
     (M 78)
     'Then there-is the other girl who has not done her
     thesis;...'

(188d) Aquí hay eso que buscas. (spontaneous conversation)
     here there-is that that you-are-looking for
     'Here is what you are looking for.'

The sentences in (188) exhibit a definite NP argument modified
by a relative clause. In (189) there are some examples in
which the modification is achieved by a prepositional phrase.

(189a) ...en muchos casos, ni siquiera hay la proyección a
     través de la radiotelevisión. (VEA b 114)
     '...in many cases, there-isn't even the broadcast
     over the (radio-) television.'

(189b) Ya no había para ellas las tertulias al atardecer.
     'For them there-were no longer the gatherings at
     sundown.'

(189c) Siempre hay la tendencia a la inercia ¿no? (VEA 51)
     'There-is always the tendency towards inertia, isn't
     there?'

(189d) Espero que todavía hay ese programa de las cinco.
     'I hope that there-is still that program at five.'

Regardless of whether the definite NP argument governed by
hay is limited by a relative clause or a prepositional phrase,
the result is the same. Since this NP argument would most
likely turn out to be new information at the discourse level,
postmodification plays a decisive role in helping with the

identification of the NP referent and, as a corollary, with the
naturalness of the utterance. Out of context, without this
modification hay sentences are regarded as awkward or even
ungrammatical by native speakers.
Observe the examples in (190).

(190a) *Hay el par de horas.
'There-are the couple of hours.'

(190b) ?*Aquí hay eso.
'Here there-is that.'

(190c) *No había las tertulias.
'There-weren't the gatherings.'

(190d) *Siempre hay la tendencia.[75]
'There-is always the tendency.'

The sentences in (190) are judged ungrammatical not because
of their syntax--if that were the case, there would be no
principled way to reject (190) while accepting (188) and (189);
they are unacceptable because of their interpretation. These
sentences appear to be uninformative; they do not say enough.
The use of the definite determiner indicates that the noun
referent should be identifiable, but at the same time not
enough information is provided to complete this identification
successfully. Cannings (1978) is of the same opinion. In
discussing French il y a and definiteness, he suggests that
the problem is not one of form but of interpretation. These
sentences do not violate a rule of grammar; they are merely
platitudinous statements which violate Grice's (1975) principle
of quantity. This principle reads: 'Make your contribution
as informative as is required (for the current purposes of the
exchange). Do not make your contribution more informative
than is required' (1975:45).

Consequently, my contention is that the speaker employs
cataphoric modification when introducing an object into the
discourse when the addressee can identify it with a little bit
of help (thus, the combination of definite determiner and post-
noun modification). Both relatives (188) and prepositional
phrases (189) contribute to the proper identification of the NP
referent.

1.3.1.3.1.3 **Anaphoric reference.** Linguistic reference can
be not only cataphoric (forward reference) but also anaphoric
(backward reference). Anaphoric reference is bound to a
previous introduction of a noun. The compatibility of this
type of reference with existential sentences must now be
examined.

Breivik (1975:69) explains that, from the viewpoint of functional sentence perspective, existential sentences with there

plus a definite NP seem to have the function of recalling the referent into the focus of attention. Bolinger (1977:115) believes likewise, since he states, 'There can bring something BACK into awareness as well as make us aware of it for the first time'. Keeping this in mind, consider example (191).

(191) ¿Hay tal sistema en su país? (VEA b 143)
       'Is there such [a] system in your country?'

It is obvious that a question like (191) would not be appropriate unless the conversation centered on (types of) systems. One could not ask (191) out of context. Possible replacements of tal with other instances of definite modification come to mind.

(192) ¿Hay $\left\{\begin{array}{l}\text{ese sistema}\\ \text{el sistema ese}\\ \text{el sistema equivalente}\\ \text{ese sistema tan complicado}\\ \text{el mismo sistema}\end{array}\right\}$ en su país?

      'Is there $\left\{\begin{array}{l}\text{that system}\\ \text{that system}\\ \text{the equivalent system}\\ \text{the so-complicated system}\\ \text{the same system}\end{array}\right\}$ in your country?'

The speaker in (191) and (192) is using anaphoric reference to identify the referent adequately. In other words, given the discourse situation, it is possible to make the NP definite because of its identifiability. Examples such as these could be considered cases of 'reentries'.

Object clitics provide another instance of anaphoric reference in existential sentences. These clitics supply a way of avoiding redundancy through mere reference to something previously expressed.[76] Clitics constitute a second mention; they are, therefore, definite. Some examples are given in (193).

(193a) Era una muchacha como ya no las hay. (CT 155)
       she was a young-woman like already no them (f. pl.)
       there-is
       'She was a young-woman the likes of whom no longer exist.'

(193b) Es cierto que ha habido muchas dificultades y que
       las hay para que la mujer pueda desarrollarse...
       (VEA 79)
       'It-is true that there-have been many difficulties and
       (that) they-exist so that women may improve themselves...'

(193c) ...problemas los hay en todas partes. (VEA 37)
        problems them there-are everywhere
        '...problems, they exist everywhere.'

In (193a) las ('them' f. pl.) stands for muchachas 'young
women' (f. pl.), extrapolated from the previously stated singular of the same noun. In (193b) las refers to its antecedent
muchas dificultades 'many difficulties'; and in (193c) los (m.
pl.) equals problemas 'problems' (m. pl.).

The examples in (193), then, are instances in which hay
reintroduces information. The original reference for this reentry may be located in the immediately previous context or it
may be farther away, as evidenced in the following taped conversation.

(194)   ...En Mallorca...los turistas han ido allí desde hace
      mucho tiempo...o sea...el turista rico...típico
      inglés etc. esto es del siglo pasado,...iban a
      Mallorca...
      --...con su...
      --Los...los había mucho tiempo antes. (VEA 59)
      '...In Mallorca...the tourists have gone there since a
      long time ago...that is...the rich tourist...typically
      English etc. this is from the last century...they
      went to Mallorca...
      --...with their...
      --They were there from a long time before.'
      (Lit.: them...them there-were...)

In (194) los is coreferential with los turistas, from which it is
considerably removed. Thus, distance per se does not seem to
be a factor in limiting reentry.

Although I do not agree with Breivik's point of view that all
instances of existential sentences with definite modification are
'recalls' or 'reminders', there seem to be some cases of hay
sentences to which his proposal applies. This is the case
where hay cooccurs with anaphoric reference. The anaphoric
noun or clitic reasserts the appearance of the object NP by reintroducing it into the discourse.

1.3.1.3.1.4 Lists. Lists may be of several kinds: incomplete or complete, a list of one or of several items.[77] Lists
may provide answers to questions, but this is not an absolute
requirement; they are also likely to occur in narrative. I now
turn to some examples.

(195a) --¿Cómo voy al centro?
      'How do I go downtown?'

(195b) --Pues, hay el (colectivo) 7 en la esquina y el subte
a dos cuadras...pero a esta hora es mejor caminar
porque todo viene lleno.
'Well, there is the (bus number) 7 at the corner and
the subway two blocks away...but at this hour it is
better to walk because everything comes full.'

(195c) --Bueno, hay el colectivo...pero mejor te llevo.
'Well, there's the bus...but I'd better give you a
ride.'

To a question like (195a), one can answer with a (presumably)
complete list (195b), or with an incomplete one (195c). The
distinction is achieved through the intonational pattern: while
colectivo in both (195b) and (195c) has the rising intonation
which indicates incompleteness, the second item in (195b)
carries falling intonation and thus signals the end of the series.
What is the purpose of a list? The person who formulates
question (195a) assumes that there is a way to go downtown.
The answer, (195b) or (195c), simply specifies the way to get
there. Thus, although the speaker assumes that 'something'
exists, s/he more often than not has no knowledge about the
specific items. The items listed in the answer flesh out the
assumption.
Another instance of incomplete listing is example (196).

(196) ...acaso en sus ojos hay esa vaga melancolía, esa
dulzura... (SXX 30)
'...maybe in her eyes there-is that vague melancholy,
that tenderness...'

It is also possible to cite a list which contains a unique item,
as in (197).

(197) Todos están de acuerdo. En el mundo de la ópera
hay sólo la Sills.
'Everybody is in agreement. In the world of (the)
opera there is only (the) Sills.'

The lists in (198) either contain more than one item or they
imply that more items exist.

(198a) Hay, pues, primero la necesidad de conocer para
vivir. (Bull 1943:122)
'There-is, then, first the need to know in order to
live.'

(198b) Además de este yerro hay en esta frase el otro no
menos chocante del plural habían. (Bello 1970:264)
'Besides this mistake there-is in this sentence the
other one not less shocking of the plural "habían".'

(198c) Además de los numerosos impuestos acumulados, hay
la molestia para el automovilista de tener que cambiar
las placas y... (VEA b 130)
'Besides the numerous accumulated taxes, there-is the
bother for the driver of having to change license
plates and...'

(198d) Para los compradores solteros o los casados falderos,
también hay el atractivo de observar a las legiones
de vendedoras,...
'For the unmarried buyers or for the married skirt-
chasers, there-is also the attraction of looking at
the legions of (female) sales clerks,...'

Observe the choice of cues that speakers use to indicate
'this is not the only item'. In (198a) the word used is
primero 'first'; in (198b) and (198c), además 'besides, on top
of', and in (198d) the cue is también 'also'.
Example (199) is provided, despite its length, to show that
items in a list may be anaphoric. The writer, after pointing
out that Spanish America is not a homogeneous whole, goes on
to list three 'distinct' Spanish Americas. Although these three
'items' are coreferential with the previous mention of Spanish
America, they provide new information: the addressee does
not know what 'kinds' of Spanish Americas are about to be
enumerated (notice the cataphoric modifiers); therefore, they
are typical instances of the presentative function.

(199) Acaso ningún error sobre Hispanoamérica esté más
generalizado que el de confundir dentro de una misma
y vaga imagen, al conjunto de sus diversos países
y la pluralidad de sus variadas regiones. Porque
en puridad, no hay una, sino muchas Hispanoaméricas.
Hay la Hispanoamérica de los grandes imperios
precolombinos, la de los antiguos Mayas, Aztecas,
Incas y Chibchas que dejaron, como testimonio de
su pasado esplendor, las ruinas de sus imponentes
templos y una interminable variedad de piezas de
oro, piedra y cerámica.
Hay la Hispanoamérica de los Conquistadores, de
las magníficas catedrales revestidas de oro y de
plata y de los apacibles claustros monacales; la
Hispanoamérica de tantas ciudades donde, a despecho
del progreso urbano, aún perduran latentes las
puras esencias coloniales en la majestad de sus
plazas y en el incomparable embrujo de sus
empedradas y sinuosas callejas.
Hay la Hispanoamérica de los grandes espectáculos
de la naturaleza, la de los ríos que forman horizontes
y de los lagos más altos que las nubes, de las selvas
aún inexploradas y de las cimas nunca escaladas.
(LP 184)

> Perhaps no misconception about Spanish America is
> more generalized than that of mistaking in a single
> vague image the entirety of its diverse countries
> and the plurality of its diversified regions. Be-
> cause, strictly speaking, there isn't one but many
> Spanish Americas.
> There is the Spanish America of the great pre-
> Colombian empires, the one of the ancient Mayas,
> Aztecs, Incas, and Chibchas who left, as testimony
> of their past splendor, the ruins of their imposing
> temples and an endless variety of gold, stone, and
> ceramic objects.
> There is the Spanish America of the Conquerors,
> of the magnificent cathedrals adorned with gold and
> silver and of the peaceful monastic cloisters; the
> Spanish America of so many cities where, in spite
> of urban progress, there still exist concealed the
> pure colonial essences in the majesty of their
> squares and in the incomparable spell of their
> cobbled and sinuous alleys.
> There is the Spanish America of the great
> spectacles of nature, the one of rivers that form
> horizons and of lakes higher than the clouds, the
> one of jungles not yet explored and of summits
> never scaled.

Although all the examples of lists offered in (199) have
definite arguments, I do not want to leave the reader with the
impression that this represents the only possibility. Hay can
also list indefinite items, as in (200).

(200a) ...pues en el pueblo había dos farmacias, notario,
   estación de ferrocarril... (VEA 5)
   '...well, in the town there-were two pharmacies,
   (a) notary, (a) train station...'

(200b) Sí, hay caza de oso, hay jabalí, hay corzo, hay
   ciervos... (VEA 30)
   'Yes, there-is bear hunting, there's wild boar,
   there's roe, there-are deer...'

Whether the items are definite or indefinite depends on
whether or not the speaker assumes that the listener is apt to
identify the entries. Observe that all of the examples of lists
with definite determiners are adequately modified so that the
addressee would presumably have no difficulty in finding the
correct referent. To make this point transparent, compare the
difference in appropriateness of the two answers provided for
the question in (201a).

(201a) ¿De qué cosas tienes que deshacerte antes de
      mudarte?
      'What do you have to-get-rid-of before you move?'

(201b) ??Pues, hay la cómoda, el sofá y un par de sillas.
      'Well, there-is the dresser, the sofa, and a couple
      of chairs.'

(201c) Pues, hay la cómoda que está en el sótano, el sofá
      destartalado de la sala y un par de sillas.
      'Well, there's the dresser which is in the cellar, the
      busted sofa in the living room, and a couple of
      chairs.'

In (201b) the items of the list are definite but carry no further
modification. The result is a highly awkward sentence, if not
a completely ungrammatical one.[78] On the other hand, the
items in (201c) are cataphorically modified; the hearer can
adequately identify the referents, and the sentence causes no
problems. Furthermore, notice the balance the author (Bioy
Casares) has achieved in the list in (202).

(202)   Había el silencio, el ruido solitario del mar, la
      inmovilidad con fugas de ciempiés. (IM 24)
      'There-was the silence, the solitary noise of the sea,
      the immobility with the flight of centipedes.'

Although the first item in the list (el silencio) is not modified,
the author counters this bareness by modifying the remaining
two items. Notice also that these latter items constitute an
elaboration of the first one. The author is effectively conveying the idea of tranquility.
   There are also times when, although the items are morphologically definite, semantically they are more akin to cardinality
and thus to indefiniteness, as in example (203).

(203a) Hay gente para todos los gustos. Hay los que gustan
      de madrugar y hay los que gustan de transnochar.
      Yo pertenezco al segundo grupo.
      'There's a person for every taste. There-are those
      who like to get up early and there-are those who
      like to go to bed late. I belong to the second
      group.'

(203b) Hay los que pintan esos programas como una
      traición a los fundamentos de la Revolución.
      'There-are those who portray those programs as
      treasonous to the principles of the Revolution.'

In (203) the referent of los que is some unspecified number of
not very identifiable persons.

1.3.1.3.1.5 **Conclusion.** The fact is that semantic definiteness is a pragmatic concept which ranges along a graduated scale; it is not a mere point on a measuring stick. Bolinger (1977:118-119), after asking how definite is definite in English, offers an increasing scale for the use of there by listing in descending order of semantic definiteness the morphological definites.[79]

The scale for Spanish in (204) is also meant to show the appropriateness of hay with syntactic definites.[80] The items do not correlate exactly with semantic definiteness ((204g) is less definite than either (204h) or (204i)), but with intuitive feelings of frequency of use.

(204a) generics
(204b) nonclitic third person pronouns
(204c) unmodified proper names
(204d) common nouns with unique referent
. . . .
(204e) cataphoric nouns with universal quantifiers
(204f) superlatives
(204g) el/la que, los/las que with no expressed antecedent
(204h) cataphoric nouns
(204i) anaphoric clitic pronouns

Contrary to the case in English, Spanish is able to use hay only with (204e-204i) (the dotted line in (204) indicates this fact).[81] Some representative examples appear in (205).

(205a) *Hay las vicuñas en los Andes. (generic meaning)
'There-are the vicuñas in the Andes.'

(205b) *Hay ellos.
'There-are them.'

(205c) *Hay Paco y María.
'There-are Paco and Maria.'

(205d) *Hay el presidente.
'There-is the president.'
. . . .

(205e) Hay todos esos juegos electrónicos que me vuelven
loca.[82]
'There-are all those electronic games that drive me
crazy.'

(205f) Hay los mejores medios de comunicación...
'There-are the best means of communication...'

(205g) Hay los que siempre llegan tarde.
'There-are those who always arrive late.'

(205h) Hay el caso del estudiante que...
'There-is the case of the student who...'

(205i) Sí, los hay.
'Yes, there-are (them).'

Leaving aside for the moment (205i), it is possible to explain the compatibility of hay with the morphologically definite nouns of (205e-205h) by the fact that such sentences can be properly interpreted as presentationals, that is, as heralding the NP referent into the universe of discourse. Clitics by their very nature are anaphoric; in the context of hay, clitics act as re-entries, reminding the hearer that the same object is still under consideration while also reasserting the existence of the NP. This is the explanation for (205i). Obviously, since (204) exemplifies a pragmatic scale and since the grammaticality of hay sentences depends on their being read as presentationals, the ungrammatical sentences in (205a-205d) cannot be discarded at the level of sentence semantics (i.e. LF). On the contrary, one must wait until SI-2, the level of total semantic representations, to arrive at a principled decision. The NP object of hay sentences needs to be understood as novel information at SI-2--novel not in the sense of brand new necessarily, but new to the segment of the discourse under consideration. Re-entries are appropriate in this sense because they function as reminders. To say it still in another way, the referent must not be completely known to the hearer in that particular discourse.

To drive this point home, let us consider some examples. As shown in (204c) and (205c), proper names by themselves cannot appear as arguments of hay because they stand for a unique referent, a referent which is considered to be already in the discourse. For example, a child who utters (206a) cannot be reminded of those who love him with the hay sentence in (206b).

(206a) ¡Nadie me quiere!
'Nobody loves me!'

(206b) Bueno, eso no es completamente cierto. *Hay
Pepe y Paco y yo por lo menos.
'Well, that is not completely true. There-is Pepe and
Paco and me at least.'

Nevertheless, if the proper noun is modified so that it can be interpreted as being a relatively new referent that is being introduced in the discourse, then the sentences are considered well-formed. So, given the situation in (207a), (207b) is an acceptable answer.

(207a) --Estoy cansada de ver siempre las mismas caras, ¿a
quién puedo invitar para la cena del viernes?

'I'm tired of always seeing the same faces, whom could
I invite for the dinner on Friday?'

(207b) --Hay ese Paco que nos presentaron el otro día.
'There-is that Paco that was introduced to us the
other day.'

Even common nouns with unique reference behave in this
way. Although (205d) is unacceptable because it immediately
picks as referent whoever happens to be at the White House at
the time, the sentences in (208) are fine. In the latter case,
although the NPs are given sufficient modification to facilitate
their identification (and thus ultimately allow the selection of
unique referents), they can still be interpreted as novel to the
pertinent discourse segment (that is, the sentences are presentationals).

(208a) Hay el presidente de esa compañía que se acaba de
mudar a Ithaca. Me pareció muy simpático.
'There-is the president of that company which just
moved to Ithaca. He impressed me as being very
nice.'

(208b) Hay el presidente de Morse Chain quien dijo...
'There-is the president of Morse Chain who said...'

Furthermore, it must be said that because of the existential
assertion hay sentences carry, their NP object can at times be
read as specific.

(209a) Hay un español con quien me quiero casar;...
'There-is a Spaniard with whom I'll get married;...'

(209b) ...se llama Paco.
'...his name is Paco.'

(209c) ...pero aún no me lo presentaron.
'...but he hasn't been introduced to me yet.'

(209d) *...pero aún no lo he encontrado.
'...but I have not found him yet.'

Indefinite nouns are opaque as to their specificity; that is,
[± specific] is not a syntactic feature proper to these nouns.
Just as for semantic definiteness, specificity is better analyzed
as a matter of pragmatic interpretation, because on occasion
one must resort to the total discourse in order to decipher its
intended reading. Now observe that the indefinite NP object
in (209a) can only be read as a specific extant reality; thus,
(209b) and (209c) are appropriate rejoinders to (209a). In
both of these examples, one knows of the existence of this

Spaniard and one can pinpoint who he is. On the other hand, because (209d) forces a nonspecific reading of (209a) which leaves open the question of his existence, this rejoinder is not considered appropriate.

The question of specificity examined in (209) shows that Guéron's (1980) analysis of There-Insertion in English cannot be correct. She claims that there sentences can only have nonspecific indefinites and attributive definites as their NP argument. As a matter of fact, a counterexample is included in her article itself: 'There's a certain person I want you to introduce me to' (1980:660). The translation of this sentence also produces a grammatical haber sentence in Spanish, a fact which confirms my hypothesis while showing Guéron to be incorrect.

(210) Hay una cierta persona que quiero que me presentes.

There is another fact which automatically falls out of this analysis and explains a problem which has puzzled many a linguist. I am referring to the impossibility of obtaining hay sentences with a generic reading (cf. (204a) and (205a)). As has been stated repeatedly, hay sentences assert the existence of whatever is referred to by their NP argument. Moreover, I have just shown that this referent necessarily receives a specific interpretation at times. Recall that in Section 1.3.1.3 it was mentioned that although generic statements refer to classes, they do not necessarily commit the speaker as to the existence of any member of the class X (cf. examples in (176)-(178)). In other words, generic statements do not entail existence; they can easily refer to possible individuals instead of actual ones. This is because generic statements are nonspecific by nature. Consequently, it is obvious that the existential reading required by hay sentences clashes with the lack of existential entailment of a generic statement. Moreover, the hay sentence imposes a specific interpretation on the NP introduced by a definite determiner. The foregone result is that an explanation for the incompatibility of hay with a generic reading has been reached, as in (211).

(211a) Hay las vicuñas en los Andes.
        'There-are the vicuñas in the Andes.'

(211b) Hay la vicuña en el valle.
        'There-is the vicuña in the valley.'

(211c) Hay vicuñas en las montañas.
        'There-are vicuñas in the mountains.'

All of the sentences in (211) are grammatical, but none of them receives a generic reading. Sentence (211a) refers to a specific

group, (211b) refers to a specific animal, and (211c) refers to
an unspecified (but existing) number of animals. [83]
To reiterate, the complete explanatory behavior of impersonal
haber sentences can only be found at the level of total semantic
representation. These sentences assert the existence of the
referent of their NP and must be interpreted as introducing
this NP into the universe of discourse, that is, they must be
interpreted as presentationals. This semantico-pragmatic characterization satisfactorily accounts for their nonoccurrence with
a generic interpretation and for the inappropriateness of some
hay sentences with syntactically definite modifiers. For ease
of exposition the discussion of definiteness was divided into
four parts: superlatives, cataphoric reference, anaphoric
reference, and lists. The notion of semantic definiteness
(i.e. anaphoricity or identifiability) as a gradient concept was
also presented.

1.3.2 The Definiteness Restriction.

After what has been
discussed in the previous sections, it should be evident that
there is little of merit in the Definiteness Restriction (DR).
Nevertheless, since this notion is so pervasive in the literature
(see references in Section 1.3.1.3), for the sake of completeness I take one of the most comprehensive analyses of the DR,
that of Milsark (1977), and show that it cannot be maintained.
Following a lead suggested by Chomsky (1975), Milsark rules
out there-be sentences with definite modifiers by appealing to
the notions of quantification vs. cardinality. He hypothesizes
that strong NP determiners are actually expressions of universal quantification, while the weak group of NP determiners
are better considered expressions of cardinality. Among the
strong determiners he includes (1977:21):

...overt expressions of universal quantification such as
each, every, all, covert universals such as the various
definite determiners and the universal reading of the
mass/plural ∅; the quantifier most; and the 'some vs.
others', 'many vs. others' senses of some and many, together with the analogous readings of similar expressions
such as lots of, few, plenty of.

The division between quantifiers and expressions of cardinality
allows Milsark to claim that he has found the way to explain
the DR on existential sentences (ES). He elaborates (1977:24):

If we assume, in common with many others, that the expression there be is in relevant respects equivalent to an expression of existential quantification, an ES containing a
strong NP would have two quantifications on the NP, one
from the existential expression there be, and another from
the strong determiner. A proposition containing such a
thing should certainly be expected to be anomalous under

any semantics which makes use of the notion quantification
at all...On a theory of this form, violations of the definiteness restriction would be ruled out of the language by reasons of their uninterpretability, and there would be no need
to state the D[efinite] R[estriction] independently. All that
is necessary is the quantification/cardinality distinction among
determiner types...

There are problems with Milsark's proposal. In the first
place, it completely ignores all instances in which there-be
cooccurs with definite NPs, such as those given in (212).

(212a) There is always the chance that he might come.
(212b) There was the usual argument in class today.
(212c) There was the most surprising odor in the closet today.
(212d) In England there was never the problem that there
        was in America.
(212e) Who do we have to help us clean up the garage?
        Well, there's John and Mary. And then there's
        the man in the garden. [84]

To claim that examples such as those in (212) are grammatical
because they are instances of 'lists' is to shy away from the
issue. [85] Existential sentences function to signal the appearance of the object in the universe of discourse; this object
might represent one item, several of the same items, or several
different items of the same category. In the latter case, the
list reading ensues, as should be expected. And if the objects
introduced into the discourse form a list, it is natural that the
sentence adopts the intonation proper to lists. Furthermore,
notice that (213) is every bit as much a list as those in (212).

(213)   There's a book, several papers, and a journal on top
        of my desk.

Thus, there is no motivation whatsoever for segregating list
existential sentences from the rest, both types being perfect
instances of the presentative function.
    It is obvious, then, that Milsark's hypothesis does not pro-
vide a satisfactory solution to the problem of there existential
sentences. Milsark's hypothesis does not work for Spanish
either. A few examples with the purported strong determiners
(cf. Section 1.3.1.3 for more) are given in (214).

(214a) No hay ya los grandes poetas de otros tiempos.
        (Bello 295)
        'There do not exist anymore the great poets of
        yesteryear.'

(214b) Había la necesidad imperiosa de resolver este caso.
       (spontaneous conversation)
       'There was the demanding need to solve this case.'

(214c) Hay también esa opinión tan difundida.
       'There is also that widespread opinion.'

(214d) Hay todo tipo de estudiante en esta universidad.
       'There is every kind of student in this university.

(214e) Había ambas opiniones en la familia.
       'There were (existed) both opinions in the family.'

(214f) Cuando fui a buscar mi abrigo me sorprendió que
       hubiera algunos de los invitados en el dormitorio.
       ¡Y estaban a oscuras!
       'When I-went to get my coat I was surprised that
       there-were some of the guests in the bedroom.
       And they were in the dark!'[86]

Second, there is an inconsistency in Milsark's analysis.
He lists demonstratives, pronouns, and possessive DETs as
strong determiners (1977:8), but these items are not included
among the expressions of quantification later on. Even if this
omission is due to an oversight, it is extremely difficult to picture the foregoing determiner tokens as quantifiers. Hence, it
might be that the distinction between quantifiers and expressions of cardinality does not obviate the DR after all.

Finally, there remain the problems that Milsark himself points
out (1977:25-29): his novel use of the term 'quantifier', and
the lack of consistency in differing truth conditions for items
such as sm and some in some instances.

Consequently, my analysis in this chapter is simpler and
more general and consistent than Milsark's proposal for several
reasons. First, the analysis here leaves open the debatable
claim that the definite determiner must be considered a universal
quantifier in all instances (and the problem that this analysis
would entail). Second, it renders any restrictions on definiteness unnecessary, and thus facilitates the explanation of the
cases in which hay emerges with definite modified NPs without
contradictions, without appeal to exceptionality, and without
disregarding the definite examples. And finally, it treats expressions of totality (Milsark's universal quantification) in the
same way as possessives and demonstratives; this unification
eliminates the cumbersome division[87] of strong determiners into
the two groups of quantifiers and remaining definites.

In short, both English and Spanish allow for the cooccurrence
of existential sentences with definite and/or quantified determiners. What any explanatory hypothesis of existential sentences should achieve is a unified treatment of this type of
sentence, a treatment which encompasses all of their possible

uses. This in turn means that the explanation is not to be
found in terms of quantification vs. cardinality. It is my contention that the main fault of the explanations for existential
sentences in English resides in the fact that they attempt to
account for usage at the level of sentence semantics. This
cannot be successfully done. I have already shown (for
example, in Section 1.3.1.3.1.5) that pragmatic factors must
also be taken into consideration; therefore, a consistent explanation of existential sentences must take into account the discourse and must interpret these sentences in SI-2. Hence,
there is no place for the DR (or any of its alternatives) in
either the grammar of English or the grammar of Spanish.

Part of the confusion which characterizes analyses of existential sentences might have arisen as a consequence of having an
idealized image of this sentence type. The argument could go
as follows: since there-be/haber sentences denote the appearance of the object in the world of discourse, it should be the
case that this object must be new, and thus indefinite. But
the fact that this object is indefinite in the overwhelming
majority of cases is a mere statistical fact which reflects a
general (and logical) tendency. Moreover, the object being
introduced does not necessarily need to be brand new, just
'not sufficiently shared by speaker and hearer at that point
in the discourse'. As shown by the numerous examples provided during the discussion of definite modifiers in hay sentences, definiteness and newness are compatible in this sense.
For example, all of the underlined NPs in the sentences of
(215) introduce new information into a particular discourse
segment, despite their definiteness.

(215a) Hablé con tu estudiante ayer.
       'I talked with your student yesterday.'

(215b) Compramos la casa de techo rojo.
       'We bought the red-roofed house.'

(215c) Vino el electricista.
       'The electrician came.'

Consequently, definiteness (or universal quantification, for
that matter) is not pertinent to the grammaticality or appropriateness of an hay sentence. As an illustration, picture the
following situation: the husband says to his wife, who is just
walking in at nine in the evening:

(216) Los niños ya están en casa.
      'The children are already home.'

The shared knowledge between them might be of two, five, a
dozen or whatever the number of children they have, but it is

bound to be the same number for both persons. Consequently, there is no point in saying, given the same scenario:

(217) Hay los niños en casa.
       'There are the children at home.'

Knowledge of <u>los niños</u> is too well shared to be appropriately conveyed by an <u>hay</u> sentence.

I submit a final point before concluding this section. I have already mentioned (Section 0.1.2) that in the unmarked case the dichotomies of subject vs. predicate, theme vs. rheme, and old vs. new tend to coincide. Thus, subjects generally constitute the theme of the sentence (what the speaker is talking about), and as such they are most likely to be definite, since what they stand for is normally known to both speaker and hearer (cf. Keenan 1976). Hence subjects tend to represent thematic information at the post-LF level of sentence grammar, and old information at the level of total semantic representation. Schematically, this ideal system can be displayed as in (218).

(218) Subject: Predicate:
       theme   rheme
       old   new
       [+definite]   [-definite] object

Now let us reconsider <u>hay</u> sentences. In the first place, they are subjectless, and secondly, they are presentationals, since they denote the appearance of the referent of the NP object in the universe of discourse. Moreover, this 'object' stands for something the hearer is not aware of, or something that the speaker has no reason to believe that his addressee is aware of at that time in the discourse. Consequently, this 'something' is part of the rheme at the post-LF level, and new at SI-2.[88] Furthermore, as a first mention it is indefinite in the overwhelming majority of cases. Therefore, <u>hay</u> sentences approximate the ideal system (218) quite closely.

(219) Subject: Predicate:
       Ø   [$_{Rheme}$ hay NP]
                           new information
                           [-definite] object (95%)

Thus, Spanish has found a (nearly perfect) way to correlate syntax, semantics, and pragmatics in <u>hay</u> existential sentences. Note that their one argument is a direct object, primarily a rhematic position. Hence, their subjectlessness makes a lot of sense, since subjects generally express thematic, old information. But although the 95 percent incidence of indefiniteness in the NP corroborates the fact that indefiniteness and newness tend to work together, this does not mean that one does not have to account for the remaining 5 percent, in which the argument is syntactically definite. This analysis gives support to the contention that there is no room in the grammar of Spanish for something like the Definiteness Restriction. No incompatibility arises between hay and definiteness as long as the function of hay sentences is not violated.

1.4 Impersonal *haber* in nonstandard Spanish. In contrast to standard usage, where finite hay is frozen in the third person singular form, in nonstandard Spanish, this verb may appear in the third person plural when it has a plural NP argument. In other words, agreement takes place between haber and its NP.

If one is to believe what many scholars have said, it might very well be that verb agreement is the norm in the colloquial speech of Spanish America and of certain areas of Spain. For example, Kany (1969:256), after stating that this 'faulty agreement' is occasionally found even in Old Spanish, goes on to say:

> In Spanish America,...,it is extremely common everywhere, in speech and in writing, and the lashing of grammarians seems to have done little to eradicate it...very few regions have escaped this popular usage and in a good many it can be found side by side with the correct form among cultured folk and in some of the foremost writers.

Kany (1969:257-259) provides a variety of literary examples from different parts of Latin America. Some of them are given under (220).

(220a) El paisanaje supuso que habrían (3 pl., conditional) nuevas elecciones.
'The country-people assumed that there-would-be new elections.'

(220b) ¿...quiénes hayan (3 pl., present) adentro?
'...who (pl.) are-there inside?'

(220c) En el suelo habían (3 pl., imperfect) dos hermosos gallos.
'On the ground there-were two beautiful roosters.'

(220d) ¿Es posible que haigan (3 pl., present subjunctive) cobardes...?
'Is-it possible that there-be cowards...?'

(220e) Sí, han habido (3 pl., present perfect) otros hombres.
'Yes, there-have been other men.'

(220f) Le preocupaba el número de personas que habían (3
pl., imperfect) allí.
'It worried him/her the number of people that there-
were there.'

If a speaker pluralizes hay to agree with a plural NP, s/he
is also likely to establish this same type of agreement across
modal and aspectual verbs, as well as across the subject-
raising verb parecer 'to seem'. All examples, with the exception of the last one, come from Kany (1969).

(221a) En el mar deben (3 pl., present) de haber hombres
así.
in the sea must of there-be men like that.
'At sea there must exist men like that.'

(221b) Podrán (3 pl., future) haber cien alumnos en la
escuela.
be-able there-be 100 students in the school
'There might be one hundred students in the school.'

(221c) Suelen (3 pl., present) haber niños desobedientes.
used-to there-be children disobedient
'There commonly are disobedient students.'

(221d) Comienzan (3 pl., present) a haber desagrados en
el matrimonio de enfrente.
begin to there-be unpleasantries in the couple
across-the-way.
'There begin to be unpleasantries in the couple across
the way.'

(221e) Parecen (3 pl., present) haber más casas...
seem there-be more houses
'There seem to be more houses...'

That examples like those in (220) and (221) have always
existed in the language cannot be doubted.[89] What needs to
be established is to what degree hay in the plural has en-
croached upon standard usage, and whether this usage is as
common as Kany leads us to believe. Since no sociolinguistic
studies of this phenomenon exist to date, this question must
remain unanswered for the time being. Nevertheless, I would
like to point out that my data rendered just three examples of
plural concord.

(222a) Ahora yo encuentro que han habido (3 pl., present
perfect) montones de charlas en la radio. (VEA 55)
'Now I find that there-have been lots of talks on the
radio...'[90]

(222b) Hubieron veinte mil peripecias ¿no? (M 207)
'There-were twenty thousand mishaps, weren't there?'

(222c) No habían las libertades que hay ahora. (M 296)
'There-weren't the liberties that exist now.'

The second point of interest raised by these examples has
to do with the function of the plural NP. Two logical possibilities exist: (1) that this NP is the subject, or (2) that it
is the object. Each possibility is considered in turn.

Keenan (1976) establishes a dichotomy of subject properties:
coding or morphosyntactic ones, such as nominative case and
verb agreement; and behavioral or transformational ones, such
as the ability of the NP to control reflexivization, deletion
under identity, and subject-raising rules. I use his classification of these properties for testing subjecthood and apply
them to contemporary nonstandard usage of hay in an effort
to determine the subject or nonsubject status of the argument
of this verb.

1.4.1 Coding properties. The only coding property obligatory for all subject noun phrases in Spanish is verbal agreement. Therefore, the hypothesis that the plural NP constitutes the grammatical subject of these nonstandard sentences
gains credence because of the plural verb marking. In other
words, this NP seems to be triggering the usual rule of
subject-verb agreement (cf. (220) and (221)). Since only
subjects invariably command agreement in Spanish, this evidence favors the subject status of the NP argument.

Nevertheless, the foregoing conclusion is contradicted by case
assignment. As is well known, surface case is practically non-
functional in Spanish. The only vestiges of it are found in the
pronominal system. If one takes the subject forms of the pronouns to be the remnants of nominative case, one has a second
coding property with which to test the purported subjecthood
of the NP under scrutiny.

Consider, then, the generalization that human subjects may
be referred to by means of subject pronouns. This observation
is corroborated by the acceptability of the pair of sentences in
(223), which in turn leads one to expect the examples in (224)
if the NP argument in question is functioning as a subject.

(223a) Llegaron unos niños.
       arrived (3 pl., preterit) several children
       'Several children arrived.'

(223b) Llegaron ellos.
       arrived they
       'They arrived.'

(224a) Habían unos niños. [91]
'There-were several children.'

(224b) *Habían ellos.
'There-were they.'

Although anticipated in this pattern, (224b) is nevertheless impossible. Moreover, observe the two examples from Kany (1969:257) in (225).

(225a) Habían 25 plateros, 25 lomilleros...Los habían por robo...
there-were 25 silversmiths, 25 harness-makers...them there-were because-of thievery...
'There were 25 silversmiths, 25 harness-makers...They were had (detained) for stealing.'

(225b) Pero don Zacarías...era rehacio al matrimonio como los hubieron pocos
but don Zacarías...was opposed to marriage as them there-were few.
'But don Zacarías was opposed to marriage as few others had been.'

Both examples exhibit a direct object clitic los ('them', pl.) whose referent cannot be other than the same plural NP that caused the plural agreement on the verb to appear. Consequently, these object clitics are anaphoric to the alleged subject argument, a fact which seems to be a contradiction at any plausible level of analysis. [92]

1.4.2 Behavioral properties. [93] Since reflexivization by nature requires that the verb be at least a two-argument verb, it cannot be used as a test for impersonal haber, which is a one-argument verb. But there is another test which can be used instead: impersonal se. Any Spanish verb which can take a human subject can be constructed with the impersonal se, irrespective of the number of arguments it takes. Therefore, on the model of (226), one could expect the pattern in (227) to be grammatical. This is not the case.

(226a) Paco trabaja mucho en esa fábrica.
'Paco works a lot in that factory.'

(226b) Se trabaja mucho en esa fábrica.
'One works ⎫
'People work⎭ a lot in that factory.'

(227a) Habían unos niños en el parque.
'There-were several kids in the park.'

(227b) *Se habían en el parque.

Sentence (227b) seems to indicate quite clearly that, in spite
of the plural agreement on the verb, the NP unos niños does
not behave as a true subject.

Next, let us assume that Equi is an operation which deletes
an NP which is referentially identical to an NP in the higher
clause (cf. (228a)). [94] Under this assumption, if the NP of
hay were a subject, it would delete under Equi. But once
more (228b) and (228c) show that this is not possible (regardless of word order).

(228a) Unos niños querían jugar en el parque.
'Some kids wanted to-play in the park.'

(228b) *Unos niños querían haber en el parque.
'Some kids wanted to there-be in the park.'

(228c) *Querían haber unos niños en el parque.

Furthermore, the NP argument of hay also fails to undergo
deletion under subject identity conditions.

(229) *Habían y olían agradablemente dos docenas de
rosas. [95]
there-were and smelled pleasingly two dozens of
roses

Thus, the NP of haber fails another of the behavioral tests
for subjecthood, the one that tests the ability of an NP to
undergo and to trigger deletion under identity (cf. (228) and
(229)).

There remains one more pertinent behavioral property: the
capacity to undergo subject raising. As already noted in (221),
the NP argument with hay seems to undergo subject raising and
causes the pluralization of the verb parecer 'to seem' (cf.
(221e)). Other examples are given in (230).

(230a) Parecía que habían más rosas el año pasado.
it-seemed that there-were more roses the year last
'It seems that there were more roses last year.'

(230b) ?Más rosas parecían haber el año pasado.
more roses seemed (3 pl.) there be the year last
'There seemed to be more roses last year.'

(230c) Parecían haber más rosas el año pasado.
seemed (3 pl.) there-were more roses the year last
'There seemed to be more roses last year.'

That is to say, (230a) is a sentence with <u>parecer</u> as a main verb and an <u>hay</u> complement clause. In (230b) and (230c), <u>muchas rosas</u> seems to have been subject-raised, because <u>parecer</u> shows agreement with this plural NP. (Notice that in (230b) the NP appears before the verb complex, but in (230c) it remains postposed.) Thus, at first glance, the argument of <u>hay</u> passes the subject-raising test and qualifies under one of <u>the</u> behavioral properties of subjecthood.

By phrasing the observations of this last paragraph in such tentative language, I have tried to convey my doubts about the validity of this last argument as a real test for the subject status of the NP with <u>hay</u>. Notice that despite the relatively 'free' word order allowed in Spanish, (230c) is a far more natural sounding example than (230b). Sentence (230b) minimally requires contrastive stress on <u>más rosas</u>, a fact which is not the norm for subject-raised subjects in initial position (cf. (231)).

(231a) Los niños parecen estar dormidos.
'The children seem to be asleep.'

(231b) Las hojas parecen estar secas.
'The leaves seem to be dry.'

Both examples in (231) have a natural sentential stress which falls on the last word (<u>dormidos</u> and <u>secas</u>, respectively), and there is no need to stress contrastively the subject NPs (<u>los niños</u> and <u>las hojas</u>) to improve the acceptability of the sentences; they are already fully grammatical and natural sounding. In short, the fact that the nominal cannot readily appear preverbally (230b), contrary to the usual privileges of subjects, creates serious doubts about both its subject status and the validity of subject raising as a reliable test in this case. Observe that since word order does not confirm the raising hypothesis, the only reason for claiming that the postverbal NP has been raised in (230c) is subject-verb agreement, a coding property.

As a matter of fact, this coding property might not be a foolproof test for subjecthood in Spanish if the sentence is an impersonal one. For example, after analyzing another type of Spanish impersonal sentences, those with impersonal SE, Aissen (1973) argues for an analogic formulation of object agreement. Her rule reads:

A verb in S_1 agrees with an NP which is not its subject, NP_1, just in case S_1 is structurally identical to an S of a different derivation whose subject occupies the position corresponding to that of NP_1 (1973:15; see also Otero 1972; Contreras 1973; and Suñer 1976a; for a different point of view).[96]

To sum up, the survey of coding and behavioral properties of the NP argument of hay has uncovered just one property which appears to support its subject function: namely, its capacity to trigger plural agreement on the verb (a coding property).[97] On the other hand, there are several tests that militate against the subjecthood of this noun. Aside from its inability to cooccur with impersonal se and to control deletion under identity, the fact that it cannot be replaced by a subject pronoun (cf. (224b)) but can be replaced by an object clitic (cf. (225)) speaks against its subject status.

It appears, then, that the NP argument of haber has a 'blurred' grammatical function in nonstandard Spanish. It might very well be that the types of sentences found in (220) and (221) are a 'blend', a 'hybrid' construction which adopts certain characteristics of subjectless sentences and at the same time assumes some characteristics of sentences that do take a subject. This might be an indication of an area of flux in the language; these sentences with plural agreement might be evidence of an incomplete syntactic change.

1.4.3 Speculations. At this point, it seems pertinent to speculate as to the nature of this apparent syntactic change. It is evident that this is not restructuring, that is, it is not a change in the base component (Lightfoot 1976a, 1977). If it were, the NP would have to have divested itself of all object properties and to have acquired the full range of subject properties. Therefore, this is most likely a change taking place in the transformational subcomponent; this change is probably causing the addition of a rule that has the effect of establishing verb agreement with the only NP argument present under certain circumstances. This new rule might very well be analogic[98] in character. Considering that impersonal (i.e. subjectless) sentences constitute a minute portion of all sentence types in Spanish, it might be that speakers feel these sentences are somehow unnatural; in an effort to make them conform with the norm (i.e. sentences with subjects), speakers may unconsciously find a pseudosubject with which to make verbal agreement. My own analysis concurs with Kany's speculation (1969:256):

> There was from the beginning an evident discrepancy between the psychological concept (the noun as subject) and the grammatical expression (the noun as object). It is not surprising, therefore that speakers should often allow the psychological concept to dominate, making the impersonal verb agree with its grammatical object as if it were a grammatical subject.

Moreover, when one takes into account Keenan's (1976) multifactor characterization of subjecthood, together with the fact that hay has only one NP whose grammatical function is that of object, it is not difficult to understand why speakers would tend to assign one of the most prominent and transparent properties of subjecthood to the sole NP found in the sentence.

Further evidence for an explanation which maintains that this agreement is a surface phenomenon is found in the historical facts. When one considers that examples of impersonal haber with plural agreement have been documented at least since the fourteenth century (cf. note 89), one may wonder why the NP in this type of construction has not progressed further along the continuum from object to subject.[99] Certainly, enough time has elapsed to complete the change, and there already existed the pattern NP-V-LOC, as exemplified by ser. It might just be that speakers (unconsciously) never considered this NP a true subject.[100]

To summarize, hay sentences in nonstandard Spanish show agreement between their NP argument and the existential verb. In spite of this fact, it is impossible to establish unequivocally the grammatical function of the NP as that of subject, because the NP lacks most of the coding and behavioral properties proper to subjecthood.[101] This discovery leads to the suspicion that this might be a hybrid construction, a conclusion supported by the fact that this purported syntactic change has hardly evolved at all during the last six centuries.[102] The hypothesis is that it is a more or less surface phenomenon, triggered in a manner analogous to sentences with subjects.[103]

1.5 Summary. In this chapter it has been established that impersonal haber is an existential verb which serves to assert the existence of its only NP argument. Furthermore, hay sentences constitute the presentational construction par excellence in Spanish; they herald the appearance of the referent of their NP object in the universe of discourse. Haber can be characterized as a subjectless verb which surfaces only in the third person singular form of any tense and aspect in standard Spanish. Its obligatorily subcategorized NP displays the grammatical function of direct object; and, contrary to what is the norm for Spanish, this object never occurs with the so-called personal a.

The subcategorization of haber is given in (232).

$$(232) \quad \text{haber}, + V, + [\_\_NP \ (\begin{Bmatrix} PP \\ AP \\ \bar{S} \end{Bmatrix})]$$

Statement (232) was arrived at after an examination of the constituent analysis of hay sentences. It was discovered that hay not only occurs with relative clauses, both headed and headless, but also with $\bar{S}$ complements. This observation is supported by the incidence of sentences having the structure clitic + hay + $\bar{S}$, by different extraction results, and, furthermore, by the double interpretation that gerundive complements

receive as adjectival vs. adverbial. The term AP is included
to account for participial modification (but see Section 1.2.2.3).
Clitics and word order possibilities were also examined briefly.
   It was maintained that the syntax of hay sentences is extremely simple, since this construction is base-generated.
What is interesting is the interpretation that these sentences
receive, because it takes place in stages and at different levels
within the total grammar. In LF, their existential import is
checked and the rules of Focus Assignment and Complement
Linking take place. Afterwards, Rhematization marks the verb
and everything which follows it within the sentence as rhematic,
i.e. in the scope of assertion; this rule operates at a post-LF
level but still within sentence grammar. On the other hand,
Presentational Sentence Interpretation applies at the level of
total semantic representation (SI-2), because it must make use
of the discourse and other extralinguistic and pragmatic facets
which contribute to complete communication.
   Determiners were examined. As expected, it was found that
hay sentences are compatible with expressions of cardinality.
Moreover, it was shown that, contrary to what has been repeatedly claimed, they are also congruous with syntactically
definite modification as long as the function of these presentational sentences is not violated. It was concluded that the
Definiteness Restriction is not valid.
   This chapter closes with a look at impersonal haber sentences
in nonstandard Spanish. In this case, the existential verb
agrees in number with its NP. Since, apart from agreement,
the NP does not exhibit any other coding or behavioral characteristics peculiar to subjects, it was hypothesized that this
agreement is analogical and that it is established with the object NP. Some support for this position comes from surveying
other impersonal constructions which show this same type of
agreement.
   It had already been said that impersonal haber sentences are
THE Spanish presentational construction. However, this does
not mean that they constitute the only such construction. The
next chapter is devoted to examination of another very common
way in which NP referents are introduced into the world of
discourse.

   NOTES

   1. It becomes necessary to distinguish between impersonal
haber 'there-be' and haber 'to-have' which is used to form the
perfect tenses in Spanish, as in (i) and (ii).

   (i) Paco ha llegado recién.
       'Paco has arrived just-now.'

(ii) (Ellas) habían decidido ir al cine.
'They (f. pl.) had decided to-go to-the movies.'

2. Hay is the present tense form of this verb. Historically, it arose from the combination of ha plus the particle y (from Latin ibi > i'i > i > y), a locative which meant 'there'.

3. Throughout this chapter, the terms 'impersonal haber' and 'hay' used as an abbreviation for all of the 3rd person singular forms of haber (había, habrá, hubo, etc.) are used interchangeably.

4. Its use in nonstandard Spanish is discussed in Section 1.4.

5. The reader should not be misguided by the English glosses which require the verb to be in the plural; in the Spanish examples the verb form remains in the singular.

6. It appears possible that English existential there sentences may be headed in the direction of the Spanish construction. Notice that in casual speech, there often governs a singular verb form even when the following NP is plural. The following examples are found in Quirk et al. (1972):

There's some people in the waiting room. (p. 958)
There's hundreds of people on the waiting list. (p. 359)

Singular concord also prevails in there with lists:

There's Paco and Pepe, and a couple of other guys also.

7. At times, this you is explicitly stated in the command:

(i) You get out of here!

The same occurs in Spanish:

(ii) ¡Salga Ud. de aquí!
You (formal) get out of here!

¡Tráeme tú eso!
You (familiar) bring me that!

Notice that an example such as (iii) does not constitute a counterexample to my claim.

(iii) ¡Que haya luz!
that there-be light!

Sentence (iii) is a wish with no implied or explicit you. Examples like this last one have also been classified as 'indirect commands'.

8. These verbs, used only in the third person singular form, have been given various labels. The most frequent seems

to be 'impersonal', but the RAE calls them 'unipersonales'
(unipersonals) and Moliner, 'terciopersonales' (third personals).
   9. I refer the reader to Appendix B for a formal treatment
of verbs without an explicit subject in surface structure.
   10. The reader should not be confused by the wording of
this last statement. I am of the opinion that clitics are base-
generated and not derived from NPs.
   11. The rules which govern the use and nonuse of personal
a (also called accusative a) are far too complex to present in
full in this discussion. For details, I refer the reader to any
of the traditional grammars, or to one of the more recent
treatments (Isenberg 1968; Roldán 1971a; Luján 1978).
   12. Notice that it is quite impossible to prove this hypothesis conclusively. Other impersonal verbs never appear with
human direct objects (cf. (16)).
   13. Another example with haber in the progressive follows:

Yo creo que sí está habiendo cierto cambio en el mundo,...
   (M 268)
I believe that, yes, there-is being (a) certain change in
the world,...

   14. This claim can be maintained even for impersonal haber
sentences which appear in the conditional and the subjunctive.

(i) Desearía que hubiera más sol.
     I-would-like that there-be (subjunctive) more sun
(ii) Habría más dinero si trabajaras.
     there-would-be (conditional) more money if you-worked
        (subjunctive)

Example (i) implies that it is not sunny, and (ii) implies that
there is not much money. Nevertheless, the assertion of existence still holds on the assumption that conditional and subjunctive are just two of the 'modalities' which provide a logical
operator outside the assertion. This extracted operator modifies the assertion. Schematically:

Op(erator) [hay NP]
           assertion

Another operator which modifies the assertion is NEG, i.e.
the negative particle.
   15. I am using topic in a nontechnical sense here.
   16. The NP exists in the universe of discourse, which does
not necessarily reproduce or parallel the real world. (Cf.
Había un unicornio en el jardin. 'There-was a unicorn in the
garden.')
   17. Spanish is a Subject PRO-Drop language. Therefore,
subject pronouns are often deleted after subject-verb agreement has taken place.

18. To the best of my knowledge, Babby (1978) was the first to apply the notions of scope of assertion and scope of negation (Givon 1975a) to existential sentences.

19. There are no compelling reasons to believe that impersonal haber should be anything but a basic nonderived verb (but see Section 1.3.1.1). This is in marked contrast to analyses of English there be. English existential there sentences have given rise to two factions: those who argue in favor of a phrase-structure analysis--Jenkins (1975), Bolinger (1977), and Stowell (1978)--and those who advocate a transformational analysis. The latter group has the larger number of proponents. Among the linguists who support this position are: Breivik (1975), Kimball (1973), Kuno (1971), McCawley (1970), Milsark (1974 and 1977), Emonds (1970), and Perlmutter (1970).

20. This semantic interpretation is refined and completed in Section 1.3.

21. An example such as the following does not constitute a counterexample to the obligatoriness of the object argument.

...el daño sicológico que hace el ruido de fondo que hay en la ciudad... (VEA 3)
'...the psychological damage which the background noise produces in the city...'

In this example hay is embedded in a relative structure where the second instance of ruido 'noise', so to speak, has been relativized. More about this type of construction appears in Section 1.2.2.2.1.

22. This shows that adverbs in Spanish are capable of functioning as NPs in some instances.

23. There is abundant literature to support this view. Perhaps the first article on the subject was by Lakoff and Peters (1969).

24. It is not my intention to claim that all possible word orders are equally appropriate in all circumstances, nor that all of them are base-generated.

25. Statement (45) represents an attempt to characterize the maximum possible string; it is not meant to express the strict subcategorization for hay. Only what appears within the VP would be strictly subcategorized by hay.

26. Kuno equates thematic with old information, a claim which has been disproved (see Introduction).

27. Although it is not crucial for my purposes to choose among the three most widespread analyses of relative clause formation (NP-S, Nom-S, or Art-S), I have selected Ross' analysis for convenience of exposition. For a good summary of the advantages and disadvantages of these different hypotheses, I refer the reader to Stockwell, Schachter, and Partee (1973:Chap. 7). For some of the most recent proposals within EST, see Chomsky (1977) and Bresnan (1977).

28. This contrast was pointed out to me by Marisa Rivero.
Sentence (62) violates Subjacency because the moved element
needs to go across both an S̄ and an NP boundary. The Complex NP Constraint is due to Ross (1967); it says, 'No element
contained in a S dominated by a NP with a lexical head noun
may be moved out of that NP by a transformation.'
29. Sentence (63) is coined after a sentence reported in
Jenkins (1975:105-106) and attributed to Chomsky. The sentence given there is: This problem which there are many
people interested in.
30. Akmajian (1977) discusses some of the peculiarities of
the complement structure of perception verbs in English in
structures such as We saw the moon rising over the mountain.
31. Jenkins' analysis raises serious questions, because he
has to resort to the very suspect rule of Whiz Deletion (cf.
Williams 1975). For a rebuttal of Jenkins' work, see Stowell
(1978).
32. More explicitly, the RAE (1974:526) says:

Frequently, the relatives que and quien are used without
an explicit antecedent, either because it is unknown or
indeterminate, or because it is of no interest to the speaker,
or because the words causa 'cause', razón 'reason', motivo
'motive', hombre 'man', or similar ones are easily understood
... [my translation, M.S.]

33. Examples (84), (85), and (86) are adapted from Hirschbühler and Rivero (1980a), and (87) from Hirschbühler and
Rivero (1980b).
34. Hirschbühler and Rivero (1980b:8-9) write the following
about hi ha, the Catalan equivalent of Spanish hay:

We think that the NP that follows hi ha is not subcategorized
in the way other direct objects of transitive verbs are; for
example, no thematic role seems to be assigned by ha to the
NP, and no semantic relationship appears to be established
between the matrix verb and the complement. However, we
propose no concrete analysis for this case, and simply conclude tentatively that it does not look like a counterexample
to our hypothesis.

I disagree with nearly everything in the foregoing quotation.
As shown in the development of this chapter, haber does
strictly subcategorize its object NP, which receives an objective thematic relationship. Moreover, this matrix verb most
certainly establishes a semantic relationship with its NP; it
asserts that the referent of the NP exists in the universe of
discourse (cf. Section 1.1.2). Example (87) means 'there is
an indeterminate body of people for whom I would not vote';
the relationship between the indeterminate group (PRO in my

terms) and the relative is obvious. Consequently, (87) constitutes a true counterexample to their proposal.
35. Soñar con is what is known in Spanish as a 'verbo de régimen'.
36. As opposed to the obligatory deletion in (89) and (91), in (i) the preposition is optionally deleted.

(i) (en) el lugar en el cual nos encontramos...
    in the place in the which we-met...

The obligatoriness of the deletion in the former sentences follows from the independent principle which prohibits dangling prepositions in Spanish.
37. The gerundive phrase in sentence (94a), for example, can be interpreted as directly modifying mujer 'woman' (relative clause interpretation), or as a manner adverbial modifying the whole VP (see diagram (101)).
The so-called representation or picture verbs also seem to allow this double interpretation.

Paco la dibujó sonriendo.
Paco her (acc.) drew smiling
'Paco drew her smiling.'

38. Only the VP constituent of the sentences is included to facilitate the comparison between hay and ver.
39. I indicate coindexing between the gerundive and mujer in order to exclude the interpretation in which the PRO subject of the gerund is coindexed with the subject of ver. More is said about this later.
40. In these tests I limit myself to the hay examples, the immediate topic of concern. The same sentences can be used to test the constituency of perception verbs.
41. Akmajian (1977) uses these and other tests to establish that complements of perception verbs also behave as single and double constituents in English. Nevertheless, by positing the simple structure [[NP NP VP]] for sentences such as We saw the moon rising over the mountains, he misses, in my opinion, several generalizations and parallelisms with full clauses (cf. Section 1.2.2.2.2).
42. There is one aspect of this sentential hypothesis for gerundive complements with which I have not dealt: the absence of tense but the presence of -ndo. For a possible answer to this, see Luján (1980:Chap. V, 5.4). For a sketch of an alternative which suggests a nonsentential source for gerundive complements, see Jackendoff (1977:Chapter 9).
43. Luján (1980) presents the most thorough analysis to date of adjectives in Spanish. She is of the opinion that all adjectives in Spanish have a sentential source. To this effect, she offers several enticing arguments. Nevertheless, some problems and questions remain unanswered.

44. Williams (1975) uses a similar observation to argue against Whiz Deletion (in English). Luján (1980) maintains that Whiz Deletion (also known as relative clause reduction) is not a transformation of Spanish. Rather she claims that the same outcome is achieved by two independently motivated deletion rules: COMP Deletion and Copula Deletion.

45. As a matter of fact, the nouns in (123a) and (123b) appear in their noncount usage. But their shape is singular, and this is the trait which the clitics seem to pick up.

46. Impressionistically, it seems that Topicalization is more frequent than Left-Dislocation in hay sentences. This is probably due to the fact that the NP argument of hay is more often than not indefinite.

47. Obviously, both Milsark and Chomsky are concerned with there-be and not with Spanish hay. Although these verbs behave very similarly in both languages, English there-be seems to be more constrained than its Spanish counterpart. Moreover, analyses of there-be seem to be plagued by problems (cf. Milsark 1977, Jenkins 1975, Stowell 1978, among others). For example, Milsark (1974) lists the following five restrictions: the NP Restriction, the Semi-Modal Restriction, the Leftmost Restriction, the Predicate Restriction, and the Definiteness Restriction. The first three are syntactic in character and the latter two are semantic. Only the Definiteness Restriction has some bearing on Spanish hay.

48. The analysis in (134) has to be taken as a rough approximation. Note that 'tense' has to be somehow indicated in (134).

49. This is contrary to what happens in the analysis of there-be sentences, where a rule of There-Insertion is posited (see discussion in Chomsky 1980a:4-5). That all NPs should be in argument position in LF is an empirical hypothesis which must be confirmed by further research. As is seen in Chapter 2, intransitive presentationals do not support Freidin's hypothesis.

50. See Section 1.2.2.4 for discussion of the term AP.

51. The format of my rules of SI-1 and SI-2 has been heavily influenced by Guéron's work (1978, 1980). Since to my knowledge no explicit theory of LF exists, it is to be expected that all rules are subject to revision as more becomes known about LF (i.e. sentence semantics).

52. It is obvious that both (140) and (141) are devised exclusively for hay sentences. I attempt to make them more general after discussing another type of presentational sentence in Chapter 2.

Since the PP, S̄, and Adv under consideration all perform an adverbial function, an alternative way of expressing (141) is as follows:

Mark any adjectival or adverbial expression to the right of [hay + NP] Complement of the Focus of S.

53. For justification of this PRO and the one in (145d), see Jaeggli (1980). Another possibility comes to mind; for example, (145c) could be assigned the structure in (i) and by general convention weak pronouns (i.e. clitics) would have to be moved in front of the finite verb.

(i) ayer había [$_{NP}$ las]

Notice that (i) would still fulfill the subcategorization requirement of hay and the statement of rule (140). Nevertheless, this movement alternative becomes problematical when considering instances in which both the clitic and the NP appear in the same sentence.

(ii) Lo$_i$ vi a él$_i$
     him (acc.) I-saw him (acc.)
     'I saw him.'

(iii) Les$_i$ compré un regalo a las niñas$_i$.
      them (dat.) I-bought a present to the girls
      'I bought a present for the girls.'

54. Alternatively, the whole relative clause in (145a) is marked as Focus of S.
55. I find that the specification 'inside of S' is necessary in order to avoid marking as rhematic the underlined segment in the following sentence:

-Sí los había, esos tomates.
 Yes them (m. pl.) there-was, those tomatoes.
 'Yes they-were there, those tomatoes.'

Esos tomates is uttered with very low intonation as a clarification or afterthought. I take it that it should be base-generated as a right-dislocated constituent. Moreover, it should be thematic and not rhematic.
56. Guéron (1980) arrives at the same conclusion.
57. Utley's one-page article (1954) is merely a reiteration of Bull's hypothesis. Most Spanish textbooks--if they address the problem at all--also make use of Bull's rules.
58. The five examples included in Bull's quote translate as follows:

(i) There-is, then, first the need to know in order to live...
(ii) ...without this one there-isn't that one.
(iii) At his side was an ancient gentleman.
(iv) A hundred times he said that he didn't want to see any more Indians; and even less one that was there...
(v) Some are at the doors...

59. I say 'rough' because nonidentifiable does not seem to cover absolutely all the cases of indefinite (predicate nominatives, for example).

60. In this section I have drawn many insights from Bull's (1965) Chapter 17, 'Mathematical organization of entities'.

61. It is not the purpose of this section to examine in detail all expressions of cardinality in all of their uses. The ensuing discussion is meant to serve as an illustration of the compatibility of hay with cardinality and not as an exhaustive treatment of cardinality per se.

62. Spanish also allows for the juxtaposition of more than one modifier. In general, it appears that the first modifier tends to be definite.

(i)   los otros libros
       'the other books'
(ii)   los otros tres libros
       'the other three books'
(iii) estos tres libros
       'these three books'
(iv)   mis tres libros
       'my three books'
(v)   todo el mundo
       'all the world~everybody'

However, there exist cases where indefiniteness is preserved throughout:

(vi)   otros tres libros
        'other three books'
(vii)   algunos otros libros
        'some other books'
(viii) unos tres libros
        'some three books~about three books'

63. As is common in Spanish, one can also find examples with double negation:

...no hay ningún fenómeno que... (VEA 54)
...no there-is no phenomenon which...
'...there is no phenomenon which...'

64. For English, see Milsark (1977).

65. This definiteness restriction adopts many guises. Some scholars completely ignore the problem (Bresnan 1970, Wasow 1975); others require that the NP be indefinite in order for There-Insertion to apply (Kuno 1971, among others). Milsark (and Jenkins follows suit) demands that the NP be [-quantified]; this restriction is discussed later on. Some allow for the 'list' reading of there sentences (Milsark; Jenkins; Rando and Napoli

1978). Notable exceptions to any kind of syntactic constraint
are Bolinger (1977) and Cannings (1978).

66. In (168) the speaker introduces new information with an
indefinite NP; then, because s/he goes on to mention the same
entity again (shirt in this case), it is necessary to use the
definite determiner. For English, Quirk et al. (1972:155)
label this use as 'anaphoric the'.

67. I make no claim as to the exhaustiveness of the cases
included in this discussion.

68. As a matter of fact, the examples given in (176) are
ambiguous. Besides the generic interpretation, they may mean
a specific total under consideration in the case of (176a), or
a specific animal in the case of (176b). Although it is more
difficult to picture (176c) and (176d) as nongeneric, given
appropriate background information I am sure it could be done.

Notice that in Spanish, as opposed to English, generics require the definite determiner. English generics such as
Beavers build dams, I hate chewing gum always require the
definite determiner when translated into Spanish: Los castores
construyen diques, Odio la goma de mascar. Consequently,
'bare plurality' is not one of the ways to express totality in
Spanish (cf. Chomsky 1975:79).

69. This does not imply that a given name could not have
been assigned to more than one individual.

Observe, moreover, that since identifiability or anaphoricity
has been defined from the speaker's point of view as an assumption that s/he makes as to whether the addressee can or cannot
identify a given referent or referents, it is possible for the
speaker to be wrong in his/her assumption. For example, the
person who utters (171a) takes for granted that the hearer
knows of the existence of this daughter; the information centers
around the losing of the teeth. In other words, mi hija is
thematic information. This fact does not bar the addressee
from coming back with:

¡No sabía que tenía(s) una hija!
'I didn't know you had a daughter!'

Sentence (170a) would be completely inappropriate unless
shared knowledge about the tools existed. Therefore, the
addressee who retorts:

Yo no tengo herramientas.
'I do not have (any) tools.'

is either being facetious or is indicating that the addresser
made the wrong assumption. The same might happen with
proper names. After (179) has been said, the listener could
ask:

¿Y quién es Pepe?
'And who is Pepe?'

70. As seen in this example, the absolute superlative of adjectives is formed by adding the suffix -ísimo. For example, simple 'simple', simplísimo 'very simple'.
This absolute superlative corresponds to the English indefinite superlative:

Hay un hombre rarísimo a la puerta.
'There-is the strangest man at the door.'

Notice that while Spanish uses an expression of cardinality (un), English employs 'the indefinite exclamatory the'. Some English native speakers preserve this 'the' even if the NP is further modified by a numeral:

Hay dos hombres rarísimos a la puerta.
'There-are the two strangest men at the door.'

71. This is essentially what Milsark claims for examples such as:

There has not been the slightest protest.

He calls them 'crypto-indefinites'. And the description also applies to Quirk et al.'s (1972) 'the indefinite exclamatory the'.
72. This is not to say that they are synonymous. Examples (183a) and (183b) provide an extra dimension precisely because of the superlative.
73. Actually, the literal translation for Spanish ningún/a is 'no' or 'none'.
74. I return to the idea of degree of definiteness in Section 1.3.1.3.1.5. It should be pointed out that Fauconnier (1975) has discussed pragmatic scales in reference to English superlatives.
75. But notice that an example like:

Siempre hay esa {tendencia. / queja.
'There-is always that {tendency.' / complaint.'}

is completely acceptable. It appears that the stronger deictic force of the demonstrative is sufficient to identify the referent. I return to this point later.
76. Actually, the previous mention of the noun and the form used as reentry need not be strictly the same. Quirk et al. (1972:703-707) point out that the noun phrases may be co-referential without being identical:

His <u>wife</u> walked slowly by his side. <u>The old woman</u> stooped
  slightly.
<u>The chap with a wart on his nose</u> is in my class. <u>The boy</u>
  is extremely clever.

As a matter of fact, in some cases the identity is extracted by
mere implication:

We visited the Browns yesterday and saw the miserable
conditions under which they live. The authorities should
abolish such houses.

In Spanish, the same conditions prevail. Notice example (193)
in the text, where there is no strict identity between <u>una</u>
<u>muchacha</u> (f. sg.) and the clitic <u>las</u> (f. pl.).
  77. See Rando and Napoli (1978) for a discussion of lists
with <u>there</u> sentences in English. Observe also that these
authors claim that in order for <u>there</u> sentences to be grammatical their NP argument must <u>be</u> nonanaphoric (in the wider
sense of the word 'anaphoric') (1978:310). This explanation
will never do for Spanish, since instances of <u>hay</u> with clitics
are legion (cf. the previous section).
  78. The native speakers consulted did not like (201b); they
claimed that <u>estar</u> should be used. One of them explained that
(201b) might <u>be OK</u> if there were only one unique dresser and
one unique sofa in the house. Of course, when consulting
native speakers one always faces the danger that they might
not imagine a possible situation in which the sentence would be
perfectly natural.
  79. Bolinger's scale is the following:

1. Third person anaphoric pronouns. The referent is
    agreed upon by both speaker and hearer and must al-
    ready have been mentioned in the context.
2. Personal names and anaphoric nouns. The speaker
    assumes that his hearer will be able to make the con-
    nection with the referent immediately, though mention
    within the context is not essential.
3. Cataphoric nouns with <u>the</u>. Something needs to be
    added to delimit the <u>noun</u>.
4. Cataphoric demonstratives. The determiner does no
    more than point to a clause as something designating a
    thing that is known to exist but about which nothing
    is presupposed: <u>that which</u>, <u>those who</u>.
5. The indefinite superlative, called by Quirk-Greenbaum
    'the indefinite exclamatory <u>the</u>', as in There's <u>the oddest-</u>
    <u>looking man standing at the front door!</u> (419). (This
    probably stems from the cataphoric <u>the oddest-looking</u>
    <u>man you ever saw</u>.)

80. This pragmatic scale is reminiscent of Ross' work on squishes (1972 and 1975, for example), and of Fauconnier's already mentioned work (1975).

81. At this point, it is only possible to speculate as to why the two languages behave differently. The explanation might lie in the organization of the lexicon in each language. To the one verb be of English, Spanish opposes three different lexical items--hay, ser, estar. This fact might justify the more specialized uses in Spanish.

Another possibility is that both languages might have a different degree of tolerance for the cooccurrence of hay/ there-be with readily identifiable unique persons. This latter possibility seems to be linked to the fact that Spanish hay never cooccurs with 'personal a'. The items in (205b-d) are human and specific, two factors which, when combined in an object NP, demand the presence of this marker.

With respect to (204a), although Rando and Napoli maintain that in English 'no generics may appear in existential sentences' (1978:310), several English native speakers I consulted contested their claim.

82. This sentence is a counterexample to Milsark's (1977) theory of (universal) quantification. See Section 1.3.2.

83. Notice that it is an accident of the Spanish language that all generic statements require the definite determiner. English expresses generics with both definite and indefinite NPs.

84. The examples in (212b-e) are all mentioned in Jenkins (1975:44).

85. Stowell (1978), for example, writes that lists 'yield interpretations which are radically distinct from those of the corresponding ES with indefinite NPs' (1978:460). And I would add, of course they are interpreted differently; definite and indefinite NPs do not convey the same meaning/information!

86. Example (214f) is included because of Milsark's starred *There are some of the people in the bedroom.

87. Cumbersome at least from the point of view of existential sentences.

88. Remember what is old and new information is decided by the speaker. S/he makes an assumption as to whether something is present (therefore, old) or not present (therefore, new) in the addressee's consciousness at the moment the exchange takes place. 'Old' should not be equated with what the addressee is supposed or expected to know already. And 'new' is not what the hearer is not believed to know (cf. Chafe 1976).

89. Kany (1969:256) cites the following two examples:

Algunos ouieron que...quisieron disfamar al rey de Navarra.
some there-were who...wanted to-discredit the king of
    Navarra.

...en ella hubieron cosas dignas de memoria...hubieron
palabras (1605)
...in her there-were things worthy of memory...there-were
words

90.   This example comes from recorded speech.   In addition
to the sources of data listed at the end of this manuscript, I
read five contemporary plays that exemplify the colloquial
speech of the River Plate region, and listened to four hours
of taped speech from Buenos Aires, in the hope of finding
more examples.   None were encountered.   Examples (222b)
and (222c) come from the tapescripts of the Norma Culta Project in Mexico City (1971).   They are the only two I found in
the 447-page volume.   (Observe that the second instance of
haber in (222c) is not pluralized despite the fact that it also
refers to the plural noun libertades.)   Of course, there always
remains the possibility that my data is either not representative,
or accidentally devoid of the phenomenon under discussion.   It
is also worth noticing that most of Kany's examples from Ar-
gentina are illustrations of the stereotyped literary 'gaucho'
speech.
91.   Since nonstandard Spanish is being examined, all the
examples with hay appear in the third person plural form.
92.   Or perhaps it is not as contradictory as it seems.   W.
Harbert informs me that English me thinks seems to have become I think over an intermediate stage me think, with 1 sg.
agreement but object case.
93.   Contrary to what Keenan states, I do not consider most
of these tests to be transformational.   However, they are still
behavioral.
94.   I take this position for ease of exposition.   The argument still holds under a different characterization of Equi.
95.   Compare the grammatical sentence:

Irradiaban luz y olían agradablemente [dos docenas de
   rosas] subj
gave-out light and smelled pleasingly two dozens of roses
'Two dozen roses sparkled and gave forth a pleasant
   fragrance.'

96.   This analogic rule is prompted by examples such as the
following, where a plural NP which is not the object of the
finite verb can trigger subject-verb agreement on that verb:

(ia) Se quieren/*quiere encontrar parejas.
     PRO wants pl./*sg. to find couples
(ib) Se comenzaron/*comenzó a preparar los mapas.
     PRO began pl./*sg. to prepare the maps
(ic) Se oyeron/*oyó doblar las campanas toda la tarde.
     PRO heard pl./*sg. the bells tolling all afternoon

(id) Siempre se tratan/?trata de cantar las canciones cortas
   primero.
   PRO always tries pl./?sg. to sing the songs short first

(The examples are from Aissen 1973:13, with her judgments of
grammaticality. Many speakers find the asterisked alternatives
grammatical.)
  97. The fact that hay seems to have acquired a coding
property before acquiring any (conclusive) behavioral properties, might provide a counterexample to the claim that behavioral subject properties are acquired prior to subject coding properties (Cole et al. 1978). However, if agreement in
impersonal sentences is analogical, then this test is not a de-
pendable subject coding property in this case, and the acquisition hypothesis remains unchallenged by the Spanish data.
  98. The analogy would be to presentational sentences with
true syntactic subject:

  (i)   Aparecieron tiburones.
        appeared (3 pl.) sharks
        'Sharks appeared.'
  (ii) Crecian rosas.
        grew (3 pl.) roses
        'Roses grew.'
  (iii) Cayeron unas piedras enormes.
        fell (3 pl.) some stone huge
        'Some huge stones fell.'

This type of sentence is discussed in detail in Chapter 2.
  99. How this impersonal construction came about constitutes
in itself an interesting topic. In Latin, habere was a personal
transitive verb that indicated possession, although already in
Vulgar Latin it began to be used impersonally with a noun in
the accusative:

Guia jam multum tempus haberet.
In arca Noe habuit homines. (Bourciez 1910:274)

Bassols (1948) seeks the reason for this change in Latin itself and speculates that it was the result of a blend caused by
the substitution of an inanimate subject for a human one.
Briefly, the hypothesized process would be as follows:

  (a) dominus habet multum vinum
      the-owner has a-lot-of wine

  (b_1) domus habet multum vinum
         the-house has a-lot-of wine

  (b_2) domi est multum vinum
         in-the-house exists a-lot-of wine

(c) domi habet multum vinum
   in-the-house there-is a-lot-of wine

In (a), the conjunction of a human subject plus <u>habere</u> conveys the idea of possession; however, the replacement of <u>dominus</u> by the inanimate <u>domus</u> (b₁) causes the concomitant shift in verbal meaning from possession to existence. Thus, the meaning of (b₁) comes to coincide with that of (b₂), which uses <u>essere</u>. These two verbs were used interchangeably to the point that <u>domus habet</u> adopted the same construction as <u>domi est</u>, insofar as the subject of <u>habere</u> became a locative just as was the case with <u>sum</u>. Therefore, (c) arose, with a locative, a verb of existence, and an argument in the accusative.

Although in Old Spanish both uses of <u>haber</u> (possession and existence) were kept, the possession use of this verb became archaic by the 1600s (Lapesa 1968:257).

100. <u>Haber</u> is not the sole member of the class of impersonal verbs that exhibits this type of agreement. Other syntactically subjectless verbs also appear with it in nonstandard Spanish.

   (i) Hace<u>n</u> diez años que llegué.
      make (3 pl.) ten years that I-arrived
      'I arrived ten years ago.'

   (ii) Hace<u>n</u> lluvia y viento.
      make (3 pl.) rain and wind
      'It is rainy and windy.'

For a treatment of subjectlessness in standard Spanish, I direct the reader to Appendix B.

101. As a matter of fact, if this agreement is analogical-- as I think it is--then the NP occurring with <u>haber</u> would have no coding or behavioral properties.

102. The only progress that this construction seems to have made is the 'feeling' that plural agreement appears to be more and more common (cf. Kany 1969). However, these feelings have not been supported by sociolinguistic studies or by our data.

103. It should be pointed out that the phenomenon of plural agreement is not exclusive to impersonal sentences. Spanish seems to display a certain propensity toward pluralization. For example, this tendency also manifests itself in clitics. Because an expression like <u>se lo dimos</u> is not clear as to the number of SE (since SE is invariable), and because number is felt as important, some people:

   ...insist on indicating plurality of the indirect object SE by adding s to the immediately following direct object <u>lo</u> or <u>la</u> making them <u>los</u> or <u>las</u>, even though the object referred to is singular. The pluralizing -<u>s</u> is added to <u>lo</u> or <u>la</u>, though

the plural number belongs to the other pronoun, because los
and las are thoroughly familiar forms and a form ses would
be unthinkable. (Kany 1969:141)

Thus,

Se lo digo (a Uds.).
to-you (pl.) it I-tell (to-you (pl.))
'I am telling it to you (pl.).'

is often rendered as: se los digo.
Furthermore, Kany also provides data to illustrate another
way of pluralizing clitics. This time an -n is added. Some
people say siéntensen or siéntesen for the standard siéntense.
Kany (1969:144) explains it as follows.

In siéntense the feeling of plurality is unfulfilled for many
speakers who see in the combined form a single verbal concept and not a combination of verb and pronoun; these
speakers expect the feeling of plurality to be satisfied at
the very end of the word, as happens in the majority of
such imperative forms: hablen, vengan, coman...The -n
is added here for the same reason that -s was added to lo
in se los (for se lo): without it the legitimate feeling for
number is frustrated. The sound -n satisfies the feeling
of plurality for third person verbs, just as -s satisfies the
same feeling in nouns and pronouns.

2

FURTHER PRESENTATIONAL SENTENCES

2.0 Introduction. Having quite exhaustively examined the presentational-existential construction par excellence--impersonal <u>haber</u> sentences--it is time to look at other ways in which Spanish can convey this type of information. Consider the sentences in (1).

(1a) Apareció un hombre.
appeared (3 sg.) a man
'A man appeared.'

(1b) Asomó el sol radiante.
peeked (3 sg.) the sun radiant
'The radiant sun peeked out.'

(1c) Llegaron unos paquetes.
arrived (3 pl.) some packages
'Some packages arrived.'

(1d) Pasaron diez perros.
passed (3 pl.) ten dogs
'Ten dogs passed by.'

The foregoing examples have intransitive[1] verbs and post-verbal subject NPs. Moreover, their communicative function is that of affirming the existence of the NP referent, and in this process the existence of the NP referent is being asserted.[2] In other words, the sentences in (1) are presentational as well as existential.[3] The difference between this type of presentational and the one with <u>hay</u> discussed in the preceding chapter lies in the fact that in <u>hay</u> sentences the verb itself acts as an existential quantifier, whereas in this other construction the existential interpretation is derived from the assertion. Furthermore, the grammatical function of the asserted NP is

that of object in impersonal <u>haber</u> sentences, while in (1) the
NP functions as subject (see Section 2.6.2 for a comparison of
both presentational subtypes). Notice, however, that the word
order of both presentational constructions is the same.

(2a) hay $[NP]_{obj}$.

(2b) V_{intr}. $[NP]_{subj}$.[4]

This fact suggests that the word order for presentational sentences is V NP regardless of the grammatical function of this
NP.

Throughout this chapter the characteristics peculiar to
examples such as those found in (1) are studied. It will be
seen that presentationals in general constitute a distinct type
of sentence, since they behave differently from declaratives
with respect to word order, stress and focus, the <u>hacerlo</u>
construction, and the scope of negation. Constraints which
at first glance appear to be lexical or structural turn out, upon
closer examination, to be pragmatic in nature; these 'constraints'
automatically follow from the function of this type of sentence.
Thus, the grammar of these presentational sentences is a maximally simple one which consists of one syntactic movement rule
--Subject Postposing--and several rules of semantic interpretation. During the development of this chapter several other
points of theoretical interest are considered, such as the nature
of the Subject Postposing rule, the resultant derived constituent
structure of this movement rule, and the implications of having
a leftward trace in surface structure.

The work in this chapter was inspired mainly by Anna
Hatcher's pioneering monograph *Theme and Underlying Question: Two Studies of Spanish Word Order*, where she justly
complains that 'the "existential" type of (intransitive) predication in Spanish has, so far, received no attention' (1956:6).[5]

2.1 **Presentational characterization.** There can be little
doubt that the sentences in (1) constitute instances of the
'presentative function' (Hetzron 1975; see also further discussion in Section 1.1.2). As such, they present to the hearer
an 'object' for consideration. This 'object' is embodied (in this
particular case) in the subject argument. The verb serves to
introduce the subject referent to the scene; it is like the tray
on which a delicacy is presented: no one pays much attention
to the tray, everyone concentrates on what is being presented.
Besides presenting the 'object', this construction carries an
existential assertion, since it asserts that the 'object' exists in
the universe of discourse. And just as was the case with <u>hay</u>,
this existential assertion may be absolute or relative.

(3a) Apareció un hombre. (absolute assertion)
     appeared (3 sg.) a man

(3b) $\left.\begin{array}{l}\text{Ayer}\\\text{A las tres}\end{array}\right\}$ apareció un hombre.   (relative assertion,
                                         time is stated)

     $\left.\begin{array}{l}\text{yesterday}\\\text{at three}\end{array}\right\}$ appeared (3 sg.) a man

     'A man appeared $\left\{\begin{array}{l}\text{yesterday.'}\\\text{at three o'clock.'}\end{array}\right.$

(3c) En el jardín apareció un hombre. (relative assertion,
      place is stated)
     in the garden appeared (3 sg.) a man
     'A man appeared in the garden.'

Before plunging any deeper into this type of presentational sentence, it is necessary to make one point absolutely clear in order to forestall any confusion. A sentence such as (3a), Apareció un hombre, is ambiguous. In isolation, it may receive either of two meanings (cf. Kuno 1972).

(4a) Y luego $\left\{\begin{array}{l}\text{ocurrió}\\\text{pasó}\end{array}\right\}$ que apareció un hombre.
     and then it happened that appeared (3 sg.) a man.

(4b) Te dije que apareció un hombre (y no una mujer)
     to-you I-told that appeared (3 sg.) a man (and not a
       woman)
     'I told you that a man appeared (and not a woman).'

In (4a), the sentence answers questions such as those found in (5), while (4b) answers the question in (6).

(5a) ¿Qué pasó/ocurrió?
     'What happened?'

(5b) ¿Y luego qué?
     'And then what?'

(5c) ¿Qué hay de nuevo?
     'What's new/up?'

(6) ¿Apareció una mujer?
     'Did a woman appear?'

In other words, (3a) may be interpreted as a neutral description (like (4a)), or as a contrastive sentence (like (4b)). This chapter concerns itself solely with the neutral descriptive reading in which both the verb and the NP are asserted (and not presupposed)--that is to say, in which both constituents form part of the rheme. (For a discussion of contrastive sentences, see Section 3.4.) It is only the neutral description interpretation that is presentational in the strict sense of the word.

2.1.1 Word order and logical form. As was already pointed out, word order is crucial for interpreting a sentence as presentational. Given the fact that Spanish is a language which allows a certain freedom in word order, messages of the type found in (1) can come 'packaged' in two different word orders.[6]

(7a) Tres hombres aparecieron.
'Three men appeared (3 pl.).'

(7b) El sol radiante asomó.
'The radiant sun began-to-appear (3 sg.).'

(8a) Aparecieron tres hombres.
appeared (3 pl.) three men.

(8b) Asomó el sol radiante.
began-to-appear (3 sg.) the sun radiant

The sentences in (7) and (8) are not equivalent. The ones in (7) are declarative sentences that adhere to the unmarked syntactic word order of subject and predicate.[7] In the absence of a negative, the subject referents carry an existential presupposition in the world of discourse, and the VP (in this case a verb by itself) predicates something about the referents of the subject NP. The main informational focus in (7) rests on the verb, and it is this constituent which receives sentential stress under neutral conditions of stress and intonation. Thus, (7a) could be normally continued by (9a) but not by (9b).

(9a) ...y no desaparecieron.
'...and did not disappear (3 pl.).'

(9b) ≠ ...y no tres chicos.
'...and not three kids.'

On the other hand, the sentences in (8) are presentational in character: the VP predicates above all the appearance of the subject referents in the world of discourse, the subject referents carry an existential assertion, and the inversion of subject and verb causes the normal informational focus to fall on the subject NP. Nonetheless, since both the V and the NP are in the scope of assertion, (8b) could be appropriately continued only by another full sentence (10).

(10) Asomó el sol radiante, desaparecieron los nubes y...
     began-to-appear (3 sg.) the sun radiant, disappeared
     (3 sg.) the clouds, and...
     'The radiant sun appeared, the clouds disappeared,
     and...'[8]

The two word orders represented in (7) and (8) are not exclusive to main clauses; they are found in embedded sentences
as well.

(11a) Me dijeron que el Papa llegó.
      to-me they-said that the Pope arrived
      'They told me that the Pope arrived.'

(11b) La niña cree que los fantasmas existen.
      'The girl believes that (the) ghosts exist.'

(12a) Me dijeron que llegó el Papa.
      to-me they-said that arrived (3 sg.) the Pope

(12b) La niña cree que existen los fantasmas.
      the girl believes that exist (3 pl.) the ghosts

The subordinate clauses in (11) are declarative, while those in
(12) are presentational. Therefore, whatever means are necessary to derive and differentiate these two types of sentences
should take care of the phenomena in main and embedded clauses
alike.
The need for classifying sentences into what I call declarative
and presentational has long been recognized in the literature.
For example, Kuroda (1972:154) follows the Brentano-Marty
theory of judgment and divides judgments into 'categorial' and
'thetic':

Of these, only the former conforms to the traditional paradigm of subject-predicate, while the latter represents simply
the recognition or rejection of material of a judgment. Moreover, the categorial judgment is assumed to consist of two
separate acts, one, the act of recognition of that which is
to be made the subject, and the other, the act of affirming
or denying what is expressed by the predicate about the
subject. With this analysis in mind, the thetic and the
categorial judgments are also called the simple and the
double judgments.

Shou-Hsin (1976) agrees with Kuroda and recognizes that at
the logical level sentences are 'bi-constituent' and 'uni-
constituent'.[9] Guéron (1978) catalogs English sentences into
predication and presentation sentences, each having a distinc-
tive logical form. Babby (1980) subdivides them into declarative and existential.

The close correspondence among all these classifications becomes clear in (13).

(13)   declarative   presentational   (Spanish)
Kuroda (1972)   categorial   thetic   (Japanese)
Shou-Hsin (1976)   bi-constituent   uni-constituent   (Chinese)
Guéron (1978)   predication   presentation   (English)
Babby (1980)   declarative   existential   (Russian)[10]

The difference between Spanish declarative sentences (cf.
(7)) and presentational sentences (cf. (8)) becomes totally
transparent at the level of logical form (LF), the level of linguistic representation incorporating those aspects of meaning
stipulated exclusively by linguistic rules (Chomsky 1977b,
1980a).

(14) $(_{S'}(_S(NP) \ (VP)_S)_{S'}$ Declarative

(15) $(_{S'}(_S \ [_{NP}...e_i...] \ [_{VP}(VP) \ (NP_i)])_S)_{S'}$ Presentational[11]

The constituent $[_{NP}...e...]$ is the trace left behind by the
Subject Postposing rule which, forming a new VP, positions the
NP subject after the original VP.[12]   The term VP is included
in both (14) and (15) instead of just V, because the LF in (14)
is meant to accommodate transitive sentences also (in which case
the informational focus falls on the object NP).   And the LF in
(15) allows for sentences with a VP-adverbial, such as those in
(16).

(16a) Andan sueltas por ahí unas lengüecitas... (H14)
      go (3 pl.) untied around there some little-tongues...
      'There is a lot of gossip going around...'

(16b) Acaba de entrar en el parque la carroza... (H10)
      finished (3 sg.) of to enter in the park the carriage...
      'The carriage...has just finished entering the park.'

Furthermore, observe that the LFs of both types of sentences
mirror the surface word order of Spanish (and, I would add, of
probably most of the languages known as having 'free word
order').[13]
   The dissimilarities between the LFs in (14) and (15) corrobo-
rate the 'categorial' vs. 'thetic' opposition (Kuroda 1972) of
double vs. simple judgments, as well as the 'bi-constituent'
vs. 'uni-constituent' partitioning (Shou-Hsin 1976).
   Moreover, by identifying the scope of assertion with 'rheme'
(see discussion in the Introduction), the LFs already point out
the differences in scope of assertion: in (14) the VP is the
one which is in the scope of assertion, the subject being unasserted (i.e. thematic); while in (15) both the VP and the NP

subject are in the scope of assertion, and thus the subject NP is being asserted (existential assertion). The post-LF representations (LF with theme/rheme assignment indicated) of declarative and presentational sentences are given in (17) and (18).

(17) $(_{S'}(_S \underset{\text{Theme} \leftarrow | \ | \rightarrow \text{Rheme}}{\text{(NP)} \qquad \text{(VP)}})_S)_{S'}$ Declarative

(18) $(_{S'}(_S [_{NP} \cdots e_i \cdots] [_{VP}\text{(VP)} \ (NP_i)])_S)_{S'}$ Presentational

Theme $\longleftarrow$ ─┤ ├─$\longrightarrow$ Rheme

To conclude, two types of sentences have been contrasted and discussed: declaratives and presentationals. After calling attention to some of their differences--differences in word order, differences in the position of the main informational focus, differences in the unasserted vs. asserted status of the referent of the subject NP, their LFs were advanced. It was hypothesized that these LFs reflect the surface word order of the constituents,[14] as well as revealing the differences in scope of assertion.

2.1.2 Semantic conditions on the verb. Although most verbs used in presentational sentences tend to fall into natural semantic classes, such as existence, appearance, emergence, occurrence, and presence, there is no single classification capable of encompassing all the verbs that might occur in this type of construction.

Hatcher found nearly 300 verbs that 'in their context, tell us only or mainly that the subject exists or is present, is absent, begins, continues, is produced, occurs, appears, arrives' (1956:7). For example, verbs that appeal to our senses of vision and hearing are encountered in her data.

(19a) ...brillaba un lucero de plata. (H 17)
      ...shone (3 sg.) a star of silver
      ...'A silver star was shining.'

(19b) ...mientras en los (ojos) del marqués relampagueaba
      una franca aversión. (H 17)
      ...while in the (eyes) of-the Marquis flashed (3 sg.)
      a frank dislike
      '...while a frank dislike flashed in the Marquis' eyes.'

(19c) Pues irremisiblemente sonará el trueno. (H 16)
      then unpardonably will-sound (3 sg.) the thunder
      'Then the thunder will resound unpardonably.'

(19d) ...crepitaban las conversaciones... (H 16)
      ...crackled (3 sg.) the conversations...
      '...the conversations crackled...'

Verbs of movement are also often found in presentationals, as shown in (20).

(20a) ...surgió una luna redonda, pesada. (H 13)
      ...emerged (3 sg.) a moon round, heavy
      '...a round heavy moon emerged.'

(20b) Por las paredes de la casa trepaban enredaderas con
         flores quietas. (H 14)
      by the walls of the house climbed (3 pl.) vines with
         flowers quiet
      'Vines with quiet flowers climbed up the walls of the
         house.'

(20c) Llega el tren... (H 10)
      'The train arrives...'

Her data also include verbs which deny the existence of something, like desaparecer 'disappear', faltar 'lack', and escasear
'to be scanty'. The difference between the verbs that introduce a new element and those which subtract an element is a
difference in point of view: the first group adds a positive
quantity, the second a negative quantity (cf. Hatcher 1956:
22).

(21a) Desapareció su buen humor. (H 20)
      disappeared (3 sg.) his good humor
      'His good humor disappeared.'

(21b) ...transcurrieron los minutos... (H 20)
      '...the minutes passed...'

(21c) ...escaseaban el hierro y la madera. (H 8)
      '...iron and wood were scarce.'

(21d) Falta dirección, sobra gente. (H 8)
      'Guidance is missing, people are in surplus.'

Therefore, it is not the case that verbs in the lexicon can
be assigned a feature for entering into a presentational construction, because it is not the verb per se that is presentational but the sentence.[15] Context is of utmost importance in
judging whether a sentence is presentational or not. As a
case in point, witness the differences between the (a) and (b)
sentences in (22) and (23).

(22a) Viajaba Paco por tren.
      travelled (3 sg.) Paco by train
      'Paco travelled by train.'

(22b) Por el ancho cielo viajaba un humo tenue que...
     vislumbraba. (H 14)
     through the wide sky travelled (3 sg.) a smoke
     tenuous that...glimmered (3 sg.)
     'Through the wide sky travelled a thin smoke that...
     glimmered.'

(23a) Le tiemblan las piernas.
     to-him tremble (3 pl.) the legs
     'His legs tremble.'

(23b) ...mientras allá lejos..., altas y seguras, tiemblan
     las estrellas.
     ...while there far-away..., high and secure, tremble
     the stars
     '...while over there far away, high and secure, the
     stars tremble.'

At first glance, few would think about the verbs viajar and temblar as entering into presentationals; but nevertheless, given an appropriate context, they do. While (22a) predicates the means of transport Paco was using, and (23a) states what somebody's legs were doing, both (22b) and (23b) predicate above all the introduction of humo and estrellas into the world of discourse. Consequently, there is no possible lexical constraint statable at any level which captures all (and only) the verbs that may occur in presentational sentences.[16]
Nonetheless, these verbs share certain general properties which naturally follow from their pragmatic function as introducers of the grammatical subject into the discourse. In the first place, these verbs are characterized by a weakening of their semantic content.[17] Regardless of their primary lexical meaning, they come to represent different shades of existential appearance which suggest mere presence. This is why dynamicity gives way to nondynamicity and motion verbs yield to 'crystallized movement' (Hatcher 1956:14). Even ir 'to go' enters this pattern, as shown in (24).

(24a) Ahí van señas de mi mujer... (H 12)
     there go (3 pl.) personal description (pl.) of my wife
     'Enclosed you find a description of my wife...'

(24b) ...y finalmente va una bibliografía... (H 12)
     ...and finally goes (3 sg.) a bibliography...
     '...and finally a bibliography is found...'

Moreover, many examples give a photographic impression. The action has been frozen and a description which generally appeals to our senses has been left in its place (cf. (19), (20), (22b), and (23b)).

The semantic weakening coupled with the nondynamicity of
the verbal element, and the photographic impression created
by the sentence as a whole, are the reasons for claiming that
these verbs tend to depict the 'natural functioning' of the subject nouns (Hatcher 1956:18), and that the processes are to a
certain degree inevitable or predictable. One finds instances
like those listed here.

blanquea la niebla 'the fog whitens'
verdean las huertas 'the orchards turn-green'
florecen, crecen, brotan, nacen flores 'flowers flower,
    grow, bud, are born'
arde, quema la pasión 'passion burns, scalds'
humea, arde la hoguera 'the bonfire smokes, burns'
brillan, titilan, resplandecen las estrellas 'the stars shine,
    twinkle, glitter'
cesa, acaba, continúa la música 'the music stops, finishes,
    continues'

Examples could be cited ad infinitum. Babby (1980:134) en-
counters the same phenomenon in Russian. He says that what
these verbs have in common is that they 'denote the subject
noun's most typical action from the point of view of the human
participants in the speech event'.

As a consequence of the foregoing, and despite the fact that
it is the sentence and not the verb by itself which is presentational (impersonal haber might be considered the only exception since it is the essence of 'presentationalism'), few native
speakers experience any problems in picking out presentational
sentences.

2.1.3 **Syntactic conditions on the verb.** The type of presentational sentence examined in this chapter seems to be confined
to intransitive verbs. Is this a necessary requirement?
Hatcher (1956:7) states explicitly that she is dealing with intransitive verbs which predicate the existence of the subject.
On examining her data, however, one finds that some of her
examples include verbs which are not inherently intransitive;[18]
for example: habitar 'to inhabit', subir 'to go up, ascend',
cruzar 'to cross', romper 'to break', susurrar 'to whisper',
irradiar 'to irradiate', hervir 'to boil', finalizar 'to finish,
finalize', among others. Nevertheless, all of them appear in
her examples in their intransitive usage.

(25a) ...las montañas, en cuyos hondones húmedos todavía
        habitaba la noche. (H 8)
      ...the mountains, in whose glens humid still inhabited
        (3 sg.) the night
      '...the mountains, in whose humid glens (the) night
        still reigned.'

(25b) ...y de ella subía una escalera de caracol. (H 12)
...and from it went-up (3 sg.) a stair of snail
'...and from it a winding stairway went up.'

(25c) Por la mirada de Arco cruzó una sombra. (H 13)
through the glance of Arco crossed (3 sg.) a shadow
'Across Arco's glance a shadow passed.'

(25d) ...ya rompieron las hostilidades otra vez. (H 16)
...already broke out (3 sg.) the hostilities again
'...the hostilities already broke out again.'

The next question that comes to mind is whether it is just a coincidence that all the verbs in Hatcher's corpus are either inherently intransitive or used intransitively, or whether this is a significant fact for presentational constructions. One way to test the relevance of intransitivity is to check some transitive verbs for a presentational interpretation.

(26a) ≠ Habitaban la casa los fantasmas.
inhabited (3 pl.) the house the ghosts
'Ghosts inhabited the house.'

(26b) ≠ Habitaban los fantasmas la casa.

(27a) ≠ Subía una escalera de caracol María.
ascended (3 sg.) a stairs of snail Mary
'Mary was going up a winding stairway.'

(27b) ≠ Subía María una escalera de caracol.

(28a) ≠ Cruzó la calle una sombra.
crossed (3 sg.) the street a shadow
'A shadow crossed the street.'

(28b) ≠ Cruzó una sombra la calle.[19]

What (26)-(28) show is that transitive verbs with two arguments[20] are not adequate as presentationals even when the subject appears in sentence-final position (the (a) examples). This inadequacy naturally follows from the function of presentational sentences. Recalling that the primary task of presentationals is to herald the appearance of the NP referent on the scene (the grammatical object in hay sentences, the grammatical subject in the sentences under discussion in this chapter), it is apparent that this function requires that only one NP be on stage at a time. Since there are two NPs competing for attention in (26)-(28), these sentences are unable to receive a presentational interpretation.

While discussing the constraints on PP Extraposition from subject position, Guéron (1978:31-32) notices that it is not the mere presence of an object but rather its semantic role which blocks the operation. Thus, if the V + NP form a semantic unit, PP Extraposition is allowed (cf. (29b) vs. (30b), Guéron's examples).

(29a) A book by Chomsky is making the rounds.
(29b) A book is making the rounds by Chomsky.

(30a) A book by Charles delighted Mary.
(30b) *A book delighted Mary by Charles.

Moreover, if the VP + NP unit can be interpreted both as a semantic unit and in a more literal sense, only the first meaning is kept after PP Extraposition (her examples again).

(31a) A book by Chomsky hit the newsstand.
      (Ambiguous between a literal meaning and an idomatic 'appearance' meaning.)

(31b) A book hit the newsstand by Chomsky.

This same kind of ambiguity between a literal and an idiomatic meaning arises in Spanish with the expression dar señales de vida.

(32a) Luego de diez años dio señales de vida mi tío Federico.
      after of ten years gave (3 sg.) signs of life my uncle
      Federico.
      'After ten years my uncle Federico appeared.'

(32b) Luego de darlos por muertos dieron señales de vida
      tres de los soldados.
      after of to-give-them for deads gave (3 pl.) signs
      of life three of the soldiers.

      Ambiguous between:

      (i) 'After giving them up for dead, three of the
           soldiers appeared.' and
      (ii) '...three of the soldiers made some movements.'

(32c) Al abrir los ojos dio señales de vida el niño que se
      desmayó.
      to-the to-open the eyes gave (3 sg.) signs of life
      the boy who himself fainted
      'By opening his eyes, the boy who fainted
      ⎰gave signs of life.'
      ⎱*appeared.'

As shown in (32), the expression <u>dar señales de vida</u> is consonant with a presentational interpretation in (a) and (b), but not in (c). This presentational reading arises only when the expression can be diagnosed as equivalent to 'appear'. But notice again that it is only after taking the whole sentence into consideration that it becomes possible to read <u>dar señales de vida</u> in its literal or idiomatic sense, a fact which shows once again that context is of utmost importance in judging whether or not a sentence is presentational.

Other expressions which lend themselves to a presentational interpretation are <u>hacer su entrada</u> 'to make one's entrance', <u>tener lugar</u> 'to take place', and <u>tomar cuerpo</u> 'to take shape'.

(33a) A las diez en punto hizo su entrada el maestro de
      ceremonias.
      at 10 o'clock sharp made (3 sg.) his entrance the
      master of ceremonies
      'At 10 o'clock the master of ceremonies appeared.'

(33b) En esa esquina siempre tienen lugar accidentes.
      on that corner always take (3 pl.) place accidents
      'On that corner accidents always occur.'

(33c) Está tomando cuerpo en mi mente una sospecha
      perniciosa.
      is taking shape in my mind a suspicion pernicious
      'A pernicious suspicion is growing in my mind.'

To sum up, it would not be accurate to state that verbs in presentational sentences must be structurally intransitive.[21] The most one can require is that they be semantically intransitive and taken as carrying overtones of appearing, existing, or occurring. It should be clear that one cannot specify lexical or structural constraints on presentationals; the 'constraints' are not formal (lexical, syntactic, or semantic) but follow naturally from the pragmatic function of this type of sentence.[22]

The conclusion that there are no lexical or structural constraints on the verbs used in presentational sentences allows the reaping of an unexpected profit. It permits placement of both impersonal <u>haber</u> and the 'semantically' intransitive sentence type of this chapter under the same rubric: that of presentationals. The sole requirement is that there be only one semantically heavy NP,[23] the one whose appearance on the scene is being signalled, as (34) shows.

(34a) hay   <u>NP</u>

(34b) [V + (NP)] <u>NP</u>[24]

The underlined NP is the semantically heavy one, the one that carries sentential stress, the one that is being introduced into the discourse. Observe the structural parallelism between (34a) and (34b): they both consist of a V and an NP in that order. The grammatical functions of these NPs--in (34a) that of object, in (34b) that of subject--is practically irrelevant. And so is the fact that an inversion (of subject and verb) has operated in (34b) but not in (34a).

2.1.4 Adverbials. Since the foremost mission of presentationals is to introduce the referent of the NP onto the scene, it is relatively easy to explain why temporal and spatial adverbs (cf. Hatcher 1956:11) abound in these sentences. These adverbial expressions help in locating the 'object' in the world of discourse; they relativize the existential assertion. The prime position for these scene-setting adverbs is, therefore, sentence-initial position in the underlying structure.[25] The same collocation of the adverbs at the surface level allows for focus and normal sentence stress to fall on the grammatical subject; this is the ideal type of presentational sentence.

> (35a) De vez en cuando asoma el sol. (H 10)
> from-time-to-time peeks the sun
> 'The sun appears from time to time.'

> (35b) En el horizonte asoma el sol.
> on the horizon peeks the sun
> 'The sun appears on the horizon.'

When such adverbials appear in sentence-final position (regardless of whether they are base-generated or have been moved there), they form part of the rheme, thereby becoming a secondary point of attention. This is true even when the subjects are also postposed. To state it differently, the postposed subject is still the prime focus and the adverbial, in specifying or relativizing the existential assertion, benefits from a 'second wind', so to speak, and receives secondary focus (cf. Kirkwood 1977). Schematically, the intonation of this type of sentence is as shown in (36).

> (36) Cayó granizo otra vez.
> fell (3 sg.) hail again
> 'It hailed again.'

Observe that (36) is still interpreted as presentational, although this subtype is somewhat less ideal than the pattern exemplified in (35). This fact is reflected in Hatcher's corpus where, among the large number of examples with sentence-initial adverbials, there are only 13 instances of the pattern Verb-Subject-Adverbial. Some of these are found in (37).

(37a) ...susurraba el viento entre los pinos. (H 16)
...whispered (3 sg.) the wind among the pines
'...the wind whispered among the pines.'

(37b) ¡Vuelve la alegría a la casa! (H 11)
returns the happiness to the house
'Happiness returns to the house!'

(37c) Y acaso entonces asomará una lágrima a estos ojos.
(H 10)
and maybe then will-appear (3 sg.) a tear to those
eyes

(37d) Ayer salió su nombramiento en la Gaceta. (H 13)
yesterday came-out (3 sg.) his/her appointment in the
Gazette

There is yet a third possibility for adverb placement in
presentational sentences: the adverbs may be located after
the verb but before the subject. Hatcher's corpus is rich in
this pattern.

(38a) En la obscuridad emerge a lo lejos, de la masa negra
..., la viva luz de un escaparate. (H 10)
in the dark emerges in the distance, of the mass
black..., the alive light of a window-shop
'In the dark, the bright light of a window-shop emerges
from the black mass far away.'

(38b) ...roncaron luego motores de camiones. (H 16)
...roared (3 pl.) then motors of trucks
'...truck engines roared then.'

(38c) ...empezaron a llover sobre ellos cuentas... (H 16)
...began (3 pl.) to rain over them bills...
'...bills began to rain over them...'

(38d) De cuando en cuando, penetraba en el alma de aquellos
hombres...un sentimiento romántico. (H 11)
from time-to-time penetrated (3 sg.) in the soul of
those men...a sentiment romantic
'From time to time, a romantic sentiment penetrated the
souls of those men.'

(38e) De la hermosa boca...desciende hacia el mundo cálido
buen humor. (H 12)
from the beautiful mouth...descends to the world warm
good humor
'From the beautiful mouth...warm good humor descends
to the world.'

Notice that although some examples also have a (surface) sentence-initial adverbial (38a, d, and e), there does not have to be one there in order for one to be placed after the verb (38b and c). Some of the adverbs in (38) are likely to have originated as sentence adverbials (a lo lejos in (38a) and luego in (38b)); but others are undoubtedly VP adverbials (sobre ellos in (38c) and en el alma de aquellos hombres in (38d)).

To repeat, place and time adverbials are common in presentational sentences because they are perfectly compatible with the primary function of a presentational construction--namely, that of introducing the subject referent on the scene. From this it follows that other types of adverbials are less frequent, because they are less consonant with the presentative function; they stress something other than mere scene-setting. This prediction is warranted by an examination of Hatcher's data, which contain very few examples with adverbials other than spatial and temporal ones.

(39a) ...y duraba aún la ovación a Gallardo. (H 9)
...and lasted (3 sg.) still the ovation to Gallardo
'...and the ovation to Gallardo lasted still.'

(39b) En ello intervenía también la diferencia entre... (H 11)
in that intervened (3 sg.) also the difference between...

(39c) Estallaban otra vez las risas. (H 16)
burst (3 pl.) again the laughs
'Again the laughter burst out.'

(39d) Quisiera...que murieran para siempre diferencias de
formas y de palabras. (H 20)
I would like...that die (3 pl. subjunctive) for always
differences of forms and of words
'I would like differences between forms and words to
die forever.'

(39e) ...ahí viene precisamente un C. (H 10)
...there comes (3 sg.) precisely a C

(39f) Flota, sacudido por la brisa, un suave vaho de calor.
(H 15)
floats (3 sg.), shaken by the breeze, a soft vapor of
heat

(39g) Palpitaba suave y gris el resplandor primero del día.
(H 15)
palpitated (3 sg.) soft and grey the radiance first
of-the day
'The first radiance of the day throbbed soft and grey.'

(39h) Desfilaban <u>rápidamente</u>...los olores de la calle.   (H 13)
      paraded (3 pl.) quickly...the smells of the street

(39i) reventaban <u>bravíamente</u> las ortigas.   (H 16)[26]
      ...burst (3 pl.) bravely the nettles

In only two of the nine examples, (39h) and (39i), do the adverbs unambiguously stress the verbal activity by calling
attention to the way in which the activity takes place. That
the corpus should render only two instances of adverbials
emphasizing the verbal activity should come as no surprise
when one takes into account that presentationals involve both
the semantic weakening of the verb's lexical meaning and the
predominance of nondynamicity in the verb (cf. Section 2.1.2).
Notice, however, that in all the sentences in (39) the subject,
as expected, remains in sentence-final position. If the subjects
occurred preverbally, the sentences would not qualify as presentationals.
   The impossibility of constraining (by rule or in the lexicon)
the types of adverbials that may cooccur in presentational constructions is evident. Their acceptability depends on the total
context. The more the adverbial helps in setting the scene,
the more compatible it will be with presentationals; the more
the adverbial stresses the verbal activity, the less compatible
it will be. Thus, activity-centered adverbs like <u>a propósito</u>
'on purpose', are less likely to appear with presentationals.[27]

   (40a) ?≠(De repente) apareció <u>a propósito</u> un hombre.
         (Suddenly) appeared (3 sg.) on purpose a man
         '(Suddenly), a man intentionally appeared.'

   (40b) ≠ (De repente), apareció un hombre <u>a propósito</u>.

But other adverbials may also raise difficulties in the interpretation of a sentence as presentational.

   (41a) ?≠Crece <u>sin cesar</u> el pasto.
         grows (3 sg.) without stopping the grass
         'The grass grows endlessly.'

   (41b) ≠ Crece el pasto <u>sin cesar</u>.

   (42a) ?≠Llegó <u>tarde</u> el tren.
         arrived (3 sg.) late the train
         'The train arrived late.'

   (42b) ≠ Llegó el tren <u>tarde</u>.

   (42c) *<u>Tarde</u> llegó el tren.

(43a) ≠ Apareció <u>blanco de rabia</u> Juan.
   appeared (3 sg.) white with anger John
   'John appeared white with rage.'

(43b) ≠ Apareció Juan <u>blanco de rabia</u>.

(43c) * Blanco de rabia apareció Juan.[28]

To sum up, adverbials are compatible with presentationals as long as they do not unduly draw attention away from the introduction of the referent of the NP into the world of discourse.

2.1.5 Recapitulation. Presentational sentences in Spanish are characterized by the surface word order V NP, which is mirrored by the order of the elements in LF. This order captures the fact that, in a presentational construction of the subtype being discussed in this chapter, both the verb and the grammatical subject are in the scope of assertion. It is not possible to specify lexical or structural constraints on the verbs of presentationals, because the interpretation of these sentences depends on more than just the verb; it depends on the total context. Although the constraints are not formal in nature, they are consistent with the function of presentationals, namely, that of heralding the referent of the NP into the world of discourse. The appropriateness and abundance of spatial and temporal adverbials in presentationals also follows from the presentative function. These adverbs relativize the existential assertion by locating the referent of the NP in space or time. Again, there is no way to constrain the type of adverbial that might appear in a presentational sentence. In general, any adverbial is compatible with presentationals provided it does not detract from the main function of these sentences.

Thus, a type of sentence is being examined in which factors of a different nature (lexical, structural, contextual, etc.) must converge so that the total meaning--that of introducing the NP referent into the world of discourse--manifests itself explicitly.

2.2 Presentationals vs. declaratives. This section explores several phenomena which confirm the hypothesis that presentational sentences are distinct from declaratives.

2.2.1 Word order. The importance of word order was discussed in Section 2.1.1. While the normal word order for presentationals is verb-subject (or even more generally, V NP), that of declaratives is subject-verb. Consider (44) vs. (45).

(44) Llegó el tren.   Presentational, VS
   arrived (3 sg.) the train
   'The train arrived.'

(45) El tren llegó.   Declarative, SV
      'The train arrived (3 sg.).'

In Section 2.1.1 it was also hypothesized that these different
word orders are reflected in the LFs of these two types of
sentences, and that the scope of the assertion (i.e. the rheme)
can be read from those LFs.

2.2.2 **Stress and focus.** As a consequence of the difference
in word order, and in keeping with the principle of neutral
(i.e. noncontrastive) stress assignment, sentential stress falls
on the subject noun in presentationals (i.e. tren in (44)) but
on the verb in (intransitive) declaratives (i.e. llegó in (45)).
In other words, stress assignment applies regularly, and the
last elements in (44) and (45) get sentential stress. However,
since the last element in each of the foregoing sentences is a
constituent of a different nature (subject vs. verb), stress becomes correlated with the information load of each sentence
type. Presentationals announce the appearance on the scene
of the referent of the NP. Thus, the noun is stressed and in
focus; the verb is semantically weak and nondynamic (cf. Section 2.1.2), although it is still part of the rheme. On the
other hand, declaratives presuppose the existence of the subject referent and emphasize the verbal activity; thus, the verb
gets the main stress. These patterns show that the focus of a
presentational sentence is the subject NP, while the focus of
declarative sentences is in the VP. Deviations from these stress
patterns result either in ungrammaticality (cf. (46)) or in a
contrastive utterance (cf. (47)).

(46)   *LLEGO el tren.

(47)   EL TREN llegó. (vs. el ómnibus 'bus' or anything
        else)
       'The train arrived.'

Observe that the subject NP el tren receives sentential stress
in both (44) and (47). However, this stress is contrastive in
(47), while it simply represents the neutral stress pattern for
presentationals in (44). Therefore, (44) carries no contrastive
implication; it merely implies that the subject NP is the semantic
'focus', the highlighted part of the utterance.[29]
    The significance of word order and its correlation with focus
and stress (under conditions of neutral stress and intonation)
are evidenced in example (48).

(48)   La guerra acabó y ahora sonríe la paz. (H 18)
       The war ended (3 sg.) and now smiles (3 sg.) the peace
       'The war ended and now peace is smiling.'

The first conjunct in (48) is a declarative sentence; focus (and stress) fall on the verb, which signals the end of the referent of the unasserted NP subject (guerra). In the second conjunct the spotlight falls on paz; this is the most important part of this message. The main task of the verb (sonreír 'to smile') is to introduce the subject NP; its weakened lexical content is a simple overtone of haber 'there be' or existir 'to exist'. The perfect balance of this conjoined structure, with its focus on the verb in the first portion but on the NP in the second, succinctly illustrates the differences between declaratives and presentationals.

2.2.3 The *hacerlo* construction.[30] There is a curious difference in behavior between declaratives and presentationals with respect to the hacerlo construction. In declaratives, it is possible to replace (part of) a VP in the second conjunct of a sentence with lo plus the verb hacer 'to do, make' in the appropriate tense, aspect, and mood. For example, the sentences in (49) can be restated as in (50).

(49a) Pepe compró una casa y Paco también compró una casa.
'Pepe bought a house and Paco also bought a house.'

(49b) Pepe llegó con María y Paco llegó con Trini.
'Pepe arrived with Maria and Paco arrived with Trini.'

(50a) Pepe compró una casa y Paco también lo hizo.
'Pepe bought a house and Paco also did (it).'

(50b) Pepe llegó con María y Paco lo hizo con Trini.
'Pepe arrived with Maria and Paco did (it) with Trini.'

It is not possible to resort to the same kind of operation in presentational sentences. Notice that the sentences in (51) cannot be reworded as in (52).

(51a) Sobraba dinero y también sobraba tiempo.
was-in-excess money and also was-in-excess time
'There was money to spare and there was also time to spare.'

(51b) Comenzó el año y también comenzaron mis vacaciones.
started (3 pl.) the year and also started (3 sg.) my vacations
'The year started and my vacations also started.'

(52a) *Sobraba dinero y también lo hacía tiempo.
was-in-excess money and also did so (3 sg.) time

(52b) *Comenzó el año y también lo hicieron mis vacaciones.[31]
started (3 sg.) the year and also did so (3 pl.) my vacations.

The examples in (52) clearly show that presentationalism is in conflict with the hacerlo construction. Moreover, the sentences in (53) may be interpreted as either presentational or contrastive.

(53a) Brillaba la luna y también brillaba Venus.
shone (3 sg.) the moon and also shone (3 sg.) Venus
'The moon was shining and Venus was also shining.'

(53b) Apareció un fantasma y luego apareció el maestro de ceremonias.
appeared (3 sg.) a ghost and then appeared (3 sg.) the master of ceremonies.
'A ghost appeared and then the master of ceremonies appeared.'

The sentences with hacerlo in (54), however, can only be interpreted as contrastive, since what is being asserted is the identification of the NPs with some x^{32} and not the appearance of the NP referent in the world of discourse.

(54a) Brillaba la luna y también $\begin{cases} \text{lo hacía Venus.} \\ \text{Venus lo hacía.} \end{cases}$
'The moon was shining and so was Venus.'

(54b) Apareció un fantasma y luego lo hizo el maestro de ceremonias.
'A ghost appeared and then the master of ceremonies did so.'

To what can this difference in behavior be attributed? There is a very natural semantic answer to this puzzle. It should be remembered that the verbs in presentationals are semantically weak, and that they deemphasize dynamicity (Section 2.1.2) precisely because they are only the means by which the referent of the NP is introduced on the scene. Hence, these non-dynamic verbs cannot be appropriately replaced by such a dynamic action verb as hacer 'to do, make'. On the other hand, the hacerlo construction is perfectly harmonious with most declarative sentences, because the verbs in this type of sentence keep their full lexical force. In other words, hacerlo requires an action verb as its antecedent, which explains its incompatibility with the stative interpretation given to verbs in presentational sentences.[33] Moreover, this pro-VP expression assigns the property of the verb it replaces to the logical subject. However, presentational sentences do not have a logical subject; strictly speaking, only e (i.e. an empty category) is in that position at the level of LF. Therefore, since it makes no sense to interpret the VP as a property of e,[34] presentational sentences are incompatible with hacerlo.

2.2.4 Scope of negation. It has been noted repeatedly in the literature that the scope of negation differs in declaratives and presentationals (Givón 1975b, Babby 1980, Guéron 1978). This difference in scope also correlates with the difference in rheme of these two types of sentences. Recalling that the rheme of an affirmative presentational sentence coincides with the scope of assertion (cf. Section 0.1.2) and that 'in the case of negation the assertion is negated' (Jackendoff 1972:257), it becomes feasible to state that the scope of negation in a negative assertive sentence is defined by the scope of assertion of the corresponding affirmative sentence (Babby 1980). In other words, what is negated is the rheme of the sentence. Consider examples (55) and (56).

(55a) [Apareció Paco]$_{Rh}$ Presentational
appeared (3 sg.) Paco
'Paco appeared.'

(55b) No [apareció Paco]
not appeared (3 sg.) Paco
'Paco didn't appear.'

(56a) Paco [llegó]$_{Rh}$ Declarative
Paco arrived (3 sg.)

(56b) Paco no [llegó]
Paco not arrived (3 sg.)
'Paco didn't arrive.'

In the presentational (55b) the negative particle no denies the rheme, which consists of the verb plus the NP subject; while in the declarative (56b) no denies only the act of arrival specified by the rhematic verb. Intuitively, this is correct. As noted by Jackendoff (1972:349), the scope of negation 'consists of everything commanded by the negative morpheme and to its right'.

The foregoing discussion entails that NEG is an operator which may command either S or VP. This is the same conclusion reached by Guéron (1978:13). She maintains that it is impossible to have instances of VP negation in presentational sentences. The only type of negation left, then, is sentence negation. This contention becomes transparent if one analyzes the LFs of both (55b) and (56b).[35]

(57) LF of (55b)
$[_{S'}NO[_S[_{NP}...e_i...] [_{VP}(_{VP}$apareció) $(\underline{Paco_i})]]]$[36]
Focus

(58) LF of (56b)

$$[_{S'}[_S(\text{Paco})\ \text{NO}\ [_{VP}\underline{\text{llegó}}]]]$$
$$\phantom{[_{S'}[_S(\text{Paco})\ \text{NO}\ [_{VP}}\underset{\text{Focus}}{}$$

Example (57) cannot represent an instance of VP negation because NO has been extracted and commands the whole sentence;
both the verb and the grammatical subject (in this case Paco)
are within its scope.[37] Consequently, sentence negation results.[38]

By contrast, (58) exemplifies a case of VP negation, in which
the unasserted subject NP is both outside the VP and outside
the rheme, and as a result outside the scope of negation.

2.2.5 Recapitulation. Four criteria that distinguish declaratives from presentationals have been surveyed: word order,
stress and focus, the hacerlo Pro-VP expression, and scope of
negation. Together they formally confirm the intuition that one
is dealing with two different sentence types. Moreover, they
give support to the different LFs postulated for these two sentence types. At the same time, the post-LF theme/rheme concepts help us see the very tight correlation that exists between
the scope of assertion and 'informativeness.'

2.3 Subject Postposing. Taking into account that the presentational sentences under study in this chapter have a surface word order of Verb + Subject, three questions need to be
answered. (1) Is a rule necessary or could presentationals be
directly generated in the base? (2) If a rule is necessary, what
type of rule would it be? (3) Provided there is a rule of Subject Postposing, what would its effect be?

2.3.1 Base generation or movement rule. It might be argued
that since the characteristic word order of these presentational
sentences is V(erb) S(ubject), they should be base-generated,
in which case no movement rule would be involved. If this
hypothesis is accepted, the underlying word order for presentationals would differ from the characteristic word order displayed by active declaratives, which is SVO. In other words,
this proposal would make the claim that Spanish word order
manifests a markedly ergative pattern in which objects of
transitive clauses and subjects of intransitive clauses would
occupy the same position.

There are several problems with this proposal. In the next
paragraphs I show that adoption of such a pattern for underlying word order can only lead to loss of generalizations.

2.3.1.1 Word order and grammatical relations. In the first
place, although it is definitely correct to claim that the characteristic word order for the presentationals in this chapter is VS,
the same cannot be maintained for haber presentationals. The
latter type exhibit VO word order. Nonetheless, in both cases

the sentences are undoubtedly presentational in nature. Therefore, a linguistic generalization is missed if one clings to grammatical relations as the way to capture the presentational
character of these sentences. Grammatical relations are to a
certain extent a consequence of the lexical items themselves:
it is a fact of Spanish that impersonal haber is a subjectless
verb (cf. Section 1.1.1.2); therefore it cannot adopt VS word
order. It is also a fact of the verbs discussed in this chapter
that they take only one NP argument and that this argument is
the grammatical subject; consequently, given the relative 'freedom' of word order in Spanish, they can and often do conform
to VS word order. But what is crucial for presentationals is
that they introduce the referent of the NP into the world of
discourse, and this is done *regardless* of the grammatical function of the NP. That both hay and these mostly intransitive
verbs are chosen to introduce the referent of the NP is a
logical consequence of their 'uni-argument' nature, which allows
them to introduce only one NP. This single NP then appears
in focus position in the rheme.

2.3.1.2 Lexical classification. Secondly, 'presentationalism'
is not an inherent feature of intransitive verbs. On the contrary, as was shown repeatedly during the development of this
chapter, presentationalism depends on the interpretation of the
entire sentence. Thus, although an intransitive verb exhibiting
VS word order normally triggers a presentational interpretation
for the utterance, this is by no means the only word order
shown by intransitive verbs. They can also display SV word
order (cf. discussion of example (48)). As a matter of fact,
it is not unusual to find a verb exhibiting both word orders
in a single passage.

(59) A. --Acaba de llegar mi primo.
         finished (3 sg.) of to-arrive my cousin
         'My cousin has just arrived.'

     B. --¿Cómo?
         'How?'

     A. --Llegó en el avión de las diez.
         He-arrived (3 sg.) in the plane of the ten
         'He arrived on the ten o'clock plane.'

In the first sentence speaker A introduces the NP referent mi
primo with the verb llegar 'to arrive', and the word order is
VS. To speaker B's question A replies with the same verb but
with the different word order SV, because it is no longer mi
primo which is in focus (on the contrary, he is presupposed)
but the means of transport. The exchange in (59) illustrates
one of the principles of discourse: rhematic material tends to
become thematic in subsequent sentences.

Consequently, it would be inaccurate to claim that the typical word order for intransitive verbs is VS, because they do also exhibit SV word order.[39] Furthermore, even if this difficulty were disregarded, there still remains another stumbling block. Suppose one assumes that the underlying word order for presentationals is VS. How is this to be captured? As established in Section 2.1.2, it is impossible to provide an airtight classification for all and only those verbs used in presentational constructions.

Summing up, to claim that the basic word order for all intransitive verbs is VS would be inaccurate, since they do appear with SV word order as well. To claim that underlying VS word order is an exclusive property of presentational verbs is fruitless, because presentationalism is not a feature of verbs but an interpretation which depends on the entire sentence and on discourse factors.

2.3.1.3 Transitives in presentationals. Finally, basic word order is further complicated when one considers transitive verbs that may be used intransitively in presentationals (cf. (25)), or expressions with transitive verbs such as dar señales de vida, which may be used as equivalent to 'to appear' and can thus be semantically intransitive (cf. Section 2.1.3).

In the first case, the adoption of underlying VS word order for intransitive verbs would force us to enter verbs such as habitar 'to inhabit', romper 'to break', subir 'to ascend', etc., in two different types of configurations--VS and SVO--which are not collapsible by any of the usual abbreviatory devices.[40] Hence, a generalization would be lost: the two configurations would make it seem like an accident that the verbs (in their transitive and intransitive usage) have the same phonological and morphological shape and, to a great degree, the same semantic range. Furthermore, this might imply an unnatural (and unnecessary, I may add) duplication of lexical entries in the generative dictionary: each transitive verb which enters into presentational constructions might need to be listed twice, once in its transitive usage and once in its presentational usage.

The case of dar señales de vida and other expressions is similar to the foregoing, although it is compounded by the fact that in this instance the object of the verb is always present (see examples (32) and (33) in Section 2.1.3). These expressions would also require a double lexical listing plus the two (unrelatable) configurations SVO and VOS. Should it turn out that the idiomatic reading of these expressions was based on an analysis of them as complex verbs, double listing with two different word orders (SVO and VS) would still be mandatory.[41]

In summarizing this section, one must conclude that base-generation of the VS order results in a loss of linguistic generalizations, creates unnecessary duplications, and attempts to place on the verb a presentational reading which is not in fact verb-specific but rather sentence- and discourse-dependent (cf. Sections 2.1.2, 2.1.3, and 2.1.4). To put it differently, base-generation of VS pushes to the lexical level the dichotomy of theme/rheme, which is much more appropriately handled at the post-LF sentence level of analysis. All of these facts point in the same direction: the word order VS must not be basic but must be derived by a movement rule.

  2.3.2 Type of rule. Having demonstrated that base-generation of VS word order has unwanted implications for the grammar of Spanish, one must now consider the possibility of deriving presentationals through a movement rule. At this point, I assume without further discussion that the underlying or basic word order for Spanish is SVO (but see Chapter 4 for a detailed discussion), and that the VS order displayed by presentationals is arrived at by a movement rule which postposes the subject.
  Central to this section is the consideration of what type of rule Subject Postposing (SP) might be. Two possibilities become immediately apparent: either SP is a stylistic rule or it is a grammatical rule.

  2.3.2.1 Stylistic rules. Emonds (1976:9-11) describes some of the formal properties of stylistic rules.[42] They apply after all other syntactic transformations (including Agreement and Case Assignment); they cannot introduce or delete morphemes (except under identity); they cannot be triggered by a specific morpheme; and they obey some version of the 'up-to-ambiguity' principle. They apply more readily in literary and poetic style than in conversational language, and normally 'their inputs appear to be systematically as acceptable or more acceptable than their outputs'.
  Rochemont (1978) argues that stylistic rules apply to surface structures and do not interact with formal syntactic or semantic processes. Moreover, 'stylistic rules are discourse bound, in the sense that the acceptability of sentences derived by the application of stylistic rules is crucially dependent upon their appropriateness to the contexts of utterance' (1978:V).[43]
  Given these properties of stylistic rules, could it be the case that Subject Postposing qualifies as a stylistic rule? I consider some of the aforementioned properties before coming to a decision. The discussion is divided into three subsections: general properties, syntactic properties, and semantic properties. This examination forces us to conclude that Subject Postposing cannot be a stylistic rule.

  2.3.2.1.1 General properties. Recall that Subject Postposing is the movement rule which derives the V NP word order associated with (intransitive) presentational sentences. This rule does not create any differences in acceptability between the input and the output: example (60a) is as well formed and as acceptable as (60b).

(60a) Paco apareció.
      'Paco appeared.'

(60b) Apareció Paco.
      appeared Paco

What happens is that these sentences are interpreted as different sentence types; as such they are used under different situations, because their information load is different. Therefore,
Subject Postposing is not a stylistic rule in the sense that the
input is just as acceptable as the output.

Moreover, the way this property of stylistic rules is stated
gives the impression that the input is basic. Although I
assume that the basic word order for Spanish is SVO, I would
not want to claim that presentationals are derived from another
type of sentence (such as declaratives, for instance). The way
I envision the process is that there is a nonsurface structure,
such as (61) (details omitted), to which Subject Postposing may
apply.

(61)

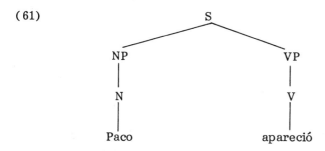

If it does apply, focus assignment falls on the postposed subject and the sentence is eventually interpreted as presentational.
If Subject Postposing does not apply, focus falls on the V and
the sentence is interpreted as declarative. In other words, although it might be true that a presentational and a declarative
sentence might have had the same underlying (or nonsurface,
in any case) origin, there is no stage in the derivation in which
one is derived from the other because sentence-type interpretation does not take place until the level of total semantic interpretation, that is, the level SI-2 in the EST model (cf. Section
2.4 for discussion).

Let us now examine Rochemont's claim that stylistic rules are
discourse bound. I find this characterization too broad to help
in discriminating between stylistic and grammatical rules. To a
degree, most if not all movement transformations seem to be
'dependent upon their appropriateness to the contexts of utterance'. For example, Williams (1977:102-103) mentions the
following 'discourse conditioned' rules: Passive, WH-Movement
in questions, Topicalization, Clefting, and Pseudoclefting.[44]
That is to say, these rules are sentence-grammar rules (as is

Subject Postposing), and not discourse-grammar rules. Naturally, when placed into connected contexts, the product of any
of these rules might be judged inappropriate.

(62a) A: What did John do?
(62b) B: ??The artwork was done by John.
(62c) B: John did the artwork.

Although both (62b) and (62c) are grammatical sentences,
(62b) is inappropriate as an answer to the question posited in
(62a).
Certainly, the same type of inappropriateness might arise in
connection with Subject Postposing.

(63a) Finalmente apareció el tren.
finally appeared the train.
'Finally the train appeared.'

(63b) Llegó el tren con tres horas de retraso.
arrived the train with three hours of delay.
'The train arrived three hours late.'

(63c) Llegó con tres horas de retraso.
it-arrived with three hours of delay
'It arrived three hours late.'

Within the discourse, (63c) may be a more 'natural' or appropriate sequel to an opening statement such as (63a). Because
el tren has already been introduced in (63a), it should become,
following one of the unwritten conventions of discourse, part of
the theme in the follow-up sentence. Notice that the inappropriateness of both (62b) and (63b) seems connected to the role of
focus assignment. In sum, 'discourse-boundness' is not an exclusive trait of stylistic rules, since syntactic rules are affected in the same way. Hence, this property is not useful
for segregating stylistic from syntactic rules.

2.3.2.1.2 Syntactic properties. Stylistic rules are said to
apply after all other syntactic transformations, including Agreement and Case Assignment; or, in Rochemont's words, they do
not interact with formal syntactic processes. This is a point
which may be hard to prove or disprove conclusively. If
transformations form an unordered set (Chomsky 1980a and
references therein, Chomsky and Lasnik 1977), and if Subject
Postposing is a transformation (as I believe it is), then I do
not think there is any way of knowing exactly when Subject
Postposing applies. I have not been able to find any conclusive evidence which shows that Subject Postposing must apply
either before or after Agreement and Case Marking in Spanish,[45]
but such evidence does exist in other languages, a fact which
might provide a clue to the status of some reordering rules in

general. For example, in Zenéyse (the dialect spoken around Genoa, Italy) the position of the subject with respect to the verb affects Subject-Verb Agreement, so that subject placement must operate before Subject-Verb Agreement (Browne and Vattuone 1975). And in Russian, Case Assignment in existential sentences varies, depending on whether the subject is in the scope of negation or not; hence Case Assignment must apply after the positioning of the subject (Babby 1978 and 1980). Moreover, Babby (1980:226) mentions that in certain Russian dialects the verb is automatically marked with the third person singular neuter ending (i.e. it does not agree with its subject) whenever the subject is part of the rheme. Thus, although there is no conclusive evidence of which I am aware to test the relative ordering of Subject Postposing, Agreement, and Case Assignment in Spanish, evidence from other 'free word order' languages seems to indicate that positioning of the subject (whether by a postposing or a preposing rule) can certainly play a role in Agreement and Case Marking.

More interesting, from the point of view of Spanish, might be the interaction of Subject Postposing with Head Start. It has been hypothesized that Head Start is a transformation which preposes the embedded subject to preverbal position without triggering verb agreement in the matrix subject (Aissen and Perlmutter 1976). Example (64b) is obtained by this rule from the structure in (64a).

(64a) Parece que los invitados llegarán tarde.
  it-seems that the guests will-arrive (3 pl.) late
  'It appears that the guests will arrive late.'

(64b) Los invitados parece que llegarán tarde.
  the guests it-seems (3 sg.) that will-arrive (3 pl.) late
  'The guests, it seems that they will arrive late.'

Let us observe what happens when the subject of the embedded clause has been postposed, that is, when the embedded clause is presentational.[46]

(65a) $\left.\begin{array}{l}\text{Parece}\\\text{Resulta}\end{array}\right\}$que a las ocho aparecerá el cometa.
  it-turns out that at 8 o'clock will-appear (3 sg.) the comet

(65b) ??El cometa $\left\{\begin{array}{l}\text{parece}\\\text{resulta}\end{array}\right\}$ que a las ocho aparecerá Δ.
  the comet it-turns-out that at 8 o'clock will-appear
  (3 sg.)

(66a) De repente resulta que a la puerta ya estaban los
      invitados.
      suddenly it-appears that at the door already were
      the guests

(66b) ??De repente los invitados resulta que a la puerta ya
      estaban Δ.
      suddenly the guests it-appears that at the door
      already were

On the basis of examples like (65) and (66), it seems that
once Subject Postposing has operated, the subject is no longer
available to the Head Start process. This impression is confirmed by examples (67) and (68), which show that Head Start
applies without any difficulties when the embedded clause is
declarative.

(67a) $\left.\begin{matrix} \text{Parece} \\ \text{Resulta} \end{matrix}\right\}$ que el cometa aparecerá a las ocho.
      'It appears that the comet will appear at 8 o'clock.'

(67b) El cometa $\left\{\begin{matrix} \text{parece} \\ \text{resulta} \end{matrix}\right\}$ que Δ aparecerá a las ocho.
      'The comet, it appears that (it) will appear at
      8 o'clock.'

(68a) De repente resulta que los invitados ya estaban a la
      puerta.
      'Suddenly it-appears that the guests already were at
      the door.'

(68b) De repente los invitados resulta que Δ ya estaban a la
      puerta.
      'Suddenly the guests, it-appears that (they) already
      were at the door.'

Examples (67) through (68) therefore seem to demonstrate that
Subject Postposing must apply before Head Start, thereby bleed-
ing possible sequences from the realm of this rule. This proposal is inviting because it would supply some evidence to show
that Subject Postposing operates before another syntactic rule.
However, I do not think it provides the correct analysis.
    If Head Start were a movement rule, it would be in violation
of the Propositional Island Condition (PIC) (Chomsky 1977b),
since it extracts the embedded NP subject out of a tensed
clause.[47] This fact has led Rivero (1980) to hypothesize that
examples like those found in (67b) and (68b) are instances of
Left-Dislocations with a structure like that in (69).

(69) $_{S''}[_{TOP}[\ldots] \; _{S'}[_{COMP}[\ldots] \; _S[\ldots \left\{\begin{matrix}\text{Pro}\\\text{NP}\end{matrix}\right\}]]]$

That is to say, the NPs el cometa and los invitados are base-generated in TOP position, there is a pronoun or an epithet in the embedded S, and a rule of semantic interpretation establishes the required anaphoric relation. But there is no pronoun in either (67b) or (68b). On the basis of similar examples, Rivero claims that the base-generated subject pronoun is deleted by the very general rule that applies to nonemphatic subject pronouns. Therefore, (67b) and (68b) would at one point have the structures found in (70) and (71), respectively.

(70)   El cometa parece que él aparecerá a las ocho.

(71)   Los invitados resulta que ellos ya estaban a la puerta.

The pronoun in (70) must delete, because normally surface subject pronouns are not used in Spanish to refer to inanimate referents; (71) is a perfectly grammatical sentence. Rivero provides us with other examples of Left-Dislocation in which the subject pronoun is retained at the surface level.

(72)   Esos hombres, dice María que ellos no pueden votar.
       'Those men, María says that they cannot vote.'

(73)   Juan, lo que dicen que parece que él quiere estudiar
       es la biología.
       'Juan, what they say that it seems that he wants to
       study is biology.'

Although this Left-Dislocation analysis accounts for the data without violating PIC, and thus is to be preferred, there still remain the less than felicitous examples in (65b) and (66b), repeated here as (74) and (75).

(74)   ??El cometa parece que a las ocho aparecerá Δ.
       the comet it seems that at 8 o'clock will-appear
       (3 sg.)

(75)   ??Los invitados resulta que a la puerta ya estaban Δ.
       the guests it-turns-out that at the door already
       were (3 pl.)

One can 'restore' the subject pronouns in an attempt to improve the grammaticality of the sentences (I am replacing the inanimate el cometa by el mago 'the magician' so that the subject pronoun is acceptable at the surface level).

(76)   ??El mago parece que a las ocho aparecerá él.

(77)   ??Los invitados resulta que a la puerta ya estaban
       ellos.

As seen in (76) and (77), even the pronouns do not make the sentences less awkward.

Summarizing, I have discussed two analyses that have appeared in the literature. According to Head Start, examples (64b), (67b), and (68b) are generated by a movement rule; according to Left-Dislocation, these sentences are base-generated. Nonetheless, the fact remains that the outcome is not fully grammatical if the embedded sentence is presentational (cf. (74), (75), (76), and (77)). Within the Head Start analysis, a plausible explanation is that after Subject Postposing has operated, the embedded subject is out of the reach of other movement rules. Within the Left-Dislocation analysis, one might hypothesize that Subject Postposing somehow impedes the establishment of the anaphoric relation between the phrase in TOP position and the subject pronoun.[48] The first case would show the interaction of Subject Postposing with another syntactic rule, the second the interplay of Subject Postposing with semantic interpretation (i.e. with the binding of the phrase in TOP to S).

The second proposal is not only consistent with the EST but also more explanatory if one also takes into account the theme/ rheme status of sentences like (74) to (77). Left-Dislocated structures are inherently thematic, that is, they are never in the asserted part of the sentence. On the other hand, the NP subject of the embedded presentational sentences under discussion is in the scope of assertion, that is, it is rhematic.[49] This creates a conflict of interest because 'linkage' must be established between a preposed theme and a postposed rheme, and the resulting sentence is less than felicitous.[50] This explanation once again underlines the role of theme/rheme in linguistic analysis and, although it does not support the interaction of Subject Postposing with another syntactic rule, it provides evidence of its interaction with rules of interpretation (the topic of the next subsection).

2.3.2.1.3 Semantic properties.

Finally, I want to investigate the claim that stylistic rules do not interact with construal. In relation to the problem that concerns us here, this means that Subject Postposing qualifies as a stylistic rule if it does not interplay with the semantic processes exclusive to sentence grammar, that is, with LF.[51]

In the first place, and assuming the model of grammar put forth by Chomsky (Chomsky 1976, Chomsky and Lasnik 1977, and references therein), I show that questions of scope, such as Neg-Interpretation and the interpretation of quantifiers, interact in a crucial way with Subject Postposing. As noted in Section 2.2.4, the scope of negation is not the same in declarative and presentational sentences. What is negated in both instances is the rheme. But while the rheme of a declarative sentence is the VP, that of a presentational sentence

encompasses the VP and the postverbal subject NP. This may
be represented schematically as follows:

Declarative: NP no̲ [VP]$_{Rh}$

Presentational: no̲ [VP NP]$_{Rh}$

Hence, under conditions of noncontrastive stress and intonation, VP negation obtains in declaratives while sentence negation obtains in presentationals. Therefore, the two different
word orders must be made available before Neg-Interpretation
can take place, which in turn means that Subject Postposing
must have applied before rules of semantic interpretation can
start operating to render LFs.
   A completely parallel argument can be made with other quantifiers in relation to their scope, as shown in example (78).

(78a) A la tarde pasan $\begin{Bmatrix} \text{muchos} \\ \text{tres} \end{Bmatrix}$ trenes.

       in the afternoon pass (3 pl.) $\begin{Bmatrix} \text{many} \\ \text{three} \end{Bmatrix}$ trains

(78b) $\begin{Bmatrix} \text{Muchos} \\ \text{Tres} \end{Bmatrix}$ trenes pasan a la tarde.

       $\begin{Bmatrix} \text{'Many} \\ \text{'Three} \end{Bmatrix}$ trains pass (3 pl.) in the afternoon.'

In (78a) muchos and tres form part of the scope of assertion
of the sentence, and the quantifiers are interpreted noncon-
trastively as stating that 'In the afternoon, the trains that go
by are many/three'. In (78b), on the other hand, the quantifiers are outside of the rheme, and the reading that obtains
can be best expressed as 'Many/Three among the trains are
such that they go by in the afternoon'. In other words, only
in (78b) do the quantifiers act as restricted modifiers which
establish an implied contrast with some total. Since this difference in the scope of the quantifiers depends crucially on the
word orders exemplified in (78), Subject Postposing must have
applied before quantifier interpretation. Hence Subject Postposing interacts with rules of semantic interpretation.
   Lastly, it seems that the rule of Focus Assignment must apply
before the level of LF. Understanding focus according to the
definition in Section 0.1.3 (i.e. the 'information point' of a sentence), and restricting ourselves to the type of focused element
that eventually receives the noncontrastive sentential stress,
this rule of Focus Assignment must be one of the rules of semantic interpretation that operates on S-structures and is sensitive to structural configurations. What this rule would do is
assign focus to the NP which follows the VP in the structure
$[[t_i] \text{ VP NP}_i]_S$ and assign focus to the VP in the structure

[NP VP]$_S$. In other words, (unmarked) focus is established solely on the basis of the surface configuration; in a sense it is predetermined by the configuration itself. But notice that configurations can only predetermine (unmarked) focus assignment if the postposing of the subject has already taken place, a fact which indicates that Subject Postposing must have already operated by the time the derivation reaches the level of surface structure.

Observe that if one assumes that Subject Postposing is a stylistic rule, normal focus assignment would apply beforehand. It would automatically fall on the VP (as predetermined by the configuration), then the stylistic rule of Subject Postposing would apply, and, since the original focus (F_1) would be incorrect, a second ('corrective') rule of focus (F_2) would need to operate. The sentence would consequently have two focused segments. This is shown schematically in (79).

(79a) Un fantasma apareció   SS
'A ghost appeared (3 sg.).'
↓
(79b) Un fantasma APARECIO. F_1
↓
(79c) APARECIO un fantasma.   Stylistic rule of Subject
↓   Postposing

(79d) APARECIO un FANTASMA. F_2

Example (79d) illustrates the conflict in focus assignment that would result if Subject Postposing were a stylistic rule. How could this conflict be resolved?

One could say that F_2 prevails because it is the last focus assigned. This 'solution' would solve the present problem but would create others in the area of contrastive stress. Consider a sentence like (80).

(80) Sólo Paco apareció.
'Only Paco appeared.'

The sentence in (80) is contrastive: heavy stress falls on Paco (sólo 'only' is one of the elements that attract focus; see Chapter 3 for further discussion). Observe how focus assignment could proceed in this type of example.

(81a) Sólo Paco apareció.   SS
↓
(81b) Sólo Paco APARECIO. F_1
↓
(81c) Sólo PACO APARECIO F_2
↓
(81d) Sólo PACO apareció.   C

In (81b) the regular rule of focus assignment based on surface configuration applies; since there is only a verb in the VP, it receives focus (F_1). In (81c), F_2, sensitive to sólo, applies and creates a conflict in focus. The output in (81d) exemplifies the solution to the conflict: F_2 prevails over F_1, but the outcome is contrastive focus (C), and not unmarked focus. In this way one has an intuitively satisfying way (although admittedly very sketchy) of dealing with contrastive focus as opposed to unmarked focus.[52]

Contrastive focus does not depend on structural configurations; it depends on lexical items, beliefs, discourse properties, etc. Hence it might belong to a realm different from sentence grammar. Notice that sentences with contrastive focus are more 'loaded'; they contain more assumptions than noncontrastive sentences do. For example, (81d) is appropriate in a context in which the speaker has assumed that more people than just Paco were going to arrive; or it could be given as an answer to a question like ¿Vino Pepe? 'Did Pepe come?' The person uttering Apareció Paco with normal focus on Paco does not need to presuppose anything; the sentence could be an isolated opening statement.

In sum, normal focus assignment should operate on surface structures on the basis of structural configurations; it belongs to sentence grammar. It should be distinguished from contrastive focus, which is sensitive to conditions other than configurational ones (but see Chapter 4 for further refinements). If this outline of an analysis is on the right track, then one has further evidence for claiming that Subject Postposing is not a stylistic rule but a syntactic rule which must operate before the level of S-structure.

2.3.2.2 Conclusion. It must be clear that throughout this section I have not been arguing against the existence of stylistic rules. What I have been seeking to substantiate is the status of Subject Postposing as a nonstylistic rule. Subject Postposing does not conform to the formal properties assigned in the literature to stylistic rules. First, it does not obey their general characteristics, because it functions at all levels of language, from literary and poetic to conversational. Although it is 'discourse-bounded' as are stylistic rules, it was found here that 'discourse-boundedness' is not a useful trait for distinguishing between stylistic and syntactic rules. Second, although it may not be possible to demonstrate conclusively that Subject Postposing interacts with other syntactic transformations in Spanish, there is some evidence from other languages that subject positioning does indeed play a role in Agreement and in Case Assignment. Furthermore, the rule of Subject Postposing interacts with the semantic interpretation rule which establishes an anaphoric relation between a left-dislocated phrase and an embedded subject pronoun, and with other rules of semantic interpretation such as those that read

the scope of the negative particle no and the scope of other
quantifiers. If it were a stylistic rule, it would have to apply
only after all other syntactic transformations, and could not
interact with formal syntactic or semantic processes. Finally,
it was also hypothesized that the rule of noncontrastive Focus
Assignment must have operated before the level of LF, only on
the basis of structural configurations; in order to generate
correct noncontrastive focus, Subject Postposing must apply
before Focus Assignment.

For all of these reasons, and on the basis of the evidence
examined, it must be concluded that Subject Postposing is a
syntactic rule (see also Section 2.3.3.1.2).

2.3.3 **The rule of Subject Postposing.** In Sections 2.3.1 and
2.3.2 presentational sentences were derived by means of a
movement rule, and furthermore, it was shown that this rule
must be a syntactic rule because it does not comply with the
properties of stylistic rules. This section looks at the formulation of this syntactic movement rule of Subject Postposing,
and discusses its effect on the grammar of presentational sentences in general.

(82) Rule of Subject Postposing (syntactic rule):

$$NP \quad V^n$$

$$1 \quad 2 \quad ==\Rightarrow \quad e \ 2 \ 1$$

Subject Postposing moves the subject NP rightward to a position after V^n,[53] leaving a trace behind in accordance with the
postulates of trace theory. Note, however, that this trace is
in an unorthodox position for traces, since it precedes its
'antecedent' (see Section 2.5 for discussion of the theoretical
implications of this leftward trace). The moved subject NP and
its trace are coindexed by convention (Chomsky 1980a:4).
Rule (82) is another instance of the very generalized rule,
'Move α,' and as such it gives credence to Chomsky's (1976)
hypothesis which aims at restricting the power of transformations. Notice that (82) is strictly local, and that there are no
conditions attached to it. Furthermore, it needs to be emphasized that the rule is formulated to mention V^n specifically in
order to limit this movement rule to NP subjects,[54] for I believe
that there exists a crucial difference in the effects of postposing a subject as opposed to postposing a nonsubject NP. For
example, as discussed in Section 2.3.2.1.3, Subject Postposing
interacts with semantic rules that interpret the scope of negation and of quantifiers in general; this is not necessarily the
case with movement of nonsubject NPs.[55] If I am correct in
assuming that Subject Postposing is a case of 'Move α,' then it
seems to follow that this rule forms part of core grammar.

Since rule (82) is optional, at the level of S-structure the two types of structures in (83) and (84) would have been produced.

(83)   NP   VP   Declarative: no movement rule
        la luna   apareció   involved
        'the moon'   'appeared'

(84)   e$_i$ VP   NP   Presentational: Sub-
                     apareció   la luna   ject Postposing has
                     'appeared'   'the moon'   applied

Before plunging into an extensive discussion of the grammar of presentational sentences, it is imperative to explore the effect of Subject Postposing, with special attention to the topic of the derived structure created by this movement rule.

2.3.3.1 The effect of Subject Postposing. There are several questions that require answers with respect to the posited rule of Subject Postposing: what is its function? does it obey the condition of Subjacency? and what is its structural output?

2.3.3.1.1 Function. In the first place, what is the function or purpose of this rule, and why should Spanish have such a rule, as opposed to a language like English, which does not? The answer to these two questions is rather simple. The rule reorders the elements in a sentence so that the surface structure can comply with the general principle that the most important information, the 'weightiest', comes toward the end of the sentence.[56] Thus, the 'information point', the focused element (which in this case happens to be the grammatical subject) is placed in the most prominent position: toward the end of the sentence. The rule moves the NP subject from an essentially thematic and unasserted site to a rhematic, and therefore asserted, location. In this new location, the NP gets the spotlight, so to speak--the attention consonant with the fact that it is being introduced onto the scene, into the world of discourse. Spanish has this luxury of aligning the surface structure and LF (i.e. sentence semantics) with degree of communicative dynamism (Prague School) precisely because it is a language with relatively free word order. On the other hand, English does not have a similar rule because it is a language with a much more rigid word order; moreover, English requires the subject position to be filled in surface structure.[57]

2.3.3.1.2 Subjacency. Another matter of interest with respect to Subject Postposing is that if it is a syntactic movement rule, it should obey Subjacency. Subjacency was proposed (Chomsky 1973) as a general condition on transformations in order to restrict their application either to a single cyclic node or to immediately adjacent cyclic nodes.

(85) Subjacency (Chomsky 1977b)

A cyclic rule cannot move a phrase from position Y
to position X (or conversely) in:

...X... [$_\alpha$...[$_\beta$...Y...] ...]...X...

where α and β are cyclic nodes.

Subjacency predicts and explains the fact that the subject NP
of S can be postposed within the boundaries of S_1 but not into
S_2, since it would be jumping over two cycles. This prediction
is borne out by the examples in (86).[58]

(86a) Paco apareció cuando nosotros ya estábamos por salir.[59]

'Paco appeared when we were already about to leave.'

(86b) En la última semana, tres accidentes tuvieron lugar

donde está la parada de ómnibus

'During last week, three accidents took place where
the bus stop is.'

Since Subjacency is a property of cyclic rules, it follows that
Subject Postposing applies in embedded as well as matrix sentences. The examples in (87) confirm this hypothesis (postposed subjects are underlined).

(87a) Paco expuso la teoría de que en 1984 aparecería
      un cometa.
      Paco expounded the theory of that in 1984 would-appear
      (3 sg.) a comet

(87b) En 1984 aparecerá un cometa.[60]
      in 1984 will-appear (3 sg.) a comet

The conclusion that Subject Postposing obeys subjacency, a
general condition on transformations, provides a further argument for its status as a syntactic movement rule.[61]

2.3.3.1.3 Derived constituent structure. One very relevant
question concerning the rule of Subject Postposing has to do
with the derived structure created by this rule. The structural
input to the rule is known; but what is the structural output?
Or, stated differently, to what node does the postposed NP
attach? There are two logical possibilities: the subject NP
attaches to the VP, or it attaches to S. The first possibility
breaks down into several options: (1) the movement rule could
be structure-preserving, in the sense of Emonds (1970, 1976),

and it could insert the moved NP into the direct object position
of the VP (Section 2.3.3.1.3.1); (2) the subject NP could be
attached to the existing VP at a higher level than the direct
object position, as made possible by the X̄-theory (Section
2.3.3.1.3.2); (3) the moved element could be attached to S
(Section 2.3.3.1.3.3). Each of these alternatives is examined
in turn.

2.3.3.1.3.1 The traditional structure-preserving alternative.
Within this view, the subject NP moves to an NP position
generatable by the phrase-structure rules within the VP: that
is, the NP is inserted in direct object position.[62]

(88)

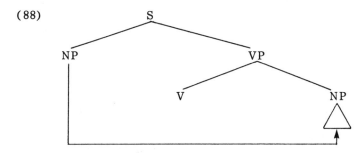

If this were the correct analysis, the fact that verbs used in
presentational sentences (cf. Section 2.1.3) are intransitive
(i.e. never have an object) or are used intransitively (i.e. no
object in the presentational use) would be automatically explained, because if they had a stated object there would be no
empty NP slot into which the subject NP could move. Attractive as this proposal looks at first glance, it is not devoid of
problems.

In the first place, as was already pointed out in Section 2.1.3,
although the great majority of verbs in presentationals are indeed intransitive or used intransitively, it appears that no syntactic conditions should be imposed on the verbs that enter into
presentational constructions due to the existence of expressions
like dar señales de vida which can be used presentationally in
spite of their object argument. Since Subject Postposing may
apply over a direct object and produce grammatical sentences
just in case the sentence is interpreted as presentational by a
rule in SI-2, the presence or absence of an object cannot be
used to explain the ungrammaticality of certain sentences. Of
course, this argument crucially depends on the analysis of expressions like dar señales de vida. There remains the possibility that señales de vida is not a true direct object but rather
the complement of a complex verb. That is, the contrast is
illustrated by [$_{VP}$[$_{V}$dar] [$_{NP}$señales de vida]] vs. [$_{V}$[$_{V}$dar]
[$_{NP}$señales de vida]]. In view of the discussion in Section
2.1.3, where it was shown that (at least) some of these expressions are ambiguous between a literal and an idiomatic reading,

let us assume that these expressions are analyzed both as complex verb and as verb plus true direct object. What remains to be determined is whether this double analysis is already lexical, or whether there is restructuring at some later stage. Since one must wait until SI-2 to interpret a sentence as presentational, the simplest assumption one can make is that only the complex verb analysis is compatible with a presentational reading. This implies that unless the complex verb has been inserted in the base, the sentence does not get a presentational interpretation. Acceptance of this reasoning would remove these expressions from the area of potential problems for the structure-preserving hypothesis.

Nonetheless, problems remain. Setting aside presentational sentences for a moment and taking a wider perspective, it becomes evident that the postposed subject cannot (and should not) be inserted in direct object position.

(89a) Comió <u>Pepe</u> una manzana.
ate Pepe an apple
'Pepe ate an apple.'

(89b) Dijo <u>Paco</u> que ese profesor era un desastre.
said Paco that that professor was a disaster
'Paco said that that professor was a disaster.'

The examples in (89) contain truly transitive sentences, exhibiting the word order verb-subject (underlined)-direct object. Assuming that either the rule of Subject Postposing (82) or a similar rule is responsible for this word order, it becomes evident that the traditional structure-preserving hypothesis does not account for the facts of Spanish.[63]

On a more theoretical level, both Freidin (1978) and Jayaseelan (1979) have pointed out some drawbacks to the traditional structure-preserving hypothesis as conceived by Emonds (1976). Freidin (1978:537) postulates a Functional Uniqueness principle: In a sentence S_i, no lexical NP may fill more than one argument position for any given predicate in the logical form of S_i. This principle rules out movement of the subject NP into object position. Freidin also points out that, under trace theory, rightward movement of an NP (he is discussing NP movement around be) need not be structure-preserving in the sense of Emonds (1976). 'All that is required is that a rule of interpretation maps the moved NP onto an argument position in LF' (1978:544). This observation applies equally well to Subject Postposing in Spanish.

Jayasselan (1979) notes that Emonds makes use of two types of empty nodes: those which are mandatorily ignored by semantics and subcategorization, and those which are mandatorily not ignored. Jayasselan suggests that the only interpretation that should be kept is the one in which empty nodes play a role in both semantics and strict subcategorization (see also

Grimshaw 1979). If his proposal is correct, intransitive verbs in Spanish could never be entered into a tree with an empty object NP.

In conclusion, the foregoing discussion suggests that (88) is not the correct derived structure created by Subject Postposing.

2.3.3.1.3.2 Attachment to VP within the $\bar{X}$-theory. The $\bar{X}$-theory originated with Chomsky (1970) and was developed by Jackendoff (1977).[64] One of its advantages is that it assumes that every lexical category X must be dominated by a hierarchy of categories $X', X'', \ldots X^n$; the number of relevant levels is subject to empirical evidence.[65] Another important asset of the $\bar{X}$-theory is that it eliminates the need for the structure-building capacities of rules (such as what Subject Postposing would need to have if the subject argument were Chomsky-adjoined) by providing enough levels of embeddings from the start to accommodate the relevant data in a principled way.

Assume that the base structure rules of Spanish generate the structure in (90) (leaving open to future research the exact number of levels required for Spanish).

(90)

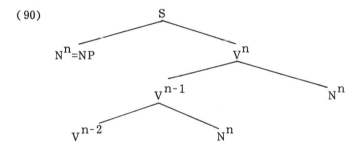

The following trees demonstrate how the data on presentational sentences can be accounted for.[66]

(91) Dio señales de vida mi tío Federico.
gave signs of life my uncle Federico
'My uncle Federico appeared.'

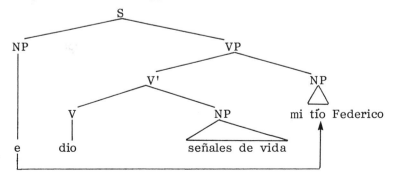

(92)   Concurre con 'menar' en los primeros textos
       medievales 'menear'. (H 18)
       'Menear coincides with menar in the first medieval
       texts.'

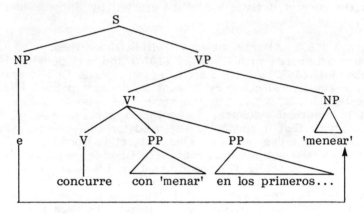

(93)   En ese momento llegó con su entrenador el campeón
       mundial de peso pesado.
       'At that moment the world heavyweight champion arrived
       with his coach.'

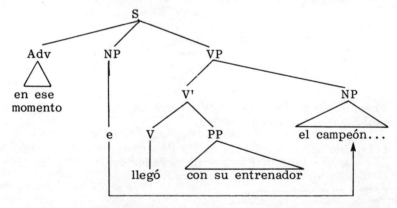

Furthermore, if one assumes that there are VP adverbs as
well as sentence adverbs, this proposal also accounts for the
examples in (94) without any difficulty (cf. Section 2.1.4).

(94a) Aquí sopla el cierzo todo el día. (H 16)
       here blows the cierzo all the day
       'Here, the cierzo blows all day long.'

(94b) ...ya rompieron las hostilidades <u>otra vez</u>. (H 16)
    already broke the hostilities again
    '...The hostilities already started again.'

(94c) Ayer salió su nombramiento <u>en la Gaceta</u>. (H 13)
    yesterday appeared his appointment in the Gazette

The subject NP would be attached to a VP level and the underlined adverbial would be directly attached to S. This is shown
schematically in (95).

(95)

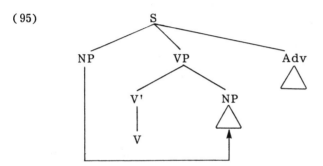

But what distinguishes sentences like those in (94) with a
sentence-final adverbial from those in (96), in which the adverbial occurs before the postposed subject?

(96a) Acaba de entrar <u>en el parque</u> la carroza... (H 10)
    'The coach has just entered the park.'

(96b) ...penetraba <u>en el alma de aquellos hombres</u> un
    sentimiento romántico. (H 11)
    'A romantic feeling penetrated the souls of those men.'

(96c) ...cayeron <u>de sus ojos</u> unas como escamas. (H 21)
    'Something like scales fell from his eyes.'

Is there any independent evidence to prove that the first are
sentence adverbs while the latter are VP adverbs? Kuno (1975)
has already recognized the difficulties in providing independent
evidence. He states that since most sentences which exhibit
the pattern of <u>She was robbed in London</u> (i.e. Subj. V Adv.)
are potentially ambiguous, 'all syntactic tests which are expected to distinguish between constituents and nonconstituents
or between higher adverbs and lower adverbs end up applying
indiscriminately to all such sentences' (1975:167).
    Thus, in Spanish one finds pairs of examples like those in
(97) through (99), where the adverbial expression surfaces at
times in final position and at other times in what looks like VP
position.

(97a) ...ya rompieron las hostilidades <u>otra vez</u>. (H 16)
     already broke-out the hostilities again

(97b) Estallaban <u>otra vez</u> las risas. (H 16)
     burst again the laughs

(98a) ...desde que cayera la revista <u>en sus manos</u>. (H 12)
     since that fell (subjunctive) the magazine in his
     hands
     'since the magazine fell into his hands'.

(98b) Comenzaban a caer <u>en el redondel</u> botellas, naranjas
     y... (H 12)
     started to fall in the ring bottles, oranges and...

(99a) Entonces comenzó una lluvia de proyectiles <u>sobre la
     gente</u>. (H 8)
     then started a rain of projectiles on the people

(99b) ...empezaron a llover <u>sobre ellos</u> cuentas que habían
     quedado pendiente de pago. (H 16)
     started to rain on them bills that had remained
     unpaid

Granted that in some instances, given the relative freedom of word order that Spanish exhibits, the adverbials could have been moved around the postposed subject by a late stylistic rule. The motivation for such a rule remains a mystery to me, however. For example, the 'heaviness' of the constituent cannot be consistently adduced because, even though someone might want to use this concept to explain (99b), 'heaviness' would not account for (99a), or for (97a) vs. (97b). And alongside examples like those in (100), one finds those in (101).

(100a) Desde muy temprano humeaba una hoguera <u>en la
     pradera, junto a la fragua</u>. (H 18)
     since very early was-smoking a bonfire in the
     prairie close to the forge

(100b) Arriba centelleaban los astros <u>en la densa calma
     del espacio</u>. (H 17)
     up-there sparkled the stars in the thick calm of-the
     space

(100c) Crepitaban las conversaciones <u>en este grupo, en el
     otro</u> (H 16)
     crackled the conversations in this group, in the
     other

(101a) Y creo que no saldrían <u>con toda la tiza que hay en la</u>
  <u>casa</u> las manchas de los candelabros. (H 20)
  and I-believe that no would-come-out with all the
  chalk that there-is in the house the stains of the
  candelabra

(101b) Concurre con 'menar' <u>en los primeros textos medievales</u>
  'menear.' (H 18)
  coincides with <u>menar</u> in the first texts medieval
  <u>menear</u>

Thus, the answer to both positions of the adverbials is not to
be found by invoking heaviness.[67]
Furthermore, there is some evidence that perhaps two types
of adverbials are involved: VP adverbials and sentence adverbials. I take two sentences and permutate the order of
their constituents.

Declarative sentences:

(102a) La carroza entró en el parque. (VP adverbial)
  'The coach entered (in) the park.'

(102b) Paco reapareció en 1970. (Sentence adverbial)
  'Paco reappeared in 1970.'

Optimal presentational sentences:

(103a) En el parque entró la carroza.

(103b) En 1970 reapareció Paco.

Adv-Subj-V (unmarked focus on V):

(104a) ?En el parque la carroza entró.

(104b) En 1970 Paco reapareció.

V-Adv-Subj (focus on Subj):

(105a) Entró en el parque la carroza.

(105b) ?Reapareció en 1970 Paco.[68]

Presentationals: V-Subj-Adv order:

(106a) Entró la carroza en el parque.

(106b) Reapareció Paco en 1970.[69]

Assuming that the (a) sentences contain a VP adverbial and
the (b) sentences a sentence adverbial, the strangeness of
(104a) and (105b) can be explained as follows: in (104a) it is
due to the preposing to sentence-initial position of a VP adverbial; in (105b) it is due to the switching of a sentence adverbial with the postposed subject (which was in the VP).   In
(106a) a late stylistic switch of the two elements in the VP
might have taken place.   The preference of (106b) over (105b)
gives some support to the sentence-level source for en 1970.

Therefore, and even though the evidence is subtle, from now
on I assume that there are two sources for the adverbials in
presentational sentences: VP and S.

In sum, attaching the postposed subject to a VP level seems
to account for all the data without any of the drawbacks associated with the traditional structure-preserving hypothesis.[70]

2.3.3.1.3.3 Attachment to S within the X̄-theory. Still to be
examined is the alternative which considers the postposed subject to be attached to S, as in (107).

(107)

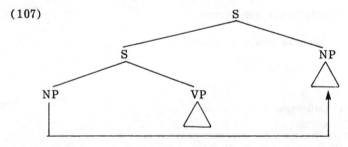

This proposal circumvents the criticisms levelled against Emonds'
hypothesis. It would also comply with Schwartz' (1972:37)
Boundary Attachment constraint, which says, 'a phrase moved
out of its phrase cannot attach to anything but the boundary
of the next highest phrase', because the next highest phrase
for the subject NP is S. Nonetheless, I see some problems
with this approach.[71] First, the subject needs to be attached
as the last element of S, even after any sentence adverbials,
if there are any. This has the very awkward effect of claiming
that an example such as (105b) would represent a natural sequence, a claim which is obviously incorrect. Then, an apparently otherwise unwarranted movement rule has to switch the

postposed subject with the sentence adverbial so as to produce
(106b).

There is another piece of evidence which suggests that
attachment of the postposed subject to S might not be desirable. Kayne (1980:87) reports on a principle introduced by
Van Riemsdijk, which stipulates that adjoining of a category X
to a category Y that dominates X is prohibited. This principle would imply that the postposed subject NP cannot adjoin to
S (or S̄) but only to VP. Since attachment of the postposed
subject to a VP level handsomely accounts for the data that
constitutes my main concern, I reject the attachment to S
alternative in favor of the previous one. In other words, from
now on I assume that the postposed subject is attached to VP
and that the correct derived structure is the one represented
in (108).[72]

(108)

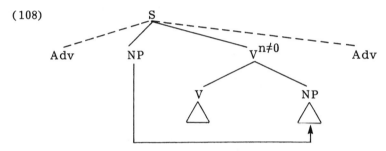

2.4 The grammar of presentational sentences. Assuming the
correctness of the revised EST model of grammar (cf. (109)) as
specified by Chomsky (Chomsky 1976:366, also Chomsky and
Lasnik 1977, Chomsky 1980a), it is hypothesized that the grammar of presentational sentences is composed of the syntactic
rule (i.e. transformation) of Subject Postposing (cf. Section
2.3.3) and several rules of semantic interpretation, some of
which belong to SI-1 and others to SI-2.

(109) Model of grammar:

$$\xrightarrow{\ B\ } \text{base structures} \xrightarrow{\ T\ } \text{surface structures} \xrightarrow{\ SI\text{-}1\ }$$

LF (LF, and other cognitive representations)

$$\xrightarrow{\ SI\text{-}2\ } \text{semantic representation}$$

After Subject Postposing applies, the two surface structures
(83) and (84), repeated here as (110) and (111), obtain.

(110) NP   VP   Declarative

(111) e_i VP NP_i Presentational

At this stage, and only on the basis of surface configurations, the interpretive rule of Focus Assignment operates to pick out the unmarked 'informational point' of the sentence.

(112) Focus Assignment (SI-1)

Mark the last constituent in the (higher) VP Focus of S.[73]

Thus, given the structures in (113), Focus Assignment has the effect noted in (114).

(113a) $[_S[_{NP}$la luna] $[_{VP}$apareció$]]_S$ Declarative
      'the moon   appeared'

(113b) $[_S[_{NP}...e_i...]$ $[_{VP}[_{VP}$apareció] $[_{NP}$la luna$_i]]_{VP}]_S$ Pre-
                         'appeared   the moon'
      sentational

(114a) $[_S[_{NP}$la luna] $[_{VP}\underline{apareció}]]_S$
                       Focus

(114b) $[_S[_{NP}...e_i...]$ $[_{VP}[_{VP}$apareció] $[_{NP}\underline{la\ luna}_i]]_{VP}]_S$
                                          Focus

In the absence of a higher VP and of any complements, (112) picks out the verb as the focused element in (114a). In (114b) it marks the postposed subject--the only constituent in the higher VP--as the Focus of S.

Observe that if the declarative sentence is transitive, (112) correctly marks the object as the focused element, because the object is the last constituent in the existing VP (cf. (115)).

(115) $[_S[_{NP}$Paco] $[_{VP}$compró $\underline{un\ libro}]]_S$ Declarative
                               Focus

Whenever a presentational sentence has a VP adverbial, Focus Assignment still picks out the postposed subject, because the VP adverbial belongs in the lower VP (cf. (92) and (96) in Section 2.3.3.1.3.2). Consider example (116).

(116) $[_S[_{NP}...e_i...]$ $[_{VP}[_{VP}$entró [en el cuarto]] $[_{NP}\underline{un\ perro\ enorme}_i]]_{VP}]_S$
                             Adv   Focus
           'entered the room   a dog enormous'

Focus assignment is also correctly indicated when the presentational sentence occurs with a sentence adverbial, because the postposed subject is still the last constituent in the higher VP, since the sentence adverbial is by definition outside the VP (cf. (95) and (96) in Section 2.4.1.3.2), as example (117) illustrates.

(117) $[_S[_{NP}\cdots e_i\cdots]$ $[_{VP}[_{VP}$rompieron$]$ $[_{NP}\underline{\text{las hostilidades}_i}]]_{VP}$ otra vez$]_S$
$\phantom{(117) [_S[_{NP}\cdots e_i\cdots] [_{VP}[_{VP}}$rompieron$]$ $[_{NP}$ Focus
$\phantom{(117) [_S[_{NP}\cdots e_i\cdots] }$'broke $\phantom{[_{VP}[_{VP}}$ the hostilities again'

Section 2.1.4 discussed sentence adverbials (such as otra
vez in (36)) which appear after the postposed subject. What
is needed is an interpretive rule which makes their status as
secondary focus or information point explicit and which links
the adverbial to the Focus of S, so that their relationship becomes transparent. This rule of Adverbial Linking could be
stated as in (118).

(118) Adverbial Linking (SI-1):

Mark any adverbial to the right of the (higher) VP,
Complement of the Focus of S.

Rule (118) marks otra vez in (117) as Comp of the Focus of S,
so that the adverbial receives the appropriate interpretation.
Thus, there is a rule of Focus Assignment (112) which correctly marks the focus of the sentence, and another rule of
Adverbial Linking (118) which assigns the special status to
sentence adverbials which appear after the postposed subject
in the surface structure. Both of these rules are interpretive
and belong to the level of LF.
In the Introduction it was hypothesized that the dichotomies
subject vs. predicate, theme vs. rheme, and old vs. new play
a role at three different levels of analysis: the syntactic level,
a level after LF but still within sentence semantics, and the
pragmatic level, respectively. Consequently, the next rule of
semantic interpretation of interest to the discussion is the one
which assigns theme vs. rheme.

(119) Rhematization (post-LF):

Mark as Rheme the VP and anything that follows it
(inside of S).[74] Anything outside the Rheme becomes
part of the Theme.

Rhematization,[75] a rule of sentence grammar which determines
the scope of assertion, has the following effect on the structures (120) and (121).

(120) $[NP]_{Th}$ $[VP]_{Rh}$ $\qquad$ Declarative

(121) e_i $\qquad$ $[VP\ NP_i]_{Rh}$ $\qquad$ Presentational

Observe that Rhematization formally captures the already discussed differences in the scope of assertion of declaratives and

presentationals, since the rheme encompasses both the VP and the postposed subject in the latter (cf. (121)), but only the VP in the former (cf. (120)).

The adequacy of both Focus Assignment and Rhematization can be illustrated by showing the workings of these rules in example (122).

(122) La guerra acabó y ahora sonrie la paz. (H 18)
'The war ended and now smiles the peace.'

Focus Assignment and Rhematization:

$[_S[\text{la guerra}]_{Th}\ \underset{\text{Focus}}{[\text{acabó}]}_{Rh}]_S$ y $[_S[\text{ahora}]_{Th}\ [\text{sonríe } \underset{\text{Focus}}{\text{la paz}}]_{Rh}]_S$

Here Focus Assignment correctly picks out the V as focus in the first conjunct and the postposed NP in the second, while Rhematization encompasses just the V in the declarative sentence (i.e. first conjunct) but includes both the V and the postposed subject in the presentational one (i.e. second conjunct). Thus, these two rules of sentence grammar formalize the intuitive feelings expressed by native speakers about where the weight of the information lies in each type of sentence.

The effect of these two rules is incorporated at the post-LF level.

(123) $(_{S'}(_S[(NP)]_{Th}\ \underset{\text{Focus}}{[(VP)]}_{Rh})_S)_{S'}$ Declarative

(124) $(_{S'}(_S[NP\cdots e_i \cdots]\ [(VP\ \underset{\text{Focus}}{(NP_i)})]_{Rh})_S)_{S'}$ Presentational

Observe that although I have been labelling the sentences as declarative and presentational throughout, neither Focus Assignment nor Rhematization makes use of this typology. In other words, both rules operate independently of sentence types. This is a definite advantage, considering that the interpretation of a sentence as presentational or declarative goes beyond the realm of sentence grammar, due to the fact that this interpretation has to take into account pragmatic and discourse factors. Consequently, it is necessary to wait until the level of SI-2 for a rule which reads a given sentence as belonging to one or the other type.

(125) Presentational Sentence Interpretation (SI-2):

Interpret S as presentational if it asserts above all the appearance of the referent of the NP in the world of discourse. This NP should carry the Focus of S.

(126) Declarative Sentence Interpretation (SI-2):

Interpret S as declarative if the VP predicates
something about the unasserted subject. The
Focus of S must be located in the VP.

Note that (125) avoids reference to subjecthood. This has the
advantage of allowing the grammar to characterize subjectless
impersonal hay sentences as presentationals by means of the
same rule, thus avoiding the loss of generalization which the
positing of a different rule of presentational interpretation for
each subtype would imply.

Thus, the grammar of presentational sentences is a maximally
efficient one that can be visualized as a four-step process.
The first step takes place in the syntactic component, where
the rule of Subject Postposing (optionally) applies. The second
step operates at the level of LF and consists of the interpretive
rules of Focus Assignment and Adverbial Linking. Immediately
after LF and still within the realm of sentence grammar, the
rule of Rhematization applies. And the fourth step happens
beyond sentence grammar, when other cognitive systems, beliefs, context, situation, etc., are taken into consideration, and
the sentence is interpreted as asserting (or not asserting)
above all the appearance of the pertinent NP in the world of
discourse--that is, as presentational or declarative. Observe
that only Presentational Sentence Interpretation might be exclusive to the grammar of presentational sentences. This would
be true just in case Subject Postposing plays a role in the
derivation of other sentence types with postposed subjects
(cf. (89) in Section 2.3.3.1.3.1, for example). Moreover,
Focus Assignment, Adverbial Linking, and Rhematization apply
to presentational and declarative sentences alike.

Before bringing this subsection to a close, I examine six sentences in order to further test the adequacy of the rules developed in this section.

(127) Casi al anochecer un tigre enorme apareció de entre
       las matas.
       'Almost at dusk an enormous tiger appeared from
       among the bushes.'

(127a) Focus Assignment and Rhematization:[76]

$[_{ADV}$Casi al anochecer] $[_{NP}$un tigre enorme] $[_{VP}$

                                                      Th↤↦Rh

apareció de entre las matas]
                 ‾‾‾‾‾‾‾‾‾
                  Focus

(127b) Sentence Interpretation (SI-2):

> Example (127) does not assert above all the appear-
> ance of the referent of the semantically heavy NP in
> the world of discourse; on the contrary, the VP
> predicates something about the unasserted subject
> (that it appeared from among the bushes). Moreover,
> the Focus of S falls in the VP. Consequently, this
> sentence receives a declarative reading by rule (126).

Compare (127) with (128), a sentence where Subject Postposing
has applied.

(128)   Casi al anochecer [t_i] apareció de entre las matas
        almost at dusk appeared from among the bushes

        [$_{NP_i}$ un tigre enorme]
        an enormous tiger

(128a) Focus Assignment and Rhematization:

$$[_S[_{Adv}\text{casi al anochecer}]\ [_{NP}t_i] \mid [_{VP}[_{VP}[_V\text{apareció}]$$
$$\text{Th}\leftarrow\!\!\longrightarrow\text{Rh}$$

$$_{PP}[\text{de entre las matas}]]\ [_{NP_i}\ \underline{\text{un tigre enorme}}]]_{VP}]_S$$
$$\underline{}\atop\text{Focus}$$

(128b) Sentence Interpretation (SI-2):

> Example (128) is interpreted as presentational by
> rule (125), since the sentence asserts above all the
> appearance of the NP <u>un tigre enorme</u>, which also
> carries sentential Focus.

(129)   [t_i] Preceden a cada fragmento [$_{NP_i}$ unas notas]   (H 11)

        precede (3 pl.) to each fragment some notes
        'Some notes precede each fragment.'

(129a) Focus Assignment and Rhematization:

$$[_S[_{NP}t_i] \mid [_{VP}[_{VP}[_V\text{preceden}]\ [_{PP}\text{a cada fragmento}]]$$
$$\text{Th}\leftarrow\!\!\longrightarrow\text{Rh}$$

$$[_{NP_i}\underline{\text{unas notas}}]]_{VP}]_S$$
$$\underline{}\atop\text{Focus}$$

(129b) Sentence interpretation (SI-2):

This example is interpreted as presentational by rule (125).

(130) Ayer [t$_i$] salió [$_{NP_i}$ su nombramiento] en la Gaceta.
(H 13)
yesterday appeared his appointment in the Gazette.

(130a) Focus Assignment, Adverbial Linking (cf. (118)), and Rhematization:

$$[_S[_{Adv}ayer] \ [_{NP}t_i] \ | \ [_{VP}[_{VP}[_V salió]] \ [_{NP_i}\underline{su}$$
$$Th \longleftrightarrow Rh$$

$$\underline{\underline{nombramiento}}]]_{VP} \ [_{Adv}\underline{en \ la \ Gaceta}]]_S$$
$$Focus \qquad\qquad Comp \ of \ Focus \ of \ S$$

(130b) Sentence Interpretation (SI-2):

This example is interpreted as presentational by rule (125).

(131) (Cuando ya nadie la esperaba,) hizo su entrada la novia.
(when already nobody her waited,) made her entrance the bride
('When nobody yet expected her,) the bride appeared.'

(131a) Focus Assignment and Rhematization:

$$[_S[_{NP}t_i] \ | \ [_{VP}[_V[_V hizo] \ [_{NP}su \ entrada]]_V$$
$$Th \longleftrightarrow Rh$$

$$[_{NP_i}\underline{la \ novia}]]_{VP}]_S$$
$$Focus$$

(131b) Sentence Interpretation (SI-2):

This example is interpreted as presentational by rule (125). Note that <u>hacer su entrada</u> is in this case equivalent to 'to appear'. The relevant NP is <u>la novia</u>.

(132) Ayer [t$_i$] compró una casa [$_{NP_i}$ Paco]

yesterday bought a house Paco
'Yesterday Paco bought a house.'

(132a) Focus Assignment and Rhematization:

$$[_S[_{Adv}\text{ayer}][_{NP}t_i] \mid [_{VP}[_{VP}[_V\text{compró}]$$
$$\text{Th} \longleftrightarrow \text{Rh}$$

$$[_{NP}\text{una casa}]]_{VP} \; [_{NP_i} \underset{\text{Focus}}{\text{Paco}}]]_{VP}]_S$$

(132b) Sentence Interpretation (SI-2):

> This sentence cannot be interpreted as presentational,
> because it does more than introduce the referent of
> the NP into the world of discourse. Notice that it
> cannot be interpreted as declarative either, because
> there is no predication about an unasserted subject
> (cf. (126)).

Observe that since Subject Postposing is an optional rule
without any conditions, nothing prevents its application to a
sentence such as (132). Focus Assignment and Rhematization
apply as usual, so that it is only at the level of SI-2 that the
sentence can be flagged as ill-formed (for a presentational),
since the focused NP cannot be interpreted as having been
introduced on the scene. This corroborates the adequacy of
the rules postulated, since under conditions of normal stress
and intonation example (132) is an ungrammatical sentence.

2.4.1 Summary and conclusion. In examining the grammar
of presentational sentences, it was discovered that a syntactic
movement rule which postposes the subject NP is required.
This rule applies optionally and has no conditions attached to
it. Furthermore, as expected for a movement rule, Subject
Postposing is cyclic and obeys Subjacency. Its function is to
align surface structure elements in accordance with the very
general and intuitive principle that the less informative elements come first, while more informative elements come toward
the end of the utterance. In other words, the rule moves the
subject to what turns out to be a focused rhematic position.
After investigating several alternatives, it was decided that
attaching the postposed NP to V^n best accounted for the data
under consideration.

Once surface structures are produced, rules of semantic
interpretation assign the focus of S and determine the rheme
of the sentence. These operations take place independently of
sentence types. It is only at the level of SI-2 that the sentences are judged as presentationals or not, depending on
whether or not their primary purpose is to introduce the referent of the NP into the world of discourse or not.

A grammar structured in this manner supports Chomsky's
autonomy hypothesis, because it renders conditions on syntactic

well-formedness independent from conditions on semantic well-formedness. Notice that Subject Postposing applies freely and unconditionally. This is because no semantic or syntactic conditions should or could be placed on the verb (cf. 2.1.2 and 2.1.3), or on other constituents of the sentence (cf. 2.1.4). It is only after considering the total context (and other pragmatic factors) that the semantic well-formedness of a presentational sentence can be considered. And this is achieved at the level of SI-2, beyond the sentence semantics of LF.

2.5 Theoretical implications of leftward [$_{NP}$...e...].[77] During the development of this chapter, and in accordance with the postulates of trace theory, it has been assumed that the movement rule which postposes the NP subject leaves a trace behind, as shown in (133) (cf. (82)).

(133) Subject Postposing

NP V^n

1   2 ===⇒ e 2 1

That is, Subject Postposing moves the category NP (under S) and its contents, yet at the same time this category remains in place with the null symbol e. This is shown schematically in (134).

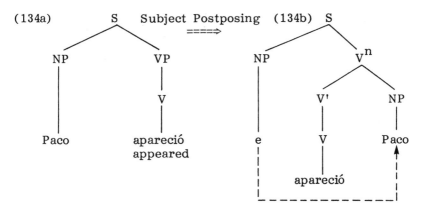

The broken line which joins e to the postposed subject indicates the path followed by Paco. As shown in (134b), e is the trace left behind by Paco, and e is dominated by the category NP, just as Paco was and still is.

The relationship between the moved NP and its trace is that of bound anaphora (Chomsky 1977b and elsewhere, and Fiengo 1977, among others). In other words, this relationship has to meet the conditions on binding. Binding is established by the coindexing of the relevant categories; in example (134), it must

take place between Paco and its trace. Due to the fact that
Subject Postposing is a movement rule, the coindexing of the
trace and the moved element happens automatically by virtue of
the movement rule (references just cited, also Chomsky and
Lasnik 1977).[78] Therefore, this coindexing can be made explicit in the rule itself.

(135) Subject Postposing

NP V^n

1 2 ===> e_i V^n NP_i

Despite this perfectly transparent way of indexing the NP and
its trace, there is one problem that arises with the structure
created by Subject Postposing. The trace is not considered to
be properly bound.[79] Proper binding of trace is achieved when
the NP precedes and C-commands its trace (see references cited;
also Lightfoot 1976b, and Dresher and Hornstein 1979). Thus,
although (136a) is considered to allow for proper binding, (136b)
usually is not considered to do so.[80]

(136a) $...NP_i...t_i...$

(136b) $...t_i...NP_i...$

It is precisely because of proper binding that Fiengo (1977:45)
postulates the metatheoretical condition shown in (137).

(137) In surface structure S_α, if $[e]_{NP_n}$ is not properly

bound by $[...]_{NP_n}$, this S_α is not grammatical.

If (137) were valid for Spanish, it would have the result of
rendering all presentational sentences discussed in this chapter
ungrammatical. Note that (137) would effectively disallow any
rightward movements of NP, because an NP to the right of its
trace would be assumed to be improperly bound.

This has led several investigators (Lightfoot 1976b, Fiengo
1977, Dresher and Hornstein 1979) to hypothesize that leftward
traces need to be obliterated in some way, so that no violations
of proper binding result in surface structure. For example,
assuming that Passive is a two-part rule of English, the trace
left in subject position by NP Postposing (cf. (138a)) is deleted
by Direct Object Preposing (cf. (138b)), and no leftward trace
appears in the well-formed surface structure (cf. (138c)).

(138a) $[_S[_{NP}e_i]$ $[_{VP}$was bought $[_{NP}$the car] $[_{PP}$by John$_i]]]$

(138b) $[_S[_{NP}$the car$_j]$ $[_{VP}$was bought $[_{NP}e_j]$ $[_{PP}$by John$_i]]]$

(138c) The car was bought by John.

Parallel reasoning is used to explain the insertion of there once
the subject NP is moved to the right.

(139a) $[_S[_{NP}e_i]$ $[_{VP}$is $[_{NP}$a bunch of grapes$_i]$ $[_{PP}$on the
table]]]

(139b) $[_S[_{NP}$there] $[_{VP}$is $[_{NP}$a bunch of grapes$_i]$ $[_{PP}$on the
table]]]

As a matter of fact, Fiengo (1977:47) speculates that since
there deletes the offending trace, 'trace theory would explain
why the insertion of there is apparently obligatory'.
A similar argument is put forth by Dresher and Hornstein
(1979) with respect to Extraposition. The only difference is
that in this case the inserted element which obliterates the
trace is it.

(140a) $[_S[_{NP}e_i]$ appears certain $[_{NP}$that John is a genius$_i]]_S$

(140b) $[_S[_{NP}$it] appears certain $[_{NP}$that John is a genius$_i]]_S$

The similarities between There-Insertion and Extraposition lead
Dresher and Hornstein (1979:68) to conclude that 'rightward NP
movement is possible when no violations of proper binding occur at SS; more specifically, when the vacated NP position is
filled by a lexical item'. This conclusion is later formalized as
a principle which is stated in (141).

(141) Only designated NP elements can erase traces.
       (1979:80) [81]

Most theoretical postulates in grammatical theory have been
forwarded with the grammar of English in mind. Trace theory
is no exception. The metatheoretical condition in (137) and the
principle in (141) have been motivated by English data. As
already pointed out, however, if leftward traces are considered
to be improperly bound, (137) would rule out Spanish presentational sentences. They have a trace which precedes its coindexed NP, and this trace is not erased by any grammatical
formative (such as English there and it) at any point in the
derivation. Where do these facts lead us with respect to the
grammar of Spanish and also with respect to trace theory?

A central difference between the Spanish and English emerges
upon examination of the Spanish equivalents of English There
sentences and Extraposition.

(142) Hay un racimo de uvas sobre la mesa.
       'There-is a bunch of grapes on the table.'

(143) Parece seguro que Paco es un genio.
       'It-appears certain that Paco is a genius.'

Sentence (142) is an instance of a completely subjectless sentence (cf. Chapter 1). If (143) is derived by extraposing
que Paco es un genio, then there is an improperly bound trace
left in the matrix subject position. Alternatively, if the clause
is generated in place, then there is no subject NP in the matrix
S. Observe that in both sentences the (matrix) verb takes the
unmarked third person singular ending. What (142) and (143)
point out is that, contrary to the English norm, all Spanish
sentences do not require an underlying subject argument. This
fact seems of utmost importance, because it explains why Spanish does not conform to either (137) or (141).[82] Given that
there already exist in the grammar underlyingly subjectless
sentences--such as impersonal haber (cf. (142)), sentences
with impersonal hacer 'to do, make', and maybe even those of
the type found in (143)--then there is no constraint against
having an empty subject position in surface structure.[83] In
other words, Subject Postposing creates a structure that is
isomorphic to an already existing (and base-generated) structure. Therefore, in spite of the unorthodox trace, the sentences generated by this rightward movement rule are fully
grammatical.

There is further evidence that (141) has no place within the
grammar of Spanish. In the first place, Dresher and Hornstein
(1979:68) speculate that perceptually there and it announce that
There-Insertion and Extraposition have applied and thus facilitate the processing of the sentences. Note that in Spanish
presentationals the subject can no longer be defined as the NP
under S, since it has been moved into the VP. This postposed
subject is coded with the corresponding Case, person, and
number markers so that no information is lost by removing it
from preverbal position. Therefore, regarding perceptual
strategies, it seems that verb inflection in Spanish may perform a task similar to that of There- and It-Insertion in English. The difference in the strategies stems, once again, from
the fact that English has a relatively fixed SVO word order,
with the further requisite that a subject is necessary in surface
structure for every tensed sentence. Spanish, on the other
hand, is a 'free word order' language that does not have the
subject requirement.

In the second place, one of the implicit claims of trace theory
is that grammatical relations can be identified on the basis of

surface structures (Chomsky 1977b, Fiengo 1977, among others). This identification could be achieved in more than one way. For instance, grammatical functions may be detected purely in terms of configuration (as in the case of subject as the NP under S or the NP of the Agential by-phrase) or by means of the binding relation between a trace and its antecedent (such as the case of the direct object in <u>what did you say t</u>). But I would also like to claim that in some languages subjecthood might be identified by Case marking and/or by verbal inflection. In Spanish, the subject status of the postverbal NP is transparent because of the inflection on the verb.

> (144)   En la lejanía t_i aparecieron varios jinetes$_i$.
>   in the distance appeared (3 pl.) various persons on
>   horseback

Both the verb and the NP coincide in their coding for person and number (i.e. third person plural).[84] Therefore, the fact that the trace *precedes* its coindexed NP is irrelevant, since this trace is not crucial to the identification of grammatical relations. Chomsky (1977a:9), following a suggestion of John Goldsmith, adopts the convention 'that erasure of a trace is permitted only when the grammatical function of its antecedent is indicated in the phrase-marker independently of the trace'. Notice that this quotation is prompted by English data and that it specifically mentions 'antecedent', since it assumes proper binding conditions for traces. But the spirit of the Goldsmith-Chomsky statement and my claim are identical. By modifying the convention to encompass Spanish presentational sentences, it is possible to maintain (145).

> (145)   Erasure of a (non-Case-marked) trace is permitted
>   only when the grammatical function of its coindexed
>   NP is transparent independently of the trace.[85]

In sum, it is hypothesized here that even though cases exist in which the trace precedes its NP, these sentences should be grammatical, since the sequence of trace and NP neither hinders perceptual strategies nor obscures grammatical relations. This hypothesis is corroborated by the Spanish data.

The specific way in which trace deletion is to be achieved is open to various similar alternatives. Chomsky and Lasnik (1977) suggest that if a language has a rule of Subject-Pronoun Deletion, it will also delete null subjects of the type [$_{NP}$e].[86] Or the trace could be deleted by general convention if it conforms to (145). Chomsky (1979b) postulates a rule which deletes non-Case-marked traces as part of the 'avoid-pronoun-principle'.

If my analysis is on the right track, traces may precede their coindexed NP just in case they comply with convention (145).

Recently, Chomsky (1979b) has also suggested that verb inflection can bind an empty element in subject position. Specifically, he proposes that a language like Italian has indices on AG(reement) which can properly bind [$_{NP}$e] in subject position.[87] He formalizes this type of binding as in (146).

(146)　[$_{NP_i}$e] ... AG$_i$

This statement not only makes explicit that the trace is bound but also complies with the requisite that empty NPs must be governed, given the characterization of (proper) government shown in (147) (Chomsky 1979b).

(147)　α properly governs β if α governs β and
　　　(a) α = [±N, ±V]
　　　(b) α is coindexed with β

Furthermore, notice that the fact that the trace precedes its coindexed NP does not hamper Case assignment. The postposed subject NP receives Nominative Case[88] regardless of its position, since by a general convention on Case assignment, the lexical NP inherits its Case from its trace.[89]

There is a further theoretical implication created by the existence of grammatical sentences with traces which precede their coindexed NPs. This has to do with the often mentioned fact that traces and bound anaphors (i.e. reflexives and reciprocals) behave exactly alike with respect to binding conditions (Chomsky 1976 and elsewhere). The question is: is the parallelism kept, that is, are there instances in which bound anaphors precede their coindexed NPs? The answer is affirmative. Consider examples (148) through (150).

(148a)　Paco$_i$ se$_i$ está bañando.
　　　　Paco himself is bathing
　　　　'Paco is bathing.'

(148b)　Se$_i$ está bañando Paco$_i$

(149a)　La leche$_i$ se$_i$ volcó.
　　　　the milk itself spilled
　　　　'The milk spilled.'

(149b)　Se$_i$ volcó la leche$_i$.

(150a)　Paco y Trini$_i$ se$_i$ respetan.
　　　　Paco and Trini themselves respect
　　　　'Paco and Trini respect each other.'

(150b)　Se$_i$ respetan Paco y Trini$_i$.

In the (a) cases of these examples, the antecedent precedes the anaphor; but in the (b) instances the postposing of the subject results in the anaphor preceding its coindexed NP. Therefore, it is the case that traces and anaphors behave analogously with respect to binding. Thus, one of the motivations for trace theory stands unperturbed.

Other evidence adduced in favor of trace theory is that it captures the left-right asymmetry of movement rules that results from the conditions on proper binding (Dresher and Hornstein 1979). In other words, since it was assumed that the trace must be preceded by its coindexed NP, it is a natural consequence--so the argument went--that there be many more leftward movement rules than rightward movement rules. As a matter of fact, 'it would be a strong evidence in favor of trace theory if it turned out that rightward movement rules were allowed just in those cases in which no violations of proper binding occurred at SS' (Dresher and Hornstein 1979:66). Since it has been argued in this section that the configuration obtained by the rule of Subject Postposing (i.e. $[_{NP_i}e]...NP_i$) does not violate proper binding, the Spanish case confirms the Dresher and Hornstein hypothesis. Nevertheless, the fact remains that left-right asymmetries exist. Notice that the sequence $t_i...NP_i$ occurs only in those cases in which the necessary information (such as subjecthood) is recoverable by other means, be it verb inflection, Case marking, or both. Moreover, these $t_i...NP_i$ configurations which arise through rightward movements appear to be confined to simple one-clause structures; the moved element never seems to cross sentence boundaries (cf. Section 2.3.3.1.2) and thus it is never lowered into an exhausted cycle. On the other hand, leftward movement rules are known to move elements up the tree into higher cycles (e.g. WH-Movement). Schematically, the possibilities in (151) are realized.

(151)

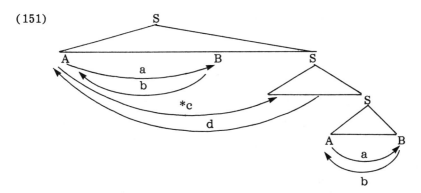

Both leftward movements (b) and (d) are permitted, the first being clause-internal, the second from lower to upper clause. Both (b) and (d) are in principle compatible with proper

binding conditions.[90] The rightward movement (c) is not permissible, since it inserts material into an exhausted cycle. The
rightward clause-internal movement (a) is allowed, provided no
loss of necessary information results. Thus, t_i...NP_i is allowed
only in a very specific and restricted number of cases--a fact
which upholds the left-right asymmetries of movement rules.

To conclude, the fact that the rightward movement rule of
Subject Postposing creates a structure in which the trace precedes its antecedent does not create any problems for trace
theory, because the trace is properly bound by the verb inflection. It is hypothesized that this binding property through AG
follows from the fact that Spanish is a 'free word order' language which codes person and number in the verb and, most
importantly, allows for completely subjectless sentences. As a
consequence, leftward traces neither hinder perceptual strategies nor obscure grammatical relations. The relatively restricted environment and conditions under which leftward traces
are permitted allow us to retain the generalization that trace
theory captures the left-right asymmetry of movement rules resulting from proper binding. Finally, the parallelism in the
behavior of traces and anaphors further supports this theory.

2.6 Conclusion

2.6.1 **Summary.** This chapter has examined the intransitive
type of presentational sentence in Spanish.[91] These sentences
are derived by means of the syntactic rule of Subject Postposing, and they are interpreted in stages. Focus Assignment and
Adverbial Linking contribute to their interpretations at LF,
Rhematization operates at a post-LF level still within sentence
semantics, and finally, Presentational Sentence Interpretation
applies at the level of complete semantic interpretation, which
goes beyond sentence grammar. No lexical or structural conditions can or should be placed on the verbs that enter into presentational sentences, since the presentational interpretation
falls out automatically from the function these sentences perform.
This allows the syntactic rule(s) to apply freely and uncon-
strainedly. The different rules which play a role in the derivation and interpretation of presentationals show how the different
subcomponents of the grammar interact and how these sentences
function in the act of communication.

It was also demonstrated that presentational sentences form a
sentence type in their own right, since they behave differently
from declarative sentences regarding word order, stress and
focus, the hacerlo construction, and the scope of negation and
other quantifiers.

Other issues of general theoretical import were also dealt with
in this chapter. The properties of stylistic rules were considered at length before the decision was made that Subject
Postposing must be a syntactic movement rule proper. The
derived constituent structure of these presentational sentences

was investigated through an analysis of different attachment
possibilities for the moved subject. It was decided that the
subject must remain within the VP and hang from $V^{n\neq0}$, as
made possible by the $\bar{X}$-theory.[92] Finally, the theoretical implications of leftward traces were weighed. It was concluded
that verbal inflection properly binds the trace left behind by
the moved subject; this fact follows from the active verb morphology that Spanish displays, as well as from the existence
of completely subjectless sentences (cf. Chapter 1 and Appendix B), and the relatively 'free' word order that this language
permits. As a result of these factors, leftward traces neither
hamper perceptual strategies nor obscure grammatical functions.

**2.6.2 Comparison of *haber* presentationals and intransitive
presentationals.** I would like to compare and contrast the grammar of both types of presentational sentences studied: impersonal *haber* sentences (Section 1.3), and the ones examined in
this chapter (Section 2.4). Because they are both presentationals, they function to introduce the referent of the NP into
the universe of discourse. Remaining to be determined are
any other similarities or differences between these two subtypes. For the purpose of this comparison I start with their
logical forms. An *hay* sentence was hypothesized to have the
LF given in (152), whereas an intransitive presentational was
given the LF in (153).

(152)   LF of *hay* presentationals:

$$[_S[_{VP} \exists [NP] \underset{\text{Focus}}{} [(\left\{\begin{array}{l}PP\\AP\\\underline{S}\end{array}\right\})]]_{VP}]_S$$

(153)   LF of intransitive presentational sentences:

$$[_S[_{NP_i} e] [_{VP}[VP] \underset{\text{Focus}}{[NP_i]}]_{VP}]_S$$

These LFs immediately point out one characteristic of presentationals. They have no subject at the level of LF, that is,
they are thetic (Kuroda 1972; also see Section 2.1). This
correlates with several other characteristics of presentationals--
for example, the fact that only sentence negation occurs in them
and the fact that they are incompatible with the *hacerlo* construction. Their thetic nature translates at post-LF level into
their being rhematic in character. Moreover, observe that their
LF also reflects the fact that their word order is invariably V
NP, which confirms our claim that V NP is the word order for
presentational sentences regardless of the grammatical function
of the NP (cf. Section 2.0). Therefore, their very similar LFs
explain not only their eventual presentational interpretation but
also some of their defining traits and behavior.

At the same time, the dissimilarities between these LFs should explain why the two subtypes are not identical in all respects. Three points of divergence between (152) and (153) emerge. First, the verb haber, itself being inherently existential, is interpreted as an existential quantifier; the same does not happen with the verbs that occur in (153). Although these verbs also serve to assert the existence of the NP referent, their existential assertion is inferred and not inherent.

In the second place, hay sentences are basic; their constituents remain in the order in which they are generated by the phrase-structure rules. By contrast, the rule of Subject Postposing must move the subject NP into the VP for (153) to result; therefore, intransitive presentational sentences are derived. As a consequence of this difference, and of the different verbs that play a role in this construction, the NP whose appearance in the world of discourse is being heralded performs a direct object function in hay sentences but a subject function in intransitive presentationals.

A third difference between (152) and (153) surfaces when the focused element in both subtypes is considered. The Focus Assignment rules postulated to achieve this aim are repeated here as (154) and (155). Note that (154) picks the object NP of hay sentences as Focus, but (155) selects the postposed subject as Focus.

(154) Focus Assignment (hay presentationals):
Mark the NP argument of hay sentences Focus of S.

(155) Focus Assignment (intransitive presentationals):
Mark the last constituent in the (higher) VP Focus of S.

It would be easy to collapse (154) and (155) by forming (156).

(156) Mark the nonoblique argument in the VP Focus of S.

Rule (156) selects the object in (152) and the postposed subject in (153), that is, it gives us the correct results. Nevertheless, recalling that (155) also correctly assigns Focus to declarative sentences, and realizing that (156) would not,[93] one can question the advisability of subsuming (154) and (155) into (156). Accepting (156) would mean that other rule(s) of Focus Assignment would need to be devised for declarative sentences. Since the interpretation of a sentence as presentational or declarative does not take place until SI-2, I see no valid reason to give up (155) (which works independently of sentence type)[94] in favor of (156) and another (unstated) rule. It is already known that impersonal haber is a peculiar verb (cf. Section 1.1) which works as an existential quantifier, and that it gives rise to the presentational construction par excellence;[95] thus, it might not be totally out of the question for it to require

its own rule of Focus Assignment. Therefore, until more research dealing with other sentence types is conducted, I prefer
to maintain the two original rules of Focus Assignment (154)
and (155).[96]
  To sum up this far, hay presentationals differ from intransitive presentationals in that haber is inherently an existential
verb, in that hay presentationals are base-generated, and in
that each necessitates its own rule of Focus Assignment. They
are similar in that they are subjectless in LF and in that they
adhere to V NP word order.
  Since comparing the rules of Focus Assignment showed a dissimilarity between the grammars of the two presentational subtypes, it might prove fruitful to examine the rest of the rules.
For hay sentences the second rule of SI-1 is (157), and for
intransitive presentationals it is (158).

  (157) Complement Linking:

      Mark any PP, AP, $\bar{S}$, or Adv to the right of
      [hay + NP], Complement of the Focus of S.

  (158) Adverbial Linking:

      Mark any adverbial to the right of the (higher)
      VP, Complement of the Focus of S.

The motivation for positing (157) and (158) is obvious. Rule
(157) establishes the relationship between the optionally subcategorized elements of haber or between sentence adverbials
and the NP in focus, and (158) does the same between the
focused postposed NP subject and any adverbial that might
follow it. The main difference between the two rules is that
(157) links VP complements as well as S complements, but (158)
only links S complements with the NP in focus. However, this
is an artifact of the position which the Focus NP occupies;
consequently, it is feasible to combine (157) and (158) into the
single rule (159) by deleting reference to complement types.

  (159) Complement Linking:

      Mark any complement to the right of the Focus NP,
      Complement of the Focus of S.

The rest of the rules are shared by hay presentationals and
intransitive presentationals. They are listed here for ease of
reference.

  (160) Rhematization (post-LF):

      Mark as Rheme the VP and anything that follows it
      inside of S. Anything outside the Rheme becomes
      part of the Theme.

(161)   Presentational Sentence Interpretation (SI-2):

Interpret S as presentational if it asserts the
appearance of the referent of the NP in the universe of discourse.

Thus, both presentational subtypes are interpreted in stages.
Some of their interpretive rules belong to sentence grammar in
that they are part of formal semantics. Others pertain to the
realm of complete semantic representation (discourse grammar);
in other words, pragmatics built on sentence grammar.

Finally, there is one difference between haber and intransitive presentationals which can most likely be linked to the basic
character of the former as opposed to the derived character of
the latter. This difference has to do with the kinds of NPs
these two subtypes may appropriately herald into the discourse.
Intransitive presentationals impose no restrictions whatsoever
on their NPs. They may introduce any NPs, from those completely devoid of any modification (162) to proper names (163)
to NPs of which the speaker and hearer share knowledge (164).

(162a) Caen piedras.
        fall (3 pl.) stones
        'Stones are falling.'

(162b) Salía sangre.
        came-out (3 sg.) blood
        'Blood was coming out.'

(163a) Apareció Paco.
        appeared (3 sg.) Paco
        'Paco appeared.'

(163b) Iba anocheciendo; surgía Madrid...   (H 13)
        was becoming-dark; emerged (3 sg.) Madrid...
        'It was becoming dark; Madrid was emerging...'

(164a) Llegaron los niños.
        arrived (3 pl.) the children
        'The children arrived.'

(164b) Apareció la luna.
        appeared (3 sg.) the moon
        'The moon appeared.'

In contrast, although hay presentationals do occur quite freely
with syntactically definite NPs (cf. Section 1.3.1.3.1), they
establish a semantic condition on their NPs: these NPs must be
novel in the discourse, and they must not be sufficiently shared
by speaker and hearer. These observations support my claim
that semantic definiteness is a gradient concept (see Section

1.3.1.3.1.5). This is a pragmatic constraint that can only be appropriately checked in SI-2 (cf. Section 1.3.2). Therefore, hay sentences do not occur with proper names (165), strong pronouns (166), or NPs which identify a unique referent shared by addresser and addressee (167).

(165)   *Hay Paco.
        'There-is Paco.'

(166)   *Hay ellos.
        'There-are them.'

(167)   *Hay el presidente.
        'There-is the president.'

How can this discrepancy between the kinds of NPs intro-duced by the two presentational subtypes be explained? I would like to maintain that it should be explained by consider-ing haber presentationals THE presentational construction in Spanish. Haber sentences are base-generated and they can only display this presentational function; therefore, they can and do dictate that their NPs be novel.[97] On the other hand, intransitive presentationals are derived; but for their word order they would be declarative (recall that the order V Su is presentational, Su V is declarative). They are less con-strained, because their base structure is indeterminate as to their ultimate discourse function.

The grammatical function embodied by the NP whose appear-ance is being heralded into the discourse automatically accounts for the different results obtained regarding deletion/interpreta-tion.[98] As expected, the NP which is deleted/interpreted in intransitive presentationals (168) performs a subject function, but it is the object in haber presentationals (169).

(168a) --¿Cayó mucha nieve?
        --Sí, Δ cayó.
        '--Did much snow fall?
        --Yes, (it) fell.'

(168b) Llegó la policía cuando menos esperábamos que Δ
        llegara.
        'The police arrived when we least expected that
        (they) would-arrive.'

(169a) --¿Había mucha nieve?
        --Sí, (la) había Δ.
        '--Was-there much snow?
        --Yes, there-was.'

(169b) Hubo una crisis cuando menos esperábamos que la
hubiera Δ.
'There-was a crisis when we least expected that
there-would be (one).'

The Δ is meant to indicate informally the site of the deletion/
interpretation.
This ends the comparison of haber and intransitive presentationals. Undoubtedly, there are other processes that can
demonstrate that the two constructions do not behave in a
totally parallel fashion,[99] but the main point has been made:
although these two presentational subtypes perform the same
function at the discourse level (that of introducing the NP
referent into the universe of discourse), one subtype is basic
whereas the other one is derived. Consequently, it should
come as no surprise that they are not identical or that they
do not behave totally alike. Their similarities can be explained
by their very comparable logical forms ((152) and (153)) and
by their discourse function. Their points of divergence are
a consequence of different lexical items, their basic vs. derived
status, and other interpretive and pragmatic mechanisms.

NOTES

1. But see Section 2.1.3.
2. That the NP referent is being asserted can be shown by
the behavior of presentational sentences under negation (see
Section 2.2.4). What obtains is a case of S-negation in which
both the V and the NP are negated. Thus, under the negative
presentational interpretation, (1a) could be expanded as (i)
but not as (ii).

(i) No apareció un hombre, en realidad no apareció
    absolutamente nada.
    no appeared (3 sg.) a man, in reality no appeared (3
    sg.) absolutely nothing
    'A man didn't appear, as a matter of fact absolutely
    nothing appeared.'

(ii) No apareció un hombre, apareció una mujer.
     no appeared (3 sg.) a man appeared (3 sg.) a woman
     'A man didn't appear, a woman appeared.'

Sentence (i) entails that 'a man doesn't exist', that is, it
asserts that the NP has no referent. Sentence (ii) is a contrastive sentence (see Section 3.4) which asserts that the NP
has a referent different from the one identified.
3. The claim is therefore that presentational sentences are
by implication also existential (presentational ⊃ ∃). This implication is unidirectional--i.e. ∃ ⊅ presentational--because there

are Ǝ sentences which are declarative and not presentational, as in example (i).

(i) Estoy segura que <u>los espíritus existen</u>.
'I'm sure that (the) ghosts exist.'

Todos me aseguran que <u>Dios existe</u>.
'Everybody assures me that God exists.'

The embedded sentences in (i) are <u>lexically</u> Ǝ but declarative in form.

4. This schema will be refined as the discussion progresses (cf. Section 2.1.3).

5. Hatcher confines herself to the existential sentence consisting of intransitive verbs and inanimate subjects, but as was already seen in (1), this construction also occurs with animate (1d) as well as human (1a) subjects. Hatcher's data come from over 70 volumes of prose published between 1908 and 1954. Excluded from my discussion are any instances of sentences with <u>se</u>.

6. Some frequency studies have been done on the subject-verb vs. verb-subject word order. Bull et al. (1952) estimated that out of 1,351 sample sentences, 77 percent followed the order subject-verb and 23 percent showed inversion of verb-subject; but since this study neither differentiated statements from questions nor took meaning or environment into account, it is of little value.

More revealing is Hatcher's statement to the effect that 80 percent of her examples of existential sentences display 'inversion of thing-subject with intransitive verb' (1956:21).

7. Subject-predicate is the unmarked syntactic word order on the assumption that Spanish is an SVO language. This assumption has been questioned recently (cf. Bordelois 1974, Contreras 1976). For a full discussion of Spanish basic word order, I refer the reader to Chapter 4.

8. That is to say, (8a) in its presentational interpretation could not be continued by (i) because (i) makes (8a) a contrastive sentence.

(8a) Aparecieron tres hombres...
     appeared (3 pl.) three men...

(i) ...y no tres mujeres.
     ...and not three women

A sentence like (ii), (suggested to me by Rivero, personal communication) could be an instance of either a presentational or a contrastive sentence conjoined with a declarative one in which the unemphatic subject pronoun has been deleted. That is to say, <u>tres hombres</u> is (part of) the rheme in the first conjunct, but <u>it</u> is the theme in the second.

(ii) Aparecieron tres hombres y no desaparecieron nunca más.
appeared (3 pl.) three men and not disappeared (3 pl.)
never again
'Three men appeared and (they) didn't disappear ever
again.'

Sentences like (ii) prompt me to cite this quotation from Halliday (1967:205):

> A distinction may...be made between unmarked focus, realized as the location of the tonic accented lexical item, which assigns the function 'new' to the constituent in question, but does not specify the status of the remainder, and the marked focus, realized as any other location of the tonic, which assigns the function 'new' to the focal constituent and that of 'given' to the rest of the information unit.

Taking into account that Halliday is using the term 'new' as 'textually and situationally nonderivable information' and not as previously mentioned (cf. Section 0.1.2), what he is saying in the foregoing quote is that focus may be marked (by heavy contrastive stress, for instance) or unmarked ('normal' or unmarked stress), and that marked focus only correlates with given (i.e. presupposed) information.

In (ii), unmarked focus goes with a presentational interpretation of the first sentence (and the whole S is rhematic), while marked focus goes with a contrastive interpretation (in which case only the NP is rhematic, and the V is thematic).

9.   Shou-Hsin considers 'uniconstituent' sentences to be subjectless at the level of logical form.

10.   For the benefit of the reader, I have added in parentheses the languages that enter into the discussion of these classifications. The fact that different linguists working from the vantage points of different languages have proposed this type of classification lends support to the need for such cataloging.

11.   Detailed discussion of the derived constituent structure of presentationals is delayed until Section 2.3.3.1.3.

12.   The implications of this 'improperly' bound trace for the theory are discussed in Section 2.5. The rule of Subject Postposing is dealt with in Section 2.3.3.

13.   In this respect, it is very interesting to compare the LFs posited in (14) and (15) with those advanced by Guéron (1978:3) for English (not a free word order language).

(i) $(_{S'}(_S(NP)\ (VP))_S)_{S'}$ Predication

(ii) $(_{S'}(_S VERB_i(NP)\ _{VP}(...v_i...))_S)_{S'}$ Presentation

Thus, while (i) and (14) coincide, (ii) and (15) do not. (In (ii), a rule operates at the level of LF to extract the V from the Presentation Sentence and place it in the leftmost position in S.) The dissimilarities in LF seem to be a by-product of the different word order possibilities allowed in each language. It remains to be seen whether tailoring the LF (ii) to resemble the Spanish (15) would accommodate the facts of English as well as (15) takes care of and explains the facts of Spanish.

14. This fact seems to be a desirable consequence and should be expected (at least for noncontrastive sentences) if LFs are obtained from S-structures (i.e. surface structures which contain traces) by rules of construal. Of course, the determination of LFs and their properties is subject to empirical testing. As such, all LFs postulated in this study are susceptible to further refinements and modifications.

15. Contreras (1976) makes precisely this mistake. His grammar attaches the feature [+ presentational] to verbs by a lexical redundancy rule. See my discussion in Section 4.3.2.1.2.

16. Dubský (1960:114) presents the following cataloging of verbs which he found with the verb-subject word order:

38% de verbes de mouvement, 10% de verbes d'apparition ou de disparition, 10% de verbes de bruit ou de son, 4% de verbes d'affirmation, 18% de verbes auxiliaires ou semi-auxiliaires; le reste (20% de cas de l'inversion verbe-sujet que nous avons observés au cours de nos recherches) est representé par de verbes qu'on ne peut ranger dans aucune des categories citées plus haut.

17. Guéron (1978:7) writes that the verbs are pragmatically emptied of all semantic content besides appearance in the world of discourse. Babby (1980) talks about 'desemanticization'. And Dubský (1960) characterizes them by their 'affaiblissement communicatif et dynamique'.

18. By 'inherently intransitive' I mean a verb which is never subcategorized for an object argument.

19. The symbol ≠ indicates that the sentences cannot be interpreted as presentationals. In general, the order V Obj. Su ((a)-sentences) is not favored at all in Spanish. The most natural reading for these sentences is either one in which the Su has been right-dislocated (and therefore carries very low intonation), or one in which the Su is contrastive. The (b)-sentences are definitely grammatical.

20. The clarification 'with two arguments' is necessary because, as can be seen in (25), the same verbs may be used intransitively, in which case they appear with just one argument. The examples in (25) should not be confused with sentences in which these verbs are used transitively but in which only the object argument occurs at the surface level. In this case, the subject argument has been deleted by the quite general rule which deletes nonemphatic subjects once subject-verb agreement has operated. For example:

(i) Subían una escalera.
   ascended (3 pl.) a stairs
   'They were going up a stairway.'

(ii) Cruzó la calle.
   crossed (3 sg.) the street
   'He/She/It went across the street.'

It is totally impossible to interpret examples such as (i) and (ii) as presentational.
   21. It could be argued that expressions like dar señales de vida, hacer su entrada, etc., should be analyzed as [$_V$[$_V$ hacer] [$_{NP}$ su entrada]], in which case they would be intransitive. Furthermore, one could maintain that only the complex verb analysis of these expressions is compatible with a presentational sentence interpretation. Even if this is the right tack, I would not want to state categorically that only intransitive verbs may appear in presentationals. Recall the verbs in the sentences in (25) and impersonal haber (Chapter 1).
   22. Bolinger (1977:102) arrives at the same conclusion with respect to English there-sentences.

There is a notably low percentage of active transitive expressions in presentative constructions. If the transitive verb is part of a phrase that is a kind of semantically analytic intransitive, that is, one that amounts to a single verb, its appearance here is normal enough so long as the sense is appropriate:

(141) In that realm (there) held sway (= ruled) a hated despot.
(142) There was slowly making its way toward (= was approaching) us a figure in black.
(143) Near here (there) have taken place (= occurred) some of the most striking events in the state's history.
(144) In the tower there strikes the hour a clock of many chimes.

But elsewhere the transitives seem to involve too many entities, and to violate the loose constraint against saying more than one thing at a time.

   23. By 'semantically heavy NP' I mean an NP which keeps all of its lexical meaning. This is as opposed to NPs like the one in dar [$_{NP}$ señales de vida] which lose their literal meaning whenever they enter into an idiomatic interpretation.
   24. The notation V + (NP) is meant to capture the type of semantic unit which can arise from expressions such as dar señales de vida, already discussed in note 23.

25. Kuno (1978) calls these adverbs 'thematic', as opposed to the ones that originate in VP-internal position, which are labeled time- or place-specifying adverbs.

26. These nine constitute the total number of items of this kind found in Hatcher's enormous corpus, with the exception of the following two which I eliminated because sólo, although an adverb, behaves in a peculiar way (cf. Section 4.3.5) and permanecer latente forms the expression 'to be alive'.

(i) Yacen sólo los despojos... (H 15)
lie (3 pl.) only the remains...
'Only the remains lie...'

(ii) ...en el ánimo de todas permanecía latente aquella angustia... (H 9)
in the spirit of all (f. pl.) remained (3 sg.) latent that anguish
'In everybody's spirit that anguish was alive.'

Even if these two examples were listed, it would bring the grand total to only 11, an insignificant number when compared to the rest of the corpus.

27. Guerón (1978:32) notices that sentence adverbs allow for PP Extraposition but VP adverbs do not. This distinction (sentential vs. predicative) does not seem to play a decisive role in the phenomenon I am discussing, although at times it helps in describing unacceptability (cf. (41)).

28. Under neutral stress conditions, (42c) and (43c) are ungrammatical because they display a 'conflict of interest': the postposed subject receives sentential stress, but at the same time the preposing of the adverbials causes them to be highlighted and thus contrastively stressed.

29. I consider 'stress' to be the phonological counterpart of the semantic notion of 'focus' (see also Section 0.1.3).

30. The use of this construction as a criterion for distinguishing declaratives from presentationals was prompted by Guéron's (1978) discussion of VP Deletion. But, of course, since English and Spanish presentationals differ considerably, the argumentation is not completely parallel. Hacerlo is the Spanish equivalent of the English Pro-VP expression 'to do so/it'.

31. The way to avoid the redundancy in the examples in (51) is by leaving the verb of the second conjunct out (i.e. by Gapping).

Sobraba dinero y también tiempo.

This same kind of deletion (or maybe interpretation) is available to the sentences in (49) also.

Pepe compró una casa y Paco también.

32. For a characterization of contrastive sentences, see Section 3.4.

33. Therefore, it should be the case that if a declarative sentence contains a verb which is interpreted statively, the sentence will be incompatible with the hacerlo construction. This is precisely what happens with the stative verb estar 'to be, remain'.

Paco estaba en la fiesta y Pepe también estaba allí.
'Paco was at the party and Pepe also was there.'

*Paco estaba en la fiesta y Pepe tambien lo hacía allí.

The crucial point is that because of desemantization and loss of dynamicity, the verbs that enter into presentational sentences always receive a stative interpretation which blocks the possibility of their cooccurrence with hacerlo. It is beside the point that some declarative sentences (precisely those which have a statively interpreted verb) are also incompatible with hacerlo.

34. I direct the reader to Williams (1977) for details.

35. While Jackendoff (1972) maintains that the scope of negation is determined in surface structure, Guéron (1978) argues for it being determined on the level of LF. This is a moot point, since LF is obtained from S-structures. Moreover, word order reflects theme/rheme structure much more closely in Spanish than in English; thus, both surface structure and LF coincide in the arrangement of the elements in Spanish presentationals.

36. Once again, it is interesting to compare the way our posited LF for presentational (57) differs from Guéron's LF for English (1978:14).

$$[_{S'}[_{S} \text{ APPEAR}_i \text{ }_{NP}\underline{\frac{(\text{A BOOK})}{F}} \text{ }_{VP} (\text{NOT} \ldots v_i \ldots)]_S]_{S'}$$

Guéron claims this LF is uninterpretable because the focus NP is not in the scope of the negative particle; consequently, no VP negation obtains for presentationals.

37. Notice that I have been claiming that the scope of NEG coincides with the rheme or asserted part of the sentence. Strictly speaking, NO in (57) commands both the theme (i.e. $_{NP}\ldots e_i \ldots$)) and the rheme (i.e. apareció Paco)). But since the theme is empty, NO has an actual effect only on the rhematic part of the sentence. Thus (57) is equivalent to:

$$[_{S'}\text{NO}[_{S}(_{VP}\text{apareció Paco})]_S]_{S'}$$

38. Givón (1975b) refers to sentence negation proper as external negation, and so does Babby (1980).

39. Moreover, there are some intransitive verbs whose lexical meaning tends to bar them from entering into presentational constructions, for example, <u>toser</u> 'to cough', <u>fracasar</u> 'to fail', <u>caminar</u> 'to walk'. These verbs are more likely to adhere to <u>SV word</u> order (in noncontrastive, noninterrogative sentences).

40. In contrast, parentheses make clear that a transitive verb may also be used intransitively + V [+__(NP)].

41. In this second alternative, double listing would be required in any case: one listing of the idiomatic expression as a complex verb, the other as a transitive verb. But it would complicate matters even more (with no obvious gain) if in addition to this, one were to specify that the complex verb alternative has only VS word order, while the transitive verb might enter into SVO and VOS word orders.

42. His discussion is based on Banfield's (1973) *Stylistic transformations in 'Paradise Lost'*, University of Wisconsin unpublished dissertation.

43. Other scholars who have dealt with stylistic rules are: Chomsky and Lasnik (1977), Koster (1978), and Kayne and Pollock (1978). But some of their supposedly stylistic rules are not really stylistic by the criteria discussed further on.

44. Kuno (1979) maintains that all syntactic rules are discourse-determined.

45. Nevertheless, on the assumption that nonoblique Case Assignment applies on S-structures, it seems reasonable to suppose that Subject Postposing must have already operated. Note that the relative order of Subject Postposing and Subject-Verb Agreement is not crucial. If this latter rule precedes Subject Postposing, agreement is established with the [NP, S]. On the other hand, if Subject Postposing precedes, agreement can be achieved with the NP which carries Nominative Case.

46. Notice that (65b) and (66b) include preverbal adverbials (<u>de repente</u> and <u>a los ocho</u>). This is to insure that the embedded clause is interpreted as presentational (see Section 2.1.4 in this chapter). I use Δ to show the supposed removal site.

47. Additionally, Head Start would also be structure-building unless it moves the embedded subject into some sort of empty node.

48. The answer to this puzzle as to why the subject of presentationals does not seem to enter into an anaphoric relation with the phrase in TOP might be found within Bordelois' (1974: 10) Crossing Constraint (interpreted as a constraint on construal).

Prevent the application of any rule resulting in the following configuration:

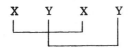

where X and Y are constituents under a given sentential
node, relating to their respective traces by means of a
rule and where obligatory control is operative within the
scope of the crossing paths.

Notice that the paths cross (or at least 'coincide') in examples
such as the ones I have been discussing.

Los invitados resulta que a la puerta [t] ya estaban ellos.

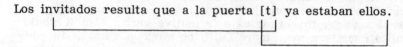

49. Recall that all presentational sentences have both the V
and the NP in the scope of assertion.

50. I owe this observation to C. Rosen. Note that our
reasoning also explains why the anaphoric relation between the
thematic phrase in TOP position and the thematic preverbal
PRO subject of declarative sentences can be established without any problems (cf. 67b) and (68b)).

51. Notice that if theme/rheme determination belonged to LF
(that is, if scope of assertion were established independently
of speaker's intention and communicative force), then the
explanation found in the last paragraph of the previous subsection would show that Subject Postposing cannot be stylistic.
It might very well be that further research and a better understanding of the role of theme/rheme in linguistic analysis would
indicate that these notions pertain to LF instead of being post-
LF. Until that time, I continue to adopt a more conservative
stand and consider theme/rheme as belonging to an immediately
post-LF level of analysis within sentence grammar.

52. Contrastive focus would also result when both F_1 and
F_2 coincide in assigning focus to the same word.

53. Discussion of the derived constituent structure that this
movement produces is taken up in Section 2.3.3.1.3.

54. This goes against Kayne and Pollock's (1978) formulation
of Stylistic-Inversion for French.

$$NP \quad X \implies e \quad 2 \quad 1$$
$$1 \quad 2$$

These authors maintain that the foregoing rule 'will automatically
apply to object NPs as well as subject NPs' (1978:619), which
will permit them to 'dispense with the heretofore separate rule
of "Heavy NP Shift"' (1978:618). For a critique of Kayne and
Pollock, see Dubuisson (1978-1979).

55. This implies that there is something basic in the partition subject/predicate. Arguments in the predicate can be
moved around within this constituent without major consequences;
but if the subject argument crosses the 'frontier' and goes into
the VP, it has an effect sometimes even in grammaticality (cf.
Section 4.3.2.3 for discussion).

2 Further Presentational Sentences / 201

56. This is not even a universal property within the
Romance languages. Italian obeys it, and French does in a
much more limited way. I suspect it correlates heavily with
the relative 'freedom' of word order a given language allows.
57. This requirement has a couple of well-known exceptions
such as commands. Recall that Spanish, as opposed to English,
even allows for syntactically subjectless sentences (impersonal
haber, impersonal hacer).
58. The prohibition against 'lowering' morphological material
into an exhausted cycle dates from Chomsky 1965:146 (for a
Spanish-related discussion of this condition, see Suñer 1976b).
Chomsky (1973:243) rules out lowering by means of the Strict
Cycle Condition (for recent discussion of the SCC, see Freidin
1978).
59. There is a grammatical sentence (i), but it does not
have the same meaning as sentence (ii).

(i) Apareció cuando nosotros ya estábamos por salir, Paco.
    he-appeared when we already were about to-leave Paco

(ii) Apareció Paco cuando nosotros ya estábamos por salir.
    appeared Paco when we already were about to-leave

Sentence (ii) is a presentational sentence with focused Paco
followed by a when-clause. Sentence (i) is a declarative sentence with a deleted nonemphatic pronominal subject, followed
by a when-clause, followed by a right-dislocated element
(Paco) which is coreferential with the deleted matrix subject.
This Paco is not in focus; on the contrary, it carries low
intonation and is separated from the preceding clause by a
comma-like pause.
    On the assumption that the postposed subject attaches to V^n
(see Section 2.3.3.1.3.2), the ungrammaticality of the blocked
outputs in (86) cannot be explained by saying that the subject
cannot attach to the highest S node (in which case, Subjacency
would not play a role).
    This is as good a place as any to point out that the posited
rule of Subject Postposing is not necessarily meant to generate
all instances of sentences which exhibit a postverbal subject.
Besides cases like (i), with a (base-generated) right-dislocated
phrase, there are sentences like (iii) and (iv).

(iii) Grande fue mi sorpresa.
    big was my surprise

(iv) ¿Compraste tú la mesa?
    bought you the table

In (iii) the preposed adjective carries emphatic stress; the
subject appears to be thematic and most likely needs to be
semantically definite. Sentence (iv) is a question in which the

preferred order seems to be Verb-Subject-Object. It remains to be determined whether (iv) is a case of Subject Postposing or of Verb Preposing.

60. If one assumes that Subject Postposing not only enters into the derivation of sentences which are eventually interpreted as presentationals, but also into the derivation of those in which the subject gets an exhaustive reading interpretation (hence, contrastive), one has sentences in which both the matrix and the embedded subjects are postposed.

Descubrió Paco que en 1984 aparecerá un cometa.
discovered Paco that in 1984 will-appear a comet
'Paco (and nobody else) discovered that a comet will
    appear in 1984.'

61. For arguments in favor of abandoning the notion of Subjacency for the Bounding Condition, see Koster (1978).

62. This is the position that Emonds (1976:39) adopts for stylistic inversion in French and for some English sentences.

63. Although it is highly desirable to have only one rule which postposes the subject, it might turn out to be incorrect to do so. Notice that the NP subject is postposed to the end of the VP in presentational sentences but ahead of the direct object in (89). Nevertheless, (89) still indicates that Emonds' structure-preserving hypothesis runs into problems.

64. Thus, it should be kept in mind that the X̄-theory was not available to Emonds.

65. Jackendoff (1977) assumes a Uniform Three-Level Hypothesis. He demonstrates its validity for English by showing the correlation between syntax and semantics in the complement system. According to him, it is possible to single out the correct position for any given complement by its degree of articulation with its head: thus, X' corresponds to functional arguments, X" to restrictive modifiers, and X''' to nonrestrictive modifiers.

66. From now on, I am assuming the X̄-theory and its labeling convention even though I use the traditional node labels for ease of exposition whenever confusion does not threaten.

67. Notice that this leaves open the possibility that heaviness might cause a switch in the order of the constituents in some instances.

68. Example (105b) sounds completely natural if a comma-like pause is inserted after en 1970 and Paco gets low intonation (i.e. if it is right-dislocated).

69. Exchanging en 1970 in the (b) sentences for a place expression such as en Nueva York leaves the argumentation intact.

70. Of course, it is still to be determined exactly at what VP level the postposed subject attaches. This has to wait until sentences other than presentationals are studies in detail. There is also the possibility that the exact level should be left

undetermined; the postposed subject attaches to different levels, depending on the degree of articulation of the other constituents present in the VP (if any) with their head.
71. Schwartz himself comments that there are problems with the notion 'next highest S' (1972:45-46).
72. One possible problem with the structure in (108) has to do with the question of government and C-command.

(i) Government: α governs β iff α minimally C-commands β and there is no S̄ or NP between α and β

α = [±N, ±V], or tns
(Koster 1979 Summary of Chomsky's Pisa lectures)

(ii) C-command:
A node α C-commands a node β if neither dominates the other and if the first branching node dominating α dominates β (Reinhart 1976).

The definitions in (i) and (ii) make it obvious that V does not minimally C-command the postposed subject in (iii); on the other hand, V does minimally C-command the postposed un hombre in (iv).

(iii)

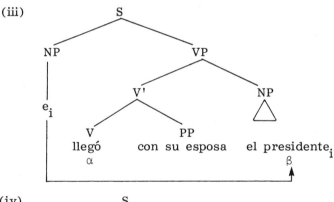

(iv)

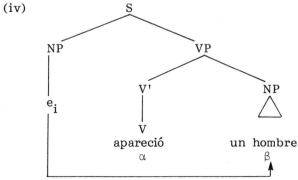

In other words, V does not govern the postposed subject provided the lower node branches, but it does so if it is immediately followed by the postposed subject. In spite of this
problem, no ill consequences arise (that I can see), because
the postposed subject receives nominative case and not objective case (see discussion in Section 2.5).

73. Guéron (1978:4) has an interpretive rule of focus marking which reads 'Mark the last constituent following the V within
the VP focus of S. If nothing follows the verb, mark the verb
focus of S.' Given that the LF she posits for her Presentation
sentences is:

$$(_{S'}(_S \text{VERB}_i \text{ (NP) } _{VP}(\dots v_i \dots))_S)_{S'}$$

the rule of focus marking--which she proposes (1978:3) applies
to LFs--could not apply to the LF of a Presentation S, because
there is nothing within the VP. Alternatively, if whatever is
assigned to the V_1 is inherited by VERB_1, then the verb is
what is marked focus of S. Either option renders the wrong
result; therefore, her rule of Focus Assignment works for Predication sentences but not for Presentation ones. The rule was
modified in Guéron (1980:650) to read as follows:

(a) Mark the last argument in the C-command domain of the
    verb 'Focus of S'.
(b) Mark VP 'Focus of S'.

One problem with this rule is that it distinguishes between
Presentation and Predication sentences before SI-2, that is, it
does not work independently of sentence type.

There is an interesting contrast between English and Spanish
regarding presentational and declarative sentences. Guéron
writes (1978:4): 'Assume both Logical Forms [Predication S
and Presentation S, M.S.] to be associated with each surface
structure in English. Any S is then in principle interpretable
either as a Presentation S or as a Predication'. This fact seems
to be a peculiarity of English, no doubt due to its fixed word
order. Spanish, with its 'free word order', aligns its surface
structure elements much more closely to the corresponding
ordering in LF, and hence seems to avoid this double association.

74. The clarification 'inside of S' becomes necessary to avoid
marking right-dislocated structures as rhematic. In essence,
everything outside of S is thematic, including left-dislocated
as well as right-dislocated constituents. This is expressed
schematically as shown here.

$$\begin{bmatrix} \text{L-D} \\ \overline{\text{Th}} \end{bmatrix} \begin{bmatrix} & \text{S} & \text{V O} \\ _S & \overline{\text{Th}} & \overline{\text{Rh}} \end{bmatrix} \begin{bmatrix} \text{R-D} \\ \overline{\text{Th}} \end{bmatrix}$$

75. It must be kept in mind that this Rhematization rule is valid for noncontrastive environments. See Chapter 3 for the grammar of (some) contrastive sentences.

76. Whenever possible, I show the effect of these rules at the same time to avoid lengthening the discussion unnecessarily.

77. This section (as well as the rest of the study) was written before I became acquainted with Chomsky's Pisa Lectures and the ensuing literature that these lectures stimulated. I had independently arrived at the conclusion that verbal agreement together with the nonobligatoriness of the subject node in Spanish play a crucial role in the grammaticality of sentences with traces which precede its coindexed NP. The main point is that grammatical relations are not obscured by the rightward movement rule of Subject Postposing. I found it very gratifying to discover that Chomsky arrived at a similar conclusion when proposing that verb inflection can bind an empty element in subject position. In revising this manuscript for publication, I have incorporated and referred to some of this recent literature.

78. This coindexing is different from that established between a PRO and its antecedent; in this case, coindexing is achieved by a rule of construal.

79. But see discussion further on.

80. The qualification 'usually' is necessary because Fiengo (1977) hypothesizes that traces must be allowed to precede in the following structure:

$$\dots[\dots[e]_{NP_i}\dots]_\alpha\dots[X]_{NP_i}\dots$$

where α is a cyclic node,

because of the existence of English examples such as:

[Pictures of himself]$_{NP}$amused him.

vs.

*Herself likes her.

81. The Dresher-Hornstein Principle is restated by Freidin (1978:524) as the Trace Erasure Prohibition which says: 'A bound trace may not be erased'. Freidin assumes that trace erasure crucially involves a change of index, and he maintains that There-Insertion and Extraposition have no effect on the index of $[_{NP}e_i]$. Under this hypothesis, Agent Postposing (i.e. the first part of Passive) would not qualify as a rule of English.

82. Actually, under my proposal, Spanish conforms to (137) because the trace is bound by the verb inflection.

83. Kayne (1980) arrives at a similar conclusion for Italian.

84. This is not to say that verb agreement is an absolute indicator of subjecthood in every instance. There are two main cases in which this type of agreement is not completely trust-worthy: (i) completely syntactically subjectless sentences (e.g. impersonal haber, hacer) and the so-called impersonal se sen-tences, and (ii) equational sentences. In the first instance, an optional object-verb attraction rule may trigger agreement with a prepositionless direct object (cf. Section 1.4). In the second, given the different word order possibilities which ob-tain in Spanish, it is almost impossible to single out unequivo-cally the syntactic subject (recall that in Latin both terms of the equation took Nominative Case).

85. Convention (145) is not exclusive to Spanish. I predict that it will be needed in other 'free word order' languages which fulfill two prerequisites: (i) the language must allow null sub-jects and (ii) it must have 'overt' verb morphology--'overt' in the sense 'phonologically salient' (that is, that it survives in the spoken language). In the Romance group, (i) and (ii) correctly separate French from Spanish, Portuguese, Catalan, and Italian.

86. Chomsky and Lasnik discuss this in reference to their putative universal filter (68):

(68) $*[_{S'}$ that $[_{NP}e...]$, unless $\bar{S}$ or its trace is in the con-text: $[_{NP}NP\_...]$ which is meant to apply taking into account the following qualification:

The filter (68) is valid for all languages that do not have a rule of Subject-Pronoun Deletion, and only these. (Chomsky and Lasnik (71))

Maling and Zaenen (1978) demonstrate that the foregoing quali-fication needs to be modified as follows:

Filter (68) is valid for all languages with obligatory dummy subjects, and only these. (Maling and Zaenen (2'))

87. Of course, this leaves open the question of which lan-guages can index by AG and which cannot. And this leads me back to my convention (145) (and note 85) as a possible way to predict this parameter.

88. That the postposed NP is Nominative can be shown by the following: (i) the NP position can be occupied by a subject pronoun:
(a) Apareció ella,
    appeared (3 sg.) she
    'She appeared.'
(ii) if the NP were not Nom., it would need to be Objective (because its governing category would be the verb). That it

is not Objective can be demonstrated by the impossibility of having an object clitic:
(b) *la apareció.
her appeared (3 sg.)
and (iii), it must be remembered that the NP determines verb agreement (a subject property).

89. This Case-inheritance convention is somewhat parallel to the convention on coindexing by movement.

90. 'In principle' because they still have to obey conditions on rules and interpretation such as Subjacency, the Specified Subject Condition (SSC), and the Propositional Island Constraint (PIC) (or alternatively, the Nominative Island Constraint instead of the SSC and the PIC).

91. Intransitive because it was decided to analyze expressions like dar señales de vida as complex verbs, i.e. [$_V$[$_V$ dar] [$_{NP}$ señales de vida]]. Moreover, 'intransitive presentationals' is a convenient label to identify the type of sentence studied in this chapter.

92. This implies that the movement is from an argument position (that of subject) to one of nonargument.

93. For a number of reasons (156) would not work for all declarative sentences. The most obvious is that in the declarative sentence Paco llegó 'Paco arrived', there is no nonoblique argument in the VP. Rule (155), however, correctly selects the verb as the element in Focus.

94. Remember that I criticized Guéron's (1980:65) rule of Focus Assignment precisely because it does not work independently of sentence type (cf. note 73).

95. Notice that haber sentences, although presentational in function, exhibit the order of constituents characteristic of declarative sentences, i.e. VO.

96. Of course, this stand might prove to be wrong. Minimally, it is to be expected that further research would lead to the refinement of all the rules in this book.

97. In other words, impersonal haber could be marked in the lexicon with the feature [+presentational], because it is a verb that is very specialized. The reason I am unwilling to do so is because of consistency: intransitive presentationals very clearly show that presentationalism is not a lexical but a discourse function.

98. It is immaterial to this discussion whether the process is one of deletion or interpretation. For the latter possibility, see Williams (1977).

99. One such process is the inability of the postposed subject of intransitive presentationals to be anaphorically related to a constituent in TOP position (cf. Section 2.3.2.1.2) or to undergo Topicalization. Both processes are available to haber presentationals (cf. Section 1.2.3).

3

THE NAKED NOUN CONSTRAINT

3.0 Introduction. In the previous chapter, it became evident during the examination of presentational sentences with semantically intransitive verbs that for every presentational sentence there appears to be a corresponding declarative sentence. That is to say, given a presentational sentence like (1), it becomes possible to predict the existence of a declarative sentence such as the one found in (2). [1]

(1) Apareció la luna.   Presentational
    appeared (3 sg.) the moon
    'The moon appeared.'

(2) La luna apareció.   Declarative
    'The moon appeared.'

The purpose of this chapter is to show that although the foregoing generalization holds in the great majority of cases, there are instances in which a presentational sentence cannot be paired with an analogous well-formed declarative sentence. Compare (3) and (4).

(3a) Caen gotas. (H 12)   Presentational
     fall (3 pl.) drops
     'Drops are falling.'

(3b) Del suelo salía humedad.
     from-the ground came-out (3 sg.) humidity
     'From the ground humidity arose.'

(4a) *Gotas caen.   Declarative
(4b) *Del suelo humedad salía.
(4c) *Humedad salía del suelo.

The lack of parallelism between (3) and (4) obtains under conditions of normal stress and intonation, i.e. in nonemphatic contexts. Section 3.1 explores this lack of parallelism while establishing its pertinent parameters. Once the conditions and domain of the Naked Noun Constraint (NNC) are justified, I turn to the reasons for the NNC, the answer to which is found by examining the meaning and functions of naked nouns and preverbal subjects (Section 3.2). Since contrastive environments stand in defiance of the NNC, Section 3.3 is devoted to the various means Spanish has at its disposal to make a given environment emphatic. Section 3.4 provides a formal analysis of contrastive sentences. Finally, in Section 3.5 a comparison of the presentational and contrastive grammars is presented so that their differences can be appreciated at a glance. This last section also includes a discussion of the form and place of the NNC as a filter.

3.1 **The Naked Noun Constraint.** As a first hypothesis, the ungrammaticality of examples like those found in (4) may be attributed to the existence of what I call the Naked Noun Constraint (NNC) in the grammar of contemporary colloquial Spanish.[2] This constraint can be stated as in (5).

(5) Naked Noun Constraint

An unmodified common noun in preverbal position cannot be the surface subject of a sentence under conditions of normal stress and intonation.[3]

The following sections explore in detail each condition in this constraint: (1) common noun, (2) unmodified, (3) in preverbal position, (4) surface subject, and (5) normal stress and intonation. With the exception of (5), which is discussed in Section 3.3, each of these provisos is considered in turn. The extent to which the NNC belongs in the grammar of Spanish and why Spanish should adhere to such an unwieldly constraint are questioned.

3.1.1 **Common nouns.** It is a well-known fact of Spanish that proper nouns can appear as subjects without any modifiers.

(6a) Paco llegará mañana.
'Paco will-arrive tomorrow.'

(6b) Madrid es la capital de España.[4]
'Madrid is the capital of Spain.'

On the other hand, if common nouns appear by themselves preverbally, ungrammatical sequences result ((7), cf. also examples in (4)).

(7a) *Dirección falta.
'Direction is-lacking.'

(7b) *Brujas aparecerán en cuanto menos lo esperes.
'Witches will-appear when you least expect it.'

3.1.2 Unmodified nouns. Common nouns completely devoid of any modification, in other words, 'naked', are not allowed as subjects in preverbal position (cf. (7)). By contrast, any modification which explicitly marks partitiveness or totality produces grammatical sentences.

(8a) Unos abogados (buenos) vivían allí.
'Some (good) lawyers lived there.'

(8b) Los abogados vivían allí.
'The lawyers lived there.'

(8c) Esos abogados vivían allí.
'Those lawyers lived there.'

(8d) Tres abogados vivian alli.
'Three lawyers lived there.'

(8e) Abogados de pocas palabras vivían allí.
'Lawyers of few words lived there.'

Compare the foregoing with the parallel sentence in (9) using the naked noun.

(9) *Abogados vivían allí.

In Alonso (1954), one finds sentences like those in (10) (my underlining, M.S.), where removal of the underlined segments renders ungrammatical outputs.

(10a) Caballo de paseo no gana batallas.
horse of riding no wins battles
'Riding horses do not win battles.'

(10b) Moza bonita no paga dinero.
woman pretty no pays money
'Pretty women don't pay.'

(10c) Hombres así no debieran existir. [5]
men like-that no ought-to to-exist
'Men like that ought not to exist.'

Therefore, the 'unmodified' specification in the NNC appears to be justified. Note that each of the modifiers in (10) separates a subset from the totals denoted by the nouns.

Schematically, the modified nouns refer to the shaded portion in the diagram.

In this study, I want to capture the contrast implicit in total vs. partitive by referring to the unmodified vs. modified parameter of the NNC.[6]

3.1.3 Preverbal position. This stipulation is needed because, in contrast to the ungrammatical declaratives which have unmodified subjects in preverbal position (cf. (7), (9), and (11)), one finds corresponding grammatical presentationals with unmodified subjects in postverbal position (cf. (3), (12), and (13)).

(11a) *Niños juegan en el parque.
'Children play in the park.'

(11b) *Noticias llegaron mientras estabas de compras.
'News arrived while you-were out shopping.'

(12a) Juegan niños en el parque.
play (3 pl.) children in the park

(12b) Llegaron noticias mientras estabas de compras.
arrived (3 pl.) news while you-were out shopping.

(13a) Vivían abogados allí. (cf. (9))
lived (3 pl.) lawyers there
'Lawyers lived there.'

(13b) Allí vivían abogados.
there lived (3 pl.) lawyers.

That 'preverbal position' is the correct characterization--as opposed to something like 'sentence-initial position'--can be shown by examining examples where an adverbial occurs sentence-initially.

(14a) *Durante la mañana niños juegan en el parque.
'During the morning children play in the park.'

(14b) *Ayer noticias llegaron ...
'Yesterday news arrived ...'

The sentences in (15) show grammatical presentationals with initial adverbials.

(15a) Durante la mañana juegan <u>niños</u> en el parque.
(15b) Ayer llegaron <u>noticias</u> ...

By comparing (14) and (15) with (11) and (12), it can easily be seen that a sentence adverbial in sentence-initial position does not alter grammaticality judgments. Consequently, 'preverbal position' represents the accurate way of stating this condition.

3.1.3.1 Unmodified subjects with transitive verbs.
In addition, mention should be made of the fact that the verbs which occur in all the examples discussed so far are intransitive. The relevance of this observation must be determined. Since 'presentationalism' is exclusive to semantically intransitive verbs (cf. Section 2.1.3), and since only verbs which are characterized by the presence of just one NP allow for a presentative interpretation, it is appropriate to ask whether the postposing of an unmodified preverbal subject renders a transitive sentence grammatical. In other words, given a sentence such as (16), does postposing of the subject produce a well-formed sentence?

(16) *<u>Hombres</u> cazaron un ciervo.
'Men hunted a deer.'

As shown in (17), the answer is negative.

(17) *Cazaron <u>hombres</u> un ciervo.
*Cazaron <u>un ciervo</u> <u>hombres</u>. [7]

These findings are confirmed by other examples.

(18) *<u>Rumores</u> llenaban el cuarto.
'Rumors filled the room.'

*Llenaban <u>rumores</u> el cuarto.
*Llenaban <u>el cuarto</u> <u>rumores</u>. [8]

(19) *<u>Alumnos</u> dieron regalos a la maestra.
'Students gave presents to the teacher.'

*Dieron <u>alumnos</u> regalos a la maestra.
*Dieron <u>regalos</u> <u>alumnos</u> a la maestra.
*Dieron regalos a la maestra <u>alumnos</u>.

The suppression of merely one of the verbal arguments in (17) and (18), so that only one NP remains in the sentence, produces mixed results, but for different reasons.

(20a) Cazaron <u>hombres</u>.
hunted (<u>3 pl.</u>) men

(20b) *Llenaban <u>rumores</u>.
   filled (3 pl.) rumors

Although (20a) is grammatical, it is only because <u>hombres</u> has been reinterpreted as direct object, the subject being a deleted third person plural pronoun. Thus the sentence actually means 'They hunted men'. In (20b) such a reinterpretation cannot take place and the sentence is ungrammatical. Even if the semantic interpretation of the verb is unambiguous, the sentence is judged ungrammatical. Such is the case in (21), although the meaning of <u>leer</u> 'to read' makes it clear that one can only read things that are readable (i.e. inanimate objects containing written language).

(21) *Leen <u>alumnos</u>.
   read (3 pl.) students
   'Students read.'

It is interesting to speculate briefly as to why transitive verbs do not readily accept unmodified postposed subjects. [9] Transitive verbs by their very nature take (at least) two noun phrases, one which functions as subject, the other as object. It seems that the language avoids potential ambiguity or misinterpretation by constraining word order possibilities. To be more precise, it is not accurate enough to say that unmodified subjects of transitive sentences cannot be postposed; one must say: 'postposition is not permitted under conditions of normal stress and intonation if the outcome is the sequence V NP (NP) in which the NP(s) is/are not clearly marked as to their function'. This observation is corroborated by comparing the ungrammatical examples in (17), (18), and (19) to the grammatical sentences in (22).

(22a) La cosecha la destruyeron <u>langostas</u>.
   the harvest (f. sg.) it (f. sg.) destroyed (3 pl.)
     locusts.
   'The harvest, locusts destroyed it.'

(22b) El cuarto lo llenaban <u>rumores</u>.
   the room (m. sg.) it (m. sg.) filled rumors
   'The room, rumors filled it.'

In (22), ambiguity does not result. Every item in these sentences is clearly marked as to function: the initial NP has been left-dislocated and is 'tied' to the direct object clitic, with which it agrees in gender and number; and the unmodified subject has been postposed and agrees with the plural verb. Furthermore, there is no room for any other prepositionless NP. The meaning of the sentences is transparent.
   Notice that in the case of transitive verbs with unmodified subjects, subject-verb agreement does not seem to constitute a

sufficient disambiguating factor (cf. (20) and (21)).[10] At this point, all I can say is that the postposing of unmodified subjects with transitive verbs obeys some kind(s) of ambiguity principle(s) of which little is understood. Nevertheless, it is clear that it would be incorrect simply to bar this type of subject postposing from applying to transitive sentences. Just as it was impossible to bar completely pseudo transitive verbs from entering into presentational constructions (Section 2.1.3, e.g. dar señales de vida, hacer su entrada, tener lugar), it is equally undesirable to prevent unmodified NPs from being postposed after some transitive verbs. If one were to do this, one would be barring grammatical sentences from the language. Consider the sentences in (23).

(23a) En esta esquina, todos los días tienen lugar accidentes.
on this corner, all the days have (3 pl.) place accidents
'On this corner, every day accidents take place.'

(23b) Y ahora hacen su entrada fantasmas.
and now are-making (3 pl.) their entrance ghosts
'And now ghosts are coming in.'

In view of what was said in Chapter 2, the grammaticality of the examples in (23) should not be surprising. The reason for their grammaticality is that the verb plus the NP object form a unit--maybe even a complex verb--which may be interpreted as 'to appear' or as suggesting mere presence or existence.

In sum, 'in preverbal position' provides the correct characterization for the phenomenon reviewed. Subject postposing should not be limited to intransitive verbs, because cases exist in which transitive verbs yield a fully grammatical sentence (cf. (22) and (23)). It was hypothesized that some version of an up-to-ambiguity principle is responsible for barring some non-contrastive word order possibilities from surfacing.

3.1.4 Surface subjects. In the first place, it is necessary to determine whether or not the NNC is exclusively limited to naked nouns that fulfill the subject function, and in the second place, it must be decided whether the NNC applies to any kind of subject or only to surface ones.

As the sentences in (24) show, Spanish does allow unmodified common nouns which represent grammatical relations other than subject.

(24a) Paco es médico.
'Paco is a-doctor.'

(24b) José ha puesto tienda.   (Ramsey 1956:2.33)
'Jose has set-up shop.'

(24c) Trini compró coche.
'Trini bought a-car.'

(24d) Cobraron dividendos.
'They-collected dividends.'

(24e) Está en casa.
'He-is at home.'

(24f) Es una estatua de marfil.
'It-is a statue of ivory.'

(25g) Los caballeros iban lanza en ristre. (Lapesa 1974:298)
'The knights were going lances in hand.'

(24h) Soportamos el bombardeo cuerpo a tierra. (Lapesa
1974:298)
'We-withstood the bombardment flat on the ground.'

Hence, it is obvious that the NNC applies only to subjects.[11]
The second task is to determine what kinds of subjects the
NNC applies to. Otero (1973:553) writes: '... Spanish requires a determiner in a deep subject NP which is not a proper
name ...,' although later in a footnote he clarifies 'the determiner does not always appear in surface structure' (1973:553,
note 4).[12] First, note that it might be difficult if not impossible to prove or disprove Otero's remark conclusively. And
second, observe that he is concerned with determiners while
the NNC mentions 'modification' in general (that is to say, it
includes adjectives and relative clauses) and it also specifies
'in preverbal position'. Thus, since the NNC and Otero's statement are not quite comparable, I do not consider his statement
further here.
It appears that deep subjects are irrelevant for the NNC.
For example, notice what happens when one passivizes[13] transitive sentences with unmodified direct objects.

(25a) *Tienda ha sido puesta por José. (Cf. (20b))
'Shop has been set-up by José.'

(25b) *Coche fue comprado por Trini. (Cf. (20c))
'Car was bought by Trini.'

(25c) *Dividendos fueron cobrados. (Cf. (20d))
'Dividends were collected.'

Once these naked nouns are made into surface subjects and
placed in preverbal position, the sentences are ungrammatical.
Further proof for this point is provided by the examples in
(26).

(26a) La cosecha fue destruida por <u>langostas</u>.
'The harvest was destroyed by locusts.'

(26b) La bomba fue implantada por <u>guerrilleros</u>.
'The bomb was planted by guerrillas.'

The sentences in (26) are passives which could be taken to be
derived from the ungrammatical sentences in (27).

(27a) *<u>Langostas</u> destruyeron la cosecha.
'Locusts destroyed the harvest.'

(27b) *<u>Guerrilleros</u> implantaron la bomba.
'Guerrillas planted the bomb.'

If the constraint applied to deep structure subjects, (27) could
not be generated by the grammar of Spanish.[14] And because
(27) is generally assumed to be the source for (26), (26) itself
could not be generated.[15]

Furthermore, it should be remembered that the NNC explicitly
stipulates surface subjects <u>and</u> preverbal position, a fact which
accounts for the difference in grammaticality judgments of (28)
as opposed to (29).

(28a) *La cosecha <u>langostas</u> la destruyeron.
the harvest (f. sg.) locusts it (f. sg.) destroyed
'The harvest, locusts destroyed it.'

(28b) *La bomba <u>guerrilleros</u> la implantaron.[16]
the bomb (f. sg.) guerrillas it (f. sg.) planted
'The bomb, guerrillas planted it.'

(29a) La cosecha la destruyeron <u>langostas</u>.
the harvest (f. sg.) it (f. sg.) destroyed locusts
'The harvest, locusts destroyed it.'

(29b) La bomba la implantaron <u>guerrilleros</u>.
the bomb (f. sg.) it (f. sg.) planted guerrillas
'The bomb, guerrillas planted it.'

Another movement rule which has the potential for placing a
naked noun in preverbal subject position is Tough Movement
(the term is due to Postal 1971). This rule has the effect of
taking the object out of the embedded sentence and making it
the subject of the matrix sentence (for example, <u>It is easy to
please John</u> ===> <u>John is easy to please</u>).[17] In Spanish, (31)
would be arrived at from (30) through Tough Movement.

(30) Es imposible arreglar relojes.
'It-is impossible to-fix watches.'

(31) *Relojes son imposibles de arreglar.
'Watches are impossible to fix.'

The sentence in (31) is ungrammatical under noncontrastive stress and intonation precisely because the subject is a naked noun which appears in preverbal position.

3.1.5 Recapitulation. At this point it may be useful to review the material covered so far. Throughout the preceding sections, examples have been given to show that the NNC applies to nouns which are common (Section 3.1.1), and unmodified (Section 3.1.2), which are in preverbal position (Section 3.1.3) and which function as surface subjects (Section 3.1.4).

Assuming that Spanish is an SVO language (see Chapter 4 for discussion of this point), this collection of facts amounts to saying that naked nouns cannot occupy the basic subject position; in other words, they cannot remain in the position in which they are generated by the phrase structure rules of the language. As has been mentioned, one of the strategies used to avoid ungrammaticality is subject postposing.[18] This is shown schematically as follows.

Basic word order: S V (O)[19]

$$*N_u$$

Strategy: N_u V

Subject Postposing

By contrast, the language allows naked nouns to perform other grammatical relations (cf. (24)). Before proceeding any further, I show that the NNC is equally operant in embedded clauses.

3.1.6 NNC's domain. As one would anticipate, the NNC is not exclusive to matrix sentences; the same conditions and requirements hold for embedded clauses. A few examples suffice to illustrate this point.

(32a) La alarma sonará si entran ladrones.
the alarm will-sound if enter (3 pl.) thieves.
'The alarm will sound if thieves enter.'

(32b) *La alarma sonará si ladrones entran.

(32c) La alarma sonará si esos ladrones entran.
'those thieves'

(32d) La alarma sonará si <u>ladrones sin experiencia</u> entran.
      'thieves without experience'

(33a) Me dijeron que explotarian <u>bombas</u>.
      to-me they-told that would-explode (3 pl.) bombs
      'I was told that bombs would explode.'

(33b) *Me dijeron que <u>bombas</u> explotarían.

(33c) Me dijeron que <u>las/unas bombas</u> explotarían.
      'the/some bombs'

(33d) Me dijeron que <u>bombas de 100 kilos</u> explotarían.
      'bombs of 100 kilos'

Examples (32) and (33) are self-explanatory. The only un-grammatical sentences are the ones given as (b) in each set. These are the ones in which the naked noun is also the pre-verbal subject of the embedded clause. Thus, whatever role the NNC is assigned in main clauses, this role should also be extended to embedded clauses. Moreover, whatever explanation is discovered for the NNC, it should be operative in the grammar of Spanish in general, and not just in matrix sentences.

3.2 **Toward an explanation.** So far, the exterior details of the NNC--its symptoms, so to speak--have been dealt with. Why should a language adhere to such a complex constraint--a constraint which is specifically limited to noncontrastive patterns, which mentions totally unmodified common nouns in a specific position (preverbally), and which additionally requires that these nouns fulfill a given grammatical relation (that of surface subjects)?

In order to try to answer the 'why', I attack the problem from two fronts. First, I look at unmodified nouns in general to see what their common denominator is. Later, I look at pre-verbal subjects from a functional perspective. The combined findings of the inquiry should provide us with the explanation for the NNC.

3.2.1 **Unmodified nouns.** In the search for the common de-nominator in the usage of unmodified nouns, one must inevitably look at the determiner system of the language.[20] Alonso (1954) argues that the basic contrast in the article system lies in the presence vs. absence of the article, and not in the contrast definite vs. indefinite. Lapesa (1974) expands the opposition 'presence vs. absence of the article' to 'noun with determiner vs. noun without determiner'. This latter approach is the one to adopt, since it is more consonant with the conditions speci-fied by the NNC. Nonetheless, Alonso's and Lapesa's views are highly compatible and can be adequately summarized as in (34).

(34)

Noun with determiner: (e.g.: el perro 'the dog' reference/existence individualized identifies objective quantitative	Noun without determiner: (e.g. perro 'dog' sense/essence nonindividualized categorizes/classifies subjective qualitative[21]

As an illustration, notice the difference that presence vs. absence of a determiner in the predicate creates in (35) as opposed to (36) (Lapesa's examples).

(35) Juan es arquitecto.
'John is (an) architect.

(36) Herrera fue el arquitecto de El Escorial.
'Herrera was the architect of the Escorial.'

In (35) arquitecto classifies, it includes the subject in a given category and appraises it according to this category; it answers the question ¿Qué es Juan? 'What is John?' (cf. Lapesa 1974: 294). In Kuno's words (1970:353), this noun indicates a property and not an individual object in the universe of discourse. Instead, in (36) el arquitecto identifies; it answers ¿Quién es Herrera? 'Who is Herrera?'. The article points to the individualized existence of an entity within a given category.[22]
Thus, according to the foregoing, one of the roles of the determiner is to signal that the noun no longer merely classifies, but that it identifies. Other pertinent examples are shown in (37) and (38).

(37a) Compré casa.
I-bought house
'I bought a house.'

(37b) Compré una/la casa.
'I bought a/the house.'

(38a) ¿Tienen ropa de hombre?
have-you clothes of man
'Do you carry men's clothing?'

(38b) Extraviaron la ropa del hombre.
they-lost the clothes of-the man
'They lost the man's clothes.'

In (37) and (38), only the (b) member of each pair indicates an objective reality.[23]
Spanish allows for this contrast between sense and reference (i.e. noun without determiner vs. noun with determiner) in all

grammatical functions--for example, predicate (cf. (35) and (36)), direct object (cf. (37) and (38a)), and object of a preposition (cf. (38a)). However, this opposition is far more restricted in the case of subjects. For example, Lapesa (1974: 298) writes that contemporary Spanish rejects examples such as those in (39).

(39a) *Verano trae cosechas.
'Summer brings crops.'

(39b) *Inglés pertenece a las lenguas germánicas.
'English belongs to the Germanic languages.'

(39c) *Hierro taladró madera.
'Iron perforated wood.'

(39d) *Envidia los movía.
'Envy moved them.'

Note that all the examples in (39) are instances filtered out by the NNC. The rest of the sentences given by Lapesa have a postposed subject, with the exception of the ones in (40) (1974:299).

(40a) Hombres de calidad estudian el asunto.
'Men of quality are-studying the matter.'

(40b) Voces prestigiosas consiguieron frenar los desmanes.
'Prestigious voices managed to-stop the misbehavior.'

(40c) Cosas como ésta desaniman a cualquiera.
'Things like this discourage anyone.'

(40d) Poderosas razones me obligaron a obrar así.
'Powerful reasons obliged me to act this-way.'

But as is quite evident in (40), the underlined preverbal subjects, although devoid of determiner, are nevertheless modified; therefore, their grammaticality is to be expected because they do not violate the NNC.[24]

3.2.1.1 Telegrams, newspaper headings, and classified ads. Nonetheless, exceptions exist.[25] The first exception is found in telegrams, newspaper headings, and classified ads, where space and economy force the creation of a pseudolanguage.[26] Some examples are shown in (41). I do not deal with this case since it can hardly be considered everyday colloquial Spanish.

(41a) Niña cae de seis pisos.
'Girl falls from six stories.'

(41b) Policía trunca robo.
'Policeman cuts short robbery.'

(41c) Paquete va por barco.
'Parcel goes by boat.'

(41d) Mecanógrafa desea empleo.
'Typist wants job.'

3.2.1.2 Definitions. The second exception is made up of
definitions and the like, where any 'X' becomes a sort of label.

(42a) Bueno es un adjetivo pero bien es un adverbio.
'Good is an adjective but well is an adverb.'

(42b) Pino es un árbol de las coníferas, de tronco elevado y
recto.
'Pine is a coniferous tree, of high and straight trunk.'

(42c) En los libros, los concuerda en género y número con
el sustantivo libros.
'In los libros, los agrees in gender and number with
the noun libros.'

(42d) Hombre no es lo mismo que caballero. (Lapesa 1974:
290)
'Man is not the same as gentleman.'

Observe that 'X' does not necessarily need to be a noun, it
can be almost any 'word'. Once again, examples such as those
found in (42), although very much part of the language, cannot be considered everyday Spanish; in the words of Lapesa,
they form part of a metalanguage. Nevertheless, one cannot
help noticing that even in this metalanguage the naked 'Xs'
conform to the summary in (34): they put things into categories, and they refer to the essence of the 'X' and not to its
individualized existence.

3.2.1.3 Proverbs. The third type of exception is comprised
of proverbs, 'of which a terse style is a leading characteristic'
(Ramsey 1956:2.37).

(43a) Dádivas quebrantan montañas. (Ramsey 1956:2.37)
'Gifts move mountains.'

(43b) Pobreza no es vileza. (Ramsey 1956:2.37)
'Poverty is no crime.'

(43c) Patria es humanidad. (Alonso 1954:173)[27]
'Fatherland is humanity.'

In cases such as (43) (i.e. proverbs), the omission of the determiner is not obligatory. Proverbs with determiners do exist (Lapesa 1974:293), as illustrated in (44).

(44a) <u>Los duelos</u> con pan son menos.
     mournings with bread are less
     'Mournings without economic worries are less painful.'

(44b) <u>Todo necio</u> confunde valor y precio.
     'Every fool confuses value and price.'

As Lapesa maintains, the naked noun appears to be a remnant of times gone by (1974:292). It points to ideal objects and makes a generalization about them with supposed universal validity. In this respect, proverbs are very much like generic statements. [28]

3.2.1.4 Enumerations. The fourth type of exception concerns enumerations.

(45a) <u>Hombres y mujeres</u> aceptaron mi opinión.
     'Men and women accepted my opinion.'

(45b) <u>Niños y adultos</u> respetaban sus palabras.
     'Children and adults respected his words.'

(45c) <u>Autos, ómnibus y camiones</u> fueron paralizados por la
        inundación.
     'Cars, buses, and trucks were at a standstill because
     of the flood.'

Those conjoined NPs behave peculiarly also with respect to Subject Postposing (cf. discussion in Section 3.1.3.1); all of the sentences in (46) are grammatical.

(46a) Aceptaron mi opinión <u>hombres y mujeres</u>.
     they-accepted my opinion men and women

(46b) Respetaban sus palabras <u>niños y adultos</u>.
     they-respected his words children and adults

(46c) Fueron paralizados por la inundación <u>autos</u>, <u>ómnibus</u>
       <u>y camiones</u>.
     they-were paralyzed by the flood cars, buses and
     trucks

Why should conjoined naked nouns act differently than single unmodified nouns? [29] Observe that examples parallel to (45a) and (46a), but with a single naked noun, are completely ungrammatical.

(47a) *Mujeres aceptaron mi opinión.
'Women accepted my opinion.'

(47b) *Aceptaron mi opinión mujeres.

I think the reason for the apparent idiosyncratic behavior of conjoined naked nouns is very simple. In the first place, notice that enumerations have a characteristic intonation pattern: the first element(s) of the list has (have) a slightly rising intonation, but the last element has falling intonation. Only when considering an incomplete list does the last element show a rise in intonation. This is shown schematically in (48).

(48a)   Complete enumeration

(48b)   Incomplete enumeration

Thus, it should be the case that an incomplete list with only one element in postverbal position should produce a grammatical sentence. That this is the case is evident in (49a); contrast this example with (49b), which exhibits falling (i.e. final) non-contrastive intonation.

(49a) Aceptaron mi opinión mujeres...
       accepted my opinion women

(49b) *Aceptaron mi opinión mujeres.

In addition, it is necessary to take a look at the function of enumerations. For the most part it seems that they are used to introduce new material into the discourse. To a question like (50a) one can answer with (50b), in which several options are offered. These options represent rhematic information which attracts focus and consequently stress.[30]

(50a) ¿Cómo voy al centro?
       'How do I get downtown?'

(50b) Bueno, puedes tomar el subte, el colectivo 7 o también puedes caminar.
       'Well, you can take the subway, bus number 7, or you can also walk.'

The rhematic information is more often than not also new information in the total discourse.

The stress pattern in examples such as those in (45) can now be studied. It is obvious that each conjoined element receives strong stress, which shows that the main focus of the sentence falls on the conjoined subject NP. Compare (51a) with (51b).

(51a) NIÑOS y ADULTOS respetaban sus palabras.
'Children and adults respected his words.'

(51b) Los niños respetaban sus palabras.
'The children respected his words.'

In (51a) heavy stress and focus fall on the conjoined subject elements, but in (51b) the sentential stress and focus fall on the last element of the VP--under normal conditions. Thus, the answer for the behavior of enumerations has been found. They do not obey the NNC because they are contrastive; that is, each element of the list receives heavy stress because the focus of the sentence has been attracted to this preverbal subject position, contrary to the case for unmarked focus. [31]

It is worth indicating that these enumerations tend to convey a sense of totality; in other words, they are read as exhaustive listings. Notice that the examples in (45) mention some kind of natural group which becomes equivalent to todo el mundo 'everybody'. This is because each example either lists the main members of the group or at least enough of them to suggest 'all'. [32] Other contrastive patterns are discussed in Section 3.3, where it is shown that they, too, fail to adhere to the NNC. This is the reason why the NNC explicitly mentions 'under conditions of normal stress and intonation'.

3.2.1.5 Summary and conclusion. Conjoined NPs exhaust the so-called exceptions to the NNC. It turns out that the first (newspaper headings, ads, and telegrams) and the second (definitions) were eliminated because they conform to specific guidelines dictated by special needs outside the realm of colloquial everyday Spanish. [33] The fourth type of exception (enumerations, or lists) is also outside the domain of the NNC because these form part of contrastive environments. Hence, only some proverbs (cf. (43)) seem to stand in defiance of the NNC. This last topic is taken up again in Section 3.3.2, where it is shown that this type of counterexample is also only apparent.

This investigation shows that the NNC is well established in colloquial spoken Spanish. Nouns without determiners point to the essence of an object, not to its existence, and they categorize it but do not identify it (cf. (34) in Section 3.2.1). What remains to be done is to examine the functional characteristic of subjecthood in order to discover why unmodified nouns cannot perform the subject function in preverbal position.

3.2.2 Preverbal subjects. It has already been established that noncontrastive sentences which exhibit the pattern NP VP are declarative sentences while those characterized by the pattern VP NP are presentationals. What needs to be determined is why VP NP_u is an allowed sequence but *NP_u VP is not

(under conditions of normal stress and intonation).   Compare
(52) with (53).

(52) Caen gotas.   Presentational
      fall (3 pl.) drops

(53) *Gotas caen.   Declarative
      'Drops fall/are falling.'

One has the feeling that somehow <u>gotas</u> in (53) does not have
enough 'weight' to appear in preverbal position.   'Weight' is
the informal term I use to refer to a noun such as <u>gotas</u> which,
because of lack of modification, has no referent and is not indi-
vidualized--a noun which categorizes but does not identify; a
noun which points to the sense and not to the reference of
whatever it denotes (cf. (34) in Section 3.2.1).   Moreover, in
(53) noncontrastive sentential stress and intonation fall on the
verb, which leaves the preverbal subject unstressed; thus,
the absence of stress is another contributing factor to its lack
of 'weight'.[34]
On the other hand, what does the preverbal subject position
imply?   In a declarative sentence, the subject constitutes the
'theme' of that sentence; as such, it is the unasserted portion
and shows a great tendency toward being presupposed.   Keenan
(1976), in developing his multifactor concept of basic subjects,
points out that subjects are generally characterized by (among
other things) independent existence,[35] absolute reference,[36]
presupposed reference, by being topics,[37] and, moreover, by
being highly referential.   Although Keenan does not explicitly
differentiate between preverbal and postverbal subject position,
it is evident that these characteristics correlate more closely
with the preverbal subject position in Spanish.   Nevertheless,
notice that none of these properties fits an unmodified preverbal
subject such as <u>gotas</u> in (53).
Consequently, what appears in the case of (53)--and in any
other sentence with a naked noun in preverbal position--is a
conflict between the function of an unmodified noun and the
function of preverbal subject,[38] which explains why these sentences are ungrammatical.   Therefore, one must conclude that
naked nouns cannot be thematic subjects; when they do appear
in preverbal position they must compensate for their inherent
'lack of weight' by attracting focus.   In this way they enter
into the spotlight and attract attention to themselves; in other
words, they become contrastive (cf. Section 3.2.1.4 and Section 3.3).
Thus, by looking at that which is proper to unmodified nouns
and that which is characteristic of subjects, one arrives at the
explanation for the NNC.   Naked nouns never appear as
subjects in preverbal position because these nouns cannot be
interpreted as the theme of the sentence.   Once again (cf.
Section 0.1.2), the functional dichotomy theme vs. rheme helps

226 / Spanish Presentational Sentence-Types

explain what might otherwise be considered an accidental gap in contemporary colloquial Spanish. As already discussed in Chapter 2, Spanish, with its relatively 'free' word order, has the liberty of postposing these naked subject nouns: Subject Postposing moves these nouns to a rhematic position in presentational sentences (cf. (52)). Note that, given the meaning of naked nouns, they might be the most appropriate way of introducing something for the first time into the world of discourse, for which reason they are highly compatible with the word order VP NP.

Tangentially, it should be pointed out that the NNC is a rather recent development of the language. Lapesa (1974:302-305) writes that the article has predominated with the subject noun ever since the seventeenth century, although it is possible to find isolated examples without the article as late as the nineteenth century. It is around the seventeenth century, therefore, that the contrast between noun with determiner vs. noun without determiner came to signal the opposition reference vs. sense. Before that, the contrast merely meant individualized vs. nonindividualized (thus, generic statements carried no determiner). This shift from [+ individualized][39] to [+referential] has been completed for the basic subject position (i.e. preverbally), but the situation is not as clear-cut for other positions where the old and the new system coexist.[40] Consider example (54).

(54a) Compré casa.
  'I-bought (a) house.'

(54b) Tiene miedo.
  s/he-has fear
  'S/he is scared.'

(54c) Paco llevaba marijuana.
  'Paco carried marihuana.'

Example (54) shows that NPs in other than basic subject position can be [- individualized] (they are also referential).

It should also be noted that, although naked nouns cannot be thematic because of their 'lack of weight', modified nouns--even though determinerless--give rise to grammatical sentences. Examples were mentioned under (10) in Section 3.1.2 (partially repeated here as (55)); one can add those in (56) (Lapesa 1974:300) and (57).

(55a) Hombres así no debieran existir.
  'Men like that ought not to exist.'

(55b) Moza bonita no paga dinero.
  'Pretty women don't pay (money).'

(56a) Leyes severas habían sido promulgadas.
'Severe laws had been issued.'

(56b) Altas montañas rodean el valle.
'High mountains surround the valley.'

(57a) Hombres andan por este mundo que son el sumo de la corrupción.
'Men exist in this world who are the epitome of corruption.'

(57b) Flores crecen aquí que lo dejan a uno asombrado.
'Flowers grow here which leave one astonished.'

The examples in (57) show a noun (hombres and flores, respectively) modified by a restrictive relative clause that has been extraposed.

The explanation for the grammaticality of (55)-(57) could be that adjectival modification--regardless of whether it is exercised by an adjective or a relative clause--provides the common noun with enough 'weight' for it to appear preverbally. Stated differently, modification brings out the contrast subset vs. whole. For example, (55a) does not refer to hombres 'men' in general, but to a subset of men who are así 'like that'. Likewise, (55b) makes explicit that only pretty women out of the total pool of female human beings are exempted from paying. The rest of the examples also discriminate a subset of entities from the potential total to which the noun could refer.

Another possible explanation for the grammaticality of the examples under discussion could be that these are contrastive environments. This latter possibility gains support from Lapesa (1974:300), who maintains that 'in all these cases [examples found in (56), M.S.] anteposition entails emphasis of expressivity'. Alonso explains his examples (given in (55)) as carrying emphasis or emotion, where a particular instance is enunciated as if it were a law with universal validity (cf. Alonso 1954:178).[41] In addition, the examples in (57) seem to require a heavy stress on hombres and flores. Consequently, if all the sentences in (55)-(57) could be considered contrastive, it would be possible to state that NPs without a determiner cannot be preverbal subjects unless contrastive. This would be a broadening of my previous dictum: 'naked nouns cannot be thematic subjects'.

The final word as to which concept--naked nouns or determinerless NPs--more accurately represents the situation of colloquial contemporary Spanish is left to further research.

3.2.3 Conclusion. In essence, the explanation for the NNC has been discovered. It turns out that the NNC--as stated in (5) in Section 3.1--is a rather complicated way to capture the generalization that naked nouns cannot be thematic subjects in

Spanish. This conclusion was arrived at by extracting the grammatical meaning proper to unmodified nouns[42] and, at the same time, by taking into account the grammatical meaning of preverbal subjects.

As an illustration, reconsider example (58).

(58) *Gotas caen.
     'Drops fall.'

Sentence (58) is ungrammatical because the noun in preverbal position (gotas) is unmodified and fulfills the subject function. These facts are at odds with the thematic--and thus unasserted --nature of preverbal subjects.

In contrast, in (59) the unmodified subject noun has been postposed.

(59) Caen gotas.
     fall drops.

This move allows the N_u to fall back into the old system for determiners, where the absence of a determiner is interpreted as [- individualized]. This interpretation is in perfect harmony with presentational sentences, whose mission is to introduce the referent of the NP into the world of discourse by asserting its existence. To put it differently, uttering a presentational sentence commits the speaker to the existence of the NP referent in the world of discourse. Thus, N_u in affirmative presentational sentences must be referentially interpreted even when marked as [- individualized].

The next section examines some unambiguous cases of contrastive environments. As should be expected, the NNC is not operative in these sentences.

3.3 Emphatic environments. It should be recalled that the statement of the NNC under (5) in Section 3.1 specifically mentions 'under conditions of normal stress and intonation'. This requirement is necessary precisely because the NNC does not function in contrastive or emphatic environments. The present section explores some of the devices Spanish uses to render a situation contrastive. All of the means to be discussed here have the same effect: they turn an essentially thematic position into a rhematic one.

3.3.1 Conjoined NPs. Conjoined NPs, also known as enumerations or lists, have been discussed in Section 3.2.1.4. To the examples given there (cf. (45)), one can add others like those in (60).

(60a) Cubiertos, platos y vasos aparecieron como por milagro.
      'Flatware, plates, and glasses appeared as if by miracle.'

(60b) Cielo y tierra te contemplan.
       'Heaven and earth watch you.'

(60c) Tía y sobrina llegaron sin novedad anoche. (Hatcher
       1957)
       'Aunt and niece arrived without problems last-night.'

(60d) Vencidos y vencedores escapaban huyendo. (Hatcher
       1957)
       'Defeated and victors escaped fleeing.'

As already mentioned, each element in these enumerations receives strong stress, the total NP displays the intonation
characteristic of lists, and the main information point of the
sentence resides in the subject NP. Very similar to this in
pattern is the one in (61).

(61)   El ruido era ensordecedor: aviones volaban en lo alto,
       autos tocaban la bocina, soldados marchaban en
       desorden, músicos interpretaban marchas patrióticas,
       y la gente vociferaba cánticos; todo para celebrar el
       triunfo de la revolución.
       'The noise was deafening: planes flew up above, cars
       honked their horns, soldiers marched in disorder,
       musicians played patriotic marches, and the people
       screamed songs; all to celebrate the triumph of the
       revolution.'

The only difference between (60) and (61) is that in (60) the
conjuncts are NPs, whereas in (61) they are full sentences. [43]
Nevertheless, the effect is the same: both constitute examples
of lists or enumerations.

    3.3.2 Single naked nouns. Within this subcase, one finds
instances of what Alonso has termed 'psychological predicates',
such as the often cited lines from the 'Jura de Santa Gadea'
(1954:168).

(62)   Villanos te maten rey, villanos, que no hidalgos ...
       villains you (accus.) kill (3 pl.) king, villains, that
       not noblemen ...
       'May those who kill you be villains, King, villains
       and not noblemen ...'[44]

The intended meaning of the lines becomes transparent in the
English translation. Alonso writes that such examples illustrate
a mismatch between grammatical and psychological categories.
According to him, villanos, despite being the grammatical subject, is a psychological predicate.[45] Observe that villanos, as
well as hidalgos, categorizes without identifying; it does not
refer to existing villanos but to villanos in their essence, the

content of the lines being an emotive plea. Note also that this noun (villanos) is heavily stressed.

This last observation is confirmed by looking at instances from contemporary Spanish.

(63a) Petróleo no surgió pero sí agua.
'Oil did not bubble up but water did.'

(63b) Temor no reinaba pero si preocupación.
'Fear did not reign but worries did.'

(64a) Envidia los movía. (Lapesa 1974:302)
'Envy moved them.'

(64b) Hierro taladró la madera. (Lapesa 1974:302)
'Iron perforated the wood.'

(64c) Mujeres atendían a los enfermos. (Lapesa 1974:302)
'Women assisted the sick.'

Just as was the case in (62), in (63) the contrast is made explicit (petróleo vs. agua, temor vs. preocupación). In (64), however, the contrast is only implicit. For these latter examples to be grammatical, the naked nouns must receive contrastive stress, showing that the main information point resides on these nouns. It is possible to demonstrate the contrastive nature of the sentences in (64) by adding a disclaimer to them. For example, one natural way in which (64a) could be appropriately continued would be by means of (65a), but not of (65b).

(65a) ... y no compasión.
'... and not compassion.'

(65b) ≠ ... y no los torturaba.
'... and didn't torture them.'

The contrast manifested in (64) is also highlighted by the way in which Lapesa paraphrases these sentences in order to clarify their meaning.

(66a) Lo que los movía era envidia.
'What moved them was envy.'

(66b) Lo que taladró la madera era hierro.
'What perforated the wood was iron.'

(66c) Quienes atendían a los enfermos eran mujeres.
'The ones who assisted the sick were women.'

Although the examples in both (63) and (64) are contrastive, they exhibit two different intonation patterns. This fact indicates that their thematic structure as well as their constituent structure is different. In (63) the naked nouns have been left-dislocated; as such they are thematic. The heavy stress they receive makes clear that they are contrastive themes.[46] An example of their structure and intonation is found in (67).

(67) $[_{\bar{S}}[_{TOP}$ petróleo$_i$] $[_{\bar{S}}$ COMP$[_S$PRO$_i$ no surgió]]]

      Petróleo   no   surgió.

$\begin{bmatrix} +\text{theme} \\ +\text{contrast} \end{bmatrix}$

A left-dislocated noun is base-generated in TOP position. The proform in subject position in S is interpreted as a variable bound by the NP in TOP.[47] Note that TOP is an inherently thematic position.

In opposition to the contrastive but thematic character of the naked nouns in (63), those in (64) are contrastive but rhematic. In these sentences the VPs appear to be right-dislocated, because they are uttered with very low almost level intonation, more as an afterthought than anything else. Since these VPs occur after the intonational peak of the sentence, they are resumptive; as such they turn out to be old information at the discourse level. An example is included in (68).

(68) (¿Qué los movía?
     What moved them?)

     Envidia los movía.[48]

$\begin{bmatrix} -\text{theme} \\ +\text{contrast} \end{bmatrix}$

Hatcher (1957) provides sentences of both types.[49] Those in (69) parallel the examples in (63).

(69a) Todo es posible en la mente y en el ánimo de los
       malvados. Y malvados sobran.
      'Everything is possible in the mind and in the spirit
      of the wicked. And wicked (ones) abound.'

(69b) Si el señor quisiera darme una armita ... --Rifle no
       queda, hermano; pero ...
      'If the gentlemen would like to give me a little firearm
      ... --There aren't any rifles left, pal; but ...'

(69c) ¿Quieres dinero? --Gracias, dinero sobra ahora ...
      'Do you want money? --Thank you, I have more than
      enough money now.'

As (69) shows, these examples are far more common (and natural) in conversational Spanish in which the speaker has the opportunity to direct the attention of the addressee immediately to the point, which s/he does by placing the contrastively stressed unmodified noun in preverbal position. Notice that at times the preposed naked noun is a mere restatement of a noun which was already introduced (cf. (69a) and (69c)), while at other times it is in some kind of relationship with a previous noun (rifle to arma 'rifle' to 'firearm' in (69b)). This results in the preposed noun being analyzed as old information at the discourse level.

It is far more difficult to find naked nouns in preverbal subject position in narrative forms, since narratives are in general characterized by a more composed, careful style. This fact was noticed by Hatcher, who remarked that she found them in the writings of only one author (Blanco-Fombona). Her two examples are given in (70).

(70a) Por entonces ocurrió un incidente que tuvo
       transcendencia en la vida del usurero. Ladrones
       visitaron una media noche al avaro.
       'Around that time an incident took place which had
       consequences in the miser's life. Thieves visited
       the miser one night at midnight.'

(70b) Minutos transcurrieron. Por fin apareció ...
      'Minutes passed. Finally there appeared ...'

These sentences are akin to the examples given in (64). Observe what this author does. In (70a) he sets up the scene; he creates suspense with the first sentence so that he can shock the reader with the news: ladrones. This is the information that is highlighted; the rest of the sentence is practically unimportant, since it is assumed everybody knows what thieves do. Sentence (70b) appears to be much the same, even though it does not have as much text. Minutos catches the spotlight; note that the verb chosen (transcurrir 'to pass, elapse') is quite weak in information value. It is practically the only thing that minutes can do; therefore, the verb is delegated to the background, as shown by the very low intonation it receives.

Bolinger (1971, 1977) exploits the notion of impact, or vividness, and maintains that naked nouns with sufficient impact may carry an existential implication even if they occur before the verb (his example, personal communication).

(71) En los últimos días, cataclismos inundarán al mundo,
     abundarán horrores, muerte y destrucción
     devastarán los horizontes, y finalmente--apocalipsis. [50]

'In the last days, cataclysms will flood the world, horrors will abound, death and destruction will devastate the horizons, and finally--Apocalypse.'

To summarize, despite the various names one might coin to label these single naked nouns in preverbal subject position-- psychological predicates, nouns charged with impact, vividness, or even emotion--the exterior manifestation is the same: these nouns must receive heavy (i.e. contrastive) stress for the sentence to be grammatical in contemporary Spanish. Despite this common trait, they can enter into different syntactic patterns and perform different thematic functions. On occasion, they are left-dislocated contrastive themes (cf. (63), (67), (69)); at other times, they are contrastive rhemes (cf. (64), (68), (70)). The role intonation plays in these two types of sentences is crucial to their understanding.

Having examined the foregoing instances of contrastive naked nouns in preverbal position, one is better equipped to take another look at proverbs; although they might not be considered part of colloquial spoken Spanish, they present an interesting pattern (cf. Section 3.2.1.3). Two earlier examples are repeated here for convenience.

(72a) Dádivas quebrantan montañas.
'Gifts move mountains.'

(72b) Patria es humanidad.
'Fatherland is humanity.'

Upon studying the stress and intonation of (72), one cannot help but notice that these proverbs appear to have two stresses of about equal strength: one on the first naked noun (the subject), the other on the second (the object). Nevertheless, the second intonational peak is slightly lower than the first, as indicated in (73).

(73) ‾ ‾
     ＿ ＿ ＿ ＿ ＿ ⌐⌐
     Dádivas quebrantan montañas.

It is as if both parts of the utterance were of almost equivalent importance, thus giving rise to a nearly symmetrical pattern. The intonation shows that the subjects of the sentences in (72) are not thematic.

If this analysis is correct, then the only type of example that stood in apparent defiance of the NNC has been brought under control (cf. Section 3.2.1.5). Such an example has also turned out to belong more appropriately with emphatic environments.

3.3.3 **Pseudo-clefts.** Pseudo-clefts are equational predicates. Alongside examples such as those found in (66), there exist sentences like those in (74).

(74a) <u>Envidia</u> era lo que los movía.
'<u>Envy</u> was what moved them.'

(74b) <u>Hierro</u> era lo que taladró la madera.
'<u>Iron</u> was what perforated the wood.'

(74c) <u>Tienda</u> es lo que ha puesto José.
'<u>A shop</u> is what Joseph has set up.'

The examples in (74) have the structure NP <u>be</u> $\bar{S}$, in which NP is a focused (rhematic) naked noun and $\bar{S}$ is a thematic relative clause structure.[51]

3.3.4 **Repetitions.** At other times, contrast results from the repetition of the same heavily stressed naked noun.

(75) <u>Años</u> y <u>años</u> transcurrieron sin que ... (Hatcher 1957)
'<u>Years</u> and <u>years</u> passed without ...'

(76) Ni dios ni demonio puede anular la verdadera libertad,
pero <u>traición</u>, <u>traición</u> (sí) puede. (Bolinger, personal
communication)
'Neither god nor demon can rescind true freedom, but
treason, treason (yes) can.'

Example (75) is an instance of conjunction in which 'the addition of the second noun amounts to more of the same thing' (Hatcher 1957:329). Sentence (76) shows the mere reiteration of the same noun; that is, it is not the case of adding one <u>traición</u> to another, but just a consideration of one and the same entity. Both cases seem to be devices exploited by the language to indicate totality by means of naked nouns (cf. Section 3.2.1.4).[52]

3.3.5 **'Focus-attractors'.** There are certain adverbials in the language which have the ability to attract the main sentential focus to the element(s) they precede. The ones of interest here are: <u>hasta</u> 'even', <u>sólo</u> ~ <u>solamente</u>, 'only', <u>ni</u> 'not even', and <u>ni siquiera</u> 'not even'.[53] Some examples with preverbal naked nouns are shown in (77).

(77a) En el sótano, <u>hasta</u> hongos crecían.
'In the basement, even mushrooms grew.'

(77b) <u>Sólo</u> fantasmas habitaban el lugar.
'<u>Only</u> ghosts inhabited the place.'

(77c) Ni flores faltan.
'Not-even flowers are missing.'

(77d) Ni siquiera sangre brotaba.
'Not even blood came-out.'

By causing focus to fall on the naked nouns, these 'focus attractors' give rise to a contrastive environment which opens the way to their preverbal positioning. It might very well be that these adverbials need to be assigned a contextual feature in the lexicon, something like +[_[+focus]] (cf. note 53).
It should be noted that the effect these adverbials have is not confined to a given position or to a given grammatical relation. Accordingly, in (78) the 'focus attractors' appear with postposed naked nouns ((78a) and (78b)), with a proper name (78c), and with nouns with determiners ((78d) and (78e)). In (79) they precede postverbal direct objects ((79a) and (79b)), an idiomatic prepositional phrase (79c), and a preposed direct object (79d).

(78a) Crecían hasta hongos.
grew even mushrooms
'Even mushrooms grew.'

(78b) No brotaba ni siquiera sangre.[54]
no came-out even blood
'Not even blood came out.'

(78c) Vino hasta Paco.
came even Paco
'Even Paco came.'

(78d) No llegó ni la tercera parte.
no arrived not-even the third part
'Not even a third arrived.'

(78e) Sobrevivieron sólo los fuertes.
survived only the strong
'Only the strong survived.'

(79a) No había ni electricidad.
no there-was not-even electricity
'There was not even electricity.'

(79b) Compraba sólo lo mejor.
'S/he used-to buy only the best.'

(79c) Comieron cerezas hasta por los codos.
they-ate cherries even through the elbows
'They ate cherries in great quantities.'

(79d) Tenían una cocinera, dos criadas, una niñera y <u>hasta</u>
jardinero tenían.
'They had a cook, two maids, a nanny, and even a
gardener (they-had).'[55]

3.3.6 Conclusion. During the development of this section on
emphatic or contrastive environments, different ways of making
the preverbal naked noun contrastive were examined. The common denominator of all the devices discussed--conjoining, repetitions, pseudo-clefting, 'focus attractors'--is the heavy stress
the naked noun gains during the process as a consequence of
the against-the-norm focus assignment. With the exception of
the left-dislocated examples discussed in Section 3.3.2, all other
instances of naked nouns are part of the rheme. Although the
conclusion arrived at in Section 3.2--naked nouns cannot be
thematic subjects--stands, it is necessary to broaden its scope
to encompass left-dislocated naked nouns. As shown in Section
3.3.2, left-dislocated naked nouns are thematic but contrastive.
Therefore, the proper generalization is: naked nouns cannot
be noncontrastive themes.[56] If the examples discussed in this
section are grammatical, it is precisely because the naked nouns
do not violate the constraint as just stated.

3.4 An analysis of contrastive sentences. In exploring the
domain and ramifications of the NNC, it was discovered that
this constraint, which bars naked nouns from thematic positions, is not operative in contrastive environments. This section examines the implications of the findings. Section 3.4.1
provides evidence that presentational and contrastive sentences
behave differently with regard to several processes. Section
3.4.2 represents an attempt to formalize the grammar of contrastive sentences.

3.4.1 Presentational vs. contrastive sentences. In the first
place, observe the nonparallelism between (80) and (81).

(80a) Surgió petróleo.
came-up (3 sg.) oil
'Oil came up.'

(80b) *Petróleo surgió.

(81a) Surgió PETROLEO.
came-up (3 sg.) oil
'OIL came up.'

(81b) PETROLEO surgió.
'OIL came up.'

Example (80a) is a noncontrastive presentational sentence in which both the verb and the postposed subject NP are part of the rheme. The focus falls on the NP in accordance with the rule of Focus Assignment (112) postulated in Section 2.4. As expected, (80b) (a declarative sentence) is ungrammatical, since an N_u cannot appear in thematic subject position; that is, (80b) violates the NNC. The structure of (80a) is found in (82) (cf. Chapter 2 for details).

(82) $[_S[_{NP_i}t]$ $[_{VP}$surgió petróleo$_i]]$

theme←—┤ ├——→ rheme

On the other hand, both examples in (81) are grammatical. In both cases, the NP PETROLEO is contrastively interpreted; that is, it receives contrastive focus (represented by capitals). These sentences are not presentationals: they do not answer the questions given in (83), but they do provide an answer for the question in (84).

(83a) ¿Qué pasó/ocurrió?
       'What happened?'

(83b) ¿Y qué más?
       'And what else?'

(83c) ¿Qué novedades hay?
       what news are-there
       'What's going on?'

(84)   ¿Qué surgió?
       'What came-up?'

The sentences in (81) would not be appropriate as 'out of the blue' utterances or as discourse openers. Only the presentational (80a) would be appropriate in such a situation.

The structure of (81a) parallels that of (80a), with the exception that the noun is contrastively stressed and the verb itself is thematic.

(85) $[_S[_{NP_i}t]$ $[_{VP}[_V$surgió$]$ $[_{NP}$PETROLEO$_i]]]$
      [+contrast]

      theme ←————┤├————→ rheme

Sentence (81b), as an answer to (84), has the structure given in (86).

(86) $[_\bar{S}[_\bar{S}[_S \text{PETROLEO} \ \Delta]] \ [_{VP}\text{surgió}]]$

rheme ←———⊣⊢———→ theme

Here the VP is right-dislocated and uttered with quite low, level intonation (cf. discussion in Section 3.3.2). The sentences in (81), with their contrastive focused NP, can be readily paraphrased by (87).

(87a) Lo que surgió fue PETROLEO.
'What came-up was oil.'

(87b) PETROLEO fue lo que surgió.
'Oil was what came up.'

These paraphrases unambiguously show that the verb in (81) must be presupposed and not asserted. In (80) both the verb and the NP form part of the assertion (i.e. rheme), but in (81) only the NP is asserted (part of the rheme), while the verb is unasserted. The NP in (81) gets either an exhaustive listing or a contrastive interpretation (Kuno 1972). In the first case, (81) can be paraphrased by (88); in the second case, it is equivalent to (89).

(88a) Surgió sólo PETROLEO.

(88b) Sólo PETROLEO surgió.
'Only OIL came-up.'

(89) Surgió PETROLEO (pero no gas).
'Oil came-up (but not gas).'

For the purposes of this discussion, I collapse the notions 'exhaustive listing' and 'contrastive reading' under the common label 'contrastive', and I use 'contrastive sentences' to identify sentences of the type found under (81), (88), and (89).

As already pointed out in Section 3.3.2, there is another type of contrastive construction of interest to this discussion. As opposed to the rhematic nature of the contrastive N_u in (81), (88), and (89), the ones found in (90) exemplify a left-dislocated thematic structure, though still a contrastive one. The intonation is indicated.

(90a) PETROLEO surgió (pero no gas).
'OIL (it)-came-up (but not gas).'

(90b) PETROLEO(,)no surgió.
'OIL, (it) did not come-up.'

Example (90) appropriately answers questions like those found in (91).

(91a) ¿Qué pasa con el petróleo?
ㅤㅤㅤ¿Qué hay de nuevo con el petróleo?
ㅤㅤㅤ'What's new with the oil?'

(91b) ¿Surgió petróleo?
ㅤㅤㅤ'Did oil come-up?'

The structure of (90) is given in (92).

(92)ㅤ$[_{\bar{S}}[_{TOP}$PETROLEO] $[_{\bar{S}}[_S$ PRO surgió]]]

theme ←─┤ ├─→ rheme

Whenever it is necessary to distinguish this latter type of contrastive sentence from the ones identified previously, I do so by the label 'contrastive left-dislocated' or simply 'left-dislocated sentences'.

Presentational and contrastive sentences differ in a number of ways. In addition to the differences already pointed out in the scope of theme vs. rheme and normal vs. contrastive stress and focus, there are others. First, note that while presentational sentences are limited to semantically intransitive predicates which above all herald the appearance of the 'object' into the world of discourse (cf. Sections 2.1.2 and 2.1.3), contrastive sentences are not so narrowly restricted. Intransitive (cf. (81)) as well as transitive verbs ((93) and (94)) are allowed in them.

(93a) Lo hizo PACO.
ㅤㅤㅤit made (3 sg.) Paco
ㅤㅤㅤ'PACO did it.'

(93b) PACO lo hizo.
ㅤㅤㅤ'PACO did it.'

(94a) Rompió el vaso PACO.
ㅤㅤㅤbroke (3 sg.) the glass PACO
ㅤㅤㅤ'Paco broke the glass.'

(94b) PACO rompió el vaso.
ㅤㅤㅤ'Paco broke the glass.'

Second, presentationals are characterized by V NP word order,[57] while contrastive sentences exhibit variable word order, either verb-subject or subject-verb (cf. (81), (88), (89), (93), and (94)).[58]

Third, contrastive sentences are presuppositionally more
marked than their presentational counterparts (cf. (80) vs.
(81)). By this I mean that the speaker who utters a contrastive sentence assumes much more than s/he assumes when s/he
says a presentational sentence like (80). Recall that (80) is
appropriate as a discourse opener; it is a neutral sentence.
On the other hand, (81) assumes some kind of previous knowledge on the part of the speaker. As a matter of fact, (80) is
subsumed under (81), because in (81) the speaker presupposes
the appearance of something and what s/he asserts is that this
'something' is oil. When one searches for pragmatic situations
in which these contrastive sentences could be used, one comes
to the realization that they are often used to contradict a claim
made by the hearer[59] (95), to provide information given in the
form of 'exhaustive listing' (96), for the sake of impact or shock
value (97), as well as to clarify or reiterate a previous assertion, as in the case of the left-dislocated construction (98).

(95a) --No surgió agua, PETROLEO surgió.

(95b) --No surgió agua, surgió PETROLEO.
'Water didn't come-up, OIL came-up.'

(95c) -¿Te parece que los movía la compasión?
'Do you think that compassion moved them?'
ENVIDIA los movía y no compasión.
'ENVY moved them and not compassion.'

(96a) (Sólo) CARAMELOS trajeron.

(96b) Trajeron (sólo) CARAMELOS.
'They brought (only) CANDIES.'

(96c) Surgió PETROLEO.

(96d) PETROLEO surgió.
'OIL came up.'

(97a) MINUTOS transcurrieron. Por fin apareció ... (H:
1957)
'MINUTES passed. Finally, there-appeared ...'

(97b) En los últimos días, CATACLISMOS inundarán al mundo,
abundarán horrores ... (Bolinger:personal communication)
'In the last days, CATACLYSMS will flood the world,
horrors will abound ...

(98a) Todo es posible en la mente y en el ánimo de los
malvados. Y <u>malvados</u> sobran. (H: 1957)
'Everything is possible in the mind of the wicked.
And WICKED (ones) abound.'

(98b) Ni dios ni demonio puede anular la verdadera libertad,
pero traición, TRAICION (sí) puede. (Bolinger:
personal communication)
'Neither god nor demon can rescind true freedom, but
treason, TREASON can.'

The presuppositionally more marked status of contrastive sentences is also evidenced by their behavior under negation.

(99a) No surgió PETROLEO.
'OIL didn't come up.'

Example (99a) is not an instance of sentence negation; on the
contrary, the scope of the negative in this sentence coincides
with the contrastively focused NP. To put it differently, (99a)
is an example of constituent negation. It denies the appearance
of oil asserted by someone else (that is, it denies the assertion
PETROLEO) while still presupposing the property denoted by
the verb.[60] In effect, then, (99a) is the negative counterpart
of the affirmative contrastive sentences (99b) and (99c).

(99b) Surgió PETROLEO.

(99c) PETROLEO surgió.
'OIL came up.'

In (99b) and (99c) the verb is presupposed (thematic); the
NP is the only constituent of the assertion (rheme). What
(99a) does, then, is negate the rheme (i.e. assertion). The
presupposition--that something came up--remains constant under
negation. Thus, it is possible to state that one characteristic
of contrastive sentences is their 'shrunken' scope of assertion:
the spotlight tends to converge exclusively on the contrastive
constituent. Nevertheless, it needs to be emphasized that what,
is crucial to negation is that it operates on that part of the
sentence which is asserted.
To clarify this point, let us take a look at contrastive left-
dislocated structures. Example (90b) is the negative counterpart of (90a). Assuming that the correct analysis of left-
dislocated sentences is something like (92), it becomes obvious
that what is being negated is the property denoted by the verb,
since the verb is the rhematic part of the sentence. Consequently, thematic contrastive element(s) do not fall within the
scope of negation precisely because they are outside the rheme.

Nonetheless, since sentence negation obtains precisely in those cases in which the entire sentence is rhematic (i.e. presentational sentences), it is obvious that even in the case of contrastive left-dislocated structures one is dealing with constituent negation.

Several distinguishing characteristics which differentiate presentationals from contrastive sentences have been presented. For ease of reference, they are schematically summarized in (100).

(100)

	Presentational:	Contrastive:
Rhematic structure of V NP	all rheme	theme/rheme
Focus and stress	normal	contrastive
Applicability of NNC	NNC does not apply[61]	violates NNC
Verb types	limited to semantically intransitive verbs and <u>haber</u>	no such limitation
Negation	sentence-negation	constituent negation
Word order	invariably V NP	V NP ~ NP V

The chart in (100) makes it obvious that we are studying two very different sentence types. What remains to be done is to devise a way to capture their differences formally.

3.4.2 The grammar of contrastive sentences.[62] In Section 3.4.1 it was shown that contrastive sentences form a distinct type of sentence which exhibits behavior different from that of presentationals. It is therefore to be expected that the grammars of these two sentence types should differ in significant ways. This section represents an attempt at formally capturing their differences. As in the previous chapters, the framework used here is that adopted by the Extended Standard Theory as developed in Chomsky (1975, 1977b, 1980a), Chomsky and Lasnik (1977), Fiengo (1977), and other related papers.

The main concern is to construct a grammar which interprets sentences like those found in (101a) and (101b), and (102a) and (102b) by using the quasi-logical reading in (101c) and (102c).

(101a) Surgió PETROLEO.

(101b) PETRÓLEO surgió.
'OIL emerged.'

(101c) The x such that (x surgió) is petróleo.

(102a) Apareció UN HOMBRE.

(102b) UN HOMBRE apareció.
'A man appeared.'

(102c) The x such that (x apareció) is un hombre.

It is evident that the rules of Focus Assignment and Rhematization to be used here cannot be those postulated in Section 2.4, because those rules were meant for 'normal', noncontrastive environments.[63]   The rule of Contrastive Focus Assignment is given in (103).

(103) Contrastive Focus Assignment (CFA)[64]

$$\alpha \begin{matrix} [X] \\ 1 \end{matrix} \longrightarrow \begin{matrix} 1 \\ (+CF) \end{matrix}$$

Rule (103) applies to S-structures, that is to say, to the output of the syntactic component at the level of logical form. The symbol α is meant to represent any lexical item or phrasal category.[65]
   It must be remembered that logical form (LF) is the level of linguistic analysis which incorporates those aspects of semantic representations exclusively determined by sentence grammar. In other words, LF excludes any contributions by other cognitive systems (see references cited earlier). Thus, rules of construal, interpretive rules, and conditions on binding are generally considered to take part in the step-by-step derivation of LF. Nevertheless, in the absence of an explicit and formal theory of LF for natural languages, all the LFs to be proposed here must be taken as a first approximation subject to further empirical testing.
   The rule of CFA is one of the rules that has an effect on the semantic interpretation of a sentence, and as such it contributes to LF.   The 'contrastive focus operator' (CF_{op}) (an operator analogous in its function to a description operator) acts to replace the focused item or phrase with a variable.   The effect of this rule of semantic interpretation on the type of sentences exemplified in (101) and (102) (that is, in cases where CFA applies to NPs) is shown in the LFs (104) and (105), respectively.

(104) CF_{op} x $(x, \lambda y(_S[_{NP} \cdots e_i \cdots] \ [_{VP}[_{VP} surgió] \ [_{NP} y_i])_S$

$= \dfrac{[_{NP} petróleo]}{CF}$

(105) CF_{op} x $(x, \lambda y$ $(_S[_{NP} \cdots e_i \cdots]$ $[_{VP}[_{VP}$aparecio]

$$[_{NP} y_i])_S = [_{NP}\frac{\text{un hombre}}{CF}]^{66}$$

Strictly speaking, (104) is the LF which corresponds to (101a) and (105) corresponds to (102a). For (101b) and (102b), the terms of the equation in (104) and (105) should be reversed. I exemplify what I mean with the LF for (101b).

(106) $[_{NP}\frac{\text{petroleo}}{CF}] = CF_{op}$ $x(x, \lambda y(_S[_{NP} \cdots e_i \cdots]$

$$[_{VP}[_{VP}\text{surgio}] \ [_{NP}y_i])_S$$

The fact that (104) and (106) are exactly the same, with the exception of the different order of their terms, appropriately indicates that (101a) and (101b) mean the same thing.

Immediately after the level of LF, the rule of Contrastive Theme/Rheme Assignment becomes operative.

(107) Contrastive Theme/Rheme Assignment (post-LF)

> Mark as Theme any left-dislocated element(s) which exhibit(s) Contrastive Focus. Mark as Rheme any nonleft-dislocated element(s) which exhibit(s) Contrastive Focus.

Recall that (107) applies after LF because I have identified theme/rheme with nonassertion/assertion. This characterization opposes the nonasserted part of a sentence--what the sentence is about--to the asserted part--what is said about that thing. Therefore, this definition is associated with the speaker of an utterance. Here the concern is more with successful communication and appropriateness conditions than with formal properties of sentences and truth conditions (cf. Kempson 1975).

If one superimposes the effects of rule (107) onto the LF found in (104), (108) is obtained.

(108) CF_{op} x $[(x, \lambda y(_S[_{NP} \cdots e_i \cdots]$ $[_{VP}[_{VP}\text{surgio}]$

$$[_{NP}y_i])_S]_{Th} = [[_{NP}\frac{\text{petroleo}}{CF}]]_{Rh}$$

Example (108) brings out several important points. In the first place, note that the LFs (104), (105), and (106) have a presentational sentence as (part of) one of their terms. In (108) it becomes evident that this term is precisely the one that is identified as thematic by rule (107). This accounts for the

presupposition of the contrastive sentences under discussion.
The appearance of something is presupposed, and what is
asserted is that it was x (petróleo in (101) and un hombre in
(102)), as opposed to p or q. In other words, the asserted
part--the rheme--is used to identify the x with some referent.
As was also the case with presentational sentences (cf. Section 2.4), this level of analysis of contrastive sentences provides us with an algorithm for the interpretation of these sentences. That the interpretation of contrastive sentences is not
only different from but also more complex than that of presentationals correlates with the observations made in Section 3.4.1
(cf. (100) for a summary). Contrastive sentences are distinct
from presentationals: they are presuppositionally more 'charged'
and they exhibit different properties from presentationals.
   To illustrate this last point explicitly, let us compare a negative presentational with a negative contrastive sentence.

(109a) No surgió petróleo. Presentational
        'Oil did not emerge.'

(109b) LF plus Theme/Rheme Assignment:

$(_S[_{NP} \ldots e_i \ldots]$ no $[$surgió$]$ $[\underline{petróleo_i}])_S$
                                              CF
        $\rightarrow$Rheme

(110a) No surgió PETROLEO. Contrastive
        'OIL did not emerge.'

(110b) LF plus Theme/Rheme Assignment:

CF_{op} x $(x,\lambda y$ $(_S[_{NP} \ldots e_i \ldots]$ $[_{VP}[_{VP}$surgió$]$

$[_{NP}y_i]])_S$ = (no $[_{NP}\underline{petróleo}])$
                           CF

        Theme $\longleftarrow$ $\longrightarrow$ Rheme

As previously mentioned (cf. Sections 2.2.4 and 3.4.1), a negative sentence denies the assertion made by its affirmative
counterpart; therefore, the negative of a presentational sentence denies the existence of any referent (that is, sentence
negation obtains). While the negative of a contrastive sentence
merely denies the identification of x with the referent of the
stated NP (that is, constituent negation results), it does not
deny the possibility that a referent other than the one mentioned might exist.
   For the sake of completeness, it is necessary to discuss the
LF and Theme/Rheme Assignment of contrastive left-dislocated
sentences. It must be remembered that in this case the

contrastive element is thematic (cf. (90), repeated here for convenience, with intonation indicated).

(111a) PETRÓLEO, surgió.
'OIL, (it) came-up.'

(111b) PETRÓLEO, no surgió.
'OIL, (it) did-not come-up.'

The LF of (111a) is given in (112). The CF_{op} identifies $\underline{x}$ with the NP PETROLEO found in TOP position; moreover, since the PRO (cf. (92)) that fulfills the subject function in $\bar{\bar{S}}$ is interpreted as anaphoric to the NP in TOP position, this pronoun is translated in LF by the same variable (cf. Rivero 1980).

(112) CF_{op} $x = [_{\bar{\bar{S}}}[_{TOP}[_{NP}\underset{CF}{\underline{petróleo}}]] \; [_{\bar{S}}[_{S} \; x \; [_{VP}surgió]]]$

After LF, Theme/Rheme Assignment takes place. Both the regular rule of Rhematization[67] and the Contrastive Theme/Rheme Assignment rule interact on the structure in (112) to render (113).

(113) CF_{op} $x = [_{\bar{\bar{S}}}[_{TOP}[_{NP}\underset{CF}{\underline{petróleo}}]] \; [_{\bar{S}}[_{S} \; x \; [_{VP}surgió]]]$

Theme ←——┤ ├——→ Rheme

The LF of (111b), with Theme/Rheme Assignment marked, is given as (114).

(114) CF_{op} $x = [_{\bar{\bar{S}}}[_{TOP}[_{NP}\underset{CF}{\underline{petróleo}}]] \; [_{\bar{S}}[_{S} \; x \; no[_{VP}surgió]]]$

Theme ←——┤ ├——→Rheme

The structure in (114) captures the fact that a negative sentence negates the assertion made by its affirmative correlate. Both (113) and (114) are intuitively satisfactory; they make it explicit that the meaning conveyed by these sentences is, informally speaking, 'As for OIL, it came up/didn't come up.'

In sum, the representations postulated for contrastive sentences appropriately correlate with the properties of these sentences. They provide an intuitively satisfactory way to capture their rhematic structure, their presuppositional status, and their behavior with respect to negation.

So far, the grammar of contrastive sentences contains a rule of Contrastive Focus Assignment (103) and a rule of Contrastive Theme/Rheme Assignment (107). The first rule belongs to the

level of LF; the second one is post-LF. What remains to be
done is to provide a rule of Contrastive Sentence Interpretation which operates at the level of SI-2, because it has to take
into account the speaker's beliefs as well as other pragmatic
factors which might enter into complete semantic representations.

(115) Contrastive Sentence Interpretation (SI-2):

Interpret S as contrastive if it has element(s) marked
with Contrastive Focus.

With rule (115) the grammar of contrastive sentences (81)
and (90) is complete. It has been shown that a proper treatment of this kind of sentence is achieved by several rules which
belong to different levels of analysis, in accordance with the
modular model of grammar adopted by the Extended Standard
Theory. In the next section, I briefly discuss two other types
of contrastive sentences.

3.4.2.1 Focus-attractors and pseudo-clefts. In Section 3.4.2
the discussion was centered around contrastive sentences in
which contrastive focus is introduced by means of rule (103).
In other words, the variable needed for the semantic interpretation (sentence semantics) of these sentences is introduced by
rule. In this subsection, I show that this is not the only way
in which this variable may appear. There are (at least) two
other mechanisms by which the required variable can be made
available.
    The first mechanism is provided by what I have termed
'focus-attractors', such as hasta 'even' and sólo ~ solamente
'only'. Assuming that these adverbials are entered in the lexicon with the contextual feature +[__ [+ CF]] (cf. Section 3.3.5),
a lexical means by which the variable is introduced is obtained.
If the rule of Contrastive Focus Assignment (103) applies, it
would assign CF to coincide with the contextual feature CF
proper to the lexical items. Contrastive Theme/Rheme Assignment (107) identifies the rheme with the element(s) marked
CF. The result of applying these two rules is the post-LF
structures found in (116) and (117).

(116a) Hasta HONGOS crecían.
        'Even mushrooms grew.'

(116b) LF plus Theme/Rheme Assignment

$$(\text{hasta } [[_{NP}\underline{\underline{\text{hongos}}}]_{\underline{\text{CF}}}]_{Rh}) = x(x,\lambda y(_{S}[_{NP} \cdots e_{i} \cdots]$$

$$[_{VP}[\text{crecían}] \; [_{NP}y_{i}]])_{S})$$

(117a) Surgió sólo PETROLEO.
emerged only OIL
'Only OIL emerged.'

(117b) LF plus Theme/Rheme Assignment:

$$x \ (x, \lambda y(_S[_{NP} \ \cdots \ e_i \ \cdots] \ [_{VP}[_{VP} \text{surgió}]| \ [_{NP} y_i]])_S)$$

$$= (\text{sólo} \ [_{NP} \underline{\text{petróleo}}]) \longrightarrow \text{Rheme}$$
$$\overline{\text{CF}}$$

Observe that both (116) and (117) have an embedded presentational in their LF; this is because of their presuppositional
status. Sentence (116) means that among the things that were
growing, even mushrooms were found. Sentence (117) indicates that the thing that emerged can be identified only as
oil.[68] The difference between (116) and (117) is to be attributed to the difference in meaning of the adverbials hasta and
only; their similarities and presuppositional status can be
attributed to their identical contextual feature and parallel LFs.

The second mechanism that can introduce a variable is provided by the QU-[69] element of (pseudo-)clefts (cf. Section
3.3.3). On the assumption that pseudo-clefts are instances of
equational predicates in which one of the terms is NP and the
other $\overline{S}$, their structure is parallel to that of relative clauses.
Examples (118) and (119) both contain a sentence together with
its syntactic structure just after WH-Movement has operated
(cf. Chomsky 1977b).

(118a) Lo que surgió fue PETROLEO.
'What emerged was OIL.'

(118b) $[_{\overline{S}}[_{\overline{S}}[_{COMP} \text{ lo que}] \ [_S t \text{ surgió}] \ [_{VP} \text{fue} \ [_{NP} \text{petróleo}]]]]$

(119a) PETROLEO fue lo que surgió.
'OIL was what emerged.'

(119b) $[_{\overline{S}}[_{NP} \text{petróleo}] \ [_{VP} \text{fue} \ [_{\overline{S}}[_{COMP} \text{ lo que}] \ [_S t \text{ surgió}]]]]$

WH-Movement provides the variable required for the proper
semantic interpretation of pseudo-cleft sentences. This interpretation is given in (120).

(120) LF = for which x, x is oil, x came up

Contrastive focus falls on the NP of the equation, that is, on
the naked noun which constitutes the identification of the variable. Later on, Contrastive Theme/Rheme Assignment singles

out this same contrastively focused NP as the rheme (i.e. the assertion), while the b̲e̲ S̲ portion of the utterance is analyzed as the theme, or unasserted part.
A more explicit LF for the sentences in (118a) and (119a) is provided in (121) and (122), respectively.

(121) CF_{op} x $(x, \lambda y[_S[_{NP} \cdots e_i \cdots] [_{VP} surgió [_{NP} y_i]]])$

$= [_{NP} \frac{petróleo]}{CF}$

(122) $[_{NP}$ petróleo$] = CF_{op}$ x $(x, \lambda y[_S[_{NP} \cdots e_i \cdots]$

$[_{VP} surgió [_{NP} y_i]]])$

The attentive reader could not fail to notice that the LFs in (121) and (122) are the same as those given in (104) and (105), respectively. This is designed to capture the fact that at the level of sentence semantics these sentences with contrastive focus convey the same meaning.[70] The only difference between them resides in the way in which the variable is introduced. In (121) and (122) it is introduced configurationally, because of the inherent variable nature of the QU-element in (pseudo-) clefts, whereas in (104) and (105) the variable is introduced by means of rule (103).

3.4.2.2 Summary. The grammar of contrastive sentences consists of a rule of Contrastive Focus Assignment (103) which belongs to the level of LF, a post-LF rule of Contrastive Theme/ Rheme Assignment (107), and a rule of Contrastive Sentence Interpretation (115) which belongs to SI-2. It was found that the common denominator in all the contrastive sentences discussed in Section 3.4.2 is contrastive focus. Furthermore, this unifying property is the one which provides the variable needed for the proper interpretation of contrastive sentences in logical form. It was shown that there are at least three ways in which the required variable may be obtained: (1) by rule (103), (2) by a contextual feature, and (3) by QU-. Thus a language may have several means at its disposal to achieve the same end.

3.5 Recapitulation. By way of summary, I briefly compare the grammar of presentational sentences with that of contrastive sentences so that the reader may appreciate at a glance the differences between the two. It should be remembered that it was the violation of the NNC by contrastive sentences which led us into the exploration of the characteristics displayed by this type of sentence. The NNC expresses the fact that un-modified nouns are barred from noncontrastive thematic posi-tions in Spanish.

(123)

	Presentational grammar:	Contrastive grammar:[71]
Examples:	(a) Surgió petróleo. (Presentational) (b) *petróleo surgió (Declarative) 'Oil emerged.'	(c) Surgió PETROLEO. (d) PETROLEO surgió. (Contrastive) 'OIL emerged.'
Syntactic Component:	Subject Postposing: $\begin{array}{cc} NP & V^n \\ 1 & 2 \end{array} \Longrightarrow 2\ 1$ [72]	
SI-1:	Focus Assignment: Mark the last constituent in the (higher) VP Focus of S. $LF = [_S[_{NP} \cdots e_i \cdots]$ $[_V{}^n[VP][\ \underline{NP}_i]]]$ Focus	Contrastive Focus Assignment: $\alpha \begin{bmatrix} X \\ 1 \end{bmatrix} \longrightarrow \underset{(+CF)}{1}$ $CF_{op}\ x\ (x, \lambda y[_S[_{NP} \cdots e_i \cdots]$ $[_V{}^n\ [VP]\ [_{NP}y_i]]] = [_{NP}\frac{x}{CF}]$
Post-LF:	Rhematization: Mark as Rheme the VP and anything that follows it. Anything outside the Rheme becomes part of the Theme.	Contrastive Theme/Rheme Assignment: Mark as Theme any left-dislocated element(s) which exhibit(s) Contrastive Focus. Mark as Rheme any nonleft-dislocated element(s) which exhibit(s) Contrastive Focus.
SI-2:	Presentational Sentence Interpretation: Interpret S as presentational if it asserts the appearance of the referent of the NP in the world of discourse; this NP should carry sentential Focus.[73]	Contrastive Sentence Interpretation: Interpret S as contrastive if it has element(s) marked with Contrastive Focus.

The differences evidenced in (123) between the two grammars account for the different behavior of presentational and contrastive sentences with respect to rhematic structure, work order possibilities, negation, presuppositional status, and 'normal' vs. contrastive focus, stress, and intonation.[74]

3.5.1 The NNC as a filter. In addition to the rules I have given here (and other rules not pertinent to this study), the grammar of Spanish must incorporate the NNC as a filter so that sentences like (123b) can be ruled out as ungrammatical. The notion of a filter raises several interesting theoretical questions. Aside from the need to determine the form of the filter itself, within the model of grammar adopted by the Extended Standard Theory, there remains the question of the level at which the filter applies and the determination of which side of the grammar (left or right side) one is dealing with.

I begin by considering the form of the filter. The filter should state that 'naked nouns cannot be noncontrastive themes'. One has to consider how best to express this fact of Spanish formally. If one were to specify the filter as in (124), it could not mark sentences like (123b) as ungrammatical until after LF, because it specifically makes reference to themehood (see (123)).

(124) *[$_{NP}N_u$]$_{Th}$ unless N_u is [+CF]   (Contrastive Focus)

Waiting until this level to discard some ungrammatical sentences might present some problems as to the proper identification of these ungrammatical sentences (see discussion pertaining to (126)). Therefore, it appears desirable to have the filter oper- ate at or before LF. For this, it becomes necessary to devise a way to state the filter without making reference to themehood. The simplest characterization is found in (125).

(125) *[$_{NP}N_u$] V ... unless N_u is [+CF]

Statement (125) is consistent with the data examined in this chapter and, furthermore, it makes reference only to gram- matical structure.

The next issue that needs to be considered is the exact place for this filter. In Chomsky and Lasnik (1977), filters are postulated as well-formedness conditions for surface struc- ture belonging to the left side, or phonological component, of the grammar. They apply after deletions and concern them- selves primarily with the complementizer system. More recently, the hypothesis that filters (of core grammar) are all grouped together in the same subsection of the grammar appears to have been abandoned.[75] Chomsky, in his Pisa lectures, concludes that his Case filter applies at the level of S-structure, while the RESNIC is postulated to operate as a well-formedness condi- tion of LF (that is, it is on the right branch of the grammar). Furthermore, Rouveret and Vergnaud (1980) argue for a syn- tactic filter which checks the distribution of NPs. Therefore, the unavoidable conclusion seems to be that filters can, in principle, be activated at any stage of the derivation of a sen- tence (perhaps with the exception of base structures).

Where does the foregoing brief discussion leave us with re- spect to the NNC? It actually leaves us with a wide open field, since the NNC could apply in the phonological component, in LF, or even in S-structure before the two branches of the grammar separate. Nevertheless, there exist some indications that favor having this filter on the right side. On the assump- tion that filters are 'local' in the sense that they are blind to anything but continuous strings (cf. Chomsky and Lasnik 1977), the following sentence would be marked as ungrammatical if the NNC were on the left side after deletions.

(126) Hombres existen que son el sumo de la corrupción.
'Men exist that are the epitome of corruption.'

This is because a phonological filter would be unable to see that, in fact, <u>hombres</u> is modified by the extraposed relative clause. On the other hand, if the NNC were on the right branch of the grammar, both the WH-word and the trace of the extraposed relative would be signaling that <u>hombres</u> is not a true naked noun. Furthermore, if I am correct in assuming that enumerations and repetitions (i.e. conjunctions, such as those in (127) (cf. Sections 3.2.1.4, 3.3.1, and 3.3.4)) are in some sense indicators of totality, this fact should become explicit by the time quantifier interpretation takes place, so that these sentences would never be excluded by the filter.

(127a) Jóvenes y adultos respetaban sus palabras.
'Young and old respected his/her words.'

(127b) Años y años transcurrieron.
'Years and years went by.'

In sum, the evidence seems to indicate that the NNC is best incorporated into the grammar as a language-specific filter at the level of LF; that is to say, it belongs to the right-hand side of the grammar.

NOTES

1. This correspondence is unidirectional, i.e.:

(i) presentational $\supset$ declarative
(ii) declarative $\not\supset$ presentational

Aside from the ill-formedness of examples such as (4) in the text, there are many declaratives with transitive verbs for which there are no corresponding presentationals. As will become evident during the development of this chapter, (i) is a true generalization, provided one accepts the existence of a filter (see Section 3.5).

The reader must be reminded that any type of <u>se</u> sentence has been purposely excluded from the discussion.

2. I find it necessary to specify both 'contemporary' and 'colloquial'. Contemporary is relevant because the language has evolved greatly from Vulgar Latin times, or even since the Golden Age period. Many writings and grammars include examples from historically noted authors (such as Cervantes and Quevedo) which do not represent today's language. I ignore these examples.

Furthermore, I stipulate 'colloquial' in the sense of everyday language, because I want to avoid examples which are perceived as archaic, bookish, or highly literary by native speakers. Whenever necessary, I point out this type of example.

3. The NNC is ultimately stated as a filter. Its place and formal relationship to the rest of the model are discussed in Section 3.5.

4. Alarcos Llorach (1967:23) points out that proper names actually fall into three compartments: those which do not take an article (Paco, Madrid), those which always appear with an article (el Tajo, los Pirineos), and those which are used indiscriminately with or without an article (China ~ la China; Estados Unidos ~ los Estados Unidos). But he is quick to indicate that, since these facts are due to diachrony, proper names lack the possibility of contrast between form with article vs. form without article, a contrast which is exhibited by common nouns.

5. These examples state generalizations. I return to them in Section 3.2.2.

6. Therefore, complex lexical units render ungrammatical sentences if they cannot be interpreted as partitives (despite their appearance of being modified). Such is the case in (i).

(i) *Limpia-parabrisas estaban en venta.
    clean-windshield
    'Windshield wipers were on sale.'

By contrast, (ii) is judged grammatical if the speaker remembers the existence of molinos de agua 'water mills'.

(ii) Molinos de viento poblaban la pradera.
     mills of wind
     'Windmills covered the prairie.'

Furthermore, it is worth pointing out that contemporary Spanish requires that totality be explicitly indicated (with the definite article or the quantifier todo(s) 'all', for instance).

7. By contrast, if the subject NP has a determiner, the sentences are grammatical with a postverbal subject, although they are not presentationals.

Cazaron los hombres un ciervo.
Cazaron un ciervo los hombres.

8. These sentences improve considerably with heavy stress on rumores.

9. Lapesa (1974:300) confirms my observations that unmodified common nouns cannot be subjects in preverbal position. Two of his examples are:

(i) *Montañas rodean el valle.
    'Mountains surround the valley.'

(ii) *Rebeldes fueron apresados.
     'Rebels were captured.'

Nonetheless, he goes on to say that these sentences could be found with the subject postposed in the written language:

(iii) Rodean montañas el valle.
    Rodean el valle montañas.

(iv) Fueron apresados rebeldes.

I find examples (iii) and (iv) completely ungrammatical under noncontrastive conditions. This is one of the problems which face the researcher. Very few people have bothered to separate consistently noncontrastive from contrastive environments. The only circumstances under which (iii) and (iv) are conceivable in my opinion is as newspaper headings (cf. Section 3.2.1.1) or with contrastive stress on the underlined noun.

10. This might have to do with speakers' expectations and with perceptual strategies. In the absence of other conclusive cues, speakers try to process the postposed unmodified noun as an object (recall that Spanish is a language which allows null subjects). If the sentence makes sense, it is considered to be grammatical (cf. (20a)); if it does not, it is discarded (cf. (20b) and (21)).

11. Curiously enough, this fact parallels the historical development of the article in Spanish. Alonso (1954:153-154) points out that historically the article started by being used solely with subjects to emphasize the division of the sentence into subject and predicate. Only later did its use expand to direct objects and other complements; this latter use, slow in developing, is still not obligatory nowadays.

12. Otero made essentially the same claim in his 1966 study. Later (Otero 1976:350), he modifies his stand and maintains that 'a subject position NP without an overt determiner ... can only be construed as nonreferential ...' I think this latter remark is much more adequate; I return to this in Section 2.2.2.

In passing, I would like to mention that I (and my informants) find Otero's example (5e) (1976:345) totally unredeemable under noncontrastive intonation:

(5e) (*Los) castores construyeron esta presa.
    'Beavers built this dam.' (PROPERTY DENOTATION)

Sentence (i), however, with the naked noun out of subject position, is perfectly grammatical:

(i) Esta presa fue construida por castores.
    'This dam was built by beavers.'

In (i), castores could still be interpreted as [-Individuality, -Totality], i.e. nonreferential (a pragmatic fact); the sentence then makes no reference to individual castores but rather

'assigns some individuals (not mentioned) to the class of castores' (1976:345).
13. It is immaterial for my purposes whether Passive is one transformation or two (NP Postposing and Object Preposing). Even if the Passive relationship is to be captured by a lexical redundancy rule, the fact remains that something needs to be said about the ungrammaticality of the examples in (25).
14. Moreover, current versions of the theory of grammar exclude the possibility of formulating deep structure constraints.
15. Alternatively, if Passive is a lexical redundancy rule, some statement might need to be made to bar (27) while allowing (26).
16. Examples in (28) are grammatical with contrastive stress on the underlined noun. The nouns then receive an exhaustive interpretation (Kuno 1972).
17. Although for ease of exposition I am assuming Postal's concept of Tough Movement (also known as Object Raising), nothing crucial depends on this assumption. As is well known, there are competing formulations. Jackendoff (1972:226) entertains the hypothesis that Tough Movement might not be a movement transformation:

It is tough [$_{VP}$to please John] $\Longrightarrow$
John is tough to please

but that, alternatively, the deep structure might be:

John is tough [$_{VP}$to please $\begin{Bmatrix} \text{John} \\ \Delta \end{Bmatrix}$] (transformational theory) (interpretive theory)

'Tough movement will then be an object deletion in the transformational theory and a semantic coreference rule in the interpretive theory'. Jackendoff (for a number of reasons) adopts the movement version of the rule. Akmajian (1972) and Lasnik and Fiengo (1974) bring up the possibility of stating Tough Movement as an object deletion rule instead of a movement rule. More recently, Chomsky (1977) has claimed that Tough Movement is derived by WH-Movement. In this latter case, the structure of a grammatical sentence like (i) would be (ii).

(i) Este reloj es imposible de arreglar.
'This watch is impossible to fix.'

(ii) [$_{\bar{S}}$[$_{TOP}$este reloj] [$_{\bar{S}}$[$_{COMP}$ +WH$_i$] [$_S$ es imposible

[$_{COMP}$[t$_i$]] [$_S$ de arreglar x]]]

The structure in (ii) is interpreted by a general rule of predication which relates es imposible with the open proposition de arreglar x. The variable x is satisfied by the referent of the NP in TOP position (i.e. este reloj).

Wherever the correct analysis ultimately lies, the fact remains that sentences like the one in (31) are ungrammatical sentences and something needs to be said about them.

18. As is seen later, other strategies are also possible but they render the unmodified common noun contrastive.

19. Read N_u as unmodified common noun.

20. A complete analysis of the article and determiner system would take us too far afield from our main goal; hence I limit my discussion to those aspects which bear directly on the topic under discussion. Those interested should consult Alonso (1954), Lapesa (1974), Alarcos Llorach (1970), Sánchez de Zavala (1976), some of the Spanish traditional grammars (such as RAE (1974), Bello (1970), Gili y Gaya (1973), Ramsey (1956)), and the pedagogical treatment found in Bull (1965).

21. Alonso (1954:162) writes: 'Echando mano de la pareja de conceptos filosóficos esencia-existencia, diremos que el nombre con artículo se refiere a objetos existenciales y sin él a objetos esenciales. Con artículo, a las cosas; sin él, a nuestras valoraciones subjetivas y categoriales de las cosas.' ('Considering the pair of philosophical concepts essence-existence, we shall say that the noun with article makes reference to existential objects, and without it to essential objects. With article, to things; without it, to our subjective and categorial evaluations of things.')

Lapesa (1974:289) talks about 'virtual, categórico o esencial, aplicables en la mayoría de los casos al sustantivo desprovisto de actualizador; y actual, individuado, o referido a lo existente, propios del sustantivo con determinativos.' ('Virtual, categorical or essential, applicable in the majority of cases to the noun without actualizer; and actual, individualized, or referring to the existing, proper to the noun with determiners.')

22. Kuno (1970:351) points out that in the schema NP_1-Copula-NP_2 there are two possibilities for interpreting NP_2: (i) NP_1 has the properties of NP_2 (nonreferential), and (ii) what is referred to as NP_1 is the same as what has been referred to as NP_2 (referential). In Spanish, (i) corresponds to a noun without determiner, and (ii) to one with determiner.

23. Thus, it makes sense that proper nouns do not generally take determiners, since they are identifiers by nature. On the other hand, common nouns are classifiers by nature; hence they require a determiner to turn them into identifiers (cf. Alarcos Llorach 1967).

24. Looking ahead, it should also be noted that all of the subjects in (40) are rhematic. This is partially shown by the intonation. For example, the intonation of (40a) is the following:

hombres de calidad estudian el asunto.

25. The reader must be reminded that the discussion restricts itself (for the time being) to nonemphatic environments unless otherwise noted (cf. conjoined NPs further on).
26. Ramsey (1956:2.41) also mentions printed titles of books and articles, such as:

Tratado elemental de mecánica.
'Elementary treatise on mechanics.'

But this is not a sentence; if put in context, titles generally require a determiner:

El Tratado elemental ... es un libro muy aburrido.
'The Elementary Treatise ... is a very boring book.'

27. Lapesa (1974:292) gives the following example:

Ojos que no ven, corazón que no siente.
'Eyes that don't see, heart that doesn't feel.'

Note that both ojos and corazón are modified by a relative clause; hence they are not true instances of naked nouns.
28. Contemporary Spanish requires a determiner for generic statements:

El hombre es mortal.
'Man is mortal.'

El perro es el mejor amigo del hombre.
'The dog is man's best friend.'

It would be very difficult to draw a line separating proverbs from generic statements. At first glance, they seem to exhibit very similar (if not the same) properties.
29. In this respect, English behaves very much like Spanish. Compare (i) with (ii).

(i) Young and old fought for the king.
(ii) *Young fought for the king.

30. In Kuno's (1972) terminology, the members of an enumeration receive an exhaustive listing interpretation.
31. A sentence such as:

Ni padre ni hijo contestaron el teléfono.
'Neither father nor son answered the telephone.'

does not violate the NNC, because the negative particle n̲i̲ acts
as a quantifier regardless of stress and intonation.
    32. D. Bolinger and C. Piera separately brought this fact
to my attention.
    33. It might very well be that the contrast core vs.
periphery is in evidence here. The NNC would belong to core
grammar (and would thus constitute the unmarked case), while
newspaper headings, ads, telegrams, definitions, and maybe
even proverbs would more appropriately belong to the periphery.
    34. In contrast, recall that in a presentational sentence such
as (52), sentential stress falls on the NP_u gotas.
    35. Independent existence is explained ($\overline{1976}$:312-313) as
meaning that 'the entity that a b-subject refers to (if any)
exists independently of the action or property expressed by
the predicate'.
    36. Absolute reference is defined as follows (1976:3i7):
'In the overwhelming majority of cases, if a b-sentence is true
then we understand that there is an entity (concrete or abstract) which is referred to or has the property expressed by,
the b-subject'.
    37. Topics (1976:318) 'identify what the speaker is talking
about. The object they refer to is normally known to both
speaker and addressee, and so is, in that sense, old information'.
    38. Alonso (1954:167-168) writes: 'El artículo, con el
nombre sujeto, preforma la categoría lingüística de sujeto.
[...] se ve que la lengua, en sus convenciones, no admite
como nombre sujeto, a la vez gramatical y psicológico, uno
que no lleve artículo, con su insistencia formal en la categoría
lingüística de sujeto'. ('The article, with the subject noun,
serves as the linguistic category of subject. ... it is seen that
the language, in its conventions, does not accept as subject
noun, at the same time grammatical and psychological, one
which does not have an article, with its formal insistence in
the linguistic category of subject'.) If I change Alonso's
'article' to 'determiner', we are in complete agreement.
    39. I use the feature [+ individualized], following the lead
of Spanish grammarians. Fiengo (1977) uses the feature [+
Individual], which I take to stand for the same notion, since
he writes: 'while nouns bear the morphological contrast
+ Plural ... determiners bear the morphological contrast
+ Individual' (1977:43).
    40. There are no indications that the new system will com-
pletely replace the old one in other than basic subject position.
    41. With respect to example (54b), Alonso writes: '... pudo
decir el barquero: "por bonita, no pagas tú dinero." Pero al
decir: "moza bonita no paga dinero", se eleva aquella situación singular a la ley de pretensión general. Hay sin duda una
emoción que nos hace formular como general lo que en realidad
es individual; pero el valor especial de este giro está en su

eficacia activa: la moza no tiene más que dejarse inscribir en la ley. No es cuestión personal' (1954:178). ('The boatman could have said: "due to your beauty, you don't pay (your money)." But upon saying: "beautiful maiden does not pay money," that particular situation is elevated to a law of general pretension. There is without a doubt an emotion that makes us formulate as general that which is in reality individual; but the special value of this expression is in its active force: the maiden only needs to be included in the law. It is not a personal matter'.)

42. The grammatical meaning of unmodified nouns has reached a steady state for preverbal subject position (the position of interest for the NNC); nonetheless, it should be kept in mind that the situation is different for other positions where the old, [+ individualized], and the new, [+ referential], systems coexist (cf. (54)).

43. Note that in (61) the conjuncts are full sentences in each of which the actors do what is somehow typical of them. Furthermore, recall what was said in Section 3.2.1.4 about the implication of totality which enumerations convey. This interpretation is reinforced in (61) by the quantifier todo 'all, everything' which appears in the last sentence.

44. Of course, these lines, besides being poetry, belong to the Romancero (circa fourteenth century). They have been quoted in the literature so often (Alonso 1974, Bolinger 1969, Lapesa 1974, among others) that I feel obliged to include them. As will be seen shortly, contemporary Spanish uses this type of contrast also.

45. To quote Alonso (1954:168), 'El nombre sin artículo es predicado psicológico, aunque sea sujeto gramatical'. ('The noun without article is a psychological predicate, even though it might be a grammatical subject'.)

46. Thus, it becomes evident that a simple opposition of theme vs. rheme is not sufficient for Spanish. In addition to this, it is necessary to distinguish between [+ contrast]. These two parameters give rise to four logical possibilities: (i) [+theme, -contrast], (ii) [+theme, +contrast], (iii) [-theme, -contrast], and (iv) [-theme, +contrast]. Each of these is realized in Spanish.

(i) (¿Por qué estás tan contenta?
'Why are you so happy?')

El petróleo surge a carradas.
'(The) oil is-bubbling-up by the barrel.'

(ii) (¿Surgió petróleo?
'Did oil come up?')

Petróleo no surgió.
'Oil did-not come-up.'

(iii) (¿Qué pasó?
       'What happened?')

       Surgió petróleo.
       came-up oil

(iv) (¿Surgió agua?)
      No, surgió petróleo.
      no, came-up oil
      'No, oil bubbled-up.'

47. Notice that the subject position in S could never have a
lexical pronominal because pronouns in general cannot cooccur
with naked nouns (cf. Torrego 1979).
      Example (67) is an instance of a base-generated left dislo-
cation because (among other reasons):

    (i) it violates the Complex NP Constraint:

         Petróleo, comparto la opinión de que surgirá.
         'Oil, I share the opinion that it-will-come-up.'

    (ii) it violates the WH-Island Constraint:

          Petróleo, me preguntaron (que) por qué no había surgido.
          'Oil, I-was asked (that) why it had not come-up.'

(For further discussion, see Rivero 1980).
      48. On the assumption that right-dislocated structures are
base-generated, their structure might be something like:

$$[_{\bar{S}}[_{\bar{S}} \text{ COMP } [_S \text{ envidia } \Delta]] [_{VP} \text{ los movía}]]$$

in which Δ would need to be a variable bound by the right-
dislocated VP.
      49. Hatcher's 1957 article is a reaction to one by Bull,
Gronberg, and Abbot (1952), who maintained that out of
27,000 examples 'no example of an unmodified common noun
was found in preverbal position'. Hatcher convincingly shows
the doubtful value of the statistical method. Nevertheless, all
of Hatcher's examples are contrastive, with one qualification
that is discussed further on (cf. (70)).
      50. Observe also that (71) is a case of conjunction in which
the conjuncts are sentences (cf. Section 3.3.1).
      51. The intonation of these sentences appears to indicate
that be $\bar{S}$ has been right dislocated.
      I should make clear that I assume no transformational deriv-
ation between $\bar{S}$ be NP and NP be $\bar{S}$.
      52. Notice that (75) seems to be equivalent to (i)

(i) Los años transcurrieron ...
     'The years passed ...'

and (76) to (ii).

(ii) ... pero la traición (sí) puede.
      ... but the treason (yes) can.
      '... but treason can.'

Here the definite articles los and la make explicit that one is
talking about a total. Nevertheless, something has been lost
in (i) and (ii); gone is the dramatic tone achieved by the mere
repetition of the naked nouns.
    53. I make no claim as to the exhaustiveness of this list.
Contreras (1976) calls these elements 'rhematizers'; they are
entered in the lexicon with the contextual feature +[__[+rh]].
It must be recalled, though, that he uses rheme as synonymous
with new information, an assumption which we have proven
wrong (cf. Introduction). The contextual feature might still
be +[__[+rh]], with no equating of rheme and new information,
or the feature could be +[__[+focus]].
    54. It is a fact of Spanish that 'words' which contain a
negative element require the negative particle no when they
occur in postverbal position. Compare (78b) to (78d) and (i)
to (ii):

(i) Nadie vino.
     'Nobody came.'

(ii) No vino nadie.
      no came nobody

    55. Sentence (79d) shows that a preposed N_u object also
needs to be rhematic, or at least contrastive (cf. (i)), for the
sentence to be grammatical.

(i) Jardinero, sí tenían.
     'Gardener, (yes) they-had.'

In (i), the left-dislocated Jardinero is [+theme, +contrast].
    Notice that it is to be expected that an element displaced
from its basic position should attract the spotlight, either because it becomes rhematic (i.e. asserted) or because it is contrastive. Thus, naked noun objects are permitted to stay in
the position in which they are generated by the Phrase Structure rules, most likely because this is essentially a rhematic
environment. Schematically, some of the possibilities that obtain for objects in the language are:

Basic: (S) V N_u

$\begin{bmatrix} +\text{theme} \\ +\text{contrast} \end{bmatrix}$: N_u, (S) V   Left dislocation

$\begin{bmatrix} +\text{rheme} \\ (+\text{contrast}) \end{bmatrix}$: (focus attractor) N_u (S) V   Right dislocation
                                                      of (S) V

On the other hand, recall that naked noun subjects cannot remain in their basic position, because they would be interpreted
as thematic. Therefore, they need to be displaced (by Subject
Postposing, for example) or they have to become contrastive.
  56. Note that it would not be correct to say that naked
nouns must be contrastive, because presentational sentences
with noncontrastive (and rhematic) naked nouns are perfectly
grammatical. Recall Caen gotas (fall drops, 'Drops are falling').
Another way of stating the constraint might be: 'preverbal
naked nouns must be contrastive'.
  57. Recall that the NP may be the grammatical subject ((80)
in the text) or the direct object if the verb is impersonal
haber 'there-be' (cf. Chapter 1):

  (i) Hoy hay un viento espantoso.
      'Today there-is a terrible wind.'

  58. Since my prime concern is to compare presentationals to
contrastive sentences of the type found in (81) and (90), I am
limiting myself to those cases in which the grammatical subject
or the left-dislocated N_u receives contrastive focus.
  59. The claim need not necessarily have been explicitly
made. The speaker may infer it because of the situation or
from knowledge of what the hearer's belief is.
  60. The most natural interpretation for this contrastive sentence is that something came up but it was not oil.
  I am also aware of the controversy between presupposition
and implication and the difficulties involved in sorting out both
notions when confronting real sentences (cf. Kempson 1975,
1977). I assume this is the logical definition of presupposition,
since it seems that stating 'OIL didn't emerge' presupposes that
'something (not oil) emerged'.
  61. The NNC concerns itself only with [$_S$NP VP] word order.
This constraint is irrelevant to presentationals, because these
sentences are characterized by VP NP word order; that is to
say, they never have their presented entity in thematic position.
  62. Once again, I remind the reader that for the purposes
of this discussion I limit myself to sentences in which the grammatical subject or the left-dislocated N_u is the element being
contrasted.

63. It should be remembered that the rules of Focus Assignment and Thematization in Section 2.4 took care of noncontrastive environments in both presentational and declarative sentences.

64. This CFA rule is essentially the one given by Rochemont (1978:81), except that his Emphatic Focus Assignment applies after stylistic rules, and is therefore part of the phonological component of the grammar (left side, cf. illustration (1) in the Introduction). Our CFA, by contrast, is one of the rules of semantic interpretation which operates on S-structures and contributes to the derivation of LFs; that is, it belongs to the right side or interpretive component of the grammar.

65. In other words, rule (103) covers much more ground than just the sentences under discussion here.

66. The presence of two operators (the contrastive focus operator and the lambda-operator) in these logical forms makes a paraphrase in English cumbersome. The LF in (104) says approximately 'the x such that it is the case that it appeared was a MAN'.
For an explanation of what seems to be an improperly bound trace (since it precedes its antecedent), I direct the reader to the discussion in Section 2.5.

67. This rule is the one given in Section 2.4. It says 'Mark as Rheme the VP and anything that follows it. Anything outside the Rheme becomes part of the Theme'.

68. This is Kuno's (1972) exhaustive listing reading of the NP.

69. QU- is the Spanish equivalent of WH-.

70. Note that this statement leaves the door open for the possibility that for some pragmatic reason these sentences might differ at some other level of analysis.

71. For more details, the reader is referred to Section 2.4 and to Section 3.4.2. The examples are not exhaustive of all types of Contrastive sentences discussed earlier. The comparison is made with the derived subtype of presentationals, i.e. with intransitive presentationals.

72. The symbol V^n represents some VP level (that is, the subject NP is moved to a level lower than S).

73. At this point it should be remembered that not all the rules in this left-hand column under Presentational Grammar are exclusive to this grammar. At least Focus Assignment and Rhematization are needed for declarative sentences also (see discussion in Section 2.4).

74. At first glance, one might think that a sentence like (i) is ambiguous between a presentational reading (the whole sentence is rhematic) and a contrastive reading (only the subject NP is rhematic).

(i) Apareció un hombre.
    appeared a man

But this ambiguity is only apparent. The Sentence can be interpreted as presentational only if normal Focus Assignment has applied. On the other hand, for the Sentence to receive a contrastive interpretation, Contrastive Focus Assignment must have applied. Therefore, the application of different rules leads to different interpretations, as should be expected.

75. In fact, Perlmutter (1971) had already postulated two kinds of filters: deep and surface filters. As the theory now stands, deep structure filters are not permissible.

4

ON BASIC WORD ORDER

4.0 Introduction. I must confess to approaching the topic of
basic word order in Spanish with no uncertain amount of appre-
hension. Not only because it is a slippery subject, due to a
lack of consensus regarding what constitutes hard linguistic
evidence for or against a given hypothesis, but also because
the concept of 'basic word order' is in itself very much theory-
dependent and demands a clear definition.
   Within the Spanish tradition, grammarians have not considered
the topic of word order extensively. In general, they have
assumed a standard pattern (SVO) and have relegated any 'deviations' to the realm of stylistics, since these deviations 'are
employed, we are told, to impart vigor and elegance or to produce a poetic style' (Farley 1958:323).[1] There are some notable exceptions to this, in particular Bolinger (1952, 1954, and
1954-1955) and Hatcher (1956a, 1956b, and 1957), but their insights appear to have had very little impact until recently.[2]
   It seems to me that the assumption has always been that
Spanish is an SVO language; therefore no need was felt for
explicit studies. In essence, the topic of word order was apparently never considered worthy of investigation. The only
systematic study of word order in the pre-seventies with which
I am acquainted is due to Greenberg (1963), a non-Hispanicist.
In his already classic study, he establishes a typology with a
view toward universals. One of his criteria consists of 'the
relative order of subject, verb, and object in declarative sentences with nominal subject and object' (1963:76), to which he
adds, 'the vast majority of languages have several variant
orders but a single dominant one' (1963:76). Although Greenberg never clarifies how he decided what constitutes the dominant word order of a given language, it is clear that he would
classify Spanish as an SVO language.[3]
   The year 1970 marks the appearance of McCawley's revolu-
tionary article 'English as a VSO language'. Since then, a few

265

266 / Spanish Presentational Sentence-Types

linguists have hypothesized that Spanish is also VSO. To my
knowledge, Bordelois (1974) is the only one who gives principled reasons for adopting this position.[4]
Notice, however, that both the SVO and VSO hypotheses
share a common assumption: base structures are ordered.[5]
In contrast, Contreras (1976)[6] presents us with unordered
semantic structures and a set of rules which assign linear
order on the basis of rhematic structure.
Analyses of both ordered and unordered base are discussed
in this chapter. Section 4.2 is devoted to the problem of basic
word order within the ordered base hypothesis, while Section
4.3 considers the same topic within the unordered base hypothesis as represented by Contreras (1976). But before plunging
into a detailed examination of these two positions, it is essential to define the notion of basic word order. This is done in
Section 4.1.

4.1 Definition of basic word order. As I have already stated,
the notion of basic word order is heavily influenced by one's
theoretical inclinations. Since I am working within one of the
versions of the Chomskian Revised Extended Standard Theory,
I define basic word order as the order generated by the phrase
structure rules of the language.[7] Insofar as it is not possible
to claim intuitions about nonsurface structures, the evidence
adduced in favor of one word order as opposed to another is
(up to a certain degree) theory-dependent. The basic word
order posited for a given language should be the one which
permits the generation of S-structures with the minimum amount
of transformational apparatus but without loss of linguistic
generalizations. Moreover, on the assumption that Case assignment takes place at the level of S-structure,[8] the following diagram is obtained.

Phrase Structure rules ———→   basic word order
                        ↓
           modified by transformations
                        ↓
                    S-structures
                        ↑
                   Case assignment

In other words, S-structures should provide us with all possible Spanish word orders, with the exception of the strictly
'stylistic' ones (cf. Section 2.3.2.1).
Furthermore, note that this definition of basic word order
necessarily implies that Spanish is a configurational language
in which grammatical relations are not primitives.[9]
Naturally, the positing of one word order as basic may be
motivated not only by economy (the minimum number of transformations, for example), but ideally also by other factors,
such as frequency studies based on a representative corpus,

determination of the presuppositionally less 'charged' discourse environments, intuitive feelings about 'normal' word order, the word order adopted whenever ambiguity may arise,[10] etc. The more of these factors there are pointing to one specific word order, the more justifications one has to posit that word order as basic. Additionally, if to the foregoing rather intuitive (and hence difficult to formalize) notions one can append some substantial arguments constructed on the basis of the internal syntactic behavior of the different constituents of the language under investigation, one should end up with some reasonable evidence in favor of a given basic word order (cf. Emonds 1980).

4.2 The Ordered Base Hypothesis. In trying to decide on the basic word order of major constituents in Spanish sentences, it might be useful to examine what Kuno (1972) has termed 'neutral description sentences'. These are sentences which 'represent nothing but new information, (they) typically appear after such expressions as Oh, look!, What happened then?, and What do you suppose I saw?' (1972:298). Consequently, Spanish sentences which answer questions like those found in (1) should be considered neutral sentences, since they present the whole event (or state) as a new one.

(1a) ¿Qué pasó/ocurrió?
'What happened?'

(1b) ¿Y ahora qué?
'And now what?'

(1c) ¿A que no sabes lo que me dijeron?
'I bet you don't know what I was told?'

(1d) ¿Por qué tienes esa cara?
'Why do you have such an expression on your face?'

Nevertheless, however useful questions might be in determining the information load of a sentence, it would be a mistake to assume that neutral sentences may appear only as answers to questions of the type found in (1). These questions should be regarded solely as a convenient tool or device. All sentences that can begin a discourse, which are appropriate as 'out of the blue' utterances, are possible neutral sentences.[11]

For the sake of clarity and ease of exposition, I illustrate neutral sentences with examples in which the arguments are either nominal or strong pronominal (thus, I am excluding sentences which contain clitics).[12] Furthermore, I subdivide verbs into two groups: transitive and intransitive.[13]

Examples of neutral sentences with transitive verbs:

(2a) Paco ganó la lotería. SVO
'Paco won the lottery.'

(2b) Tu mamá mandó un paquete. SVO
'Your mother sent a package.'

(2c) (Nosotros) necesitamos más lluvia. (S)VO
'We need more rain.'

(2d) Chomsky escribió otro libro. SVO
'Chomsky wrote another book.'

(2e) Hay un unicornio (afuera). VO(Adv)
'There-is a unicorn (outside).'

Examples of neutral sentences with intransitive verbs:

(3a) José murió. SV
'José died.'

(3b) El golpe fracasó. SV
'The coup failed.'

(3c) Los invitados llegaron (tarde). SV(Adv)
'The guests arrived (late).'

(3d) La niña estuvo llorando. SV
'The girl was crying.'

(3e) Apareció un mendigo. VS
appeared a beggar
'A beggar appeared.'

(3f) Llegaron noticias de tu familia. VS
arrived news of your family
'News from your family arrived.'

(3g) Surgió petróleo. VS
came-up oil
'Oil came up.'

As one can see immediately by examining the data in (2) and
(3), neutral sentences with transitive verbs are characterized
by (S)VO word order, while those with intransitive verbs
exhibit both SV (3a)-(3d) and VS order (3e)-(3g). Apparently,
Spanish neutral sentences do not provide us with a uniform pattern of word order for major constituents. Therefore, several
postulates present themselves for discussion.

(a) Spanish has two basic word orders: one for transitive
verbs (SVO) and another one for intransitive verbs (VS).
(b) Spanish has two basic word orders: one for transitive
verbs and some intransitive verbs (SV(O)), another for
some intransitive verbs (VS).
(c) Spanish is VSO.
(d) Spanish is VOS.
(e) Spanish is SVO.

Each of these alternatives is entertained in turn.

4.2.1 Spanish is SVO and VS. The hypothesis that Spanish
has two basic word orders, one for transitive verbs and another
for intransitive verbs, appears to be immediately invalidated by
the data in (3). Why should VS order be more basic for all
intransitive verbs when (3) indicates that these verbs fall into
two categories (i.e. SV and VS)? What could justify selecting
VS as basic when the sentences in (3a)-(3d) are as neutral
as those in (3e)-(3g)? Moreover, one must also keep in mind
that the neutral pattern for transitive sentences appears to be
unequivocally SVO. If one were to accept VS as basic for intransitive verbs, to what would one attribute the preposing of
the subject in (3a)-(3d) but not in (3e)-(3g)?

As evidenced by these unanswered questions, there is little
merit in this proposal. I therefore discard it.

4.2.2 Spanish is SV(O) and VS. This second alternative
also claims that Spanish displays two basic word orders. It
differs from the first in that only some intransitive verbs are
underlyingly VS, while the rest of the intransitive verbs fall
together with transitive ones as SV(O). The question to ask
then is: which verbs would belong to the basic VS pattern?
By merely glancing at the sentences in (3), one can see that
(3e)-(3g) are presentational sentences, that is, sentences which
introduce the referent of the NP into the world of discourse.
It was precisely this type of sentence that was discussed in
Chapter 2; there the possibility of directly generating presentational sentences in the base was considered and discarded
(cf. Section 2.3.1). I briefly recapitulate the reasons given
against base generation of VS presentationals.

In the first place, although presentational sentences are
accurately characterized by V NP word order, it would be incorrect to maintain that the postverbal NP argument has to be
the subject, since it must be recalled that this NP is the object in impersonal haber sentences (the presentational construction par excellence). In other words, the presentational function is independent of grammatical relations; all that matters is
that the referent of the NP be heralded into the discourse.
Although 'presentationalism' demands V NP word order, this
word order may be exemplified by (at least) the sequences in
(4).[14]

(4a) VS   Apareció un hombre.
                appeared a man
                'A man appeared.'

(4b) VO   Había grandes esperanzas.
                there-was great hopes
                'There were great hopes.'

(4c) [V+O]S   Dió señales de vida mi tío Paco.
                gave signs of life my uncle Paco
                'My uncle Paco appeared.'

This militates against base generation of VS as the presentational word order.

In Section 2.1.2.1 I showed that it was impossible to provide an accurate and complete classification of all and only those verbs which enter into presentational constructions. Therefore, it is neither advisable nor possible to attach this kind of information to the verbs themselves.[15] This conclusion is confirmed by the fact that most intransitive verbs appear as easily in presentational sentences as in declarative ones (cf. Section 2.3.1.2). This is precisely because 'presentationalism' is not a feature of verbs; on the contrary, it is an interpretation which depends on the discourse, that is, the conjunction of sentence semantics and pragmatics (LF and SI-2, as explained in Section 2.4).

All of the foregoing arguments point in the same direction. It would be nonsensical to postulate one basic word order for presentational sentences (VS) and another one for all other sentences (SVO); such a step could only lead to unnecessary complications and loss of generalizations. Therefore, this hypothesis must also be abandoned.

4.2.2.1 Discourse conditioning. The question remains as to why the sentences in (3e)-(3g) adopt VS word order under the neutral interpretation. It does not seem unreasonable to assume that even discourse-initial sentences might be conditioned by the total discourse. Derbyshire (1977, and references cited therein) explores this possibility and concludes that, although discourse-initial sentences are the most context free, 'even here there are discourse conditioning factors that influence word order' (1977: 596). What makes Derbyshire's position even more attractive is that he is discussing a construction used 'to introduce a new participant, or to bring back into focus one who has been out of the picture in the immediately preceding context' (1977); that is, he is talking about presentational sentences.

The conditioning hypothesis is strengthened by further considerations. The examples in (3e)-(3g) are utterances that either answer a question of the type found in (1) or start a new discourse. In other words, these sentences reflect their discourse-initial character, and this influence is manifested in their VS word order. To support this point of view, notice that without knowledge of the discourse, it is impossible to decide between (5a) and (5b) as the more natural or appropriate.

(5a) Un mendigo apareció en la puerta. SVAdv
      'A beggar appeared at the door.'

(5b) En la puerta apareció un mendigo. AdvVS
      'At the door appeared a beggar.'

In a vacuum all one knows is that the information highlighted by these two sentences is different.
    Further support for the thesis that the VS word order of presentational sentences might be influenced by discourse factors is found in the argument illustrated by the data in (4). 'Presentationalism' cannot be unequivocally equated with VS word order, because 'presentationalism' manifests itself in other word orders. The fact that intransitive verbs are monovalent, coupled with the relative 'freedom' of word order that a language like Spanish allows, explains why intransitive verbs appear with equal ease in SV and VS structures. That these different word orders are paired with different rhematic structures at the post-LF level and with different information structures in SI-2 (cf. Section 0.1.2) is to be expected and is, I assume, beyond dispute at this point (compare once more (3a)-(3d) and (3e)-(3g)).
    On the other hand, notice that discourse-initial sentences with transitive verbs fall back to SVO word order, which gives us a symmetrical pattern of one NP preceding the V, the other one following it: NP V NP. This pattern has the advantage of redundantly marking grammatical relations. The subject is identified by position as well as by dominance and by subject-verb agreement; the object is recognized by its position, dominance, and at times also by the so-called 'personal a'. Thus, it makes sense for SVO to be the pattern adopted whenever the possibility of ambiguity might arise (cf. note 10 and example (32c)).

4.2.3 Spanish is VSO. The third hypothesis maintains that Spanish is basically a VSO language. Bordelois (1974) is the main proponent of this stand,[16] which she supports with three data-oriented and one theoretical argument.
    First, Bordelois states that VSO order is common in Spanish root sentences.

(6) (=B(143))
     Pronunció el embajador un discurso.
     pronounced the ambassador a speech.
     'The ambassador gave a speech.'

Second, she says that for verbs of movement and location the unmarked word order is VS.

(7) (=B(144))
    Vino Juan.[17]
    came John
    'John came.'

Third, Bordelois correctly notices that gerundives, infinitives, and participial clauses always prohibit a preposed subject.

(8) (=B(145))
    Habiendo llegado Juan, comenzó la fiesta.
    having arrived John began the party
    'John having arrived, the party began.'

(9) (=B(146))
    Al llegar Juan, comenzó la fiesta.
    to-the to-arrive John began the party
    'Upon John's arrival, the party began.'

(10) (=B(147))
    Llegado Juan, comenzó la fiesta.
    arrived John began the party
    'John having arrived, the party began.'

Her theoretical claim is that it is more economical to posit basic VSO and an optional transformation which preposes the subject in tensed clauses. According to Bordelois, this has the advantage of avoiding any contradiction of Emonds' (1970) structure-preserving hypothesis or Ross' (1972) Penthouse Principle, because no rearrangement of embedded tenseless clauses ((8)-(10)) would be needed.[18]
I now review Bordelois' arguments. Starting with the theoretical one, it is easy to show that the assumption of SVO and a rule of Subject Postposing do not violate the structure-preserving hypothesis or the Penthouse Principle, since VSO word order is not limited to root sentences.

(11a) Me dijeron que apareció otro libro de Chomsky.
      'to me they-told that appeared another book of Chomsky
      'They told me that another book by Chomsky appeared.'

(11b) Me sorprendió que apareciera otro libro de Chomsky.
      to-me it-surprised that appeared (sunjunctive) another
          book of Chomsky
      'It surprised me that another book by Chomsky
          appeared.'

(11c) Es imposible que pronunciara el embajador ese
discurso.
it-is impossible that pronounced (subjunctive) the
ambassador that speech
'It is impossible that the ambassador gave that
speech.'

(11d) El congreso en el cual participará Paco es en Caracas.
the conference in the which will-participate Paco is en
Caracas
'The conference in which Paco will participate takes
place in Caracas.'

As shown by (11), VSO word order appears in embedded sentences, both assertive (11a) and nonassertive (11b)-(11d)[19] (cf. Hooper and Thompson 1973). Hence, the rule (or rules) which postposes the subject in Spanish is not limited to main clauses. Therefore, (11) does away with Bordelois' theoretical argument in favor of VSO.[20]

From among her data-oriented arguments I start with the third--that gerundives, infinitives, and participial clauses require that the subject (if stated) appear postverbally (cf. (8)-(10))--because it is related to the preceding point. The following remarks should not be taken as comprehensive but merely as a pointer for future research, since a thorough treatment of this topic would require a chapter of its own. In the first place, I think it would be a mistake to place too much weight on an argument based on the constructions found in (8)-(10). They are examples of 'absolute clauses', and as such they are special, or 'marked'. For example, the norm for Spanish is for the subject of the infinitive[21] to be either unexpressed or to appear in a prepositional phrase.

(12a) Paco quiere salir temprano.
'Paco wants to-go-out early.'

(12b) Susana mandó comprar vino (a Paco).
Susana ordered to-buy wine (to Paco)
'Susana ordered (Paco) to buy wine.'

(12c) Pedro la invitó a bailar (a María).
Pedro her (acc.) invited to to-dance (to Mary)
'Pedro invited her (Mary) to dance.'

(12d) Paco la vió venir (a María).
Paco her (acc.) saw to-come (to Mary)
'Paco saw her (Mary) coming.'

(12e) Paco lo hizo salir (a José).[22]
Paco him (acc.) made to-go-out (to José)
'Paco made him (José) leave.'

The main verbs used in the examples in (12) are representative of large groups of verbs: subject control (12a), object control (12b, 12c), perception (12d), and causative (12e).[23] Note that none of the infinitives in these sentences takes a subject argument directly, i.e. without an intermediary preposition.[24]

Undoubtedly, it was the observation of facts such as those I have illustrated for Spanish that led Chomsky (1980a) to maintain that nonfinite verbs do not assign Case to their subjects.[25] This hypothesis is confirmed by Spanish to the extent that the underlying subjects of infinitives appear after a preposition (which serves as a Case-assigner) in order for this argument to escape the No-Case Filter (13):

(13) *N, where N has no Case   (Chomsky 1980a:25)

Furthermore, it must be recalled that the theory of abstract Case (14) does not constitute a total prohibition against assigning Case in any other environments, but rather represents the unmarked instances.

(14) NP → Nominative if governed by Tense
     NP → Objective if governed by -N (i.e. V or P)[26]

With this background it seems that I am justified in maintaining that the lexical subjects of infinitives in absolute clauses constitute a marked case. They receive Nominative Case, even though they are not governed by tense. The question that remains to be answered is why these subjects should always appear in postverbal position. First, notice that the subject of the absolute clause in (8)-(10) is different from that of the matrix clause (Juan and la fiesta 'the party', respectively). Second, observe that if the subjects in both clauses are the same, the norm is for the one in the absolute clause to be left out in surface structure. Compare (15a) to (15b).

(15a) Al ser derrocado, el tirano huyó.
      to-the to-be deposed, the tyrant fled
      'When he$_i$ was deposed, the tyrant$_i$ fled.'

(15b) *Al ser derrocado el tirano, huyó.
      to-the to-be deposed the tyrant, fled
      'When the tyrant$_i$ was deposed, he$_i$ fled.'

What this distribution of the data indicates is that absolute clauses tend to contain a lexical subject whenever this subject differs in reference from that of the matrix clause. Therefore, this subject of the absolute clause provides some crucial and nonrecoverable information; consequently, it is highlighted, that is, it needs to be in the scope of assertion. In other

words, this subject is rhematic in nature, in which case it should be expected that it be postverbal.[27]
In sum, I have countered Bordelois' third argument in favor of the VSO hypothesis by showing that there are reasons to consider absolute constructions as being marked, due to the fact that they allow their subjects to be assigned Nominative Case in the absence of tense, contrary to the norm in Spanish (cf. (12)). And secondly, I have speculated that the postverbal position of these subjects is due to their rhematic nature.

Let us now turn to the two remaining arguments adduced to provide support for the VSO hypothesis. One of them uses the presentational sentence Vino Juan. All pertinent evidence and discussion concerning this type of sentence are found in Section 2.2.2. Therefore, one is left only with the rationale exemplified by (6).

(6) Pronunció el embajador un discurso.
    pronounced the ambassador a speech
    'The ambassador gave a speech.'

It is true that VSO order appears in main clauses (and embedded ones, cf. (11)), but this does not mean that such clauses represent the norm, are more basic, or are even statistically more frequent. I am aware of only two quantitative studies on this point, one conducted by Bentivoglio and D'Introno (1978), based on the spoken Caraqueño Spanish of 24 informants, and the second done by Silva-Corvalán (1978), using eight working-class Mexican-American Spanish speakers of Los Angeles. The first study shows the results given in (16).

(16)	SVO	%	VSO	%	OVS	%	VOS	%	Total[28]
Main declarative	3082	82.60	591	15.84	38	1.01	9	0.24	3731
Tensed embedded nonrelative	1122	80.37	264	18.91	1	0.71	1	0.71	1396
Tensed embedded relative[29]	275	68.58	126	31.42	---	---	---	---	401

These statistics clearly indicate that SVO order is more frequent by more than a significant percentage in both main and subordinate clauses. Silva-Corvalán obtained the following percentages for two-argument sentences: 78% SVO, 7% VSO, 7% OVS, and 8% VOS (1978:22).[30] These two studies leave very little doubt as to which word order is the more frequent in Spanish. Therefore, quantitative studies do not support the VSO hypothesis.

Furthermore, observe that while (17a), with its SVO order, is appropriate as discourse-initial, (17b), with VSO order, is more constrained.

(17a) El embajador pronunció un discurso.
'The ambassador gave a speech.'

(17b) Pronunció el embajador un discurso.
gave the ambassador a speech.

The most appropriate context for (17b) is one in which the sentence is one of the members of a list of events (i.e. $E_1, E_2, \ldots, E_n$), as in (18).

(18) Pronunció el embajador un discurso, respondió el cónsul a las preguntas de los periodistas, y por último distribuyó un secretario unos papeles.
'The ambassador gave a speech, the consul answered the journalists' questions, and finally a secretary distributed some papers.'

And although sentences like (17b) or (18) may answer a question like ¿Qué pasó? 'What happened?', it is clear that a VSO sentence is intuitively more 'marked', more specialized than its counterpart with SVO order (cf. (17a)). Furthermore, (17b) could also be used in a situation where el embajador is focused and, therefore, contrastively stressed.[31] These facts seem to weaken the supposition that the VSO pattern is the basic one.
Up to now I have demonstrated that Bordelois' arguments for underlying VSO word order can be satisfactorily countered and, moreover, that neither statistical studies nor the notion of basic word order as defined in Section 4.1 give much support to that hypothesis. There are further complications with the VSO hypothesis. Since VSO does not leave room for a basic VP constituent, it becomes possible to argue against this hypothesis by showing that the verb and its objects form a constituent. Confirmation for a VP constituent is found in constructions such as those in (19) and (20).

(19a) Susana lo mandó comprar vino a Juan.
Susana him (acc.) ordered to-buy wine to Juan
'Susana ordered Juan to buy wine.'

(19b) *Susana lo mandó comprar a Juan vino.

(20a) Susana le prohibió fumar un cigarro a Juan.
Susana him (dat.) prohibited to-smoke a cigar to John
'Susan forbade John to smoke a cigar.'

(20b) *Susana le prohibió fumar a Juan un cigarro.[32]

If Spanish were underlyingly VSO, why should it be that the subjects (underlined) of the infinitive clauses in (19) and (20) cannot stay in their base-generated positions?[33] One very plausible explanation seems to be that since the verb and its object(s) form a constituent, the infinitive subject must be displaced, to the end of this constituent. But note that this explanation is not available to the proponents of VSO, precisely because the VSO hypothesis does not allow for a VP constituent.

More evidence for a VP constituent is provided by VP Topicalization. As shown by the examples in (21), this movement rule preposes the embedded verb and its object to TOP position, leaving a gap behind (indicated by Δ).

(21a) Cortándose un mechón, la mamá la vió Δ a su hija.
      cutting her hair, the mother her$_i$ (acc.) saw her daughter$_i$

(21b) Contando un chiste verde, la maestra lo pescó Δ a José.
      telling a joke off-color, the teacher him$_i$ caught José$_i$

Note what happens when Topicalization is applied to a sentence like (20): either the whole embedded sentence is preposed (22a), or only the (lower) embedded VP is (22b), but never the embedded V and its subject (22c).

(22a) Fumar un cigarro a Juan, Susana le prohibió Δ.
      to-smoke a cigar to John, Susana him prohibited

(22b) Fumar un cigarro, Susana le prohibió Δ a Juan.

(22c) *Fumar a Juan, Susana le prohibió Δ un cigarro Δ.

Hence, these data also support the existence of a VP constituent.

In essence, since the VSO hypothesis does not make the correct predictions with respect to displacement of infinitive subjects (cf. (19), (20)) and Topicalization (cf. (21), (22)), it must be rejected.[34]

Another question concerning a proposed basic VSO order of major constituents can be raised by an examination of different kinds of Spanish verbs. The types that are relevant here are exemplified in (23).

(23a) Verbs with two arguments: a subject and an object
      Examples: comer 'to eat', lavar 'to wash'

(23b) Verbs with one argument, such as the intransitive verbs llegar 'to arrive', toser 'to cough', aparecer 'to appear'

(23c) Verbs with one argument, such as the subjectless
verbs <u>hay</u> 'there-be', <u>hacer</u> 'to make'

Taking into account that the VSO hypothesis implies that
basic sentences have the structure (24), in which both NPs are
directly dominated by S, it appears reasonable to assume that
linear order is the only factor which differentiates the NPs
from each other.

(24) [$_S$ V NP NP],

The first NP is identified as the subject, the second as the
object. This assumption works quite well for verbs found in
(23a).

(25a) [$_S$ comió Paco caracoles]
ate Paco snails

(25b) [$_S$ lavó María al niño]
washed Maria the boy

In both sentences in (25), verb agreement is established with
the first NP; in (25b) the so-called 'personal a' is correctly
positioned before the [+human] direct object, i.e. the second
NP.[35]
Nonetheless, all does not go as smoothly with the verbs in
(23b) and (23c). These verbs are uni-argument; they differ
only in the fact that in some cases the sole argument functions
as subject (23b) and in other cases it functions as object (23c).
The contrast in function depends on the type of verb. However, this dissimilarity is lost in the VSO hypothesis, because
these sentences manifest themselves as V NP regardless of the
verb type.

(26a) [$_S$ llegó Paco]
arrived Paco

(26b) [$_S$ tosían los niños]
coughed the boys

(27a) [$_S$ había muchas flores]
there-were many flowers

(27b) [$_S$ hace un frío espantoso]
it-makes a cold terrible
('It is extremely cold.')

In other words, given that the structure produced is [$_S$ V NP],
what is there to signal that the NP in (26) is the subject and
governs verb agreement, whereas the NP in (27) is the object

and, consequently, does not rule verb agreement? The answer seems to be, 'Nothing'.[36] Nevertheless, the NPs fail to behave alike not only with respect to subject-verb agreement but also with respect to potential for pronominal replacement. The NPs in (26) are replaceable by a subject pronoun (cf. (28)), while those in (27) can be substituted by an object clitic (cf. (29)) --facts which demonstrate that linear order is not a sufficient condition for capturing grammatical relations.

(28a) El llegó.
'He arrived.'

(28b) Ellos tosían.
'They (m. pl.) were-coughing.'

(29a) Las hay.
them (f. pl.) there-are
'There are them.'

(29b) Lo hace.
it (m. sg.) makes
'It is.'

As a consequence, it is imperative that the grammar provide a way to identify the NP (or NPs) with regard to function.[37] Unless we accept Relational Grammar's claim that grammatical relations are primitives, there is no obvious direct way to capture this fact within the VSO hypothesis. But observe that there is no need to take such a drastic step;[38] the acceptance of SVO as basic for Spanish provides this as a bonus. The SVO hypothesis allows for a configurational definition of subject and object based on dominance and internal constituency. The differences characteristic of the two types of monovalent verbs (cf. (23b) and (23c)) are simply and directly captured in this hypothesis, as (30) and (31) show.

(30)

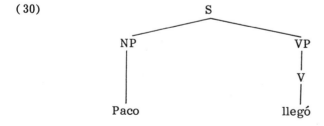

(31)

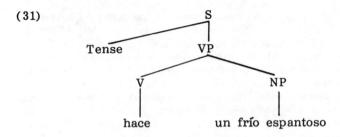

Diagram (30) clearly indicates that one is in the presence of an intransitive verb, while (31) shows that one is dealing with a subjectless verb (see Appendix B for further discussion and justification of this stand). There is no possible confusion as to the function performed by the relevant NPs.

Thus, different types of Spanish verbs furnish the data necessary to demonstrate that the identification of grammatical relations is obscured by the VSO hypothesis. The foregone conclusion is that SVO provides a more highly valued analysis of the facts for Spanish.

I now recapitulate the arguments given to refute the VSO order as basic for Spanish. In the first place, it was shown that Bordelois' reasoning for VSO weakens under close scrutiny. Second, neither quantitative studies nor the notion of 'less marked' or 'more basic' speaks in favor of VSO. Third, syntactic movement rules--such as displacement of the infinitive subject and Topicalization--lend support to a VP constituent, which is contrary to what would be expected if VSO were basic. Fourth, VSO obscures grammatical relations, especially with regard to the two kinds of monovalent verbs.[39] Together, these facts force the rejection of VSO for Spanish.

4.2.4 Spanish is VOS. The fourth alternative for basic word order is VOS. As far as I know, nobody has claimed that this order should be considered basic for Spanish. Indeed, the chances of Spanish being VOS are remote. Note what Greenberg (1963:61) has to say with respect to VOS.

Logically there are six possible orders: SVO, SOV, VSO, VOS, OSV, and OVS. Of these six, however, only three normally occur as dominant orders. The three which do not occur at all, or at least are excessively rare, are VOS [my underlining, M.S.], OSV, and OVS.

Later studies in word order typology have established that there are some languages with basic VOS (see, for example, Pullum 1977), but the fact remains that this is a rare order.[40]

In Spanish, there are no noncontrastive matrix sentences in which VOS order is natural. The only possible candidates would be the presentational expressions dar señales de vida, hacer su entrada, and the like. But these expressions might be better analyzed as complex verbs; and, moreover, there is no overriding reason to generate presentational sentences directly in their surface word order (see Sections 4.2.2, 4.2.2.1, and 2.3.1).[41] Furthermore, observe that VOS is not supported at all by the two quantitative studies previously cited: Bentivoglio and D'Introno (1978) attested only nine instances (0.24 percent) out of 3731 tokens, and Silva-Corvalán puts the percentage at 8 percent. Thus, although VOS is not susceptible to some of the arguments levelled against VSO in Section 4.2.3 (for example, it allows for a VP constituent and hence permits a configurational definition of grammatical relations), in the absence of any strong evidence in its favor, VOS does not seem to be a workable hypothesis for Spanish basic word order.

4.2.5 Spanish is SVO. This is the final alternative to be considered. By now it should be obvious that the observed facts of Spanish must support the SVO hypothesis. Because the arguments supporting SVO developed out of the criticism of untenable alternatives discussed in earlier sections, I present merely their outline for review here.

(32a) SVO is the neutral pattern for transitive sentences as well as for a good portion of intransitive sentences (all the nonpresentational ones).

(32b) As a consequence of (32a), SVO is the least context-dependent pattern for declarative sentences, i.e. the intuitively least marked and least presuppositionally 'charged' order.

(32c) SVO is the word order chosen whenever there is any possibility of ambiguity. For example, in the following sets of sentences, only word order tells us which NPs are the subject and the object.

　　(i) El auto chocó el camión.
　　'The car crashed into the truck.'

　　El camión chocó el auto.
　　'The truck crashed into the car.'

　　(ii) La recesión causó la quiebra de los bancos.
　　'The recession caused the banks' bankruptcy.'

　　La quiebra de los bancos causó la recesión.
　　'The banks' bankruptcy caused the recession.'

(32d) Generic statements also adopt SVO word order:

El frío penetra los huesos.
the cold penetrates the bones
'Cold goes through one's bones.'

(32e) Frequency studies support the SVO hypothesis over-
whelmingly.

(32f) Syntactic rules lend support to a VP constituent.

(32g) The grammatical relations of subject and object are
easily characterized within the SVO hypothesis.

The conjunction of all of the arguments cited here makes a
strong case in favor of SVO as the basic word order for
Spanish. This is even more evident when one takes into account that none of the alternatives considered proved to be
viable. Consequently, I claim that I have established SVO as
basic.
One last point needs to be restated. Throughout this section I have assumed without any discussion that the phrase
structure rules generate an ordered set of entities, or in other
words, that base structures are ordered. Nonetheless, as already mentioned in Section 4.0, there has recently been set
forth a proposal concerning word order which assumes an unordered base. This proposal, given by Contreras (1976),
needs to be evaluated and contrasted with the conclusion that
SVO is basic. I now turn to this new problem.

4.3 The Unordered Base Hypothesis. As should be expected,
this analysis is built on different premises from those discussed
in Section 4.2. This fact makes impossible a direct comparison
of both models. What can be compared, however, are the predictions they foster and the range of data they cover.
Another dissimilarity between Contreras' study and my own
resides in their objectives. That of Contreras is a much more
ambitious project aimed at accounting for the word order of all
declarative sentences, contrastive and noncontrastive alike.
On the other hand, I have delimited my goal to providing an
in-depth description and explanation of the syntax and semantics of two subtypes of presentational sentences. This difference in the scopes of the two studies must be kept in mind
throughout the discussion.

4.3.1 Contreras' *A Theory of Word Order with Special
Reference to Spanish*. To present a detailed account of Contreras' work is far from my main goal. Nevertheless, I provide enough background to warrant a fair evaluation of the
predictions made by the unordered base hypothesis as opposed
to those made by the ordered base alternative discussed in
Section 4.2. I summarize in capsule form Contreras' main proposals before introducing any of my comments.

In essence, Contreras develops a theory of word order in which a sentence is defined as consisting of a nucleus and optional adjuncts. The arguments stand for semantic notions such as agent, patient, experiencer, instrument, cause, etc.; and they are assigned a linear order on the basis of their rhematic status. The Rheme Selection Hierarchy in (33) (Contreras 1976:139), characterized as a surface structure constraint, is responsible for evaluating the ranking of arguments and adjuncts,[42] taking into account their likelihood of being used as rhemes.

(33) Rheme Selection Hierarchy (RSH)
1. Instrumental, manner adverbial, 'strong' time and place adverbial
2. Target
3. Complement, source, location, time identifier, beneficiary
4. Patient
5. Agent, cause, possessor, experiencer
6. 'Weak' time and place adverbial

Typical rheme assignment obeys the RSH; atypical rheme assignment violates it. The RSH, in conjunction with Linear Order I (which places rhemes to the right of nonrhemes) and Linear Order II (which arranges higher ranking rhemes or nonrhemes to the right of lower ranking ones), provides for normal word order. Emphatic word order requires the rule of Theme Postposing. The rule of Sentential Stress Assignment marks as [+stress] any rheme which is not directly followed by another rheme.[43] There are also some special rules meant to deal with sentences which are not linearized according to their rhematic status and several surface structure constraints devised to capture differences in acceptability manifested by sentences with atypical rheme selection. Furthermore, Contreras does away with the object category but finds it necessary to keep the subject category, which is identified not configurationally but as the argument marked with the feature [+subject] by the rule of Subject Selection (for discussion of this point, see Section 4.3.3.1).

4.3.1.1 Differences in definitions. A clarification is imperative in connection with Contreras' use of the notions of theme and rheme. His use differs from mine. While I have defined rheme as whatever is in the scope of assertion, and theme as the unasserted part of a sentence, Contreras follows Chafe (1974) and defines theme as whatever is assumed by the speaker to be in the addressee's consciousness, and rheme as the elements not assumed by the speaker to be in the hearer's consciousness. The adoption of these definitions allows Contreras to utilize these terms as equivalent to given and new information (1976:4). Moreover, he claims that theme/rheme assignment

takes place in deep structure (1976:6), while I have assumed
that theme/rheme is determined at a level immediately after LF
but still within sentence grammar. I have already shown that
theme/rheme should not be equated with given/new; the latter
dichotomy belongs to discourse grammar (cf. Section 0.1.2).

4.3.2 'Normal' word order. Because what is at stake here
is an evaluation of whether the base generates a set of ordered
entities (which by implication entails the acceptance of a basic
word order) or a set of unordered entities (in which case
there is no need to establish a basic word order), and since
basic word order as defined in Section 4.1 carries an assumption about the least marked or most neutral word order, I concentrate primarily on Contreras' claims about 'normal' word
order.

4.3.2.1 The Rheme Assignment rule. Considering that the
rules which assign normal word order to sentence constituents
do so on the basis of their rhematic status (1976:71), it is
necessary to examine the rules which mark a constituent as
rhematic. Contreras postulates four separate rules (1976:139),
shown in (34).

(34a) Rheme Assignment (obligatory)

[+rheme], X

1   2 $\longrightarrow$

$\emptyset$ $\begin{bmatrix} 2 \\ 1 \end{bmatrix}$

Condition: X is any element in semantic structure.

(34b) If the predicate has the feature [+passive], the
patient interchanges rank with the agent, cause,
possessor, or experiencer.

(34c) The predicate always ranks one step higher than the
lowest ranking argument, except when the predicate
is [+presentational], in which case its rank is lower
than that of the patient.[44]

(34d) If the verb has the feature [+presentational], the
patient interchanges its rhematic rank with that of
the other argument present.

Subsequently, the rhematic structure obtained by the foregoing
rules is checked against the RSH surface structure constraint
(cf. (33)). The result of this procedure, taken with the definition of violation of the RSH (35), supposedly accounts for
typical vs. atypical rheme selection.

(35) A structure violates the RSH if X is [-rheme] and Y is [+rheme], and X ranks higher than Y in the RSH (1976:40).

Several weaknesses are inherent in this approach.

4.3.2.1.1 The Rheme Selection Hierarchy (RSH). I first examine the RSH. Disregarding for the moment the elements in (33.6), the RSH says that the arguments identified as agent, possessor, and experiencer rank lowest in the hierarchy. Consequently, Linear Orders I and II place them in preverbal position and then Subject Selection (see Section 4.3.3.1) assigns them the feature [+subject]. The question one must ask is whether these arguments rank lowest in the hierarchy because of their semantic function or because they are the most likely candidates for subjecthood and thus tend to appear in preverbal position. Observe that, with the exception of cause, these lowest ranking arguments are at least [+animate] if not [+human], and that NPs which carry these features rank the highest in what Foley and Van Valin call the Referentiality Hierarchy.

(36) speaker > hearer > human proper > human common > animate > inanimate

(Foley and Van Valin 1977:294)

With (36), Foley and Van Valin attempt to capture what seems to be a 'universal hierarchy of topic-worthiness' (1977:294)[45] which, depending on the language, may be reflected in word order and/or by overt Case marking. In Spanish, the Referentiality Hierarchy manifests itself in word order. As a consequence, the arguments of agent, possessor, and experiencer tend to function as preverbal subjects. Besides sharing at least the feature [+animate], these arguments have another trait in common: they can be [+rheme] by themselves in two-argument sentences only if postposed (37), or if they receive heavy stress (38).

(37) [=C(5.21)]
Lo llama el DIRECTOR.
'The DIRECTOR is calling you.'

(38) EL DIRECTOR lo llama.
'The DIRECTOR is calling you.'

Either alternative renders a contrastive sentence. The facts examined appear to support the suggestion that there is something to left-to-right word order--with themes to the left of rhemes--quite independently of Contreras' RSH.

4.3.2.1.2 'Special cases'. These are constructions such as idiomatic expressions, passive sentences, presentational verbs, and negation (cf. Contreras' Chapter VI) which alter the RSH. Contreras says, 'All of these cases require special rules the precise formulation of which is not always clear ...' (1976:57). Illustrating my contention with presentational and passive sentences, I show that these 'special' cases require special rules only because Contreras disregards basic word order in favor of semantic roles.

Let us start with presentationals. Contreras states that they function to introduce the patient to the addressee's consciousness (1976:54); he attaches the feature [+presentational] to verbs by means of an optional lexical redundancy rule. But in Section 2.1.2 I showed that presentationalism is not a feature of verbs, but rather one of the whole context. Therefore, it is not at all clear what can be accomplished by means of this optional feature. For instance, suppose this feature were assigned to the verb empezar 'to begin'. I am in complete agreement with Contreras that verb-subject word order (39) is less restricted contextually than subject-verb word order (40) in this pair of sentences.

(39) (=C(6.15))
Empezó la resistencia.
'The RESISTANCE started.'

(40) (=C(6.14))
La resistencia empezó.
'The resistance STARTED.'

Nevertheless, the same cannot be said of (41) vis-à-vis (42).

(41) ??Empezó a ganar terreno la resistencia.
started to gain terrain the resistance

(42) La resistencia empezó a ganar terreno.
'The resistance started to gain terrain.'

In this case, (42) is less restricted contextually, because it is the most appropriate of the two as a discourse opener. However, since empezar meets the conditions for the optional lexical rule to operate, the feature [+presentational] could have been assigned to it in (41).[46] This, in turn would have triggered rule (34c) (and maybe even (34d)[47]) and the outcome should have been a perfectly natural 'normal' presentational sentence--which (41) is not. Moreover, the same process would have characterized (42) as somehow more 'marked' than (41); again the wrong prediction. Consequently, these results confirm my previous assertion (cf. Section 2.1.2) that it is impossible to capture all and only the presentational sentences by marking the verbs, even when this marking is done optionally.

Hence, the conclusion one must arrive at is that despite the positing of two special rules ((34c) and (34d)--rules for which no independent evidence is given) and a lexical redundancy rule, Contreras' grammar does not provide a satisfactory analysis of presentational sentences.

Another case in which a special rule is required because of a violation of the RSH is that of passive sentences. Rule (34b) states that if the predicate has the feature [+passive], the patient interchanges rank with the agent, cause, possessor, or experiencer (which in my eyes once again demonstrates the importance of linear order and the thematic tendency of subjects in preverbal position). For example, in (43) Víctor Jara is the patient which ranks lower in rhematicity than the agent los militares.

(43) (=C(6.3))
    Víctor Jara fue asesinado por los MILITARES.
    'Victor Jara was murdered by the MILITARY.'

However, in (44) the subject (patient) is in postverbal position and is the only rhematic element; that is, in this case the patient ranks higher than the preverbal agent even though the predicate has the feature [+passive].

(44) (=C(6.4))
    Por los militares fue asesinado Víctor JARA.
    'Victor JARA was murdered by the military.'

In other words, sentence (44) is in violation of rule (34). Once again, it appears that word order overrules semantic relationships, and that the rules given by Contreras do not account for the data. In a theory which assumes the existence of basic word order, (43) would be directly generated[48] and (44) would be derived by rules which alter the normal word order, thus accounting for its presuppositionally more marked status.[49]

What rules (34b)-(34d) have in common is their effort to account for typical rheme assignments despite violations of the RSH. It is interesting to note that all these 'violations' are intimately related to the fact that an NP which bears the semantic role of patient is given the subject function. This confirms my suspicion that the unifying and crucial factor is the grammatical function coupled with linear order (preverbal vs. postverbal), and not the semantic roles themselves.[50] It is evident that adherence to semantic roles at the expense of grammatical relations only leads to the proliferation of unmotivated rules.

4.3.2.2 Argument definitions. There are other problems of a slightly different nature regarding the RSH. One of them concerns the definition of the arguments in relation to their position in the sentence. For example, consider the NP la pelota 'the ball' in sentences (45) and (46).

(45) Paco rompió la ventana con la pelota.
'Paco broke the window with the ball.'

(46) La pelota rompió la ventana.
'The ball broke the window.'

Contreras would analyze la pelota as instrument in (45) but as
cause in (46). Instruments are defined as 'objects which play
a role in bringing about a process but which are not its main
instigator' (1976:35). No definition of cause is given; Contreras says only that, 'If no agent is present, a cause may appear as a surface subject ... natural forces are a common type
of cause' (1976:35). His examples are shown in (47).

(47a) (=C(4.18))
Las balas atemorizaron al pueblo.
'The bullets frightened the people.'

(47b) (=C(4.19))
Los truenos atemorizaron a la gente.
'Thunder frightened the people.'

Nonetheless, the only difference I perceive between (45) and
(46) is that la pelota is part of a prepositional phrase in the
former but the subject in the latter. The definition of instrument fits la pelota in both sentences regardless of its position
or grammatical relation. Furthermore, observe that both (45)
and (46) are perfectly 'normal', noncontrastive sentences. The
main motivation I can detect for claiming that la pelota in (46)
is a cause and not an instrument is that (46) creates problems
for the RSH, since instrument would need to appear twice:
once with a very low ranking (perhaps at the level of (33-5),
and another time with a high ranking (as in (33-1). It is so
much in the nature of instruments that they can function as
subjects that Contreras himself mentions them in his rule of
Subject Selection (1976:142).

(48) (=C(13.24b))
Assign the feature [+subject] ... to the highest ranking
argument in the following hierarchy: agent, instrument
[my underlining, M.S.], experiencer, patient, identifier. [51]

Therefore, once more the RSH fails to capture the asymmetry
in the hierarchy of rhematicity caused by preverbal vs. postverbal position of an argument, in this case the instrument.
The same type of asymmetry is explicitly acknowledged in the
RSH by a double listing of time and place adverbials (cf. (33)).
There is nothing inherently 'weak' or 'strong' in most of these
adverbials. What makes them 'weak' or 'strong' is their position

in the sentence: 'strength' correlates with sentence-final
position while 'weakness' correlates with sentence-initial position.

(49a) Saldremos de vacaciones en junio.   (Strong)
we-will-go-out on vacation(s) in June

(49b) En junio(,) saldremos de vacaciones.   (Weak)
in June(,) we-will-go-out on vacation(s)

This evidence once again shows the importance of linear order,
especially as it relates to preverbal vs. postverbal position.
What occurs is that the verb acts as the central point or
pivot of the sentence.   Preverbal constituents are much
'weaker', in the sense that they are much less likely to carry
new information than postverbal arguments.   That the verb
plays such a central task is to be expected, since under normal
(noncontrastive) conditions the verb and the elements which
follow it form the asserted part of the utterance (the rheme,
according to my definition), while preverbal elements are unasserted (and are thus thematic, according to my definition).
The acceptance of basic SVO order captures this generalization
without any complications.   Postposing rules (such as Subject
Postposing) move constituents into the scope of assertion.   On
the other hand, rules which prepose elements to preverbal
position(s), would have the effect of getting them out of the
scope of assertion. [52]
Obviously, semantic roles are crucial in the interpretation of
sentences, since each role expresses the way in which that
element relates to the verb.   Nevertheless, there are reasons
to believe that such roles are less crucial to the question of
linear word order, inasmuch as such diverse factors as interpretive status (e.g. presentationalism), morphological structure
(e.g. passivization), and even the nature of lexical entries
(e.g. the fact that change of state verbs allow an instrument
as their subject), alter the position of a given semantic role
with respect to its verb.

4.3.2.3 Sentences with three or more arguments.   Further
support for a basic word order and a weakening of Contreras'
unordered base hypothesis is derived from an examination of
sentences with three or more arguments.

(50) (=C(8.41))
Don Fermín (agent) sacó (predicate) sus espuelas
(patient) de la SALA (source).
'Don Fermín took his spurs from the ROOM.'

Under a noncontrastive reading, this sentence is grammatical and fully acceptable only if the word order is SVO. Even when one of the arguments is contrastive ([+rheme] in Contreras' terms), the most natural word order is SVO,[53] but with contrastive stress over the relevant element (which violates both the RSH and Linear Order I). From my point of view, this indicates that SVO word order is reaching the point of becoming grammaticalized in sentences which display a certain level of complexity.[54] Compare the fully grammatical sentences in (51) with the less felicitous ones in (52).

(51a) (=C(8.46))
Don Fermín sacó sus ESPUELAS de la sala.
'Don Fermín took his SPURS from the room.'

(51b) Don FERMIN sacó sus espuelas de la sala.
'Don FERMIN took his spurs from the room.'

(51c) Don Fermín SACO sus espuelas de la sala.
'Don Fermín TOOK his spurs from the room.'

(52a) (=C(8.44))
Don Fermín sacó de la sala sus ESPUELAS.
'Don Fermín took his SPURS from the room.'

(52b) Sacó sus espuelas de la sala don FERMIN.

(52c) Don Fermín sus espuelas de la sala SACO.

Contreras is aware of this shortcoming (1976:78).

[...] it could be objected that the linear order always seems to follow the rhematic hierarchy regardless of which elements are themes and which rhemes. In other words, in our example the preferred order is always agent + predicate + patient + source regardless of the rhematic structure of the sentence, and it seems uneconomical to assign a linear order on the basis of rhematic structure only to change it later to the order indicated.

Despite this statement, Contreras persists with his analysis for three reasons: (1) one-argument sentences do not always follow the rhematic hierarchy, (2) the rule of Theme Postposing[55] produces sentences whose order does not follow the rhematic hierarchy, and (3) there are instances in which Topicalization leaves behind a structure which may not agree with the RSH.

Before entering into the details of Contreras' position, it is necessary to call attention to two relevant points. First, basic SVO word order renders the RSH and the three special rules in (34b)-(34d) unnecessary. Second, assignment of linear order in terms of rhematic structure--that is, placing rhemes on the right of nonrhemes--is adequate only for normal, non-contrastive environments in which the last element of the sentence receives the sentential stress. As shown by (51), such a procedure does not necessarily work where contrast is involved (unless the contrastive element also happens to be sentence-final). With the foregoing in mind, it is possible to counter directly the three reasons which Contreras gives for adhering to his analysis. As for reason (1): one-argument sentences appear with equal ease with two word orders, SV and VS: the first order exemplifies a declarative sentence in which the verb is highlighted; the second, a presentational sentence which introduces the NP referent into the discourse.[56] As for reason (2): Theme Postposing collocates resumptive elements to the right of the contrastively highlighted element(s); the RSH is irrelevant, since the main conditions to this rule are that the sentence be assertive and that if the verb is postposed, it must appear immediately after the contrastive element.[57] And as for reason (3): the example given to illustrate this case is Sus espuelas Don Fermín las SACO de la sala 'His spurs Don Fermín (them) took from the room'. Contreras analyzes this example as topicalized las espuelas, postposed de la sala, and rhematic Don Fermín and sacó. I consider this to be an instance of misanalysis. The example shows a topicalized object plus a highlighted (i.e. contrastive) verb. The sentence follows the basic word order TOP S V Obj-clitic PP. There is no possibility for only the subject and the verb to be interpreted as carrying new information,[58] since there is no appropriate context or question which can be answered by this sentence as analyzed by Contreras.

Thus, not only do sentences with three or more arguments fail to promote the unordered base hypothesis, but Contreras' three supporting reasons also fall short of providing any conclusive evidence in favor of his position.

4.3.3 Grammatical relations. Finally, I would like to examine Contreras' use of the syntactic notions subject and object. Each is discussed in turn.

4.3.3.1 Subject. Because of its significance in verbal agreement, Contreras admits that his grammar must identify one argument as surface subject. Thus, Contreras agrees with Fillmore (1968) in not accepting the notion of deep or underlying subjects. What appears strange is that Contreras justifies the notion of surface subject on the basis of 'the existence of several transformational rules which require the identification of an argument as subject, for instance, SUBJECT RAISING, EQUIVALENT NOUN PHRASE DELETION, AND SUBJECT-VERB AGREEMENT' (1976:123). He uses the standard transformational analysis to illustrate the first two rules, a treatment which requires the notion of underlying subject. It is not clear to me

how Contreras can dispose of underlying subjects while accepting the existence of Raising and Equi as transformational rules.
He further states that the argument functioning as subject
cannot be identified by position but rather it must be assigned
the feature [+subject] by rule (53).

(53) (=C(13.24)) Subject Selection (obligatory)
Assign the feature [+subject]

    (a) in a structure with a patient and an identifier,
       (i) if one argument is [+third person] and the
       the other [-third person], to the latter;
      (ii) if they differ in number, to the argument
       marked [+plural];
    (b) in other structures, to the highest ranking argu-
    ment in the following hierarchy: agent, instrument,
    experiencer, patient, identifier.

After the proper identification has taken place, the rule of
Subject-Verb Agreement (54) is triggered.

(54) (=C(13.25))
The verb agrees in person and number with the argument having the feature [+subject].

Thus, for Contreras, subject is equivalent to the argument
with which the verb agrees. He supports his stand with the
following statement (1976:127).

First, this analysis does not require any exception features.
Second, there is no counterintuitive treatment of agreement
in terms of linear order. Third, the treatment of agreement
is unified, not split into two or three unrelated rules.
Finally, since our analysis divorces agreement from linear
order entirely, it reflects accurately the fundamental difference between the rule of agreement and other rules like
TOPIC PLACEMENT or THEME DISPLACEMENT, which are
clearly linear order rules.

This analysis suffers from several flaws. In the first place,
note that 'the treatment of agreement is unified, not split into
two or three unrelated rules' only if one could consider rule
(54) in isolation. However, this is not possible. It is obvious
that the simplification of the agreement rule has been achieved
at the expense of rule (53). In other words, rule (54) obligatorily demands the existence of rule (53). Since Contreras
explicitly states that 'the only reason [my emphasis, M.S.] an
argument must be identified as subject is so that the verb may
agree with it' (1976:128),[59] it is appropriate to question the
purported 'unification' of Subject-Verb Agreement. As a matter

of fact, (54) could be added as case (c) of rule (53) and no perceptible change would take place in the grammar.

As the next step, I examine the rule of Subject Selection to determine its adequacy. Part (b) establishes the hierarchy of agent, instrument, experiencer, patient, identifier. It is no coincidence that this hierarchy represents the near opposite of the RSH (33), since (as should be well known by now) arguments which function as (preverbal) subjects tend to rank low in the rhematic hierarchy. Compare the two hierarchies in (55).

(55)

Subject Selection:	RSH:
1. Agent	1. Instrumental
2. Instrument	2. Identifier
3. Experiencer	4. Patient
4. Patient	5. Agent, cause, possessor,
5. Identifier	experiencer[60]

In spite of the expected correlation between Subject Selection and the RSH, there are some inconsistencies. One wonders about the absence of 'possessor' and 'cause' in the Subject Selection hierarchy, and about the ranking of 'instrument(al)' in both hierarchies. Sentence (56) unequivocally shows that possessors can fulfill the subject function.

(56) Paco tiene un libro en la mano.
'Paco has a book in his hand.'

The puzzling ranking of 'instrumentals' must be related to the omission of 'cause'. As I pointed out previously, there is no justification for dividing instruments into 'cause' (when they function as subjects) and 'instruments' proper (when they appear as prepositional phrases) (cf. Section 4.3.2.2).

Since Subject Selection (53b) specifies that the feature [+subject] should be assigned to the highest ranking argument in the stated hierarchy (i.e. agent, instrument, experiencer, patient, identifier), these rules as stated would allow instrumentals to be consistently chosen as subjects over experiencers, patients, and identifiers, because instruments rank higher than these arguments. Nevertheless, this would produce many ungrammatical sentences. For example, the rules predict that, given the semantic structures in (57), the sentences in (58) should be well-formed. Obviously they are not, since experiencers have priority for subjecthood and patients prevail over instrumentals in passive sentences.

(57a) vió,   Paco   a un niño con un cuchillo
      (Predicate) (Experiencer) (Patient) (Instrumental)
      'saw'   'Paco'   'a boy'   'with a knife'

(57b) fue rota   la ventana   con una piedra
      (Predicate) (Patient)   (Instrumental)
      'was broken' 'the window' 'with a stone'

(58a) *Un cuchillo vió Paco a un niño.[61]

(58b) *Una pelota fue rota la ventana.

In sum, Part (b) of the Subject Selection rule shows some
inconsistencies or oversights which could, I am sure, be
remedied if Contreras' approach should prove to be of any
merit.

Part (a) of the rule specifically deals with subject selection
in structures with a patient and an identifier; that is, this
subpart of the rule singles out equational sentences. Hence,
two related issues must be considered: (1) one must ascertain
whether the rule is adequate, and (2) one must decide whether
this subpart should be limited to equational sentences or whether
its scope should be broadened.

Offhand, it appears that Part (a) of Subject Selection does
not account for all the Spanish data. One problem with equational sentences is that, since the two elements (patient[62] and
identifier in Contreras' analysis, subject and predicate nominal
in others) may occur in either sequence, it is quite arbitrary
at times to decide on the function or semantic role of the elements. Fält (1972), who has extensively studied verbal agreement in Spanish, writes (1972:156):

There are quite a few cases--especially the kind el primer
capítulo es la mejor parte 'the first chapter is the best part'--
in which it is extremely difficult to distinguish between the
subject and the predicate nominal and, what's worse, this
difficulty significantly increases when the two elements are
of different number. The indeterminacy which exists between
the roles of subject and predicate nominal is the origin of
several agreement problems in such attributive sentences.
When the limit between those two elements is imprecise, there
cease to function the traditional norms by which a verb must
always agree with its subject. In those instances it may
agree with the element that, in the speaker's opinion, is in
the foreground, whatever its syntactic function may be [my
translation, M.S.].[63]

As a consequence of this indeterminacy, verbal agreement is
not as clearcut as Contreras' rule leads us to believe. For
example, although there is a tendency to establish agreement
with the [+plural] argument in instances in which the two elements differ in number, it is not difficult to find examples with
singular agreement.

(59a) Mi mayor preocupación es las enfermedades.[64]
'My greatest worry is (the) illnesses.'

(59b) El problema es los militares.[65]
'The problem is the military.'

(59c) El campo de operación de estos jóvenes era principal-
mente las calles del centro de la ciudad.
'The field of operation of those youngsters was mainly
the streets downtown.'

(59d) El pueblo era solamente unos caseríos.
'The town was only several groups of houses.'

(59e) Las piscinas ha sido el tema ...
'(The) swimming pools has been the topic ...'

(59f) Las únicas señales de civilización, a trechos, era el
tendido eléctrico.[66]
'The only signs of civilization, at intervals, were the
power lines.'

Consequently, as it is not possible to make [+plural] agreement
categorical, Part (a-ii) of the rule of Subject Selection must be
modified to allow for instances of singular agreement.

Yet to be considered is Part (a-i): 'if one argument is
[+third person] and the other [-third person], [assign the
feature [+subject]] to the latter'. This statement readily accounts for the examples in (60).

(60a) (=C(13.17))
El problema eres tú.
'The problem is (2 sg.) you.'

(60b) (=C(13.22))
El problema soy yo.
the problem am I
'The problem is (I) me.'

But what about the sentences in (61) (=C(13.23))?

(61a) Yo $\left\{ \begin{array}{l} \text{soy} \\ \text{*eres} \end{array} \right\}$ tú.
'I am you.'

(61b) Tú $\left\{ \begin{array}{l} \text{eres} \\ \text{*soy} \end{array} \right\}$ yo.
'You are me.'

Example (61) is not taken care of by Part (a-i), because in
this case there are two [-third person] arguments. There

appears to be no ambivalence as to which NP determines agreement in this case. Contreras himself writes, 'If, on the other hand, the sentence includes first and second person, the verb agrees with whichever person appears in the subject position' [my emphasis, M.S.] (1976:126). But recall that Contreras' theory denies any reality to a positional or configurational analysis of subject; therefore 'subject position' is not an allowable characterization in his framework.[67] The only possibility left open for him is to claim that the first NP is the patient, since this role ranks higher in the subject selection hierarchy than the identifier. To me, examples like (61) show that whenever there is a possible conflict--note that both elements in (61) are strong personal pronouns, thus human--the basic SVO pattern predominates. If this is the correct assumption to make, (61) provides us with another argument for SVO word order.

Returning to the statement in Part (a) of Subject Selection, it is pertinent to ask whether the state of affairs described by (a-i) and (a-ii) is limited to equational sentences or whether it is part of a broader phenomenon. The second assumption is more consonant with the facts of Spanish. There appears to be a certain hierarchical correlation between verb agreement and person marking as seen in conjoined structures. The scale is first, second, third person.[68] That is, if one of the elements is [+1st], the verb must also be [+1st] (cf. (62)); if one of the conjuncts is [+2nd], it carries the verb agreement (cf. (63)); only if both elements are [+3rd] does the verb take the third person plural ending (cf. (64)).

(62) Paco y yo
     'Paco and I

     Tú y yo   llegaremos tarde.
     'You and I   will-arrive (1 pl.) late.'

     Nosotros y Juan
     'We and John

(63) Paco y tú
     'Paco and you

     Tú y ella   llegaréis tarde.[69]
     'You and she   will-arrive (2 pl.) late.'

     Vosotros y María
     'You (pl.) and Mary

(64) Paco y ella
'Paco and she

Ella y él   llegarán tarde.
'She and he   will-arrive (3 pl.) late.'

Ellos y Pepe
'They and Pepe

Naturally, these rules are disjunctively. ordered.[70]
     If agreement in equational sentences and agreement in con-
joined structures were totally unrelated, it would be a mere
accident for the same agreement hierarchy to be at work.[71]
Therefore, the grammar must somehow capture this similarity
in behavior. It is beyond the scope of this study to pursue
the phenomenon of verbal agreement to its limits; the topic
deserves a monograph in its own right.[72] Nonetheless, I have
achieved my aim of showing that the phenomenon which Contreras (unsuccessfully) tried to capture in Part (a) of his rule
of Subject Selection might be broader than one is led to believe.
     As a final point, let me question the validity of having the
rule of Subject Selection, as formulated by Contreras, apply
obligatorily. Recall that Spanish has subjectless sentences
such as those in (65).

(65a) Hace frío y viento.
      it-makes cold and wind
      'It is cold and windy.'

(65b) Había muchos estudiantes en la conferencia.
      there-was many students in the lecture
      'There were many students at the lecture.'

In standard Spanish, these sentences always have the verb in
the third person singular; no verbal agreement is established
with any NP. Nevertheless, because Subject Selection is
obligatory, the feature [+subject] would be assigned to the
plural patients in (65a)-(65b) and the verb would be pluralized,
rendering the nonstandard sentences in (66).

(66a) Hacen frío y viento.
      same as (65a)

(66b) Habían muchos estudiantes.
      same as (65b)

Accordingly, Contreras' theory makes the counterintuitive claim
that the sentences in (66) constitute the acceptable norm.
     Contreras attempts to resolve this problem by saying that 'a
lexical feature of llover "to rain" and haber "there to be, exist"

allows the optional assignment of the feature [+subject] to the patient' (1976:128). But the issue is not how to account for the sentences in which agreement with the patient has been triggered. The crux of the matter is how to prevent the obligatory rule of Subject Selection from applying to subjectless sentences, so that the sentences in (65) can be attained. Contreras does not provide an answer. It should be noticed, moreover, that contrary to his claim that 'this analysis does not require any exception features' (1976:127), he is forced to postulate special features for these subjectless verbs. In spite of this, he is still not able to account for the data in a satisfactory way.[73]

Given these considerations, I find Contreras' arguments in favor of a feature-assigned notion of subject unconvincing. His rules of Subject Selection (53) and verbal agreement (54) are incapable of accounting for all the Spanish data. There are subjects which are not included in the rule (cf. (55)), inconsistency in the treatment of the arguments instrumental and cause, and sentences which are not produced (cf. (59) and (61)-(64)), not to mention other sentences which appear to be the 'norm' when they are actually nonstandard (cf. (66)). This is exacerbated by the difficulty of properly identifying the arguments of equational sentences (cf. Fält 1972), and the failure to connect the first-second-third person verbal agreement and the hierarchy of coordinated structures to the very similar phenomenon exemplified by equational sentences. In sum, one must conclude that Contreras has failed to establish the superiority of his treatment over the more orthodox configurationally defined notion of syntactic subject.[74]

4.3.3.2 Object. While admitting the need for surface subjects, Contreras dispenses with the syntactic notion of direct object, which he characterizes as superfluous in his framework. He argues his case by examining the rule of passivization. He maintains that examples like (67) and (68) show that Passive should be formulated in terms of the semantic notion 'patient' rather than in terms of the syntactic category 'direct object', because (68) but not (67) can passivize.

(67) Paco pesa 90 kilos.
'Paco weighs 90 kilos.'

(68) Paco pesa los libros.
'Paco weighs the books.'

Contreras explains their different behavior by saying that the underlined phrase in (67) is a 'complement' while that in (68) is a 'patient'. He states that 'only patients are affected by passivization' (1976:121).

Contreras' argument would be valid only if the underlined phrases in both (67) and (68) were direct objects, a dubious

claim at best. Note that these phrases behave differently not
only with respect to passivization but also with respect to pronominalization, as shown by (69) and (70).

(69) *Paco lo pesa.

(70) Paco los pesa.
  Paco them weighs
  'Paco weighs them.'

Moreover, they answer different information questions.

(71) ¿Cuánto pesa Paco?
  'How much does Paco weigh?'

(72) ¿Qué pesa Paco?
  'What is Paco weighing?'

This shows that, while the underlined phrase in (68) is a
direct object, the one in (67) is better analyzed as an adverbial.
Therefore, one must conclude that a verb like pesar subcategorizes a direct object or an adverbial, which explains why sentence (67) does not passivize.

Consequently, Contreras provides an analysis of passivization
equivalent to the transformational one. While he resorts to the
semantic roles 'patient' and 'complement' to explain the difference in behavior between (67) and (68), a transformational
treatment will explain the same difference by invoking the syntactic notions of 'direct object' and 'adverbial'.[75] Thus, Contreras has failed to show the superiority of his treatment, and,
moreover, he falls short of providing any conclusive evidence
which forces the rejection of the syntactic notion of direct object.

Furthermore, observe that, contrary to Contreras' assumption,
there is no incompatibility between syntactic and semantic
notions. Both Gruber (1970) and Jackendoff (1972), among
others, have used a configurational framework for their analysis, to which they have incorporated 'thematic relations'; that
is to say, configurational and thematic notions can both be used
advantageously within the same model.

4.3.4 Summary and conclusion. Contreras has offered a
case grammar theory of word order into which the Praguean functional notions of theme vs. rheme have been incorporated. His
system as developed necessarily entails an unordered base as
well as a surface characterization of the grammatical relation of
subject.[76] Linear order is achieved through a series of rules
whose outputs are checked against surface structure constraints.
Much to his credit, throughout his book Contreras has highlighted the importance of prosodic factors for the determination
of normal vs. emphatic word order. His work also has the

unique merit of being the most comprehensive study of Spanish word order to date.

Nevertheless, several crucial flaws were discovered during the discussion. First, perhaps heavily influenced by one-argument sentences and by presentational sentences in particular, Contre·as embraced the unordered base hypothesis whole-heartedly. This led to a proliferation of rules which assign normal word order and to the labelling of certain sentence types as 'special' just because they do not adhere to his postulated RSH. Moreover, three- (or more) argument sentences do not uphold the RSH and/or the unordered base hypothesis.

The definition of some of the arguments and their ranking in the RSH were also questioned in the discussion. The categories of cause and instrumental, in addition to strong and weak adverbials, appear to be split quite arbitrarily in order to comply with the RSH.

Finally, Contreras' rules of Subject Selection and Verbal Agreement were considered and found observationally deficient, since they are incapable of accounting for all of the Spanish data.

On a more general basis, it seems to me that many of the problems I have pointed out during the discussion stem from the fact that Contreras defines theme vs. rheme as deep structure notions which must be carried through and must survive the effects of transformational movement rules. This requires the positing of extra rules--such as in the case of passives and presentationals (cf. (34b)-(34d))--and filters to rearrange or reassign elements according to their rhematic structure in surface structure. A considerable streamlining of this model could result if theme vs. rheme were assigned in surface structure. Whether an unordered base model modified in accordance with this suggestion could account for all the different word orders in Spanish lies outside the scope of this study and is left to future research.

To conclude, the evidence brought forth in Section 4.3 clearly indicates that Contreras' unordered base hypothesis is inferior to the ordered base hypothesis which postulates SVO word order as basic for Spanish. Many of its rules and hier-archies are not even observationally adequate and make the wrong predictions. And what is of more immediate concern to my study, this model cannot account for Spanish presentational sentences in a straightforward and non-ad hoc way. It is al-ready a premise in linguistics that, given two competing hy-potheses, the burden of proof lies with those who advance the less orthodox analysis. Therefore, for the time being and until someone brings forth forceful evidence to the contrary, I assume the superiority of the ordered base hypothesis by postulating the SVO order as basic for Spanish.

NOTES

1. Farley's article is a good summary of the literature on Spanish word order published up to about 1956.
2. Contreras devotes Chapter II, 'Linguistic theory and the study of word order' of his 1976 work to an overview of the problem.
3. Spanish was not among his 30 sample languages, although Italian was. In his Appendix II, he includes the whole group of Romance languages as SVO (1963:109).
4. Bordelois says (personal communication) that her position is not based on the same premises as McCawley's; while he postulates VSO because of simplicity, she argues for it because of the structure preserving hypothesis.
5. In his 1975 article 'Order in base structures', Bach argues against unordered base structures. I sympathize with his feeling that 'there is something inherently linear in language' (1975:338).
6. And before him Goldin (1968).
7. Thus, it should be expected that my definition is far more in harmony with the ordered base thesis.
8. It must be remembered that S-structures are surface structures which contain traces; that is, the term S-structures presupposes trace theory.
9. This is directly opposed to the tenets of Relational Grammar, according to which basic word order is obtained by linearization rules which apply after all cyclic rules but before any postcyclic ones (cf. Pullum 1977).
10. A case in point would be:

La desesperación sofocó la esperanza.
'(The) desperation suffocated (the) hope.'

Here only the first NP can be interpreted as subject. If this order is disrupted, the object argument must be explicitly marked as such:

A la esperanza sofocó la desesperación.
Sofocó la desesperación a la esperanza.

Curiously enough, generic statements also invariably adopt SVO word order:

El perro es un mamífero.
'(The) dog is a mammal.'

Los perros odian (a) los gatos.
'(The) dogs hate (the) cats.'

Since generic statements proclaim generalization with supposed universal validity, it is to be expected that they would be quite immune to discourse pressures. Hence, their word order might be a good indicator of basic word order.

11. Bolinger (1952) calls them 'first instance' sentences.

12. To state it differently, I do not consider possible neutral sentences of the type shown in (i) and (ii).

(i) Lo$_i$ vi a Paco$_i$ fumando marijuana.
   him$_i$ I saw Paco$_i$ smoking marihuana
   'I saw Paco smoking marihuana.'

(ii) José le$_i$ dio una azotaina al vecinito$_i$.
    José to-him$_i$ gave a beating to the little-neighbor$_i$
    'José beat the little neighbor up.'

13. A transitive verb is defined here as one that appears with a direct object; an intransitive verb appears without such an argument.

14. There is also the fossilized archaic presentational expression he aquí 'here's' ~ he allí 'there's', for example:

He $\left\{ \begin{array}{l} \text{aquí} \\ \text{allí} \end{array} \right\}$ tu libro.

is $\left\{ \begin{array}{l} \text{here} \\ \text{there} \end{array} \right\}$ your book

$\left. \begin{array}{l} \text{'Here} \\ \text{'There} \end{array} \right\}$ is your book.'

Nowadays this expression seems to be circumscribed to the present tense.

15. Contreras (1976) does assign a [+presentational] feature to Spanish verbs by means of a lexical redundancy rule. As expected, this procedure gets him into trouble (cf. Section 4.3.2.1.2).

16. Bordelois is the only one who, to my knowledge, justifies her position. Others have simply said that Spanish is VSO without expanding on the issue. One such example is Manteca Alonso-Cortés (1976).

Meyer (1972) was the first to advance this hypothesis in an informal paper on Spanish word order. I do not discuss her proposal in detail for various reasons, among which I can cite that the entire article was based on data provided by a single speaker. Incorrect conclusions were drawn from this set of data: for example, maintaining that it is impossible to have sentences with more than one topic, or stating that VSO is possible only if the subject is not definite. Se sentences were also used to determine basic word order. Moreover, Meyer herself states that SVO is not completely ruled out. Her strongest argument is based on the word order of interrogative sentences. An alternative analysis, such as one involving verb fronting or verb attraction, would seriously weaken her argument.

No doubt, McCawley's 1970 article is the precursor of the VSO order hypothesis for Spanish. For a critique of McCawley, see especially Berman (1974).

17. Bordelois maintains that a sentence of the type <u>Juan</u> <u>vino</u> 'John came' is interpreted contrastively as 'It was John and not Peter who came'. I find this explanation misleading. Normally, <u>Juan vino</u> highlights the act of coming (as opposed to any other action); only when <u>Juan</u> receives contrastive stress, such as in JUAN <u>vino</u>, does Bordelois' interpretation obtain. The different readings correlate with normal vs. contrastive assignment of focus and sentential stress.

18. As a corollary to her four arguments, Bordelois demonstrates that the VSO hypothesis explains the problem of the distribution of clitics in the examples in (i) and (ii).

(i) *Juan <u>lo</u> parece admirar.
    John it seems to admire

(ii) *Juan <u>me le</u> hizo escribir.
     John me to-him made write

(iii) Juan <u>me lo</u> hizo comer.
      John to-me it made eat
      'John made me eat it.'

She postulates an uninterrupted chain of verbs plus the obligatory ordering: (1) Clitic Movement, (2) Raising.

This argument is rendered vacuous if one accepts trace theory (which, moreover, does not permit ordering of transformations). Both (i) and (ii) have a specified subject (whether the NP itself, if Clitic Movement applies first, or its trace, if Raising applies first) in the path of the clitic. On the other hand, as Bordelois points out, the embedded subject in (iii) has been deleted on identity with the controller.

In sum, the data in (i)-(iii) is irrelevant to the VSO hypothesis, given the framework adopted in my study.

19. The embedded sentence in (11d) is a restrictive relative clause, and as such, nonassertive (but nonrestrictive relative clauses are assertive).

20. Bordelois (personal communication) writes that what she had in mind was a more flexible characterization of the structure-preserving hypothesis in which the notions of root/nonroot could correspond to tense/tenseless claused in some languages. Even though this interpretation of structure preservation is not developed in her dissertation, it is an interesting proposal which might merit further research.

21. I ·limit myself to the infinitive in order not to prolong
the discussion inordinately. Similar examples can be built with
participles and gerundives.

22. The element in parentheses (the underlying subject of
the infinitive) is totally optional in all of these examples. In
its absence, the subject of the infinitive is either identified
because of the total discouse, or it is interpreted as arbitrary
(for example, (12b)). Note that the matrix objects in (12c)-
(12e) provide us with some cues for the identification of these
subjects: they give us information as to person and number
(i.e. third singular), and gender.

23. For obvious reasons I have omitted examples with
Subject-Raising verbs.

24. There are no Spanish equivalents of:

John believed Peter to have lied.

This example represents a marked case for English itself.

25. Case here is 'an abstract marking associated with certain constructions, a property that rarely has phonetic effects
in English [or Spanish, M.S.] but must be assigned to every
lexical NP' (Chomsky 1980a:32).

26. In essence, I am following Chomsky's (1980a) proposal.
In his Pisa lectures, he modifies his position and says that
there are structurally assigned Cases; thus, anything in the
VP becomes objective, everything not in the VP (provided
Tense is present) becomes Nominative. It is not clear to me
whether this is really an improvement, since Tense has to be
mentioned anyway in order to establish a difference between
subjects of tensed vs. tenseless clauses; only the first kind
qualify for Case assignment.

Also notice that I am limiting myself to issues that directly
concern my line of inquiry. For example, I am disregarding
inherent cases, since they play no role in the argument I am
developing.

27. That is, the subject of these nonfinite clauses is displaced from its basic preverbal position.

28. The totals do not add up to 100 percent because OSV
and SOV orders were also considered. Since the number of
tokens for these word orders is extremely low, I have excluded them here.

29. This excludes cases in which the relative pronoun
functions as subject.

30. Furthermore, this linguist states that of one-argument
sentences, 54.2 percent of the cases have postposed subjects
and 45.8 percent have preposed subjects. One problem with
these latter percentages is that she included in this group
such diverse sentence types as: (1) intransitive sentences;
(2) se passive sentences; (3) regular, obligatory, and pseudo-
reflexive sentences; and (4) transitive sentences with an object

clitic and zero noun phrase (e.g. ellos lo hacen 'they do it')
(1978:note 4).
31. Sentence (17b) is in itself not the best example to use
an an illustration, due to the fact that pronunciar un discurso
'to give a speech' is a set expression. I have kept this example
only because it is the one given by Bordelois. Some clearer
examples of focused subjects are shown in (i)-(iv).

(i) ... creo yo que ése es el caso. (M 232)
    ... believe I that that is the case
    ... 'I believe that that is the case.'

(ii) ... no lo veo que tengan ellos el derecho de juzgar.
     (M 279)
     ... not it I-see that have (subjunctive) they the right
     of to-judge
     ... 'I do not see that they have the right to judge.'

(iii) ... decía tu mami que lo primero es ... (M 297)
      ... was-saying your Mom that the first-thing is ...
      ... 'your Mom was saying that the first thing is ...'

(iv) ... me contaba mi mamá los minutos ... (M 296)
     ... to-me was counting my mother the minutes ...
     ... 'my mother counted the minutes on me ...'

32. This sentence is ungrammatical under a noncontrastive
reading.
33. This is another difference between 'regular' embedded
infinitives and absolute constructions (cf. (8)-(10)). In absolute constructions the subject freely appears directly after the
nonfinite verb.

(i) De fumar Juan un cigarro, le daría un ataque de asma.
    of-the to-smoke Juan a cigar, to-him would-give an attack
    of asthma
    'If John were to smoke a cigar, he would have an asthma
    attack.'

(ii) Habiendo comprado Paco un auto nuevo, no le quedó
     plata para ir de vacaciones.
     having bought Paco a car new not to-him remain
     money for to-go of vacations
     'Having bought a new car, Paco was left without money to
     go on a vacation.'

Undoubtedly, the preposition gained by the underlying subjects
of regular infinitives in (19) and (20) during the derivation
has something to do with the different (noncontrastive) word
order possibilities.

34. See also Emonds (1980) for a discussion of the advantages of having NP subjects generated outside the VP.

35. Problems arise as soon as one considers complex structures in which one of the two arguments has been deleted or removed by a transformation (see Berman 1974, and especially Anderson and Chung 1977). I do not develop this area because Spanish uni-argument verbs (see discussion further on) provide sufficient evidence to show that grammatical relations cannot be accurately captured exclusively on the basis of linear order.

36. If someone were to claim that Spanish is underlyingly VSO but that there is a transformation which changes the order to SVO before any other transformation applies, my argument would be rendered as vacuous as the VSO hypothesis.

37. Anderson and Chung (1977) show that this might even be a requirement for what are claimed to be true VSO languages.

38. I feel quite uneasy about the claim that grammatical relations are primitives. Anderson and Chung (1977) very aptly state the case I support: 'Work in Relational Grammar has uncovered an impressive array of properties associated with the fundamental grammatical relations; it would appear that the interest of such a theory could only be 'enhanced by showing that these notions themselves could be reduced to other independently motivated properties such as the internal constituent structure of clauses' (1977:25).

39. But recall that this is not the only instance where this problem arises. See note 35.

40. Pullum (1977:254) lists the following languages as possible VOS: Toba, Batak, Gilbertese, Malagasy, Tzeltal, Classical Mayan, and maybe even Fijian, Mezquital Otomi, Tumbala Chol, Tzotzil, and Coeur d'Alene.

41. Within the Romance group of languages, Vattuone (1975) claims that Genoese, the language (dialect?) spoken in Genoa, Italy, is underlyingly VOS. Pullum (1977) suggests an alternative analysis in which Genoese is SVO with a rule which displaces rhematic subjects to sentence-final position. Pullum's analysis is consistent with my own analysis of Spanish presentational sentences given in Chapter 2 (although Pullum works within the framework of Relational Grammar).

42. Adjuncts are never defined formally. Nevertheless, one learns that adjuncts--as opposed to arguments, which are severely restricted by the type of predicate with which they appear--occur quite freely with any type of predicate (1976:37) and they are 'dispensable'. This behavioral definition, besides being rather weak, is further complicated by the fact that time and location adverbials function as both arguments and adjuncts. 'Dispensability' does not provide a sufficient criterion for being an adjunct, because Contreras says that in his sentence (4.34) 'the first locative phrase is an adjunct and the second an argument' (1976:37).

(4.34) En Chile, hay un dictador en el poder.
'In Chile, there is a dictator in power.'

Nonetheless, the second is as dispensable as the first:

Hay un dictador.
'There is a dictator.'

Furthermore, I do not think Contreras would say that the instrumental phrase is an adjunct in the next sentence although, as the parentheses indicate, it is perfectly dispensable:

Paco compró cigarrillos (con un billete falso).
'Paco bought cigarettes (with a counterfeit bill).'

Perhaps a better characterization of adjunct is 'not subcategorized by the verb' (or predicate, in Contreras' terms); this definition seems to obviate the problem created by optionally subcategorized arguments.

43. Contreras considers the following to be the main rules of his grammar: Rheme Assignment, Topic Assignment, Linear Order I and II, Topic Placement, Theme Postposing, and Sentential Stress Assignment (1976:137).

44. The last word in this rule is <u>predicate</u> in Contreras' work (cf. pages 54 and 139). I assume this to be a typographical error; therefore, I have replaced <u>predicate</u> with what I gather to be the correct notion.

45. Foley and Van Valin (1977) appear to use topic as synonymous with theme. They mention that this hierarchy is also known as the Natural Topic Hierarchy (Hawkinson and Hyman 1975) or the Inherent Lexical Content Hierarchy (Silverstein 1977).

46. As a matter of fact, Contreras' grammar would probably generate (i).

(i) a ganar terreno empezó la resistencia.
     to gain terrain started the resistance

This sentence has the semantic structure given in (ii).

(ii) ⎧empezar,   ganar terreno, la resistencia⎫
     ⎪Predicate   ?   Patient   ⎪
     ⎨[+rheme]   [+rheme]   [+rheme]   ⎬
     ⎩[+presentational]   ⎭

Here the lexical redundancy rule has attached the [+presentational] feature to the predicate. Rules (34c) and (34d) would then cause the constituents to be ordered as in (i). But (i) is even less appropriate than (41) as a discourse-initial sentence.

47. Rule (34d) certainly would be activated in the following sentence, provided the verb were given the [+presentational] feature.

(i) ??En lo alto bailaban una danza frenética las estrellas.
    high above danced a dance frenetic the stars
    'High above, the stars danced a frenetic dance.'

Notice that [+presentational] cannot be made conditionally dependent on the patient argument being the subject because Subject Formation applies to surface structures. Furthermore, observe that <u>bailar</u> 'dance' is compatible with a presentational reading in (ii) but not in (i).

(ii) En lo alto bailaban las estrellas.
     'High above danced the stars.'

This is because (ii) can be interpreted as introducing the subject in the world of discourse. Contreras provides no way to accept (ii) while rejecting (i) as a presentational sentence.

48. Although the active-passive relationship is most likely established by means of a lexical redundancy rule in Spanish, this assumption is not crucial to the discussion. In any theory which presupposes an ordered base, (43) is more 'basic' than (44) because its subject is in preverbal position.

49. This analysis does not exclude the possibility of semantic roles; that is, it leaves the door open for stating that passive morphology requires a patient as the subject. On the import of semantic roles within the ordered base hypothesis, see Gruber (1970) and Jackendoff (1972).

50. Notice the lack of parallelism between object and subject with respect to semantic roles. It appears that the direct object always bears the semantic relationship of patient with regard to the verb, but that subject might be represented by the semantic notions of agent, possessor, experiencer, instrument, cause, patient, etc. This leads me to believe that it might be a hopeless task to identify the subject unequivocally in terms of semantic roles, and by implication that it might prove impossible to capture linear order exclusively in these terms.

51. Notice that the inconsistency goes beyond instruments, since no mention is made of possessor or cause, although both these arguments should be included. More is said later about Contreras' rule of Subject Selection.

For the sake of economy, it would be possible to argue that agents, instruments, and natural forces should all be encompassed under the common rubric of cause, since they pattern alike, that is, all of them may function as subject and also appear after a <u>por</u> phrase. Further differences among the three roles would be accomplished by a device resembling the following rule (cf. Suñer 1973):

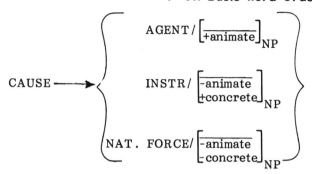

52. In Contreras' analysis, Topic Placement is an example of a preposing rule. I view the structure created by this rule as a base-generated left-dislocated structure (notice that it leaves a pronoun behind). The same applies to the structure created by Theme Postposing, although in this case it would be right-dislocated. In contrast, Topicalization proper (not discussed by Contreras) behaves as a preposing rule, since it leaves a gap in the extraction site.

53. The order needs to be SVO even more in sentences in which two constituents have been given rhematic status. Compare Contreras' (8.49) with (8.48) (1976:78).

Another complication arises when one considers that Contreras does not seem to allow for contrastive themes such as in (i).

(i) De la SALA (y no del comedor) sacó Don Fermín sus
    espuelas.
    from the living room (and not from the dining room),
    took Don Fermín his spurs

For discussion of some contrastive themes, see my Chapter 3.

54. Impressionistically, the cutoff point seems to be more than two arguments.

55. Contreras maintains that Theme Postposing optionally postposes elements which rank lower than the rheme. It applies only to assertive contexts. The following is an example:

ESO quiero yo.
THAT want I
'THAT is what I want.'

An ad hoc rule places the predicate immediately after the rheme (1976:90).

56. Contreras' first argument does not make sense even if one were to agree with his analysis. He gives as an example of a sentence which does not follow the rhematic hierarchy La resistencia EMPEZO 'The resistance STARTED'. Given that the feature [+presentational] is assigned to verbs only optionally, this example does not violate the hierarchy, provided the lexical redundancy rule has not operated. That the predicate ranks

one step higher than the lowest ranking argument (the patient in this case) is in accordance with both the RSH and rule (34c). 57. It is beyond the scope of this chapter to discuss this rule in detail. Nevertheless, a couple of observations are in order. First, there is the possibility that Theme Postposing (i.e. Right Dislocation) is not a rule but that the postposed structures are generated directly (although not necessarily in the order in which the elements appear on the surface). Obviously, more research is called for on this topic. Second, Contreras' examples seem to show that the arguments in the VP can be moved around within this constituent without producing any ill effects.

> (10.25a) Don Fermín sacó de la sala sus ESPUELAS.
> (10.25b) Don Fermín sacó sus ESPUELAS de la sala.
> 'Don Fermín took his SPURS from the room.'

> (10.27a) María cerró con llave la PUERTA.
> (10.27b) María cerró la PUERTA con llave.
> 'Mary locked the DOOR with a key.'

However, this is not the case when the postposed element is the subject, because in this instance the sentences are unacceptable if not ungrammatical.

> (10.18) Sacó sus espuelas de la sala don FERMIN.
> 'Don FERMIN took his spurs from the room.'

> (10.22) ?Cerró la puerta con llave MARIA.
> 'Mary locked the door.'

> (10.29b) ?Pronunció un discurso MARIA.
> 'MARY gave a speech.'

Contreras explains this asymmetry with the following surface structure constraint:

> (10.30) The acceptability of surface structures decreases as the number of pre-rhematic themes which outrank the rheme in the RSH increases.

I would like to explain the asymmetry as another instance which supports the basicness of the preverbal position for subjects. This position becomes more fixed as the sentence increases in complexity. Furthermore, note that the basic object position is after the verb; therefore, it is to be expected that nontopicalized objects in preverbal position produce ill-formed sentences.

> (10.41a) Sus espuelas don Fermín SACO de la sala.
> (10.41b) Sus espuelas don Fermín sacó de la SALA.
> (10.41c) Don Fermín sus espuelas sacó de la SALA.

(10.41d) Don Fermín sus espuelas SACO de la sala.

Sentences like those in (10.41) lead Contreras to postulate another surface structure constraint:

(10.45) A surface structure is unacceptable if it contains a nontopicalized patient which violates the rhematic hierarchy.

But once more, acceptance of basic SVO does away with both the constraint and the RSH.

58. Although it is perfectly conceivable for the subject, verb, and prepositional phrase to convey new information.

59. This assertion makes me wonder even more about Contreras' purpose in discussing Raising and Equi.

60. I have kept the original numbering of the RSH in order to avoid confusion. For the purposes of this comparison, I have discarded the arguments which can never function as subjects in Spanish (i.e. adverbials and those which are prepositional phrases).

61. The order of the patient and the experiencer with respect to each other in (58a) is irrelevant to the grammaticality of the sentence.

62. Contreras defines 'patient' as the argument which 'denotes something which is in a particular state or which is changing its state' (1976:33). It is hard for me to see how this definition corresponds to one of the arguments in equational sentences. Contreras attempts no definition of identifier, but does direct us to Halliday (1967-1968).

63. The exact quote follows. 'Hay no pocos casos límites--sobre todo el tipo el primer capítulo es la mejor parte--en los que resulta sumamente difícil distinguir entre el sujeto y el atributo y, lo que es más, la dificultad de hacer esta distinción crece sensiblemente cuando los dos elementos son de distinto número. La vacilación que existe acerca de los papeles del sujeto y del atributo es el origen de varios problemas de concordancia en tales frases atributivas. Cuando el límite entre los dos elementos es poco preciso, no rigen ya las normas tradicionales según las cuales el verbo debe concertar siempre con su sujeto. Entonces puede concordar con el elemento que, en opinión del hablante, está en el primer plano, cualquiera que sea su función sintáctica.'

Latin assigned Nominative case to both members of an equational sentence, thus solving the indeterminacy problem by placing both arguments on the same plane.

64. This example is cited by Moliner (1967 II:531), who also mentions the possibility of:

Mi mayor preocupación son las enfermedades.
'My greatest worry are (the) illnesses.'

65. Contreras marks this sentence as ungrammatical.
Nevertheless, several native speakers whom I consulted disagree with his opinion.

66. Examples (59c)-(59f) come from Fält (1972). I direct
the reader to this source for more examples and for a thorough
discussion of the problem of verbal agreement.

67. Thus, contrary to what he says, Contreras is not able
to 'divorce agreement from linear order entirely' (1976:127).

68. Observe that this hierarchy neatly correlates with Foley
and Van Valin's hierarchy of inherent topic-worthiness.

speaker > hearer > human proper > human common > animate > inanimate ⌐

1st p.   2nd p.   ⌣_____   3rd p.

69. The vosotros 'you (pl.)' form is not used in Spanish
America; therefore in (63) the verb adopts the third person
plural form on this continent.

70. Contreras' rule of Subject Selection does not take into
consideration conjoined structures of the type exemplified in
(62)-(64). Therefore, the rule is not even observationally
adequate.

71. Note that nonconjoined sentences follow the first-second-
third hierarchy only when the functions or roles are not
clearly delimited, i.e. in equational sentences. The only exception seems to be that illustrated in (61b), but even here
(i) follows the hierarchy and sounds considerably better than
(ii), which violates it.

(i) ?Tú soy yo.
    'You am I.'

(ii) *Yo eres tú.
     'I are you.'

It is obvious that this problem requires further study.

72. Fält's study is largely descriptive. It would prove useful to use his work as the starting point for a comprehensive
study where the facts described by him are incorporated into
a theoretical model.

73. Two other claims are made during his discussion of
subjectless verbs. First, he says 'the positional theory of
subject formation requires the optional promotion of patients in
subject position in order to generate the (b) sentences [the
ones with plural agreement, M.S.], followed by the now obligatory application of the rule of SUBJECT-PREDICATE INVERSION,
which suggests erroneously that the linear arrangement of such
sentences is less basic than that of the (a) sentences [the ones
with verbs in the singular, M.S.]' (1976:128). Although this
is a possible analysis, it is not the only one. Verbal agreement
could be established with the direct object just in case the sentence is subjectless (for details, see Suñer 1976a, and also

Section 1.4 and Appendix B of the present work). This latter
alternative avoids the unmotivated back-and-forth movement of
an argument.

The second claim with which I disagree is the 'justification' of
the optional assignment of [+subject] to the patient of verbs
like llover. Contreras states that 'this type of specification is
needed independently for verbs like gustar "to like", which
allow either the experiencer or the patient to function as subjects' (1976:128). His examples are:

(13.28a) Gusto de la música.
'I like music.'
(13.28b) Me gusta la música.
'Music is pleasing to me.'

The examples in (13.28) are instances of two different lexical
verbal entries that, although perhaps semantically related, behave quite differently syntactically. One entry is gustar de
'to like', a verb plus particle complex; the other is gustarle
(a uno) 'to be pleasing to one', a verb which obligatorily requires an indirect object. Hence, it is not just a question of
which argument functions as subject. Observe that no special
features are needed within a configurational analysis, since the
subject is the item immediately dominated by S.

74. Actually, if one analyzes Contreras' statement quoted on
page 292, one finds that none of the four reasons given in de-
fense of his theory actually hold. First, his analysis requires
special features for (at least) subjectless verbs. Second, he
must resort to linear agreement for an example such as (61b),
unless he chooses to be completely arbitrary in the assignment
of semantic roles. Third, the treatment of agreement is not
unified, because it is intrinsically dependent on the rule of
Subject Selection. And finally, even if one were to grant that
Contreras' analysis divorces agreement from linear order, this
would not reflect the fundamental difference between the rule
of agreement and rules such as Topic Placement or Theme Displacement. The fundamental difference resides in the fact that
agreement is a copying rule while the other two are movement
rules (in Contreras' framework, at least).

75. There is nothing odd in this claim. After all, not
everything that looks alike necessarily represents the same
syntactic and/or semantic notion. For example, I doubt that
anyone would claim that the underlined elements in sentences
(i) and (ii) stand in the same type of relationship to the verb.

(i) Entregaron el premio al ganador.
'They-gave the prize to-the winner.'

(ii) Entregaron el premio <u>al día siguiente</u>.
they-gave the prize to-the day next
'They gave the prize the next day.'

In (i) the underlined phrase is the indirect object, while in
(ii) it is an adverbial.

76. In all fairness, it must be noted that Contreras is not
the only one to postulate an unordered base for Spanish. He
was preceded by Goldin (1968). Working within a case grammar framework, Goldin also maintains that grammatical relations
are irrelevant at the deep level of analysis. He posits six
subject selection principles to describe the subject function and
three to capture the object function. For a comprehensive
review of Goldin's *Spanish Case and Function*, see Langacker
(1970). Interestingly enough, Langacker suggests replacing
Goldin's subject selection principles with an Agent-Dative-
Instrumental-Objective Subject Choice hierarchy, similar to the
Subject Selection hierarchy of Contreras.

5

CONCLUSION

5.1 Summary of main results. The idiosyncracies of two subtypes of presentational sentences have been described and explained in this monograph through an examination of their lexical, syntactic, and interpretive modalities. This was carried out in Chapter 1 for haber presentationals and in Chapter 2 for (semantically) intransitive presentationals. The grammars of both subtypes were contrasted in Section 2.6.2. There it was shown that their similarities are due to their function in the discourse--to signal the appearance of the referent of the NP into the universe of discourse--and to their parallel logical forms (LFs). These LFs evidence that what is common to presentationals is their 'subjectlessness' at this interpretive level. Although haber presentationals and intransitive presentationals share the foregoing traits, as well as the rules of Complement Linking (SI-1), Rhematization (post-LF), and Presentational Sentence Interpretation (SI-2), they part company in other aspects. Their differences are attributable to the lexical properties of impersonal haber as opposed to those of the verbs that enter into the other subtype of presentationals, and to the basic vs. derived character of the constructions. The rule of Subject Postposing demonstrates the derived nature of the intransitive subgroup. This rule takes the subject argument and moves it to the end of the VP, a nonargument position. Preference was shown for the postposing rule to apply freely without any constraints;[1] any ill-formed sequences that might result would be filtered out at a later stage by the pertinent interpretive rules. This stand agrees with the position of the EST, which advocates moving away from constraints on transformations in favor of more general principles and the filtering effect of the interpretive component (cf. Chomsky 1980a, and references therein).

The base-generated vs. derived quality of the presentational subtypes also explains the different kinds of NPs they are

entitled to introduce into the discourse. <u>Haber</u> requires that
there be a sufficient lack of shared knowledge on the part of
speaker and hearer regarding the NP to warrant bringing it
into Focus; this is because <u>hay</u> sentences are THE inherent
presentational construction in Spanish. This condition can
only be properly checked at the level of complete semantic
representations, which demonstrates both the inadequacy of
postulating a definiteness restriction at the level of sentence
semantics, and the appropriateness of characterizing old vs. new
as a dichotomy operant at SI-2. By contrast, intransitive
presentationals impose no constraints on their NPs. It was
hypothesized that this was due to the indeterminacy of the
eventual discourse function which the base-generated sequence
subject-verb performs: presentational (VS) or declarative (SV).
Again, this is a consequence of the fact that functional sentence interpretation cannot take place before SI-2, since the
total discourse--linguistic and extralinguistic--must be available for appraisal.

At several points throughout this manuscript it was claimed
that the presentational word order must invariably be V(+O) NP
in order that the NP whose appearance is being heralded would
be in the scope of the verb. The grammatical relation the NP
bears is secondary, since it can perform an object function
(<u>haber</u> presentationals) as well as a subject function (intransitive presentationals). Hence, the grammatical relation of the
NP is but another trait which distinguishes basic from derived
presentationals.

Throughout this study the Praguean notions of theme vs.
rheme have proved helpful. It was postulated that they play a
role at a post-LF level within sentence grammar, that they are
correlated with the unasserted/asserted portion of the sentence, and that they relate to conditions for successful communication, since the speaker is the one who decides what is
rhematic and what will 'push the communication forward'. The
sequence V NP proper of presentational sentences is rhematic,
which correlates with the thetic/subjectless character of this
type of sentence at the level of LF. Moreover, theme vs. rheme
also captures the scope of <u>no</u> and other quantifiers and explains
the impossibility of obtaining an anaphoric relation between a
left-dislocated constituent (thematic) and the postposed subject
of an intransitive presentational (rhematic) since a conflict of
interests results from a referent already under discussion being introduced into the discourse (cf. Section 2.3.2.1.2 for
examples and discussion).[2]

In an effort to establish beyond any doubt that presentational
sentences represent a distinct type of sentence, they were compared to declarative sentences, from which they differ with
respect to word order, stress and focus, the scope of quantifiers, and behavior regarding the <u>hacerlo</u> construction. This
difference is made explicit when one considers that, contrary
to the thetic or rhematic character of presentational sentences,

declarative sentences are categorial, that is, partitioned into a thematic portion and a rhematic one.

In Chapter 3 it was noted that some intransitive presentational sentences cannot be paired with a well-formed declarative counterpart. The explanation for this fact was found in the Naked Noun Constraint (NNC), a generalization which maintains that naked nouns cannot be noncontrastive themes. To arrive at this conclusion it was necessary to infer the grammatical meaning proper to unmodified nouns, and to investigate the determiner system of the language. Insofar as contrastive sentences stood in defiance of the NNC, it led us into researching the characteristics of some of these sentences. It was found that conjoining, repetitions, pseudo-clefting, and 'focus-attractors' cause an against-the-norm focus assignment which results in the naked noun receiving heavy stress. A comparison of the grammars of presentational vs. contrastive sentences shows that they vary with respect to rhematic structure, word order possibilities, negation, presuppositional status, and normal as opposed to contrastive focus, stress, and intonation. The NNC was postulated to be a language-specific filter belonging to the right-hand side of the grammar.

Spanish has always been considered a 'free' word order language because it allows for different word order possibilities and rearranging of constituents. In Chapters 1 through 3 it was demonstrated that 'free' is not so free after all. Different word orders convey different functional perspectives: subject-verb does not carry the same information as verb-subject, for example. Therefore, it was thought relevant to determine whether Spanish adheres to some basic pattern of word order. Being fully aware that the notion of basic word order is very much theory-dependent, I defined it in Chapter 4 as the word order generated by the phrase structure rules of the language. Several alternatives were considered within the ordered base hypothesis; Contreras' (1976) study was then taken as the exponent of the unordered base proposal. After careful consideration, it was decided that no compelling reasons exist to think of Spanish as representing anything other than basic SVO. The arguments that forced this conclusion were of diverse character: SVO is the neutral sentence pattern for the majority of sentences; it is the presuppositionally least marked order; it is the order adopted when ambiguity may result, and the word order assumed by generic statements; frequency studies render support to SVO; and--what is of crucial importance--syntactic rules point to the existence of a VP constituent. Finally, grammatical relations are easily captured within the SVO analysis.

During the course of this book care was taken to point out the interaction of the rules of the syntactic component with the rules which apply at different levels of semantic interpretation, those pertaining to sentence semantics as well as those proper to the discourse. It was shown how one subcomponent of the grammar builds on another until the sentences receive their complete semantic interpretation, which gives credence to the step-by-step derivation of sentences. The revised EST, supplemented by some of the notions brought forth by linguists of the Prague School, provided an adequate model of grammar which led to the discovery of some very consistent patterns of the Spanish language. Undoubtedly, this work can only be taken as a first step into the intricacies and subtleties of word order in Spanish. As such, it is subject to refinement and modification. Since much remains to be done, I feel obliged to point out a few areas which can fruitfully be explored and which may some day help us to understand completely the linguistic resources that we so proficiently and unconsciously use as native speakers.

5.2 **Areas for future research.** This study has dealt with two subtypes of presentational sentences, haber presentationals and intransitive presentationals. I happen to believe that a third subtype exists: the se presentational.[3]

(1a) Se alquilan departamentos.
se rent (3 pl.) apartments
'Apartments for rent.'

(1b) Se arreglan relojes.
se repair (3 pl.) clocks
'Clocks (are) repaired.'

(2a) Se volcó la leche.
se spilled (3 sg.) the milk
'The milk (got) spilled.'

(2b) Se cerraron las ventanas.
se closed (3 pl.) the windows
'The windows closed.'

Se sentences were excluded from the previous discussion because their analysis has stirred up much controversy,[4] and I am of the opinion that better insights are gained if one deals with clear-cut data first. Now that a theory has been developed for the two subtypes presented in Chapters 1 and 2, it is possible to go back to the more controversial areas and check to see how the theory fares when applied to them.

Although it is far from my objective to present a full treatment of the sentences in (1) and (2), I would like to show that they are presentationals. These sentences can be interpreted as denoting the appearance of their NP referent into the universe of discourse; they introduce a new participant for further consideration. As such, these sentences are appropriate neutral sentences: they can be used as discourse-openers, and constitute adequate answers to the questions in (3).

(3a) ¿Qué pasó?
'What happened?'

(3b) ¿Qué hay de nuevo?
'What's up?'

Moreover, observe that the sentences in (1) and (2) adhere to the word order proper to presentationals, i.e. V NP. Part of the controversy related to these sentences centers around the grammatical function performed by the NP in (1) and (2).[5] But notice that the decision as to whether this NP is a subject or an object is irrelevant to the presentative function. All that this functional interpretation requires is that one and only one NP referent be introduced at a time, so that this NP can be properly highlighted and receive semantic focus. To put it differently, presentationalism works independently and despite grammatical functions, as shown by haber presentationals, which introduce an object NP, and intransitive presentationals, which introduce a subject NP. The V NP word order makes it obvious that these se presentationals are subjectless at the level of LF, that is, their NPs are in the scope of the verb. This is true regardless of whether their NPs are subjects or objects. If the NP happens to be a subject, it is moved into the VP by the rule of Subject Postposing and the LF parallels that of intransitive presentationals (4). On the other hand, if the NP turns out to be an object, the LF is similar to that of haber presentationals (5).

(4) $(_S[_{NP_i} \ldots e \ldots] [_{VP} VP[NP_i]])$

(5) $(_S[_{VP} V NP])$

The LFs in both (4) and (5) have the correct structure for the post-LF Rhematization rule of sentence grammar to mark both the V and the NP as rhematic, that is, se presentationals are also all rheme, thetic, again in agreement with the two presentational subtypes investigated in this monograph. Another point worth mentioning is that one of the factors that allows the se sentences in (1) and (2) to be read as presentationals[6] is precisely that they appropriately introduce only one NP referent. This is because se changes the valence of the verbs in (1) and (2) from two to one. In other words, se signals that one of the verb arguments is not present. All the verbs which can appear in se sentences are transitive, that is, they may (minimally) take both a subject and an object.

(6a) Paco alquila departamentos.
'Paco rents apartments.'

(6b) Paco volcó la leche.
'Paco spilled the milk.'

Therefore, the se has the ultimate effect of making the sentences in (1) and (2) conform to the presentational characterization advanced in this study.[7] It remains to be determined whether these se presentationals require any other rules besides the ones postulated for haber and intransitive presentationals.

This book has dealt with two neutral word orders in Spanish, SV(O) and VS, declaratives and presentationals respectively.[8] But there are several other word orders (probably nonneutral) that deserve to be carefully researched. For example, it would be interesting to find out whether VSO is derived through a rule of Subject Postposing or through a rule of Verb Preposing. Although my sentiments run in favor of the second alternative, I have at this time no hard evidence to offer in its support.[9] Moreover, is the VSO order of the noninterrogative sentences in (7) related to the VSO word order of yes/no questions such as those in (8)? That is to say, is the mechanism that derives the former word order the same as that which derives the latter? (Subjects are underlined.)

(7a) Creo yo que ése es el caso. (M 232)
     believe (1 sg.) I that that is the case
     'I believe that to be the case.'

(7b) Tenemos nosotros la facilidad ... (M 290)
     have (1 pl.) we the facility
     'We have the facility ...'

(7c) ... no lo veo que tengan ellos el derecho de juzgar
        (M 279)
     no it (acc.) I-see that have (3 pl., subjunctive) they
        the right of to-judge
     '... I don't see that they have the right to judge.'

(8a) ¿Recuerda usted el primero? (M 105)
     remember you (sg., formal) the first
     'Do you remember the first?'

(8b) Y ¿siempre habías pintado tú? (M 234)
     and always had painted you (sg., informal)
     'And have you always painted?'

(8c) ¿No son dañinos los tintes de pelo? (M 39)
     no are harmful the dyes of hair
     'Aren't hair dyes harmful?'

Furthermore, what is the relationship between the word order illustrated by the sentences in (8) and the alternative word

order of the yes/no questions in (9)? Intuitively, it seems
that the information requested is not exactly the same, that is,
their communicative value is not identical.

(9a) ¿Él lo estableció? (M 69)
he it (acc.) established
'Did he establish it?'

(9b) ¿Y ustedes las hacen o ...? (M 90)
and you (pl., formal) them (acc., f. pl.) make or ...
'And do you make them or ...?'

(9c) ¿Y el terreno está ahí mismo? (M 95)
and the lot is there same
'And is the lot right there?'

Still left to specify is the connection (if any) between the
word order found in (8) and that of the information questions
in (10). This latter type does not have an alternative word
order parallel to the examples in (9).[10]

(10a) ¿Qué vino usted a hacer a Francia? (M 137)
what came you to do in France
'What did you come to do in France?'

(10b) ¿Adónde va usted? (M 137)
where go you
'Where are you going?'

(10c) ¿Cuántos años tiene mi tío Genaro?
how-many years has my uncle Genaro
'How old is my uncle Genaro?'

Another question which also needs to be answered is whether
any of these word orders is related to contrastive sentences,
some of which were briefly analyzed in Chapter 3.

Satisfactory answers to all of these intertwined areas of inquiry may bring us a step closer to a more complete grammar
of Spanish and, as a consequence, closer to achieving a fuller
understanding of the complexities of the human mind.

NOTES

1. Therefore, the Subject Postposing rule can operate even
if there is a direct object argument in the sentence. If this
happens, the sentence is discarded by Presentational Sentence
Interpretation (if not before SI-2) because it could not be read
as merely asserting the appearance of the NP into the world of
discourse.

2. A sentence like the following does not constitute a
counterexample to my claim:

Los dolores ya vienen ellos solos, sin que haga falta que
los llamen. (EJ 261)
the aches already come they alone without that it-make lack
that them (acc.) they-call (subjunctive)
'Aches they already come by themselves, without need to
call them.'

In this sentence the left-dislocated and thematic los dolores is
indeed anaphoric with the rhematic ellos; but this ellos is not
being introduced into the discourse; rather, it is contrastive
and as such, receives an exhaustive reading.

3. Remember that occasionally there can still be found in
the written language the archaic presentational expression he
aquí/he allí 'here it is/there it is' (cf. note 14, Chapter 4).
See also Suñer (1981).

4. For a quick appraisal of some of the material that deals
with this topic, I refer the reader to Nuessel's (1979) bibliography. I myself am responsible for a few of these articles
(cf. Suñer 1973, 1974, 1975, 1976a, 1976b, and forthcoming in
Orbis).

5. I have proposed that the NPs in (1) are direct objects.
Since these sentences never have a surface subject (see Appendix B for discussion), the verb agrees with its object ana-
logically (cf. Section 1.6, and note 24 in Appendix B). Observe that the grammaticality judgments of (i) and (ii) fall out
naturally on the assumption that clitics are base-generated.

(i) Se los vende.
se them (acc., m. pl.) sell (3 sg.)
'They are sold.'/'People sell them.'

(ii) *Se lo venden.
sell (3 pl.)

The verb in (ii) can never be plural because there is no argument with which it can agree.

By contrast, I have claimed that the NPs in (2) are subjects
(cf. Suñer forthcoming in Orbis). I call this se 'spontaneous
se'. These sentences occur with change of state verbs and
they can always be interpreted as spontaneous happenings
(whereas those in (1) demand human intervention).

Since my purpose is to suggest that both (1) and (2) are
instances of presentational sentences, I shall keep the discussion as neutral as possible in order to avoid undue controversy.

6. Naturally, they can also be interpreted as contrastive
sentences if their NP receives contrastive focus. In this case,
only the NPs are in the scope of assertion.

7. The sentences in (1) and (2) react differently under
noncontrastive conditions if their NPs appear preverbally.

(i) *Departamentos se alquila/n.
    apartments se rent

(ii) La leche se volcó.
     'The milk spilled.'

Sentence (i) is ungrammatical whether departamentos is in subject position or in TOP position (left-dislocated). This is because of the NNC, which maintains that naked nouns cannot be noncontrastive themes (Chapter 3). On the other hand, (ii) is a perfectly grammatical declarative sentence. Note that while (ii) provides evidence for the subject status of la leche, (i) is indeterminate as to the function of departamentos.

8. However, I did not treat declaratives as thoroughly as presentationals. Therefore, I do not consider that the last word about declaratives has been said.

9. This is an area I plan to work on in the near future.

10. At least, it does not have an alternative word order in most dialects. Nevertheless, in some Caribbean dialects one finds the word order: WH-word + Subject + Verb, especially when the subject is the second person singular informal, i.e. tú.

¿Qué tú tienes?
what you have
'What do you have?'

APPENDIX A

HABER, ESTAR, SER

A.0 Introduction. The purpose of this appendix is to
examine the use of this trilogy of verbs in connection with
Bull's proposal (cf. Section 1.3.1.1). Recall that Bull's main
interests focused on the formulation of practical rules which
would assist students learning Spanish. With this objective in
mind, he stated (1965:205) that the student:

> ... must learn that haber and ser are used with events,
> haber and estar with entities, and the choice between each
> member of the two pairs depends on the subset of limiting
> adjectives used. The cues are unmistakably clear: entity
> vs. event; definite vs. indefinite.

Although these guidelines are approximately 95 percent accurate, there still remains 5 percent of the data which does not
conform to them. Therefore, my aim is to refine Bull's pedagogical statement and to explain why this situation obtains.[1]

A.1 *Haber* and *estar*. According to Bull, haber is used to
locate indefinite entities, and estar definite ones. That haber
is employed to introduce indefinitely modified nouns is to be
expected, since this is in perfect agreement with its presentational function at the discourse level. However, the existence
of examples in which impersonal haber locates a definite entity
(1) (see also Section 1.3.1.3.1) and estar an indefinite one (2)
cannot be denied.

(1a) ... y allí no hay el problema ... (VEA 75)
'... and there there-isn't the problem ...'

(1b) ... en sus ojos había el fuego de la desesperación.
'... in his eyes there-was the fire of desperation.'

324

(2a) Sí, y donde está una fuente también ... (M 199)
'Yes, and where (there) is a fountain too ...'

(2b) ... entramos en una especie de ... recinto, una
cantina. Estaba una mesa de billar ... (M 203)
'... we-entered a kind of ... room, a bar. (There)
was a billiard table ...'

Before trying to find the reasons which prompt the selection
of estar and hay with different determiners, the functional
differences between hay and estar must be discussed. Hay is
essentially a one-place predicate which asserts the existence of
the entity to which its NP refers; although it is true that hay
sentences could go on to specify a location, this type of information is incidental rather than required (see Section 1.2 for
further discussion).

In contrast to hay, estar is a two-place predicate. At the
level of sentence grammar, estar requires both an NP and a
locative.[2] To show this difference, compare the two messages
in (3).

(3a) Hay un policía que quiere hablarle.
'There-is a policeman who wants to-talk-to-you.'

(3b) ??Está un policía que quiere hablarle.
'Is a policeman who wants to-talk-to-you.'

Sentence (3b) sounds quite incomplete.

Given that estar requires two arguments, and given the
relatively free word order of Spanish, at least two word order
possibilities come immediately to mind: NP-estar-Loc and Loc-
estar-NP.[3] It is to be expected that these two different word
orders would carry different informational potential; and indeed
this is the case. The structure NP-estar-Loc presupposes the
existence of the NP and asserts its location. Consider example
(4).

(4) El policía estaba en el bar.
'The policeman was in the bar.'

Sentence (4) takes for granted the existence of el policía and
asserts that he is in a particular place (en el bar) as opposed
to any other place (his home, the police station, etc.). Under
noncontrastive interpretation, the word order in (4) makes
clear that the locative is in focus. In terms of theme/rheme
the sentence is partitioned as in (5).

(5) $[_{Th}$ el policía] $[_{Rh}$ estaba en el bar]

Now compare sentence (4) with sentence (6). The latter constitutes an example of Loc-estar-NP word order. [4]

(6) En el bar estaba el policía.
    'In the bar was the policeman.'

This order has the effect of shifting the weight of the information. In this instance the NP is in focus. Sentence (6) states that in a given location (en el bar) there was el policía, as opposed to any other person. The contrast between (4) and (6) becomes totally transparent when one considers possible continuations for these sentences. Observe example (7).

(7a) ... y no en la esquina.
     '... and not on the corner.'

     ... y no durmiendo en su casa.
     '... and not sleeping at home.'

(7b) ... y no el capitán.
     '... and not the captain.'

     ... y no tu hermano.
     '... and not your brother.'

The appropriateness of the examples in (7a) as possible continuations for (4) confirms the claim that what is in focus in (4) is the Loc, while the items in (7b) lend support to the contention that the focus in (6) is the NP itself. On the basis of these examples, it is clear that under noncontrastive intonation the focus in estar sentences encompasses the argument that occurs in postverbal position. Sentence (6) has the theme/ rheme structure given in (8).

(8) [$_{Th}$ en el bar] [$_{Rh}$ estaba el policía]

What then is the interpretation of an estar sentence? Given the fact that it is a two-place predicate, its function consists of asserting either the location of an entity or the existence of the NP relative to a given location. [5] This difference correlates with the two word order possibilities explored earlier.

A.1.1 *Haber* and *estar* with indefinite subjects. The principles that determine the choice between hay and estar follow. I have already devoted part of Chapter 1 to the examination of hay sentences with definitely modified nouns (see Section 1.3.1.3.1). Therefore, since there is no controversy over the cooccurrence of estar with definite nouns, I limit this discussion for the most part to the selection of one verb over the other with indefinitely modified nouns.

I begin by pairing examples of hay (the (a)-sentences) with examples of estar (the (b)-sentences).

(9a) Hay un hombre en la puerta.
'There is a man at the door.'

(9b) Un hombre está en la puerta.
'A man is at the door.'

(10a) En la esquina hay un vigilante nuevo.
'On the corner there-is a new policeman.'

(10b) En la esquina está un vigilante nuevo.
'On the corner is a new policeman.'

(11a) Había una pecera de cristal sobre una mesita.
'There-was a glass fishbowl on-top-of a small-table.'

(11b) Una pecera de cristal estaba sobre una mesita.
'A glass fishbowl was on-top-of a small-table.'

Contrary to the prediction of Bull's pedagogical rules, the three (b) examples are grammatical. Some speakers balk at (9b) without additional context and some 'turn the sentence around' (type (10b)) to make it sound more natural.

(12) En la puerta está un hombre.
'At the door is a man.'

This inversion is not at all surprising. It makes the sentence conform to the intuitive principle that syntactically definite modification indicates shared knowledge between speaker and hearer, which should come before indefinite arguments. Because this dichotomy between definite and indefinite does not arise in (11b), the order of the elements in this sentence does not cause anyone to hesitate. This is not to say that (11a) and (11b) are synonymous. In keeping with the meaning and function of hay, (11a) asserts the existence of the NP, whereas (11b) presupposes the existence of pecera de cristal while asserting its location.

Another way to avoid any reluctance on the part of native speakers to accept (9b) is to bury it in context. Consider example (13).

(13) Debido a los disturbios hay mucho control, un vigilante está en esta esquina, dos más están en la plaza y ...
'Due to the disturbances there-is a-lot-of control, a/one policeman is on this corner, two more are on the square, and ...'

Example (13) makes the numerical value of un stand out by
contrasting the location of one policeman to that of the others. [6]
This same kind of contrast is implicit in estar sentences with
other cardinal expressions. Observe that in these estar sentences the subject argument is outside the scope of assertion;
therefore, the existence of the NP is presupposed or at least
unasserted. As expected, it is more difficult to presuppose
the existence of something not easily identifiable (i.e. indefinite). The conflict is solved by interpreting the noun
modifiers contrastively; that is, these cardinal modifiers set
apart a certain number or group of the noun referents and
contrast this group with the whole set (cf. examples in (14)).
No such contrast is detectable in the corresponding sentences
with hay in (15); in this case, the expressions of cardinality
merely refer to an unspecified number of students.

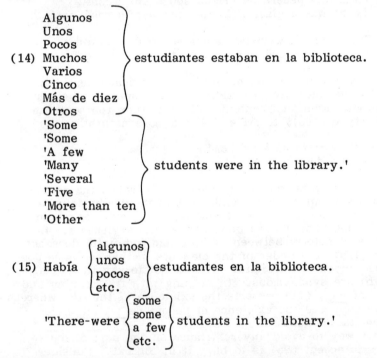

(14)
Algunos
Unos
Pocos
Muchos
Varios
Cinco
Más de diez
Otros
} estudiantes estaban en la biblioteca.

'Some
'Some
'A few
'Many
'Several
'Five
'More than ten
'Other
} students were in the library.'

(15) Había
{ algunos
unos
pocos
etc. }
estudiantes en la biblioteca.

'There-were
{ some
some
a few
etc. }
students in the library.'

In other words, in (14) the noun estudiantes is presupposed;
the 'weight' of the subject argument falls on the modifiers which
make explicit that only a portion of the possible total of the set
categorized by the noun was in a particular location. Thus,
the modifiers take their value from the cardinality of a contextually determinate set of students. [7] Sentence (15) merely
asserts that an undetermined number of students were in a
certain location; no reference to a possible total is implied.
The modifiers are not linked to any contextually determinate

set of students; their value is quite loose. This difference in the reading of the modifiers correlates with the difference in the scope of assertion (i.e. theme/rheme division). The modifiers form part of the rheme in (15), but part of the theme in (14).[8]

Making use of the very general rule of Quantifier Interpretation (16), which assigns scope to quantifiers that appear in surface structure by allowing their interpretation at the levels of both VP and S, the structures in (17) and (18) are derived.

(16) Quantifier Interpretation

$$[\ldots Q \ldots] \begin{Bmatrix} S \\ VP \end{Bmatrix} \rightarrow [Q_i(\ldots x_i \ldots)] \begin{Bmatrix} S \\ VP \end{Bmatrix} \quad \text{(Williams 1977: 126)}$$

(17) $[\text{MUCHOS}_i \ (x_i \ \text{estudiantes} \ [\text{estaban en la biblioteca}]_{Rh})]_S$

(18) $[\,[\text{MUCHOS}_i \ (\text{había} \ x_i \ \text{estudiantes en la biblioteca})]_{Rh}]_S$

The structure in (17) is representative of the examples in (14); it clearly captures the fact that MUCHOS is outside the rheme. It informally states 'Many among the students are such that they are in the library'. By contrast, (18) represents the sentences in (15); in this case the quantifier is inside the rheme. The structure in (18) is interpreted as merely saying, 'The students who are at the library are many'.[9]

Therefore, one of the reasons that lead speakers to choose between the type of hay and estar sentences in (14) and (15) seems to be the implicit contrast with the total set carried by the estar sentence with an indefinite subject in preverbal position.

Yet to be explained are the examples in (10). Could it be the case that these sentences are synonymous? Notice that both have un vigilante nuevo as part of the rheme. Nevertheless, there are some differences between the two, however minute and subtle. First, recall that although the locative is optional with hay, it is required with estar. This fact seems to influence the impression caused by an estar message of the type found in (10b). This sentence does more than merely assert the existence of the NP; it provides a description, almost a portrait--which is to say it produces the same effect as that of looking at a photograph. Although the estar sentence is presentational in character, it also functions to recreate the scene.

Atkinson (1973) refers to this impression as that of being 'on stage'. He describes Staged Activity as follows:

From the point of view of the reader, it is, when perfectly realized, that part of the narrative that gives him the

illusion of direct participation in an objective world perceptible to his senses. From the point of view of the
writer, it is the result of a technique for re-creating an
objective world. (1973:59)[10]

This trait of estar sentences is very clearly exploited (although unconsciously, I am sure) in example (19).

(19) ... te acuerdas que, pasando por el Paseo Orinoco,
    están unas piedras enormes ...[11]
    '... (you) remember that, going along the Paseo
    Orinoco, are some enormous rocks ...'

Obviously, the speaker is trying to recreate an image, to
evoke in someone's mind the picture of something already seen
as if it were there in front of them at the moment of speaking.
This is, then, an excellent illustration of the 'on stage' function of the estar sentence under consideration. This 'pictorial'
impression even affects estar sentences with other word orders.
In the following examples, hay could be exchanged with estar;
however, this replacement would cause the 'on stage' quality
to disappear (see also examples under (2)).

(20a) Allí está otra que no es ... (M 203)
    'There (there)-is another that is not ...'

(20b) --¿Cuántos soldados están aquí?--inquirió ... (SXX 110)
    '--How many soldiers are here?--he-inquired ...'

(20c) --No estaban aquí más que doce ... (SXX 111)
    no were here more than twelve ...
    'There weren't more than twelve here ...'

(20d) El Flaco mira los zapatos. Están dos pares de zapatos
    en un rincón. (stage direction; TO 257)
    'The Flaco looks at the shoes. (There) are two pairs
    of shoes in a corner.'

(20e) ...¿ no es adonde está un lugar que ... (M 200)
    '... isn't-it where (there) is a place that ...'

No doubt the difference between hay, with its colorless informational value, and estar, with its vivid, descriptive, on-stage
impact, constitutes a very subtle semantic contrast. If the
notion of markedness were duly exploited in syntax-semantics,
the hay sentences would represent the unmarked construction
and the estar sentences would be the marked member of the
pair.
Consequently, two loosely interrelated factors determine the
choice between hay and estar with indefinite subjects. The
first is the difference in readings obtained from the indefinite

modifiers, which depends on whether these quantifiers fall inside or outside the scope of assertion. Thus, the NP-estar-Loc construction implies a contrast with the total set which is absent in the Loc-estar-NP type and in hay sentences. The second factor centers around the obligatoriness of the Loc argument for estar sentences. These sentences provide a more pictorial description which produces an 'on-stage' impact. Support for this latter characterization is found in the fact that it accounts for other peculiarities related to these two presentational constructions.

A.1.1.1 Abstract subjects. It has been noticed repeatedly for English that existential there is obligatory in certain contexts. For example, Kimball (1973) requires the There-Insertion rule to be obligatory when the sentence is used to express inalienable possession. His examples are shown in (21) and (22).

(21) There is space in the manger.
    *Space is in the manger.

(22) There is fire in his eye.
    *Fire is in his eye.

Breivik (1975:63) accounts for the same facts by making There-Insertion obligatory whenever the subject is [+abstract].

(23) *No sign of life was in the house.
    There was no sign of life in the house.

Jenkins (1975), an advocate of the base generation of there, points out that many phrases lack grammatical paraphrases without the there. Some of his examples are given in (24) (1975:49).

(24a) There's an answer to the question.
    *An answer is to the question.

(24b) There's a solution to the problem.
    *A solution is to the problem.

(24c) There's a trick to it.
    *A trick is to it.

(24d) There's no point to that.
    *No point is to that.

(24e) There's nothing to it.
    *Nothing is to it.

The same distribution of grammaticality and ungrammaticality
holds true for Spanish if one generalizes these observations to
the dichotomy haber/estar. Only the hay version is possible
in examples like those in (25).

(25a) Hay un mundo de diferencia entre los dos hermanos.
      'There-is a world of difference between the two
          brothers.'
      *Un mundo de diferencia está entre ...

(25b) Ha habido mucho entusiasmo con el partido.
      'There-has been a lot of enthusiasm for the game.'
      *Mucho entusiasmo ha estado con el partido.

(25c) Hay un dejo de envidia en sus ojos.
      'There-is a hint of envy in his eyes.'
      *Un dejo de envidia está en sus ojos.

(25d) Había algo sospechoso en sus movimientos.
      'There-was something suspicious in his movements.'
      *Algo sospechoso estaba en sus movimientos.

Why should it be that indefinite [+abstract] subjects are not
allowed with estar sentences?[12] Why are they permitted in hay
sentences? The explanation for this apparent oddity is to be
found in the meaning of the estar and hay constructions. Recall that one of the functions of an estar message is to produce
a descriptive impact, to recreate a scene vividly, to put something 'on stage'. Therefore, the more concrete this description
is, the easier it is to give the hearer the feeling of participat-
ing in the scene. The prime candidates for subjects of estar
are, then, those which are perceptible to the senses; this is
why one native speaker verbalized her interpretation of the
estar examples as, 'It is like looking at a picture'. Consequently, [+abstract] subjects are not appropriate for estar
messages: they yield ungrammatical sentences because they
are too weak to produce a descriptive impact. To exploit the
metaphor, they cannot be easily captured in a photograph. In
addition, notice that [+abstract] nouns do not lend themselves
very readily to being quantified; that is, it is difficult, if not
impossible, to visualize for such nouns a contrast between a
subset of the whole and the whole. But this is precisely the
requirement that must be fulfilled by estar sentences with indefinite subjects in preverbal position.
    To further confirm my hypothesis, notice examples (26) and
(27).

(26a) Había varias personas entre los dos hermanos.
      'There-were several people between the two brothers.'

(26b) Varias personas estaban entre los dos hermanos.
'Several people were between the two brothers.'

(26c) Varias de las personas estaban entre los dos hermanos.
'Several of the people were between the two brothers.'

(27a) Había varias diferencias entre los dos hermanos.
'There-were several differences between the two brothers.'

(27b) *Varias diferencias estaban entre los dos hermanos.
'Several differences were between the two brothers.'

(27c) *Varias de las diferencias estaban entre los dos hermanos.
'Several of the differences were between the two brothers.'

The only difference between the examples in (26) and those in (27) is the [+abstract] character of the relevant noun. Sentence (26b) implies that several but not all people were at a particular location; this reading is unequivocally transmitted in (26c).[13] In contrast, both (27b) and (27c) are uninterpretable. It is as if, with estar, the noun requires a concrete outline, so that it can be pictured in one's mind.

Notice, furthermore, that it is possible to locate abstractions with estar provided that a definite determiner modifies the subject noun.

(28a) La idea ya estaba en su mente.
'The idea was already in his mind.'

(28b) La suerte de los acusados estaba en sus manos.
'The fate of the accused was in his/her/their hands.'

(28c) La autoridad de Dios está sobre nosotros.
'The authority of God is over us.'

(28d) No había diferencias entre las mujeres. Las diferencias estaban entre los dos hermanos.
'There weren't any differences among the women. The differences were between the two brothers.'

The definite determiners do not imply a contrast between a subset of the whole and the whole; on the contrary, they make reference to the whole set under consideration.

Returning now to the examples in (25), abstractions like those found there--un mundo de diferencia, un dejo de envidia, mucho entusiasmo, and algo sospechoso--are perfectly matched to an hay sentence, because this latter type of construction has the sole function of asserting the existence of its NP; it is

informational in nature, it reports a fact. Here no inconsistency arises between existence, factual information, and
abstractions. Furthermore, since the pertinent noun does not
receive a quantificational interpretation, no contrast is established.

In sum, the foregoing characterization of the differences
between hay and estar sentences explains one of the facts
that has been repeatedly noted in the literature.

A.2 *Ser.* The third member of the trilogy under scrutiny
is the verb ser. Ser is a two-argument verb; it requires an
NP subject and a locative. It is used to locate events, happenings (as opposed to estar, which locates entities). [14] By their
very nature, events are [-concrete]; therefore, the prediction
is that the juxtaposition of ser with an indefinite, abstract preverbal subject (i.e. an event) should render sequences which
are very unnatural. This is especially true when these sentences are considered in isolation (29).

(29a) ??Una reunión será en mi casa.
'A gathering will-be at my home.'

(29b) ?*Un partido fue anoche.
'A game was last-night.'

(29b)
?Más de tres
?Pocas
*Unas
?Muchas
} fiestas serán allí. [15]

'More than three
'Few
'Some
'Many
} parties will-be there.'

It must be recalled (Section A.1.1.1) that this result follows
from the fact that because it is hard to picture a contrast between a subset of the whole and the whole for such nouns,
[+abstract] nouns resist quantification.

However, some of the examples of (29) improve considerably
when they are used in contexts where the cardinal value of the
indefinite modifiers is given prominence, whether through direct
linguistic context (30), or through inference (31).

(30a) Una reunión será en mi casa a las ocho y otra en casa
de María a las doce.
'One gathering will be in my home at eight o'clock
and another at Maria's home at twelve o'clock.'

(30b) Una boda será a las cinco, otra a las ocho y una
tercera a las diez.
'One/a wedding will be at five o'clock, another at
eight o'clock, and a third one at ten o'clock.'

(31) --No te preocupes, otra boda será a las ocho, te lo
prometo [dicho cuando ya ha habido una a las
siete].[16]
'--Don't worry, another wedding will-take-place at
eight o'clock, I promise you [said when there has
already been one at seven o'clock].'

The sentences in (29) illustrate NP_{indef}-ser-Loc word order.
Although one may predict that the order Loc-ser-NP_{indef} should
produce better results, they are not forthcoming (32).

(32a) ??En mi casa será una reunión.
'At my place will-be a gathering.'

(32b) ??Anoche fue un partido.
'Last night was a game.'

(32c) ?Allí serán muchas fiestas.
'There will-be many parties.'

In contrast, definitely modified events may appear with ser
without any problems. Consider NP-ser-Loc in (33) and Loc-
ser-NP in (34).

(33a) La fiesta será en mi casa.
'The party will-be at my place.'

(33b) El partido fue a las ocho.
'The game was at eight o'clock.'

(34a) En mi casa será la fiesta.
'At my place will-be the party.'

(34b) A las ocho fue el partido.
'At eight o'clock was the game.'

Despite the awkwardness of the sentences in (29) and (32),
it is evident that the grammar must allow for their generation,
since this type of example becomes acceptable, given appropriate context (cf. (30) and (31)). Nevertheless, one may speculate as to the reasons for the resultant awkwardness. It appears that since events are inherently [+abstract], they either
demand a definite modifier (which never implies a contrast between a subset and the set), or require that the cardinality
of the indefinite modifier be sufficiently explicit, that is, that
a given value be assigned to it.

A.3 Summary. To recapitulate, it has been shown that, contrary to Bull's claim, not only <u>hay</u> but also <u>estar</u> and <u>ser</u> are compatible with indefinite arguments. However, this does not imply that all three predicates are used under the same circumstances. <u>Hay</u>, an essentially one-term existential predicate, has the primary function of introducing the referent of the NP into the discourse. The information it presents is factual and to a certain degree colorless; in terms of markedness, it would represent the unmarked construction.[17] On the other hand, <u>estar</u> and <u>ser</u> are two-term predicates; within sentence grammar each requires both an NP (the syntactic subject) and a locative. Their two-argument nature opens the door to different word order possibilities. Thus, NP-V-Loc is primarily a locative construction which presupposes the existence of whatever is being referred to by the NP, whereas the order Loc-V-NP renders a presentational pattern which asserts the existence of the NP referent. These differences in the scope of the assertion are captured at post-LF level by the rule which assigns rhematic structure to sentences.

The NP of <u>estar</u> embodies entities, that of <u>ser</u> events. Whenever this NP is preverbal and modified by expressions of cardinality, there arises an implied contrast with the total set which must be made explicit in <u>ser</u> sentences. This contrast is absent[18] when the NP argument is inside the scope of assertion (i.e. in <u>hay</u> sentences and in the case of Loc-V-NP order).

<u>Estar</u> sentences with indefinite subjects in postverbal position are presentational sentences which, among other things, recreate a scene and convey an 'on stage' impact. Due to their vividness, they appeal to our senses and to our imagination. They represent the marked construction when compared to <u>hay</u> sentences.

The inherent character of events as [+abstract] explains why <u>ser</u> sentences are more natural with definitely modified NPs or with NPs in which the contrast with another member of the set is made explicit through context or inference.

NOTES

1. This appendix has some points in common with the paper 'Existential predicates: <u>hay</u> vs. <u>estar</u>' which I presented at the Ninth Linguistic Symposium on Romance Languages, Georgetown University, March, 1979.

2. It is necessary to specify 'at the level of sentence grammar' because, given the discourse, the locative could be 'recovered' from context. For example:

(A) -¿Quién estaba contigo en el bar?
'Who was with you in the bar?'

(B) -(Estaba) Paco.
'(Was) Paco.'

Given the question asked by speaker (A), speaker (B) does not need to reiterate the locative, since it is transparent from the context.

3. There are other word order possibilities as well, but they are not crucial to the discussion.

4. The way this word order is arrived at is in itself an interesting problem. Provided I am correct in claiming that estar obligatorily subcategorizes a locative, then the word order in (6) would be derived by preposing the locative to TOP position and postposing the NP subject to the end of the VP.

5. Or to put it differently, NP-estar-Loc is a locative sentence, while Loc-estar-NP is a presentational sentence.

6. To a great degree, the facts of Spanish correlate with those pointed out by Perlmutter (1970a) for English. He claims that the indefinite article cannot occur with the subjects of certain stative predicates (*A boy is tall); only the stressed numeral is acceptable in this environment. In Spanish, the so-called indefinite article and the numeral are the same morpheme. Nevertheless, some contexts--like my (13)--make this numerical value more explicit and may, therefore, facilitate comprehension.

7. An appropriate context for structures of the type NP$_{indef}$-estar-Loc could be the following. Imagine an instructor who comes to teach a class only to find a nearly deserted building. This person asks:

--¿Y dónde está la gente hoy?
'And where are the people today?'

A very plausible answer would be:

--Hace media hora, algunos estudiantes estaban en la biblioteca pero me parece que la mayoria fue a una manifestación.
'Half an hour ago, some students were in the library but I have the impression that the majority went to a (protest) march.'

8. Thus, it should be anticipated that the modifiers in sentences with the word order Loc-estar-NP would not necessarily imply a contrast with the whole set, since they are inside the scope of assertion. This is exactly the case. Notice that (ia) would be appropriately continued with (ic) yet not with (ib).

(ia)   En la clase estaba un policia.
       'In the class was a policeman.'

(ib)   ... *y otro (estaba) en la cafetería.
       '... and another one was in the cafeteria'

(ic)   ... y no un marino.
'... and not a sailor.'

9. Observe that in (17) and (18) I have replaced VP by
Rh(eme) for ease of exposition. No consequences should be
attached to this move; note that VP and Rheme coincide in the
sentences under discussion. What the semantic interpretations
in (17) and (18) fail to make explicit is that only in (17) is
MUCHOS acting as a restricted modifier; this is due to the fact
that in (17) the quantifier takes its value from the cardinality
of a contextually determinate set of students representing a
sizeable proportion but less than totality. Perhaps (17) could
be expressed more formally with the following sublogical form:

(MUCHOS x, xε{x: estudiantes x}) (x estaban en la biblioteca)

This formula can be paraphrased in 'quasi-English' as in the
text.
10. Atkinson uses Staged Activity to discuss the two forms
of subject inversion in French:

(i) arrive X
(ii) il arrive X

Bolinger (1977: 93-94) also resorts to this distinction in order
to pinpoint the differences between

(i) Across the street is a grocery.
(ii) Across the street there's a grocery.

Sentence (i) presents something on stage, while (ii) brings
something into awareness, presents something to our minds.
In a note (1977:123), Bolinger claims that Spanish presentatives
are essentially the same as those in English. His examples are:

En el patio está una mesa.
'On the patio is (stands) a table.'

En el patio hay una mesa.
'On the patio there is a table.'

The first one is an instance of 'on stage', the second of
'bringing something into awareness'.
Although many of the native speakers I consulted have difficulties explaining the tenuous difference between examples with
hay and estar, if they are given this explanation, they agree
with it. One native speaker expressed her feeling about the
estar examples as, 'It's like looking at a still picture, it is
there in front of you'.

11. This example comes from the Norma Culta Project from Caracas, Venezuela. It is cited by Bentivoglio in her article, 'Queísmo y dequeísmo en el habla culta de Caracas'. In: 1975 Colloquium on Hispanic Linguistics. Edited by Frances M. Aid et al. Washington, D.C.: Georgetown University Press.

12. Word order is immaterial in this case. The estar sentences in (25) are equally bad when their subjects are postposed:

*Entre los dos hermanos está un mundo de diferencia.
*Ha estado mucho entusiasmo con el partido. etc.

13. But I do not mean to imply any kind of derivation between (26b) and (26c), or vice versa (cf. Selkirk 1977).

14. Since the behavior of ser is quite parallel to that of estar, except for the fact that estar locates entities and ser locates events, I have narrowed the discussion of ser to indefinite vs. definite modification in order to avoid being repetitious.

15. Parallel examples with haber are quite grammatical:

(i) Habrá una reunión en mi casa.
'There-will-be a gathering at my place.'

(ii) Hubo un partido anoche.
'There-was a game last-night.'

The language also has at its disposal the expression tener lugar 'to-take place' to express the situations given in (29).

16. I owe this example to Marisa Rivero.

17. That hay sentences constitute the unmarked construction also follows from their being basic and from their being the foremost presentational construction in the language (cf. Chapter 1).

18. More precisely, this contrast is absent under 'normal' noncontrastive intonation.

APPENDIX B

ON NULL SUBJECTS

B.0 Introduction. The euphoria and refreshing outlook that transformational grammar brought to the study of language in the 1960s led many an enthusiastic linguist to cast whatever language s/he was studying into the English mold. Only comparatively recently have some contemporary theoretical linguists come to realize that other languages besides English are worthy of in-depth investigation. Although it is reasonable to assume that languages (or more accurately grammars) share some common core which explains the human capacity for language, it is also true that languages do indeed differ. Of late, some very interesting papers have been devoted to a determination of possible parameters by means of which these differences might be explained.[1] I would like to concentrate here on some Spanish data which I hope will elucidate the properties of 'missing elements' and consequently offer insights into one of the parameters that differentiate languages.

Spanish is one of the major languages of the Romance group which allows for subjectless sentences in outer structure. The question that needs to be raised is whether these sentences are subjectless at any other level of analysis. In particular, I concentrate on the types of sentences illustrated in items (1)-(5), and I present evidence that will lead to the proper identification of the deltas.

(1) Δ comen a las diez.
    eat (3 pl.) at ten o'clock
    'They eat at ten o!clock.'

(2) Paco quiere Δ comer.
    'Paco wants (3 sg.) to eat.'

(3) Δ había mucha gente.
    existed (3 sg.) many people
    'There were many people.'

340

(4) Δ hace mucho viento.
    makes (3 sg.) much wind
    'It is very windy.'

(5) Δ apareció un hombre.
    appeared (3 sg.) a man
    'A man appeared.'

The structure of this appendix is as follows: in Section 1, sentences (1) and (2) are examined and the identity of their deltas is established. The same procedure is pursued in Section 2 with respect to sentences (3) and (4), and in Section 3 with respect to sentence (5). Section 4 provides a summary of the results arrived at as well as a comparison of the differences and similarities among PRO, [$_{NP}$e], and ∅. It also includes some speculations about PRO government and the [$\pm$obligatory subject] parameter.

B.1 PRO as underlying subject. To my knowledge, one of the first linguists to examine null subject languages within the EST framework was Taraldsen (1978). In essence, he maintains that null subjects in the Romance languages are nominative null anaphors--i.e. [$_{NP}$e]--which are bound in S' by subject-verb agreement.[2] By positing null subjects as empty NPs, Taraldsen claims that he does away with the Subject Pronoun Drop rule. Under this hypothesis then, the Spanish sentence (1) would be base-generated with a terminally null subject NP.

(6) [$_{NP_i}$e] comen$_i$ a las diez.

Here i captures the coindexing properties of AG(reement). I would like to show that such an analysis cannot be maintained and that the delta of sentence (1) should be identified with PRO and not with a base-generated null anaphor.

In the first place, postulating null subjects in structures like (1) erases certain parallelisms in behavior between matrix and embedded missing subject elements. To illustrate this point, allow me to expand on the rule of Subject-Verb Agreement (SVA). Traditionally, this rule has been thought of as a rule which copies the relevant features from the subject NP onto the verb. This becomes evident in the paradigm in (7), where person and number features are present in both the subject and the verb.[3]

(7a) (Yo)   llegué.   'I arrived.'
     $\begin{bmatrix} +1st \\ +sg. \end{bmatrix}$ $\begin{bmatrix} +1st \\ +sg. \end{bmatrix}$

(7b) (Tú) llegaste. 'You (sg.) arrived.'
$\begin{bmatrix} +2\text{nd} \\ +\text{sg.} \end{bmatrix}$ $\begin{bmatrix} +2\text{nd} \\ +\text{sg.} \end{bmatrix}$

(7c) (El) llegó. 'He arrived.'
$\begin{bmatrix} -1\text{st} \\ -2\text{nd} \\ +\text{sg.} \end{bmatrix}$ $\begin{bmatrix} -1\text{st} \\ -2\text{nd} \\ +\text{sg.} \end{bmatrix}$

(7d) (Nosotros) llegamos. 'We arrived.'
$\begin{bmatrix} +1\text{st} \\ -\text{sg.} \end{bmatrix}$ $\begin{bmatrix} +1\text{st} \\ -\text{sg.} \end{bmatrix}$

(7e) (Vosotros) llegasteis. 'You (pl.) arrived.'
$\begin{bmatrix} +2\text{nd} \\ -\text{sg.} \end{bmatrix}$ $\begin{bmatrix} +2\text{nd} \\ -\text{sg.} \end{bmatrix}$

(7f) (Ellos) llegaron. 'They (m.) arrived.'
$\begin{bmatrix} -1\text{st} \\ -2\text{nd} \\ -\text{sg.} \end{bmatrix}$ $\begin{bmatrix} -1\text{st} \\ -2\text{nd} \\ -\text{sg.} \end{bmatrix}$

Note that at times even the inherent feature of grammatical gender becomes relevant, since it manifests itself in predicative adjectives. [4]

(8a) (Ellos) son altos. '(They) are tall (m. pl.).'
$\begin{bmatrix} -1\text{st} \\ -2\text{nd} \\ -\text{sg.} \\ +\text{masc.} \end{bmatrix}$ $\begin{bmatrix} -1\text{st} \\ -2\text{nd} \\ -\text{sg.} \end{bmatrix}$ $\begin{bmatrix} -\text{sg.} \\ +\text{masc.} \end{bmatrix}$

(8b) (Ellas) son altas. '(They) are tall (f. pl.).'
$\begin{bmatrix} -1\text{st} \\ -2\text{nd} \\ -\text{sg.} \\ -\text{masc.} \end{bmatrix}$ $\begin{bmatrix} -1\text{st} \\ -2\text{nd} \\ -\text{sg.} \end{bmatrix}$ $\begin{bmatrix} -\text{sg.} \\ -\text{masc.} \end{bmatrix}$

(9a) PRO Está abierto. [5] '(It) is open (m. sg.).'
$\begin{bmatrix} -1\text{st} \\ -2\text{nd} \\ +\text{sg.} \\ +\text{masc.} \end{bmatrix}$ $\begin{bmatrix} -1\text{st} \\ -2\text{nd} \\ +\text{sg.} \end{bmatrix}$ $\begin{bmatrix} +\text{sg.} \\ +\text{masc.} \end{bmatrix}$

(cf. El libro está abierto.
'The book is open.')

(9b) PRO   Está   abierta.   '(It) is open (f. sg.).'
$\begin{bmatrix} -1st \\ -2nd \\ +sg. \\ -masc. \end{bmatrix}$ $\begin{bmatrix} -1st \\ -2nd \\ +sg. \end{bmatrix}$ $\begin{bmatrix} +sg. \\ -masc. \end{bmatrix}$

 (cf. La tienda está abierta.
 'The shop is open.')

The examples in (7), (8), and (9) make it clear that the subject position has to be occupied by a pronominal--either one with a phonetic matrix (i.e. a pronoun) or one without a phonetic matrix (i.e. PRO)--since this position contains features which are crucial to the grammaticality and interpretation of these sentences. [6]
Observe that this 'feature launching' characteristic of subjects is not exclusive to matrix subjects; infinitival subjects behave similarly with respect to their agreement with predicative adjectives.

(10a) (Paco/él) quiere Δ ser alto.
$\begin{bmatrix} +sg. \\ +masc. \end{bmatrix}$
      'Paco/he wants to be tall (m. sg.).'

(10b) (Las niñas/ellas) quieren Δ ser altas.
$\begin{bmatrix} -sg. \\ -masc. \end{bmatrix}$
      'The girls/they (f. pl.) want to be tall (f. pl.).'

In order to capture the parallel behavior of matrix and infinitival subjects, it seems reasonable to hypothesize that the same element should be responsible for the same facts. If one were to accept Taraldsen's analysis and postulate that the underlying subject of (6) is $[_{NP}e]$, then one should expect that the deltas in (10) would also be $[_{NP}e]$.
Nevertheless, on the assumption that the Empty Category Principle (11) is a valid principle of grammars, a structure such as that in (12) would be discarded because $[_{NP}e]$ is not governed.

(11) Empty Category Principle: $[_{NP}e]$ must be governed.

(12) Paco quiere $[_{NP}e]$ ser alto.

Therefore, the conclusion must be that the embedded deltas in (10) are PROs. Notice that now $[_{NP}e]$ is the subject of (6) (and (7), (8), and (9)), but PRO is the subject of (10). This analysis is counterintuitive. It postulates two different entities, depending on whether one is dealing with a finite (cf. (6) and

(7)-(9)) or a nonfinite clause (cf. (10)), despite the fact that
these entities act in the same manner with respect to the assignment of the features of number and gender to predicative adjectives (compare (8) and (9) with (10)). Consequently, let
us assume that all these sentences have PRO as subject. This
in turn implies that the deltas in both (1) and (2) must be
PRO. Failure to accept this conclusion would lead to missed
generalizations regarding the 'feature launching' property of
these PRO subjects.[7] The discussion of the theoretical implications of having a governed PRO in the subject position of
finite clauses is delayed until Section B.4.

Another argument which supports the postulation of PRO as
the missing subject element of tensed clauses can be brought
forth. Notice that when sentence (1) is embedded under a
matrix clause, the missing element can be disjoint in reference
with the matrix subject (cf. (13a)), although this is not necessarily the case (cf. (13b)).

(13a) Los hombres$_i$ dicen que Δ_j comen a las diez.

(13b) Los hombres$_i$ dicen que Δ_i comen a las diez.
      'The men say that (they) eat at ten o'clock.'

Since the interpretation of pronominals as being [+coreferential]
takes place at the level of logical form (LF), it follows that
PRO needs to be present at this stage.[8] Consequently, the
deltas in (13) must be identified with PRO.[9]

B.2 Sentences with no underlying subject. Having established that the deltas in (1) and (2) have to be PRO, sentences
(3) and (4) can be approached.

(3) Δ había mucha gente.
      existed (3 sg.) many people
    'There were many people.'

(4) Δ hace mucho viento.[10]
      makes (3 sg.) much wind
    'It is very windy.'

Both (3) and (4) are considered to be impersonal sentences.
Example (3) is an instance of impersonal haber 'there-to-be',
while (4) is an example of impersonal hacer 'to do/make'. Perhaps the principal characteristic of these sentences is that
their verbs invariably appear in the third person singular form
(in standard Spanish).

The hypothesis that I would attempt to demonstrate is that
these sentences have absolutely nothing in subject position; in
other words, their deltas should be identified with $\emptyset$. In the
first place, sentences of the type found in (3) and (4) never
show any kind of subject nominal in outer structure, whether

it be a lexical NP or a pronominal (compare this to (7), (8), (9), and (10), for example), a fact which indicates that the subject position must be mandatorily null. Second, not only must this position be phonologically null; it must also be semantically null, since it never bears any kind of relationship to the predicate. These two traits in and of themselves would not provide enough evidence to support the Ø hypothesis. However, it is possible to find some confirming evidence.

The absolute 'nullness' of the deltas in (3) and (4) can be demonstrated by several arguments. For example, the interpretation of gerundive phrases proves the absence of [NP, S] for impersonal haber. (I assume that haber and ver enter into the subcategorization frame [+ _NP S], cf. Section 1.2.2.2.2; and Suñer 1978.)

(14) Había unos chicos [$_\bar{S}$ PRO leyendo en el parque].

'There were some kids reading in the park.'

(15) PRO veía a unos chicos [$_\bar{S}$ PRO leyendo en el parque.]

saw some kids reading in the park

The gerundive phrases in (14) and (15) offer ambiguous adjectival and adverbial interpretations. In the former case, these phrases represent the $\bar{S}$ element of a relative clause (cf. (16)); in the latter, they are instances of $\bar{S}$ complements (cf. (17)).

(16) $\left.\begin{array}{l}\text{Había}\\\text{PRO veía}\end{array}\right\}$ [$_{NP}$[$_{NP}$ unos chicos] [$_\bar{S}$ PRO leyendo ...]]

(17) $\left.\begin{array}{l}\text{Había}\\\text{PRO veía}\end{array}\right\}$ [$_{NP}$ unos chicos] [$_\bar{S}$ PRO leyendo ...]

Regardless of the structure of these gerundives, in haber sentences the embedded PRO can only be coreferential with the direct object.

(18) Había unos chicos$_i$ [$_\bar{S}$ PRO$_i$ leyendo ...]

On the other hand, in the sentence with ver the PRO of the gerundive phrase can be coreferential with unos chicos, yet it can also be coreferential with the matrix PRO (cf. (19)).

(19) PRO$_i$ veía a unos chicos [$_\bar{S}$ PRO$_i$ leyendo ...]

This extra reading is available to ver but not to haber precisely because the former, as opposed to the latter, has a noun phrase subject.

Another argument which supports the total lack of a subject argument for both impersonal haber and hacer can be

346 / Spanish Presentational Sentence-Types

constructed by examining their behavior in infinitival complements. Whereas these impersonal sentences cannot appear embedded under an Equi verb (be it subject, (20), or object
control, (21)), or under a perception or causative verb ((22)),
they may appear as embedded infinitivals under the traditional
Raising verbs ((23)).

(20) *Paco cree $\begin{cases} \text{haber mucha gente.} \\ \text{hacer mucho viento.} \end{cases}$

　　'Paco believes $\begin{cases} \text{there-to-be-many people.'} \\ \text{it-to-be very windy.'} \end{cases}$

(21) *Paco mandó $\begin{cases} \text{haber mucha gente.} \\ \text{hacer mucho viento.} \end{cases}$

　　'Paco ordered $\begin{cases} \text{there-to-be-many people.'} \\ \text{it-to-be very windy.'} \end{cases}$

(22) *Los hombres de ciencia vieron/hicieron
　　$\begin{cases} \text{haber mucha gente.} \\ \text{hacer mucho viento.} \end{cases}$
　　'The scientists saw/caused
　　$\begin{cases} \text{there-to-be many people.'} \\ \text{it-to-be windy.'} \end{cases}$

(23) Debe/puede/empieza a $\begin{cases} \text{haber mucha gente.} \\ \text{hacer mucho viento.} \end{cases}$

　　'There must/can/begins to $\begin{cases} \text{be many people.'} \\ \text{be windy.'} \end{cases}$

If one were to identify the deltas of (3) and (4) with PRO,
there would be no non-ad hoc way to explain the data displayed in (20)-(23). On the other hand, if one assumes that
these deltas are 0, it is possible to venture the following hypothesis. Equi verbs as well as perception and causative verbs
impose conditions on the subjects of their embedded infinitives;
the common denominator among such conditions is that these
infinitives must minimally have a PRO subject.[11] Since impersonal haber and hacer sentences are completely subjectless,
they fail to fulfill this minimal condition; thus the ungrammaticality of (20)-(22).[12] Furthermore, this alternative provides a satisfactory answer for the compatibility of these infinitive sentences with Raising verbs (23): since Raising verbs
do not make any demands on the subjects of the infinitives (it
is a well-known fact that they do not establish any selectional
restrictions or conditions on referentiality), there is no reason
why they should not cooccur with a subjectless infinitive. The
proposed nonsurface structure would therefore be (24) (details
omitted).

(24)

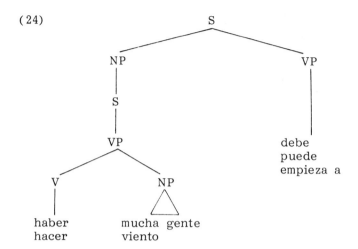

After VP-Raising[13] has applied, the structure in (24) yields the grammatical sentences in (23). This analysis provides a principled way of explaining the traditional statement that 'the infinitives and present participles of impersonal verbs communicate their impersonal effect to whatever verbs they depend upon' (Ramsey 1956: 394).

Two arguments have been presented (gerundive phrases and infinitival complements) which disqualify PRO as a plausible alternative for the identity of the delta in (3) and (4). These same arguments strongly suggest that impersonal <u>haber</u> and <u>hacer</u> are completely subjectless. However, before reaching a firm conclusion, one should consider the possibility of identifying these deltas with [Npe], that is, with a null anaphor. In tensed clauses this does not create any problems; [Npe] is properly governed since it is coindexed with the verbal inflection (Chomsky 1979). The deciding data is again to be found in embedded infinitives.

(25) Paco mandó [[Npe] haber mucha gente]
      Paco mandó [[Npe] hacer mucho viento]

(26) [[Npe] haber mucha gente] debe
      [[Npe] hacer mucho viento] debe

If the nonsurface structures of Equi and Raising verbs were (25) and (26), respectively, one would assume that all these structures should render ungrammatical sentences: they are in violation of the Empty Category Principle (cf. (11)) since there is nothing in the embedded sentences which could govern the empty NP. Nevertheless, as already discussed, this is not the way the grammaticality judgments filter through. While the examples derived from (25) are ungrammatical (see (21)), those derived from (26) produce perfectly grammatical sentences (see

(23)).[14] Hence, it must be the case that the deltas in (3)
and (4) cannot be identified with [$_{NP}$e].

By now, both PRO and [$_{NP}$e] have been discarded as possible candidates for the delta of (3) and (4). One alternative
remains: delta must be ∅. This hypothesis is in agreement
with the evidence provided by gerundive phrases (cf. (16)-
(19)) and by infinitival complements (cf. (20)-(23)).

This conclusion in turn implies that Spanish needs the phrase
structure rule shown in (27) (details aside).

(27) S → (NP) INFL VP

The environments in which the subject NP equals ∅ are rather
limited. Only some of the so-called impersonal constructions--
like the ones discussed in this subsection, and perhaps a few
others with ser 'to be' and estar 'to be' used impersonally[15]--
render grammatical sentences in the total absence of a syntactic
subject. Note that (27) provides for total parallelism between
matrix and embedded sentences: both types have the potential
for being totally devoid of a subject.

One apparent counterargument to identifying delta with ∅ may
be presented by using Subject-Verb Agreement. But notice
that the types of sentences under discussion invariably take a
third person singular verb form (in standard Spanish).[16]
Therefore, verb agreement does not constitute an insurmount-
able problem, since it can be argued that, in the absence of
a subject NP, whenever tense is chosen the verb adopts the
unmarked person and number form--i.e. the third person singular form.

Furthermore, my proposal has an advantage over that of
Taraldsen. As already pointed out (Section B.1), he postulates
[$_{NP}$e] for null subjects. This move obliges him to claim that
these null anaphors are interpreted as definite pronouns in LF.
Thus the sentences are not ruled out as independent clauses
for being open sentences 'and as such unfit for main clause
and sentential complement status' (Taraldsen 1979:12). Adoption of this interpretation would be nothing more than an arbitrary use of the theory to save Taraldsen's hypothesis. Note
that there is nothing 'definite' in the delta position of (3) and
(4). Since I have postulated that these sentences are completely subjectless, this problem of interpretation does not
arise.

As a matter of fact, it is possible to write a very straightforward and general rule, shown in (28), which would interpret the impersonal sentences under discussion.

(28) Interpret S as impersonal in the absence of [NP, S].

In short, I have argued that impersonal haber and hacer
sentences are syntactically and semantically subjectless. This

conclusion neither creates problems for the Subject-Verb Agreement rule nor interferes with the proper interpretation of these sentences. Therefore, the question, 'What is the missing element in sentences (3) and (4)?' should be given the answer, 'There is no missing element'. [17,18]

B.3 Trace in subject position. Finally, the proper identification of the delta in (5) must be established.

(5) Δ apareció un hombre.
     appeared (3 sg.) a man

Example (5) is a presentational sentence which asserts the appearance of the referent of the NP subject (in this case un hombre) in the world of discourse. The NP un hombre has been moved to postverbal position by a Subject Postposing rule. [19] This movement rule leaves behind a trace in accordance with the principles of trace theory. Hence, the S-structure of (5) is (29).

(29) $[_{NP_i}$ e] apareció un hombre$_i$

Here the trace is coindexed with the moved NP by virtue of the movement rule itself. However, notice that this is an unorthodox trace in the sense that it precedes its 'antecedent'; thus it is not properly preceded and C-commanded by this antecedent. Despite this, $[_{NP_i}$e] is properly bound; recall that Spanish is one of the Romance languages which can bind an empty element in subject position through verbal inflection (cf. Section 2.5; Chomsky 1979, among others). Therefore, the trace in subject position is fully specified in (30).

(30) $[_{NP_{i,j}}$ e] apareció$_j$ un hombre$_i$

That is to say, the trace is coindexed both with the postposed subject and with AG(reement).

The fact that the trace precedes its coindexed NP does not hinder either Case Assignment or Subject-Verb Agreement. The postposed NP receives nominative case regardless of its position, because lexical NPs inherit case from their trace by a general convention on Case Assignment. [20] And Subject-Verb Agreement can be established between the nominative NP and the verb, regardless of the position of the NP. In conclusion, the missing element in (5) has to be $[_{NP}$e]--i.e. trace.

B.4 Conclusion. The deltas of sentences (1) through (5) have been successfully identified. Although all of these deltas are completely null in outer structure, they are not identical otherwise. The results arrived at are given in (31) through (35).

(31) PRO_j comen$_j$ a las diez.

(32) Paco quiere PRO comer.

(33) Ø Había mucha gente.

(34) Ø Hace mucho viento.

(35) $[_{NP_{i/j}}$ e] apareció$_j$ un hombre$_i$.

That the evidence has forced the conclusion that there are three types of null elements should not distress us; on the contrary, their different identities are corroborated by differences in behavior. For example, one advantage of positing distinct entities for the deltas of (31) and (32) as opposed to those in (33) and (34) lies in the fact that only Ø is exclusive to nonparadigmatic sentences, in the sense that these impersonal sentences appear exclusively with the third person singular verbal form.

Furthermore, PRO differs from traces in that the latter must have an 'antecedent'[21] while the former may have one (cf. (32)) but need not (cf. (31)). Another difference pointed out by Chomsky (1979) is that while in the relationship NP-PRO each has an independent thematic role (in Gruber's 1970 and Jackendoff's 1972 sense), a trace and its 'cedent' are associated with only one thematic role since the NP inherits its role from its trace (compare (32) to (35)).[22]

There is another contrast which concerns traces and PRO which I would like to explore. This contrast has to do with the behavior of these elements in Spanish as opposed to English. If my analysis is correct, it shows that universal theory cannot mandate that PRO has to be ungoverned in every position (Chomsky 1979, 1980a). The result is that this dictum needs to be relegated to a language-specific parameter fixed through experience, and more likely reducible to other facts.

It appears to be true that a trace is always governed in both Spanish and English. On the other hand, PRO behaves differently in these languages. In English, PRO is never governed or case-marked (Chomsky 1979, 1980a,b). In Spanish, however, PRO can be [+governed] in direct correlation with [+tense]. In other words, PRO is not governed in nonfinite clauses but is governed in finite clauses,[23] as shown by sentences (32) and (31), respectively. Furthermore, the rule which deletes PRO cannot operate until after LF because of the proper interpretation of this element.[24]

(36) Las niñas$_i$ dijeron que PRO$_{i/j}$ llegarían temprano.
'The girls said that they-would arrive early.'

This in turn means that PRO must still be case-marked at this level of analysis. In this respect, PRO becomes totally parallel to traces: recall that traces can be case-marked (in which case they are variables, as in WH-Movement), or not case-marked (as in NP movement); PRO also can be case-marked or not case-marked, depending on whether it is in the environment of tense or not (for Spanish).

This parallel behavior of PRO and traces is confirmed by an examination of the positions in which these elements may appear. Each can appear in the subject position of a tensed clause or as the subject of an infinitive. For PRO see (31) and (32), and for traces see (35) and (37).

(37a) ¿Quién$_i$ dijiste que [$_{NP_i}$ e] había venido?

who said (you) that had come
'Who did you say had come?'

(37b) Paco$_i$ parece [$_{NP_i}$ e] haber salido.

'Paco seems to-have left.'

The last question that I would like to consider is this: can the different behavior of PRO in Spanish and English be ascribed to any other facts about these languages? I think it can. English requires that every sentence have a subject.[25] Moreover, these subjects need to have phonetic matrices in finite clauses. (One result of this is that the language makes use of the so-called 'dummy' subjects it and there.) In contrast, Spanish has never had this requirement,[26] and therefore null subjects are allowed not only in outer structure (cf. (31)) but also in underlying structure (cf. (33)) and (34)). PRO is one of these null subjects.

Moreover, observe that the lack of a subject requirement allowed Spanish to develop the full range of possibilities (i.e. PRO, [$_{NP}$e], and Ø) in both finite and nonfinite clauses, so that clauses behave alike with regard to 'missing elements'.[27]

To sum up, there are three kinds of null subjects in Spanish: PRO, [$_{NP}$e], and Ø.[28] Each of these 'missing elements' has distinct properties and each may appear in both finite and infinitival clauses. Both PRO and traces can be [+case]. It is hypothesized in this paper that the fact that PRO is governed in Spanish tensed clauses is a logical consequence of the lack of a subject requirement in this language. Therefore, [+obligatory subject] is one of the significant parameters along which languages may vary. PRO government is but one of the corollaries of the [+obligatory subject] end of the parameter.[29]

NOTES

1. Taraldsen (1978), Pesetsky (1979-1980), Hirschbühler and Rivero (1980), Chomsky (1979 and 1980a), among others.

2. I also arrived independently at the conclusion that verbal inflection has binding properties (Section 2.5). See also Chomsky (1979) and Pesetsky (1979-1980). Chomsky speculates that even if a language has AG(reement), it is still necessary to know whether AG has indexing properties or not. As opposed to the case for Spanish, INFL(ection) in English cannot bind, precisely because AG does not index (where INFL → $\pm$ Tn AG). Therefore, English cannot have empty subjects.

3. Parentheses around the subject NP mean that the sentence is grammatical without this argument in outer structure.

4. This captures the fact that adjectives are not inherently marked for number and gender.

Gender is also evidenced in past participles that behave like adjectives (see also examples in (9)).

(i) Los libros fueron encuadernados en cuero.
$$\begin{bmatrix} -1st \\ -2nd \\ -sg. \\ +masc. \end{bmatrix} \quad \begin{bmatrix} -1st \\ -2nd \\ -sg. \end{bmatrix} \quad \begin{bmatrix} -sg. \\ +masc. \end{bmatrix}$$

'The books were bound in leather.'

Although Spanish does not show gender in the verbal inflection, one does not want to rule out the possibility that other languages might manifest it there.

5. It is a fact of Spanish that, under normal circumstances, subject pronouns do not stand for things; thus Spanish does not have a pronoun equivalent to English it or they [-animate].

6. Notice that pronouns and PRO differ only with respect to a 'pronounceable shape' (i.e. phonetic matrix). Both elements share features of number, person, and gender (and perhaps others not pertinent to the present discussion). Taraldsen's [Npe] hypothesis appears to be incompatible with Chomsky's (1979) as a matching process conception of SVA; [Npe] supposedly has no features; therefore sentences containing it are discarded because the subject and AG do not match in features.

7. 'Feature launching' is taken in the sense that from PRO these features are copied onto the verb inflection and even onto predicative adjectives. I prefer this more traditional approach to SVA over Chomsky's Pisa proposal for a number of reasons which I do not elaborate here.

Although the argumentation does not support Taraldsen's [Npe] hypothesis, he is correct in maintaining that Spanish does not require a Subject Pronoun Drop rule. (Strictly speaking, Taraldsen made this claim for Italian). This follows

from the adoption of the strongest possible claim, namely, that
deletion rules cannot delete elements which have a phonetic
matrix. At most, what Spanish might require is a Subject PRO
Drop rule. However, since PRO is as unpronounceable as
[Npe], there might not be enough justification for a deletion
rule.
   8. Of course, my analysis also implies that PRO receives
nominative case on the assumption that case is assigned at the
level of S-structure. Chomsky (1979) maintains that the theory
demands that PRO be ungoverned (i.e. noncase-marked at the
level of LF). He speculates that it is possible to have a case-
marked PRO as long as the Delete-Pronoun rule applies to it
before LF. His rule says:

   (63) $PRO_i ===> [_{NP_i} e]$ (1979:49)

That is, PRO loses its features but keeps its index. Chomsky
elaborates (1979:49): 'Remember that the theory says that
PRO cannot be governed, i.e. case-marked at LF, but of
course there's nothing to stop PRO from being governed and
case-marked previously: you could have a base-generated PRO
which is governed and gets case and then undergoes the delete-
pronoun rule so that by the time it gets to LF it is not PRO
anymore'.
   Although this hypothesis allows for the proper interpretation
of pronominals, it raises questions as to the place of deletion
rules in the organization of the grammar. It has generally
been assumed that deletion rules belong to the left-hand branch
of the grammar because null elements play a role in semantic
interpretation (Chomsky and Lasnik 1977). If so, (63) could
have no bearing on LF because LF is on the right side of the
grammar.
   9. If one were to postulate a pronoun (as opposed to PRO)
in the deep structure of tensed sentences without a subject in
outer structure, then sentences in which the pronoun can never
appear in outer structure are left to be explained.

   (i) Los hay que (*ellos) se burlan de uno.
       them (acc.) there-is that (*they) themselves mock (3 pl.)
       of one
       'There exist those who make fun of everybody.'

   (ii) Lo vi que (*él) venia.
        him (acc.) I-saw that (*he) was-coming
        'I saw him coming.'

   (iii) Paco es mejor de lo que (*él) aparenta.
         Paco is better than what (*he) appears
         'Paco is better than he appears to be.'

(For the structure of examples like (i) and (ii), see Section
1.2.2.2.2, and Suñer 1978b.) Thus, the foregoing data appear
to indicate that the alleged Subject Pronoun Drop rule would
need to be obligatory in certain environments (yet undetermined).

10. That the arguments <u>mucha gente</u> 'many people' and
<u>viento</u> 'wind' function as direct objects can be shown by
'replacing' these arguments with the corresponding object
clitics.

   (i) --¿Habia mucha gente en la fiesta?
       'Were-there many people at the party?'

       --Seguro que <u>la</u> había.
       sure that it (acc. f. sg.)
       'Sure (that) there-were.'

  (ii) ¿Hace mucho viento por esta zona?
       'Is it very windy in this region?'

       --Sí que <u>lo</u> hace.
       yes that it (acc. m. sg.) makes
       'Sure (that) it is.'

For <u>haber</u>, see Section 1.1.1.3. When discussing impersonal
<u>hacer</u>, Ramsey (1956:410) writes, 'In speaking of the state of
the weather, <u>hacer</u> takes as its object a noun expressing the
phrase desired'.

11. I say 'minimally' because it is a well-known fact that
perception and causative verbs also allow for lexical infinitival
subjects.

   (i) Paco vio/hizo [$_{\overline{S}}$ Juan emborracharse].

       'Paco saw/made John (to)-get-drunk.'

  (ii) Paco vio/hizo emborracharse a Juan.

       'Paco {saw John getting drunk.'
             {made John (to) get drunk.'

12. Note that if PRO were taken to be in subject position of
<u>haber</u> and <u>hacer</u>, the ungrammaticality of (20)-(21) could still
be dismissed by a statement that control verbs require identity
between controller and controllee. Nevertheless, this explanation cannot do for perception and causative verbs, because
these are not control verbs. Consequently, the ill-formedness
of (22) can only be explained if these impersonal verbs are
claimed to be completely subjectless.

13. The derived structure after VP-Raising is something
like the following:

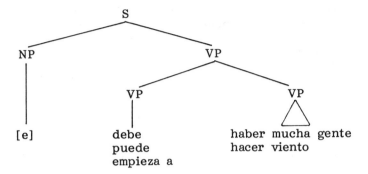

Notice that if the embedded infinitive has a subject (cf. (i)), this subject automatically becomes the subject of the matrix after VP-Raising has operated (cf. (ii)).

(i) [$_{\bar{S}}$[$_{NP}$[$_{\bar{S}}$ Paco [$_{VP}$ tocar el piano]]] puede]

(ii) [$_{\bar{S}}$[$_{NP}$ Paco] [$_{VP}$ puede [$_{VP}$ tocar el piano]]]

14. It could be argued that since the Empty Category Principle most likely operates at the level of LF, Raising should have already operated in (26). This would mean that an empty NP would be raised from the embedded subject position to the matrix subject position. The two empty NPs would be coindexed by convention and the lower [$_{NP}$e] would be governed.

[$_{NP_i}$ e] debe [[$_{NP_i}$ e] haber mucha gente]

It seems an artifact of the theory to allow movement and co-indexing of nodes which have never been filled.

15. One can cite expressions such as:

Es lástima. 'It is (a) pity.'
Está claro. 'It is clear.'
Está muy lluvioso. 'It is very rainy.'

16. Moreover, if it is assumed that impersonal sentences are subjectless, it becomes possible to formulate a very simple rule of Verb-Object Agreement that accounts for the following sentences:

(i) Habian muchas personas.
'There-were many persons.'

(ii) Hacen frío y viento.
there-make cold and windy
'It is cold and windy.'

The rule could roughly say: Verb-Object Agreement may take place in the absence of a subject. (This object must look like a subject in the sense that it must be prepositionless and cannot be an object clitic.)

Notice that if one were to maintain that the postverbal arguments in sentences (i) and (ii) are subject NPs, one would be at a loss to explain the impossibility of their being embedded under a subject control verb while preserving their impersonal interpretation.

(iii) *Muchas personas quieren haber en la fiesta.
many people want (3 pl.) to-there-be at the party

For more details on impersonal <u>haber</u> in nonstandard Spanish, I refer the reader to Section 1.4.

17. Of course, the positing of a phrase structure rule like (27), together with the interpretive rule (28), leaves the door open to the possibility of strictly subcategorizing NP subjects (cf. Suñer 1978c).

Notice that the postulation of base-generated subjectless sentences does not necessarily imply that these sentences are VPs. Since the rule says S → (NP) INFL VP, subjectless sentences are nevertheless sentences.

18. Note that among impersonal sentences I have not included weather verbs (<u>llover</u> 'to rain', <u>granizar</u> 'to hail', etc.). This is because they do not pattern exactly with the sentences considered in the text. For example, as one would expect, weather verbs do not appear embedded under control verbs (cf. (i)), whereas they do occur embedded under raising verbs (cf. (ii)). However, they also cooccur with perception verbs and the causative <u>hacer</u> 'to cause' (cf. (iii)), contrary to the situation for the impersonal sentences discussed in the text.

(i) *Paco mandó llover.
Paco ordered to-rain

*Paco prefiere llover.
Paco prefers to-rain

(ii) Puede llover.
'It can (to-) rain.'

Comenzó a llover.
'It-started to-rain.'

(iii) Los hombres de ciencia vieron/hicieron llover.
the scientists saw/caused to-rain

This patterning of the data seems to indicate that these verbs are generated with a PRO in subject position. Some confirming evidence to the effect that sentences with these verbs have a subject slot is found when one considers the readiness with which these verbs appear with lexical subjects.

(iv) Los días amanecían uno tras otro, rutinarios, sin cambios.
'The days dawned one after the other, routine-like, without changes.'

(v) El granizo llovía sobre ellos.
'(The) hailstones rained on them.'

(vi) Relampaguearon las luces antes de apagarse.
'The lights flashed before going out.'

19. For details, see Section 2.3.
20. That the postposed subject is nominative becomes evident when the subject NP is a pronoun. If the NP were objective, personal a would be required.

Apareció él/ella.
appeared (3 sg.) he/she
'He/she appeared.'

Using a slightly different framework from the one assumed in this paper, Jaeggli (1980) maintains that my sentence (5) is base-generated with its subject in postverbal position. This outcome derives from the claim that intransitive verbs which enter into presentational constructions do not assign a thematic role to the [NP, S] position, but rather assign a thematic role to the element in [NP, VP]. This treatment presupposes that presentationalism is constrained by lexical properties of verbs. In Section 2.1.2, I show that presentationalism can only be determined by taking into account the total discourse. Therefore, it would be hopeless to try to subdivide intransitive verbs in Spanish into those which do and do not assign a thematic role to [NP, S], since practically any verb used intransitively can enter into a presentational sentence (cf. Hatcher 1956).

21. Although traces in English seem for the most part (cf. Green 1980) to have a proper antecedent, the same is not true in Spanish. Traces in Spanish can have either an antecedent proper:

¿Qué$_i$ compró Paco [$_{NP_i}$ e]?
'What did Paco buy?'

or a 'postcedent' (see (35)). Therefore, one might consider abandoning the term 'antecedent' in favor of a term neutral as to whether X precedes or follows. 'Cedent' might be a good candidate.

Whether traces must be to the right of the 'cedent' (as in most English cases), or whether they may appear to either the right or the left of the 'cedent' (as in Spanish and other major Romance languages), might constitute one of the parameters along which languages differ.

22. Although Chomsky maintains that the trace and the 'cedent' are linked with only one thematic role, I am not sure this claim is accurate enough. Both Gruber (1970) and Jackendoff (1972) assert that a given NP could be specified for more than one thematic role; for example, both Theme and Agent coincide on the subject NP in Paco ran a mile in four minutes. (I owe this observation to J. Goldsmith.) Therefore, the way to state this characteristic is: the trace and the 'cedent' are linked with the same thematic role(s).

Nor am I sure that the specification of this role could not change in some well-defined and restricted cases. I have in mind examples like (i) and (ii).

(i) Un hombre apareció.
'A man appeared.'

(ii) $[_{NP_i}$ e] apareció un hombre$_i$
appeared a man

In both sentences, un hombre is the subject. But in (i) this NP is the Agent, while in (ii) its role is closer to that of Patient or Theme (in Jackendoff's sense). The difference is similar to that of the English sentences (iii) and (iv).

(iii) Three men appeared. (of their own free will)

(iv) There appeared three men. (?of their own free will)

The meaning of both (ii) and (iv) seems to be closer to 'the appearance of X happened/took place' than 'X appeared'.

This shift in meaning could be accounted for if a rule like (v) were possible.

(v) Agent → Theme in presentational sentences.

However, since the notion of thematic roles in the Chomskian government-binding theory is quite nebulous at best, my observations can only be taken as tentative until thematic roles are further specified.

23. Chomsky (1979) defines government as follows:

α properly governs β if α governs β and
a. $\alpha = [\pm N, \pm V]$
b. α is coindexed with β

PRO government falls under case b.

24. But see note 8.

25. There are some well-known exceptions to this statement: for example, imperatives. See also Green (1980).

26. French differs from all major Romance languages in that it developed from a stage in which it did not require a subject to the present stage in which a subject is needed (a few exceptions aside, see Kayne and Pollock 1978). No doubt sound changes which caused the loss of verbal inflection in the spoken language played a role in this development.

27. It remains to be determined which language constitutes the unmarked case. Intuitively, Spanish seems to be more consistent: 'null subjects everywhere'.

28. Strictly speaking, there are only two, because $\emptyset$ represents the total absence of a subject.

29. Other corollaries might be: existence of leftward traces (see Section 2.5), or indexing by AG (Chomsky 1979); violation of complementizer-trace phenomena (Pesetsky 1979-1980); and items that count as anaphors with respect to the Nominative Island Condition (Taraldsen 1978; Pesetsky 1979-1980).

REFERENCES

Abbreviations:

BLS: Berkeley Linguistic Society
CLS: Chicago Linguistic Society
LA: Linguistics Analysis
Lg.: Language
LI: Linguistic Inquiry
LSRL: Linguistic Symposium on Romance Languages
NELS: North Eastern Linguistic Society
PMLA: Publications of the Modern Language Association
of America

Adjémian, C. 1978. Theme, rheme, and word order.
Historiographia Linguistica V. 253-273.
Aissen, J. 1973. Shifty objects in Spanish. CLS 9.11-22.
Aissen, J. 1975. Presentational there-insertion: A cyclic
root transformation. CLS 11.1-14.
Aissen, J., and D. Perlmutter. 1976. Clause reduction in
Spanish. In: Harvard Studies in Syntax and Semantics, 3.
Edited by J. Hankamer and J. Aissen. Cambridge, Mass.:
Harvard University Press.
Akmajian, A. 1972. Getting tough. LI 3.373-377.
Akmajian, A. 1977. The complement structure of perception
verbs in an autonomous syntax framework. In: Culicover
et al., eds. (1977).
Alarcos Llorach, E. 1967. El artículo en español. To honor
Roman Jakobson. Janua Linguarum, Series Maior. The
Hague: Mouton.
Alarcos Llorach, E. 1970. El artículo en español. In:
Gramática funcional del español. Madrid: Gredos.
Alonso, A. 1954. Estilística y gramática del artículo en
español. In: Estudios lingüísticos, Temas españoles.
Madrid: Gredos.
Anderson, S. R., and S. Chung. 1977. On grammatical
relations and clause structure in verb-initial languages. In:

Syntax and semantics 8: Grammatical relations. Edited by P. Cole and J. Sadock. New York: Academic Press. 1-25.
Atkinson, C. 1973. The two forms of the subject inversion in Modern French. The Hague: Mouton.
Babby, L. H. 1978. Negation and subject case selection in existential sentences: Evidence from Russian. Bloomington: Indiana University Linguistics Club.
Babby, L. H. 1980. Existential sentences and negation in Russian. Ann Arbor: Karoma Publishers.
Bach, E. 1975. Order in base structures. In: Li, ed. (1975:307-343).
Banfield, A. 1973. Stylistic transformations in 'Paradise Lost'. Unpublished dissertation. University of Wisconsin.
Bassols de Climent, M. 1948. Origen de la construcción impersonal del verbo 'habere'. Revista de Estudios Clásicos de la Universidad de Cuyo, Mendoza, III.
Bello, A. 1970. Gramática de la lengua castellana. Revised by R. J. Cuervo and N. Alcalá-Zamora y Torres. Buenos Aires: Sopena.
Bentivoglio, P., and F. D'Introno. 1978. Análisis socio-lingüístico del español de Caracas: el orden de las palabras y la posición del sujeto. Unpublished MS.
Berman, A. 1974. On the VSO hypothesis. LI 5.1-37.
Bolinger, D. L. 1952. Linear modification. PMLA 67.1117-1144.
Bolinger, D. L. 1954. English prosodic stress and Spanish sentence order. Hispania 37.152-156.
Bolinger, D. L. 1954-1955. Meaningful word order in Spanish. Boletín de Filología, Universidad de Chile 7.45-56.
Bolinger, D. L. 1969. Of undetermined nouns and indeterminate reflexives. Romance Philology 22.484-489.
Bolinger, D. L. 1971. A further note on the nominal in the progressive. LI 2.584-586.
Bolinger, D. L. 1972. Accent is predictable (if you're a mind reader). Lg. 48.633-644.
Bolinger, D. L. 1977. Meaning and form. London: Longman.
Bordelois, I. 1974. The grammar of Spanish causative complements. Unpublished dissertation. Massachusetts Institute of Technology.
Bourciez, E. 1910. Éléments de linguistique romane. Paris.
Bowers, J. 1981. The theory of grammatical relations. Ithaca, N.Y.: Cornell University Press.
Breivik, L. 1975. The use and non-use of existential there in present-day English. Forum Linguisticum 7.57-103.
Bresnan, J. 1970. An argument against pronominalization. LI 1.122-124.
Bresnan, J. 1977. Variables in the theory of transformations. In: Culicover et al., eds. (1977:157-196).
Bresnan, J., and J. Grimshaw. 1978. The syntax of free relatives in English. LI 9.331-391.

Browne, W., and B. Vattuone. 1975. Theme-rheme structure and Zenéyze clitics. LI 6.136-140.
Bull, W. 1943. Related functions of haber and estar. Modern Language Journal 27.119-123.
Bull, W. 1965. Spanish for teachers: Applied linguistics. New York: Ronald Press.
Bull, W., A. Gronberg, and J. Abbott. 1952. Subject position in contemporary Spanish. Hispania 35.185-188.
Cannings, P. 1978. Definiteness and relevance: The semantic unity of il y a. In: Suñer, ed. (1978a:62-89).
Chafe, W. 1974. Language and consciousness. Lg. 50.111-133.
Chafe, W. 1976. Givenness, contrastiveness, definiteness, subjects, topics and point of view. In: Li, ed. (1976:25-56).
Chomsky, N. 1962. The logical basis of linguistic theory. In: Preprints of Papers for the Ninth International Congress of Linguists. Cambridge, Mass.
Chomsky, N. 1965. Aspects of the theory of syntax. Cambridge, Mass.: MIT Press.
Chomsky, N. 1970. Remarks on nominalization. In: Readings in English transformational grammar. Edited by R. Jacobs and P. Rosenbaum. Washington, D.C.: Georgetown University Press. 184-221.
Chomsky, N. 1971. Deep structure, surface structure, and semantic interpretation. In: Semantics: An interdisciplinary reader in philosophy, linguistics, and psychology. Edited by Steinberg and Jakobovits. New York: Cambridge University Press.
Chomsky, N. 1973. Conditions on transformations. In: A Festschrift for Morris Halle. Edited by S. R. Anderson and R. P. Kiparsky. New York: Holt, Rinehart and Winston.
Chomsky, N. 1975. Questions of form and interpretation. LA 1.75-109.
Chomsky, N. 1976. Conditions on rules of grammar. LA 2.303-354.
Chomsky, N. 1977a. Essays on form and interpretation. New York: American Elsevier.
Chomsky, N. 1977b. On WH-movement. In: P. Culicover et al., eds. (1977:71-132).
Chomsky, N. 1979a. Language and responsibility. New York: Pantheon Books.
Chomsky, N. 1979b. Pisa lectures. Unpublished Xerox MS.
Chomsky, N. 1980a. On binding. LI 11.1-46.
Chomsky, N. 1980b. On the representation of form and function. Unpublished MS. MIT.
Chomsky, N., and H. Lasnik. 1977. Filters and control. LI 8.425-504.
Cole, P., W. Harbert, G. Hermon, and S. N. Sridhar. 1978. On the acquisition of subjecthood. Studies in Linguistic Sciences 8.42-71.

Contreras, H. 1973. Grammaticality versus acceptability: The Spanish SE case. LI 4.83-88.

Contreras, H. 1976. A theory of word order with special reference to Spanish. North-Holland Linguistic Series No. 29.

Contreras, H. 1976b. Theme and rheme in Spanish syntax. In: Current studies in Romance linguistics. Edited by M. Luján and F. Hensey. Washington, D.C.: Georgetown University Press. 330-342.

Corominas, J. 1967. Breve diccionario etimológico de la lengua castellana. Madrid: Gredos.

Culicover, P., T. Wasow, and A. Akmajian, eds. 1977. Formal syntax. New York: Academic Press.

Daneš, F. 1964. A three-level approach to syntax. Travaux Linguistiques de Prague, 1.225-240.

Derbyshire, D. C. 1977. Word order universals and the existence of OVS languages. LI 8.590-599.

Dresher, B., and N. Hornstein. 1979. Trace theory and NP movement rules. LI 10.65-82.

Dubsky, J. 1960. L'inversion en espagnol. Sborník prací Filosoficka Faculta, A8.111-122.

Dubuisson, C. 1978-1979. A reanalysis of stylistic inversion in French. NELS 9, CUNY Forum 5-6. 268-275.

Emonds, J. E. 1970. Root and structure-preserving transformations. Bloomington: Indiana University Linguistics Club.

Emonds, J. E. 1976. A transformational approach to English syntax: Root, structure-preserving, and local transformations. New York: Academic Press.

Emonds, J. E. 1980. Word order in generative grammar. Journal of Linguistic Research 1.33-54.

Fält, G. 1972. Tres problemas de concordancia verbal en el español moderno. Uppsala: Acta Universitatis Upsaliensis 9.

Farley, R. A. 1958. Background notes on syntactic arrangement. Hispania 41.318-323.

Fauconnier, G. 1975. Pragmatic scales and logical structure. LI 6.357-375.

Fiengo, R. 1977. On trace theory. LI 8.35-61.

Fillmore, C. 1968. The case for case. In: Universals of linguistic theory. Edited by Bach and Harms. New York: Holt, Rinehart and Winston. 1-88.

Firbas, J. 1964. On defining the theme in functional sentence analysis. Travaux linguistiques de Prague 1.267-280.

Firbas, J. 1966. Non-thematic subjects in contemporary English. Travaux linguistiques de Prague 2.239-254.

Fish, G. T. 1959. The position of subject and object in Spanish prose. Hispania 42.582-590.

Fish, G. T. 1960. Postverbal word order in Spanish prose. Hispania 43.426-429.

Foley, W. A., and R. D. Van Valin. 1977. On the viability of the notion of 'Subject' in universal grammar. BLS 3.293-319.

Freidin, R. 1978. Cyclicity and the theory of grammar. LI
9.519-549.
Gili Gaya, S. 1973. Curso superior de sintaxis española.
Barcélona: Vox.
Givón, T. 1975a. Focus and the scope of assertion: Some
Bantu evidence. Studies in African Linguistics 6.2. 185-205.
Givón, T. 1975b. Negation in language: Pragmatics, func-
tion, ontology. Working papers on language universals 18.
59-116.
Goldin, M. 1968. Spanish case and function. Washington,
D.C.: Georgetown University Press.
Green, G. 1980. Some wherefores of English inversions.
Lg. 56.582-602.
Greenberg, J. 1963. Some universals of grammar with par-
ticular reference to the order of meaningful elements. In:
Universals of language. Edited by J. Greenberg. Cam-
bridge, Mass.: MIT. 58-90.
Grice, H. P. 1975. Logic and conversation. In: Syntax and
semantics: Speech acts, Vol. 3. Edited by P. Cole and
J. L. Morgan. New York: Academic Press. 41-58.
Grimes, J. E. 1975. The thread of discourse. The Hague:
Mouton.
Grimshaw, J. 1979. The structure-preserving constraint: A
review of: A transformational approach to English syntax by
J. E. Emonds. LA 5.313-343.
Gruber, J. 1970. Studies in lexical relations. Bloomington:
Indiana University Linguistics Club.
Guéron, J. 1978. The grammar of PP extraposition. Unpub-
lished MS. Université de Paris 8.
Guéron, J. 1980. On the syntax and semantics of PP extra-
position. LI 11.637-678.
Gundel, J. K. 1977. Role of topic and comment in linguistic
theory. Bloomington: Indiana University Linguistics Club.
Hadlich, R. L. 1971. A transformational grammar of Spanish.
Englewood Cliffs, N.J.: Prentice-Hall.
Halliday, M. A. K. 1967. Notes on transitivity and theme in
English, Part 2. Journal of Linguistics 3. 199-244.
Hatcher, A. 1956a. Theme and underlying question. Two
studies of Spanish word order. Word 12, Supplement 3.
Hatcher, A. 1956b. Syntax and the sentence. Word 12.234-
250.
Hatcher, A. 1957. Casos se han dado. Hispania 40.326-329.
Hawkinson, A., and L. Hyman. 1975. Hierarchies of natural
topic in Shona. Studies in African Linguistics 5.147-170.
Herschensohn, J. 1979. Genericness and intensionality.
Mimeo. Cornell University.
Hetzron, R. 1975. The presentative movement, or why the
ideal word order is VSOP. In: Li, ed. (1975:346-388).
Hirschbühler, P., and M-L. Rivero. 1980a. Catalan restrictive
relatives: Core and periphery. To appear in Lg.

Hirschbühler, P., and M-L. Rivero. 1980b. A unified analysis of matching and non-matching free relatives in Catalan. Paper read at NELS 11.
Hooper, J., and S. Thompson. 1973. On the applicability of root transformations. LI 4.465-497.
Isenberg, H. 1968. Das direkte objekt im Spanischen. Studia Grammatica IX. Berlin: Akademie-Verlag.
Jackendoff, R. 1969. An interpretive theory of negation. Foundations of Language 5.218-241.
Jackendoff, R. 1972. Semantic interpretation in generative grammar. Cambridge, Mass.: MIT Press.
Jackendoff, R. 1975. Morphological and semantic regularities in the lexicon. Lg. 51.639-671.
Jackendoff, R. 1977. X̄ Syntax: A study of phrase structure. Linguistic Inquiry Monographs 2. Cambridge, Mass.: MIT Press.
Jaeggli, O. 1980. On some phonologically-null elements in syntax. Unpublished dissertation. Massachusetts Institute of Technology.
Jayaseelan, K. 1979. On the role of the empty node in the structure-preserving hypothesis. LA 5.247-292.
Jenkins, L. 1975. The English existential. Linguistische Arbeiten 12. Tübingen: Max Niemeyer Verlag.
Kahane, H., and R. 1950. The position of the actor expression in colloquial Mexican Spanish. Lg. 26.236-263.
Kany, C. E. 1969. Sintaxis hispanoamericana. Madrid: Gredos.
Kayne, R. S. 1975. French syntax: The transformational cycle. Cambridge, Mass.: MIT Press.
Kayne, R. S. 1979. Rightward NP movement in French and English. LI 10.710-719.
Kayne, R. S. 1980. Extensions of binding and case marking. LI 11.75-96.
Kayne, R., and J-Y. Pollock. 1978. Stylistic inversion, successive cyclicity, and move NP in French. LI 9.595-622.
Keenan, E. L. 1976. Towards a universal definition of 'Subject'. In: Li, ed. (1976:303-333).
Kempson, R. 1975. Presupposition and the delimitation of semantics. London: Cambridge University Press.
Kempson, R. 1977. Semantic theory. Cambridge: Cambridge University Press.
Kimball, J. P. 1973. The grammar of existence. In: Papers from the 9th Regional Meeting, CLS. Edited by C. Corum et al. 262-270.
Kirkwood, H. W. 1977. Discontinuous noun phrases in existential sentences in English and German. Journal of Linguistics 13.53-66.
Koster, J. 1978. Locality principles in syntax. Dordrecht: Foris Publications.

Kuno, S. 1970. Some properties of non-referential noun phrases. In: Studies in general and oriental linguistics. Edited by Jakobson and Kawamoto. Tokyo: TEC Co.

Kuno, S. 1971. The position of locatives in existential sentences. LI 2.333-378.

Kuno, S. 1972. Functional sentence perspective: A case study from Japanese and English. LI 3.269-320.

Kuno, S. 1975. Conditions for verb phrase deletion. Foundations of Language 13.161-175.

Kuno, S. 1978. Generative discourse analysis in America. In: Current trends in textlinguistics. Edited by W. V. Dressler. Berlin: Walter de Gruyter. 275-294.

Kuno, S. 1979. Functional syntax. Paper presented at the Conference on Current Approaches to Syntax, University of Wisconsin-Milwaukee campus.

Kuroda, S-Y. 1972. The categorical and the thetic judgment. Foundations of Language 9.153-185.

Lakoff, G., and S. Peters. 1969. Phrasal conjunction and symmetric predicates. In: Modern studies in English. Edited by D. Reibel and S. Schane. Englewood Cliffs, N.J.: Prentice-Hall. 113-142.

Langacker, R. W. 1970. Review of: Spanish case and function by M. G. Goldin. Lg. 46.167-185.

Lapesa, R. 1968. Historia de la lengua española. Madrid: Escelicer.

Lapesa, R. 1974. El sustantivo sin actualizador en español. Estudios filológicos y lingüísticos, Homenaje a Angel Rosenblatt. Caracas: Instituto de Pedagogía.

Lasnik, H., and R. Fiengo. 1974. Complement object deletion. LI 5.535-571.

Li, C., ed. 1975. Word order and word order change. New York: Academic Press.

Li, C., ed. 1976. Subject and topic. New York: Academic Press.

Lightfoot, D. W. 1976a. The base component as a locus of syntactic change. In: Proceedings of the Second International Conference on Historical Linguistics. Edited by W. Christie. Amsterdam: North Holland.

Lightfoot, D. 1976b. Trace theory and twice-moved NP's. LI 7.559-582.

Lightfoot, D. 1977. On traces and conditions on rules. In: Culicover et al., eds. (1976:207-238).

Luján, M. 1978. Direct object nouns and the preposition a in Spanish. Texas Linguistic Forum 10.

Luján, M. 1980. Sintaxis y semántica del adjetivo. Madrid: Cátedra.

Luque Moreno, J. 1978. En torno al sintagma 'Haber impersonal + sustantivo' y sus orígenes latinos. Revista española de lingüística 8.125-147.

Maling, J., and A. Zaenen. 1978. The nonuniversality of a surface filter. LI 9.475-497.

Manteca Alonso-Cortés, A. 1976. En torno al se impersonal. Revista española de lingüística 6.167-180.
McCawley, J. 1970. English as a VSO language. Lg. 46. 286-299.
Meyer, P. 1972. Some observations on constituent-order in Spanish. In: Generative studies in Romance languages. Edited by J. Casagrande and B. Saciuk. Rowley, Mass.: Newbury House. 184-195.
Milsark, G. 1974. Existential sentences in English. Unpublished dissertation. Massachusetts Institute of Technology.
Milsark, G. 1977. Toward an explanation of certain peculiarities of the existential construction in English. LA 3.1-29.
Moliner, M. 1970. Diccionario de uso del español. Madrid: Gredos.
Nuessel, F. 1979. An annotated, critical bibliography of generative-based grammatical analyses of Spanish: Syntax and semantics. The Bilingual Review/La Revista Bilingüe 6.39-80.
Otero, C. 1966. Gramaticalidad y normatismo (a propósito de algunos escritos de A. Rosenblat). Romance Philology 20. 53-68.
Otero, C. 1972. Acceptable ungrammatical sentences in Spanish. LI 3.233-242.
Otero, C. 1973. Agrammaticality in performance. LI 4.551-562.
Perlmutter, D. M. 1970a. On the article in English. In: Modern studies in English. Edited by M. Bierwisch and K. E. Heidolph. Englewood Cliffs, N.J.: Prentice-Hall.
Perlmutter, D. M. 1970b. Deep and surface structure constraints in syntax. LI 1.187-257.
Pesetsky, D. 1979-1980. Complementizer-trace phenomena and the Nominative Island Condition. In: NELS 9, CUNY Forum 7-8. 137-157.
Pope, E. 1976. Questions and answers in English. The Hague: Mouton.
Postal, P. 1971. Cross-over phenomena. New York: Holt, Rinehart and Winston.
Postal, P. 1974. On raising. Cambridge, Mass.: MIT Press.
Pullum, G. K. 1977. Word order universals and grammatical relations. In: Syntax and semantics 8: Grammatical relations. Edited by P. Cole and J. Sadock. New York: Academic Press. 249-277.
Quirk, R., S. Greenbaum, G. Leech, and J. Svartvik. 1972. A grammar of contemporary English. New York: Seminar Press.
Ramsey, M. 1956. A textbook of Modern Spanish. Revised by R. K. Spaulding. New York: Holt, Rinehart and Winston.

Rando, E., and D. J. Napoli. 1978. Definites in <u>there</u>-sentences. Lg. 54:300-313.

Real Academia Española (RAE). 1974. Esbozo de una nueva gramática de la lengua española. Madrid: Espasa-Calpe.

Rivas, A. 1977. A theory of clitics. Unpublished dissertation. Massachusetts Institute of Technology.

Rivero, M-L. 1979. That-relatives and the deletion in COMP in Spanish. NELS 10. Cahiers Linguistiques d'Ottawa 9.

Rivero, M-L. 1980. On left-dislocation and topicalization in Spanish. LI 11.363-393.

Rochemont, M. S. 1978. A theory of stylistic rules in English. Unpublished dissertation. University of Massachusetts.

Roldán, M. 1971a. The double object constructions of Spanish. Language Sciences 15.8-14.

Roldán, M. 1971b. Spanish constructions with <u>se</u>. Language Sciences 15.15-29.

Ross, J. 1967. Constraints on variables in syntax. Unpublished dissertation. Massachusetts Institute of Technology.

Ross, J. 1972. The category squish: Endstation Hauptwort. CLS 8.316-328.

Ross, J. 1973. The penthouse principle and the order of constituents. In: CLS 9. Edited by Corum et al. 397-422.

Ross, J. 1975. Clausematiness. In: Formal semantics of natural language. Edited by E. Keenan. Cambridge: Cambridge University Press.

Rouveret, A., and J-R Vergnaud. 1980. Specifying reference to the subject: French causatives and conditions on representations. LI 11.97-202.

Sánchez de Zavala, V. 1976. Sobre una ausencia del castellano. In: Estudios de gramática generativa. Edited by V. Sánchez de Zavala. Barcelona: Editorial Labor. 195-254.

Schwartz, A. 1972. Constraints on movement transformations. Journal of Linguistics 8.35-85.

Schwartz, A. 1972. The VP-constituent of SVO languages. In: Syntax and semantics 1. Edited by J. P. Kimball. New York: Seminar Press. 213-236.

Selkirk, E. 1977. Some remarks on noun phrase structure. In: Culicover et al., eds. (1977:285-316).

Shou-Hsin, T. 1976. Structure and function of existential sentences. Unpublished MS.

Silva-Corvalán, C. 1978. Constraints on subject expression and subject placement in spoken Spanish. Paper read at the N-Wave Conference, Georgetown University.

Silverstein, M. 1977. Hierarchy of features and ergativity. In: Grammatical categories in Australian languages. Edited by R. Dixon. Canberra: Australian Institute of Aboriginal Studies.

Smith, S. 1969. Determiners and relative clauses in a generative grammar of English. In: Modern studies in English. Edited by D. A. Reibel and S. A. Schane. Englewood Cliffs, N.J.: Prentice-Hall. 247-263.

Solé, Y. R. and C. A. 1977. Modern Spanish syntax. Lexington, Mass.: Heath.

Stockwell, R. P., J. D. Bowen, and J. W. Martin. 1965. The grammatical structures of English and Spanish. Chicago: The University of Chicago Press.

Stockwell, R. P., P. Schachter, and B. H. Partee. 1973. The major syntactic structures of English. New York: Holt, Rinehart and Winston.

Stowell, T. 1978. What was there before there was there. CLS 14.458-471.

Strozer, J. 1976. Clitics in Spanish. Unpublished dissertation. University of California, Los Angeles.

Suñer, M. 1973. Non-paradigmatic se's in Spanish. Unpublished dissertation. Indiana University.

Suñer, M. 1974. Where does impersonal se come from? In: Linguistics studies in Romance languages. Edited by R. J. Campbell, M. G. Goldin, and M. C. Wang. Washington, D.C.: Georgetown University Press. 146-157.

Suñer, M. 1975. The Free-Ride Principle and the so-called impersonal se. In: 1974 Colloquium on Spanish and Portuguese Linguistics. Washington, D.C.: Georgetown University Press. 132-148.

Suñer, M. 1976a. Demythologizing the impersonal se in Spanish. Hispania 59.268-275.

Suñer, M. 1976b. Looking down the tree in Spanish. Lingua 39.201-225.

Suñer, M. 1976c. Change verbs and spontaneous se. Two proposals. [Forthcoming in Orbis.]

Suñer, M. 1976d. The Spanish naked noun constraint. Paper presented at the Colloquium on Hispanic and Luso-Brazilian Linguistics. Oswego, New York.

Suñer, M., ed. 1978a. Contemporary studies in Romance linguistics. Washington, D.C.: Georgetown University Press.

Suñer, M. 1978b. Perception verb complements in Spanish: Same or different? Canadian Journal of Linguistics 23.107-127.

Suñer, M. 1978c. La subcategorización estricta y los sujetos en español. Paper read at the 5th ALFAL Congress, Caracas.

Suñer, M. 1978d. Spanish hay. Unpublished MS. Cornell University.

Suñer, M. 1981. Existential predicates: Hay vs. estar. In: Linguistic Symposium on Romance Languages: 9. Edited by W. W. Cressey and D. J. Napoli. Washington, D.C.: Georgetown University Press. 105-122.

Suñer, M. 1981. On presentationals: Characterization of a Spanish sentence-type. Paper read at the 11th Linguistic Symposium on Romance Languages. San Antonio.

Taraldsen, K. T. 1978. On the NIC, vacuous application and the that-trace filter. Unpublished mimeo. Massachusetts Institute of Technology.

Torrego, E. 1979. Fronting in Spanish. Unpublished MS. University of Massachusetts, Boston.

Utley, J. H. 1954. Haber and estar. Hispania 37.225.

Vattuone, B. 1975. Notes on Genoese syntax: Kernel VOS strings and theme-rheme structure. Studi italiani di linguistica teorica ed applicata 4.335-378.

Wasow, T. 1975. Anaphoric pronouns and bound variables. Lg. 51.368-383.

Williams, E. S. 1975. Small clauses in English. In: Syntax and semantics 4. Edited by J. Kimball. New York: Academic Press. 249-273.

Williams, E. S. 1977. Discourse and logical form. LI 8.101-140.

SOURCES OF DATA

SXX   Anderson-Imbert, E., and L. B. Kiddle, eds. 1956.
Veinte cuentos hispanoamericanos del siglo XX. New
York: Appleton-Century-Crofts.

CT   Arreola, Juan José. 1961. Confabulario total [1941-
1961]. México: Fondo de Cultura Económica.

LP   Azevedo, M. M., and K. K. McMahon. 1978. Lecturas
periodísticas. Lexington, Mass.: Heath.

IM   Bioy Casares, Adolfo. 1972. La invención de Morel.
Madrid: Alianza Editorial.

R   Denevi, Marco. 1964. Rosaura a las diez. Edited by
D. A. Yates. New York: C. Scribner's Sons.

EL   Gorostiza, C. 1972. El lugar. Buenos Aires:
Sudamericana.

M   El habla de la ciudad de México: Materiales para su
estudio. 1971. México, D.F.: Universidad Nacional
Autónoma de México.

H   Hatcher, A. 1956. Theme and underlying question:
Two studies of Spanish word order.

VEA   Ingamells, L., and P. Standish. 1975. Tapescript for
Variedades del español actual. London: Longman.

VEA b   Ingamells, L., and P. Standish. 1975. Variedades
del español actual. London: Longman.

TE   Kadir, D., ed. 1976. Triple espera: Novelas cortas de
hispanoamérica. New York: Harcourt, Brace,
Jovanovich.

CH   Leal, Luis, ed. 1972. Cuentistas hispanoamericanos
del siglo veinte. New York: Random House.

EJ   Sánchez Ferlosio, R. 1975. El Jarama. Barcelona:
Destino.

TO   Tres obras de teatro. 1972. La Habana, Cuba:
Casa de las Américas.